W9-AAL-032

BROADCAST NEWS

BROADCAST NEWS

THIRD EDITION

Mitchell Stephens

New York University

HARCOURT BRACE JOVANOVICH COLLEGE PUBLISHERS

Fort Worth   Philadelphia   San Diego   New York   Orlando   Austin   San Antonio
Toronto   Montreal   London   Sydney   Tokyo

Editor in Chief	Ted Buchholz
Acquisitions Editor	Stephen T. Jordan
Developmental Editor	Cathlynn Richard
Project Editor	Kelly Riche
Production Manager	Erin Gregg
Book Designer	Melinda Huff
Photo/Permissions Editor	Annette Coolidge
Cover/Part Opener Art	Scott Sawyer

Copyright © 1993, 1986, 1980 by Holt, Rinehart and Winston, Inc.

All rights reserved. No part of this publication may be reproduced or transmitted in any form or by any means, electronic or mechanical, including photocopy, recording, or any information storage and retrieval system, without permission in writing from the publisher.

Requests for permission to make copies of any part of the work should be mailed to: Permissions Department, Harcourt Brace Jovanovich, Publishers, 8th Floor, Orlando, Florida 32887.

Address for editorial correspondence: Harcourt Brace Jovanovich, 301 Commerce Street, Suite 3700, Fort Worth, Texas 76102

Address for orders: Harcourt Brace Jovanovich, 6277 Sea Harbor Drive, Orlando, Florida 32887
1-800-782-4479 or (in Florida) 1-800-433-0001

ISBN: 0-03-079176-6

Library of Congress Catalog Card Number: 92-72321

Printed in the United States of America

6 7 8 9 0 1   016   9 8 7 6 5 4

Preface

People depend on broadcast news. Through three editions, the goal of this book has been to train broadcast journalists who can be depended on.

The book was written with the following thoughts in mind on how broadcast journalists should be trained:

- Reporting and writing skills can and should be taught, not just hinted at. Concepts such as the "feel" of writing or the "smell" of news must be demystified and defined so they can be clearly communicated.
- The basic responsibilities of all broadcast journalists are the same, no matter what the size of their station or audience. This book would be remiss if it ignored the special problems of small-town or big-city journalists, but the book would be deficient if the standards it advocates were not relevant in all broadcast newsrooms.
- Writing and reporting are best taught with frequent, precise and realistic examples. Most of the examples used in the text were used on the air.
- A book that stresses the need for clear and engaging writing should try not to be ponderous and dry.

This book uses many expressions and terms peculiar to broadcast newsrooms. My excuse for spreading jargon is a conviction that skills are easier to master once they have been named and defined. Readers will encounter these names if they find themselves in a broadcast newsroom. All unfamiliar terms are defined when they are first used in the text, and the definitions can be located through the index.

Any attempt to provide a comprehensive introduction to a field requires a broad perspective on that field. In preparing the first two editions of this book, I talked or corresponded with broadcast journalists at almost ten percent of the radio and television stations in the United States. Hundreds more were contacted for this edition in an effort to update and strengthen these discussions. I have also benefited enormously over the years from the suggestions of teachers and students who have used the book. They have helped make it by far the best-selling broadcast journalism textbook in the English-speaking world.

The organization of the book remains the same. Part I covers specifics of the actual writing process: copy, words, meanings, sentences, leads and stories. Part II examines reporting in some depth, including discussions of sources, gathering news, tape, writing to tape and coverage. Part III explains how both newscasts and public affairs programs are produced, while Part IV delves deeper into television—visuals, reporting and writing to visuals. Part V concludes the text with an in-depth look at the profession—ethics and law, programming and broadcast careers. Examples have been updated for this edition, and new material has been added on computers, satellites, video news services, data banks, polls, election coverage, reenactments, deregulation, broadcast and cable networks, cellular telephones, television visuals and computerized graphics.

Most of this new research and reporting, and a significant portion of the new writing, was done by Irwin Gratz, the former news director of WPOR in Portland, Maine. His industry and intelligence, along with his broad understanding of the workings of radio and television newsrooms, are reflected throughout these pages.

In addition, I would like to thank the following broadcast journalists for their help with the third edition: Richard Threlkeld and Tony Malara of CBS News; Frank Raphael and Arnott Walker of ABC News; Evelyn Cassidy and Steve Geimann of the Associated Press; Neil Offen of WCHL, Chapel Hill; Krys Quimby of KNX, Los Angeles; Kris Ostrowski, Bill Johnson, Chester Panzer and Wendy Rieger of WRC-TV, Washington, D.C.; Norm Fein, News 12, Long Island; Georgeanne Herbert, WBBM, Chicago; Irv Kass, John DeTarsio and Michael Settonni of KNSD-TV, San Diego; Al Blinke, Linda Cooper and Tom Loebig of WTAE-TV, Pittsburgh; Joe Gillespie, Jamie Bragg, Christy Cave, Lillie Shaw-Hamer and Judy Taub of WTOP, Washington, D.C.; Paul Beavers, Jim Valentine, Lori Dang, Angelos Papazis, Kyle Williams and Denise Wright of KUSI-TV, San Diego; Joe Rovitto and Kathy Driscoll of WTAE-TV, Pittsburgh; Roger Ball and Pat Brown of WANE-TV, Fort Wayne, Indiana; Steve Pritchett of KVII-TV, Amarillo, Texas; Mark Schneider of KEZO, Omaha; Sue McInerny of KDKA-TV, Pittsburgh; Stu Marckoon of WKSQ, Ellsworth, Maine; Elbert Tucker of WBRC-TV, Birmingham, Alabama; Alex Montano of WBKB-TV, Alpena, Michigan; Rob Cizek of WKLG-TV, Fort Wayne, Indiana; Rich Cook of KDKA, Pittsburgh; Kirk Winkler, KETV, Omaha; Paul Sands and Wayne Brown of KGTV, San Diego; Gary Wordlaw, WJLA-TV, Washington, D.C.; Steve Blum and Raymond Conover of Conus Communications; and Jim Hood of Zap News. Thanks too to Barry Smith of BASYS, to Robert Lystad of Baker and Hostetler and to Ron Tindiglia.

I am also appreciative of the detailed suggestions supplied for this edition by the following professors: Don Edwards, Syracuse University; Terry Finnegan, University of Illinois; Tom Grimes, University of Wisconsin-Madison; Richard Labunski, University of Washington; Meg Moritz, University of Colorado; and Robert E. Walker, Hampton University.

And I remain grateful for the work contributed to previous editions by the late Eliot Frankel, James T. Farley, Jr., Alan Walden, Mervin Block, Hyman Bender, Susan Linfield, Mary Quigley, Gerald Lanson, Arthur Engoron, Kathy Lavinder, David Kogan, Mitch Lebe, Dick Petrik, Liz Shanov, Dallas Townsend, Peter Flannery, Bill Diehl, Mike Eisgrau, Russell Patrick, Rick Wallace, Bob Madigan, Mike Sechrist, Wendie Feinberg, Steve Sabato, Lee Giles, Steve Sweitzer, Carissa Howland, Ed Walsh, Jeff Wald, Karen Crow, Larry Dodd, John Harding, Constance Ober, David Miller, Lou Adler, Mike Callaghan, Susan Brudick, Gael Garbarion, Walt Dibble, Tim Lennox, James L. Hoyt, Zoltan Bedy, Steve Ramsey, Jim Stimson, Marv Rockford, Sarah Toppins, William Furnell, Vincent L. Spadafora, Jr., Peter E. Mayeux, Richard D. Yoakam, H. Al Anderson, Ernest F. Andrews, John Cramer, Dan G. Drew, Robert H. Farson, George A. Mastroianni, Robert H. Prisuta, Jayne Rushin, Jay L. Schadler and Roth Wilkofsky; and by Bernard Stephens, Lillian Stephens and Esther Davidowitz.

The book is dedicated to the memory of my father, to my mother and to Esther.

Many news directors provided examples for use in this book. Here is a list of the broadcast news organizations that appear in the book.

NETWORKS
ABC
AP
BBC
CBC
CBS
CNN
INN
Mutual
National Black
  Network
NBC
NPR
PBS
UPI

ALABAMA
WAPI-FM
WBRC-TV
WERC
WNPT
WVOK

ARIZONA
KTSP-TV

ARKANSAS
KATV

CALIFORNIA
KABC
KCBS-TV
KCRA-TV
KFWB
KGO
KGTV
KLOS
KOME
KNAC
KNDE
KNSD-TV
KNX
KNX-FM
KRCR-TV
KRED
KSJO
KSMA
KTLA
KWSO

COLORADO
KCNC-TV
KOA
KREX
KVOR
KWBZ

CONNECTICUT
WSUB
WTIC
WTNH
WXLS

DISTRICT OF COLUMBIA
WETA
WMAL
WRC-TV
WTOP

FLORIDA
WHOO
WINK-TV
WKIS
WLOD
WMEL
WSPB

GEORGIA
WBBQ-FM
WSB

ILLINOIS
WBBM
WBBM-TV
WBNQ
WGN
WJVM
WLS
WLS-FM
WSOY
WXTA

INDIANA
WANE-TV
WARU
WAZY
WIFF
WISH-TV

WNAP
WNDE

IOWA
KLGA
KOEL
KWSL

KANSAS
KFLA
KLWN
KMAN
KWCH-TV

KENTUCKY
WAVE-TV
WBGN
WBLG
WFMW
WVLK

LOUISIANA
WRNO-FM
KWKH

MAINE
WPOR
WRKD

MARYLAND
WCEM

MASSACHUSETTS
WARA
WBUR
WEEI
WHDH
WIEV
WJDA
WRKO
WTEV

MICHIGAN
WDEE
WGHN
WJR
WKNR
WMUS

WSJM
WXYZ

MINNESOTA
KCLD
KCUE
KOWB
KWEB
WCCO

MISSOURI
KSIS

MONTANA
KULR-TV

NEBRASKA
KEZO
KODY
KYNN

NEVADA
KENO
KLUC

NEW MEXICO
KOB

NEW YORK
Shadow Traffic
WABC
WALK
WAXC
WBLS
WCBS
WCBS-TV
WFAN
WHEN
WINS
WMCA
WNBC-TV
WNEW
WNET
WNYW-TV
WOR
WPIX-TV
WPDM

WRFM
WTLB
WWLE

**NORTH
CAROLINA**
WADA
WCHL
WOHS
WRBX

NORTH DAKOTA
KXMB-TV

OHIO
WFIN
WLEC

OKLAHOMA
KAKC
KWHW

OREGON
KEX
KGW

KPNW
KROW

PENNSYLVANIA
KDKA
KQV
WCAU
WFLN
WJET
WKPA
WNAE
WPXI
WTAE-TV
WWWE

**SOUTH
CAROLINA**
WRHI

TENNESSEE
WIVK
WLAC
WMAK
WSIK-FM
WTVF

TEXAS
KBWD
KENR
KEYH
KFJZ
KLOL
KNOW
KRLD
KWTX
Texas State
   Network

UTAH
KWMS

VERMONT
WKVT
WSYB
WWSR

VIRGINIA
WBRG
WFFV
WFIR

WNOR
WNOR-FM
WROV
WRVA
WRVQ
WRVQ-FM

WASHINGTON
KGDN
KGMI
KREW
KWYZ

WEST VIRGINIA
WLOG

WISCONSIN
WHSM
WIBA
WSAU

WYOMING
KCWY-TV
KVOC

About the Author

Mitchell Stephens is chairman of the Department of Journalism at New York University. He has worked for NBC News and written for numerous magazines and newspapers, including the *Columbia Journalism Review*, the *Washington Journalism Review*, the *Los Angeles Times Magazine*, the *Chicago Tribune*, *Newsday* and the *Philadelphia Inquirer*. His book *A History of News* was a *New York Times* "Notable Book of the Year." The *Washington Post* called it "thorough, scrupulous and witty . . . in all respects first-rate, and original, work." He is co-author of *Writing and Reporting the News* with Gerald Lanson.

Broadcast News has been the most widely used radio and television journalism text since publication of its first edition in 1980.

Contents

Introduction

It's 6:52 in the morning. The phone rings in a room at KOEL in Oelwein, Iowa. News director Dick Petrik leans over to answer it and immediately begins typing notes as he shoots out questions:

"You don't know what stores, do you?"

"Did they have guns?"

"Okay, thanks. If you hear any more, get back to me."

It's a tip from a police dispatcher in a nearby county. The sheriff is out investigating a series of robberies, but the dispatcher doesn't have any details; he doesn't even know what stores were hit.

Petrik dials a couple of restaurants and cafés in the area to see if anyone has heard anything. Someone has: A customer at a café saw the sheriff's car leaving a local gas station. Petrik calls the gas station: "I heard the sheriff was there this morning."

"Did he say anything about any robberies in town?"

"The hardware store? Did they hit anywhere else?"

"Are you sure that was the Railroad Diner?"

He calls the hardware store: "I heard they got you last night."

"How much did they take?"

"How many were there? Do you know?"

"When did the sheriff leave?"

The Railroad Diner, and another series of questions. Petrik hooks the telephone up to a tape recorder and records the diner owner's indignant description of the mess the robbers made. Then he begins typing the story. It will be on the air by 7:30.

■ ■ ■

At 11:39 a.m. in Richmond, Virginia, WRVA reporter Dave Miller calls in on the station's direct line from the State Capitol. The story he's been covering all morning has just fizzled. A legislative subcommittee has found "a gentlemanly Virginian" way of killing a proposal to certify teachers. Miller files a story on the rejection of the plan, but a defeated plan is small news.

After he gets off the phone, Miller wanders through the Capitol looking for something hotter.

At 11:46 he stumbles onto something: A representative of one of the candidates for governor says his man is going to mount a major attack on the state's power

1

Dick Petrik has been news director of KOEL, Oelwein, Iowa, for 40 years.

company. Miller writes out a report on the upcoming attack on his pad. By 11:59 he's back on the direct line to the newsroom. His report is recorded, a lead-in is written, and it's aired on the station's 12:05 newscast.

■   ■   ■

At 3:13, Liz Shanov sits behind a typewriter at one of eight desks in WCBS's modern newsroom. She faces a picture window with a view of the East Side of Manhattan. On the walls around her are three clocks, two television sets, two maps, and one poster of King Kong climbing the Empire State Building, with the news director's head pasted over Kong's.

Shanov's fingers are driving her typewriter. On her head are earphones that allow her to audition the tapes of newsmakers and reporters that are stacked on the desk in front of her. Next to the tapes is a pile of wire copy that has been churned out of the station's many small computer printout machines—connected to the Associated Press, United Press International and Reuters. Shanov must turn this collection of wire copy into a series of stories that can be used on the air. She must write copy that integrates those tapes, and whatever additional reports her reporters come up with, into the newscasts. Shanov is responsible for two hours of all-news radio—from 5 to 7 p.m.

*Dave Miller,
WRVA, Richmond,
in a hotel lobby,
talks to a sniper
holed up in an
upper-floor room.
Miller got there
before the police,
called the sniper on
a house phone, and
the recorded
conversations were
played over the air
almost immediately.
Shortly thereafter,
the sniper shot
himself. (Amir
Pishdad, Richmond
Newspapers, Inc.)*

■ ■ ■

This book is about newswriters—like Liz Shanov—and reporters—like Dave Miller.

Newswriters take information from the wire services, tips, their own research and the station's reporters, and turn it into copy that is ready to be read on the air.

Reporters specialize in gathering information—at news events or on the telephone. They have to get the facts, usually on audio- or videotape, and turn them into reports that can be included in newscasts.

Newscasters—who read copy prepared by newswriters—and **news directors**—who are responsible for running a station's news operation—also appear frequently in the book.

At small-town radio stations such as KOEL, a newscaster like Dick Petrik will also handle the jobs of newswriter, reporter and news director. (At some stations that person also has to spin records.) Major radio stations in big cities, however, may hire different people to fill each of these roles. And in television news—a more complex undertaking—the staffs grow larger still, and the jobs get more specialized.

At 5:59 in the evening at WTNH, a television station in New Haven, Connecticut, the producer of the 6 o'clock newscast, Steve Sabato, is sitting in the control

room of the studio, staring at his script. The newscast's director, perched on a stool next to him, is checking sound levels and camera angles. The two newscasters, visible on one of the dozens of monitors stacked on the wall in front of Sabato, are settling in before the cameras. There is now less than a minute to go before air time, and Sabato still doesn't know when *SPEZIALE* will be ready. And *SPEZIALE*—a videotape report on files the police reportedly kept on a judge named Speziale—is scheduled to be the second story in Sabato's newscast.

Producers—like Steve Sabato—will also play a major role in this book. They are responsible for forming a coherent newscast out of the efforts of the team of newswriters, reporters, newscasters, assignment editors, photographers, tape editors, graphics artists and broadcast technicians employed by a station like WTNH. Producers are in charge of television newscasts. Sabato had spent his day deciding what stories to use in his newscast, fitting them into the exactly 58 minutes and 27 seconds he has to fill and approving or editing those stories as they were completed . . . if they were completed. The reporter and photographer assigned to *SPEZIALE* returned to the newsroom late and have not yet finished writing the story and editing the videotape.

Videotape on the newscast's opening story is playing on the air at 6:01 when Sabato makes a decision. "Float page four," he tells the director and, through an intercom, the two newscasters. In other words, Sabato wants them to pull the introduction to the *SPEZIALE* story, which is on page four of the newscast's script, and

Producer Steve Sabato editing a news script. (WTNH 8, New Haven)

put it aside for later in the newscast. The director and newscasters confirm that they have "floated page four."

However, at 6:02, a newswriter dashes into the control room and announces to Sabato that *SPEZIALE* has just been finished. Sabato makes another quick decision. He calls over to the director and gets back on the intercom: "Page four is back," he announces. The story is inserted back into the scripts, and 20 seconds later one of the newscasters is reading the introduction to that report on the file on Judge Speziale. The videotape, complete with the reporter's narration, plays right on schedule. It all looks perfectly smooth on the screen.

Steve Sabato watches the monitor, sighs and then begins worrying about the live report that is coming up at 6:23.

Broadcast news is not always this frantic, but it *is* always being produced under deadline pressure. Newscasts, or even public affairs shows, must be ready to air at set hours, and—whether or not the subcommittee has killed the plan or the reporter has returned late—every second should be filled with an intelligent, intelligible and accurate account of current events.

The settings for most of the action in this book are broadcast newsrooms or broadcast studios. They can be busy, futuristic rooms—like the newsroom at WCBS or the control room at WTNH—or quiet little rooms with a few desks, phones and computers—like KOEL's newsroom. But whether these rooms sit next to a soybean field or in a skyscraper overlooking Manhattan, their occupants have the same jobs: efficiently pulling information in, then promptly turning it into something interesting and understandable—*writing*, *reporting* and *producing*.

I

Copy

Can you read this sentence out loud smoothly and quickly?

> Dp. Atty. Gen. Paco Niemyer says ~~says~~ Daphne Shottenkirk was sitting on her porch on RR#1 when a truck drove by and spilled $658,439 in bills and 13 lbs. of coins on the street in front of her.

The pages that broadcast journalists produce do not just have to be read; they have to be read on the air. Abbreviations, numbers, symbols, confusing corrections, sloppiness or unclear typography—anything that causes the newscaster to hesitate or stumble—impair the newscast.

To protect newscasters and keep everything in order, broadcast newsrooms have developed style rules for their copy. Mastering these rules is the first step in producing broadcast copy; it is also the first step in understanding the special job broadcast copy has to do. This would be a much duller task if broadcast style rules were followed just because that's the way it has always been done. Fortunately, broadcast news is too young to be overgrown with traditions. Nor are these rules concerned with sprucing up the pages to please thousands of readers. Only one person will read the copy—a newscaster. As far as looks go, newscasters demand only that their copy be consistent and easy to read.

Since there are so few traditions determining the layout of the pages, finished copy varies from newsroom to newsroom. The rules discussed here are not "gospel." They have been selected because they seem the most effective or adaptable.

Consistency

There are all sorts of ways broadcast news copy could be livened up. You might imitate the poet E. E. Cummings and

type
    the
        words in
            e
            voc
            a
            tive
            patterns.

Or place the paper in the typewriter at rakish angles or capitalize every third word. Such "creativity," however, would not last long in a newsroom. Newscasters want every page of copy to look like the page before it, so that they know exactly where to look and what to read. Surprises and variations in format upset concentration and cause mistakes.

These first style rules ensure that each page of copy follows the same format. They are designed for consistency.

Computers

When Dick Petrik, phone snug against his ear, types out stories for his early morning newscasts on KOEL in Oelwein, Iowa, he now types them into a computer. KOEL abandoned its old typewriters in 1991.

Under various aliases (perhaps **VDT**, for video display terminal, or **word processor**) computers have now infiltrated most of the television and radio stations in the United States; most of the rest will be buying systems soon. News Director Joe Gillespie of WTOP in Washington admits to missing the noise of typewriters in the newsroom, but he calls computers "a godsend" for broadcast journalists.

Computer systems vary widely in sophistication. Some stations simply locate a few small personal computers in the newsroom. A basic word-processing system, like Word Perfect, then allows stories to be more easily corrected and updated. Other stations, particularly television stations, have installed complex computer networks featuring custom software that can organize and distribute scripts and zip information—changing election returns, for example—directly to monitors in the studios. Computers have probably improved the production of newscasts "a thousandfold!" exclaims Joe Rovitto, news director of WTAE-TV in Pittsburgh, with perhaps a touch of exaggeration.

The use of computers is changing some of the rules of broadcast copy style, but the first rule stays the same: Whether a newsroom features modern keyboards or still uses creaky old manual typewriters, all copy *must* be typed. On the air there is no time to figure out whether that loop was meant to be an *o* or an *e*. Whatever the quality of penmanship, handwritten copy is out.

No one cares how many fingers a writer uses to work the keyboard as long as the copy comes out clean, readable—and fast. Broadcast newswriters turn out much more copy per day than newspaper reporters; so a typing speed of less than 40 words

Newswriters prepare copy in CNN's newsroom in Atlanta. (© 1988 CNN, Inc. All Rights Reserved)

a minute is a handicap. That 5-minute newscast goes on the air at 9 o'clock sharp. There's no such thing as an extension or an incomplete.

A question on which broadcast newsrooms are clearly divided is whether to type all-caps or upper/lower case. Some use all-capital letters because the letters are larger and, they believe, easier to read. Others use the standard upper/lower case style, with which most of us are familiar, because it gives more visual information. For instance, the distinction between proper names and other words is more clear in upper/lower case:

```
The space shuttle Atlantis ended its mission three days
early this afternoon -- touching down safely at
California's Edwards Air Force Base. NASA shortened the
mission after a navigational unit failed.
                                            Forrest Sawyer, ABC
```

Most television newsrooms use all-caps copy, at least in scripts for newscasters in the studio, but there are exceptions: "Several of our anchors [newscasters] prefer upper and lower case," says Marvin Rockford, news director of KCNC-TV in Denver. "And our newswriters are instructed to accommodate them."

Which style of typing is best to learn? Although the majority of broadcast journalists probably type all-caps, there is a clear advantage to learning to type broadcast copy with the normal mix of small letters and capitals: It's much easier to switch from upper/lower to all-caps—all you have to do is press the lock on the shift of your keyboard. If a writer learns all-caps, however, and then gets a job in a newsroom that uses upper/lower, it will be necessary to regain the habit of capitalizing. Upper/lower case typing is therefore more adaptable.

One final typing rule: Always double or, better, triple space. It is easier for newscasters to read and leaves room for corrections if stories need to be edited outside of the computer. (The examples in this book are single-spaced to save space.)

Margins

Copy that is spread all over the page is difficult to read. Wide margins are best in broadcast news—they make the copy stand out. Most radio newswriters leave a one-inch margin on both the left and right side of the page, which allows room for about 55 or 60 characters per line. It's important that the length of lines of copy be consistent so that the time it takes to read a story can be determined by counting the lines.

Radio news stories tend to be short and should be centered on the page—beginning at least two and a half inches from the top.

Television news copy uses different margins. They are discussed in Chapter 16, "Writing to Visuals."

Headings

As the stories flow through the newsroom—in and out of computers, files and newscasts—the news staff must be able to identify each one at a glance. Therefore, each page of copy must have a heading that tells anyone picking it up a few things about the copy on that page. There is no time to produce an involved summary at the top of each story, but a certain minimal amount of information is necessary:

The Slug The **slug** is the name or title the writer gives the story. It's the word or words people in the newsroom use to refer to that story throughout that day and after the story finds its way into the files.

The slug will also serve as the "file name" under which that story is stored in the computer. A story about the recall of some Chevrolets might be slugged *CHEVY*.

A slug must be short. Writers rarely waste words by using a slug longer than one or occasionally two words. A statement by Senator Joseph Biden on a Supreme Court nominee may be slugged *BIDEN*. When the murderer who called himself Son of

Sam was terrorizing New York City, *SAM* was an adequate slug—no need for his full name.

A slug must be clear. The slug must clearly identify the story it heads. Don't get cute and slug a story about the city council's failure to act on the proposed highway—*NOTHING*. That may succeed in amusing colleagues, but at the risk of confusing them. Choose a word or two that clearly labels the story, in this case—*COUNCIL* or *HIGHWAY*. And watch out for slugs that might refer to more than one story in the newsroom that day. *MURDER* is not an acceptable slug in a large city—there are too many of them. Be more specific—*KNIFING* or *STRANGLER*. Similarly, the name of the president is rarely used as a slug. He is involved in too many different stories. Slug his plan for veterans—*VETS*—or his trip to Europe—*EUROPE TRIP*.

A slug must be all-caps—so it stands out from the copy below.

The Date Each story heading should include the date the story was written. Exact records are vital in the news business. Sometime in the future, someone may refer back to the *COUNCIL* story and need to know the exact date of that meeting.

The Time of the Next Newscast News loses its freshness quickly on the radio. The time—"6:30am"— in the heading tells everyone that by 10 a.m. that story is already at least 3½ hours old. That's important.

The Writer's Initials or Last Name Often newscasters or the writers of later shows will have a question about a story. A name or initials on the story tell them whom to ask. This is also the writer's way of taking responsibility for the story. It shows colleagues in the newsroom where to direct the praise or blame.

■ ■ ■

Some newsrooms omit one or two of these items; some may add an additional item; but these four make up the standard heading. They are typed in the upper-left-hand corner of the page, clearly separate from the body of the story. Stacked:

```
EUROPE TRIP
11/11
10:05am
mullins
```

Or across the top of the page:

```
EUROPE TRIP 11/11 10:05am mullins
```

Here's a page of copy with a heading for use at 6:15 p.m.:

```
7-21 shanov HEAT                                    6:15pm

    The record-breaking heat got to 66 youngsters while
they were attending the Yeshiva-Flatbush Broad Channel
Day Camp this afternoon.
    The children started complaining of headaches,
weakness and nausea . . . classic signs of heat
exhaustion. Some of them were too weak to walk to the
nearby Peninsula Hospital Center . . . so they had to be
carried into the emergency room by camp counselors.
    All the campers recovered after resting for a while
in the hospital's air-conditioned auditorium.
                         Liz Shanov, WCBS, New York City
```

Some computer systems automatically print the date at the top of stories and then prompt the writer to finish the heading.

Pages

Despite their growing use of computers, most broadcast organizations have not yet arrived at the entirely paperless newsroom. At NBC Radio, where stories could be read directly off monitors in the studio, former president Jim Farley reported that newscasters still felt more secure entering the newsroom with a script—essentially a collection of computer printouts—in hand.

In television news, computer "teleprompters" allow newscasters to read their scripts while looking directly at the camera, but those newscasters still keep paper copies of those scripts in front of them. That enables them to prepare for upcoming stories.

Most newswriters, therefore, still have to think in terms of paper, of pages, and they have to follow certain rules for preparing those pages. Here's the first: one story to a page. A newscast script will often need to be rearranged at the last minute—stories added, subtracted or just shuffled. If a few stories are written on the same page, that becomes impossible.

Few radio stories run longer than one page. Television stories often do. If the newswriter does have an opportunity to take a pen to the script, the most graphic way to indicate on the bottom of a page that the story continues onto the next page is with a heavy, dark arrow—pointing to the right. Otherwise, the newspaper cue for a continuation—*(MORE)*—can be typed at the bottom of the page.

FIRST ADD should then be included in the heading of the second page. Why not simply number the pages 1, 2, 3? Numerals are reserved for numbering the pages of the final newscast script.

How do writers indicate that the story is finished? Many type -0- or -30- or ####, centered, a few lines after the final line of the story. Others do not use any symbol to mark the end of the story. If there is no arrow or *(MORE)* at the end of a page, it is understood to be the end of that story.

Readability

The rest of the style rules covered here are designed to make the copy as easy as possible to read on the air.

Numbers

Read this out loud quickly: *$57,313.* If you had to pause for a moment, it may have been because the dollar sign, which should be read last, is written first; or perhaps because it takes time to translate the numerals into words. The seconds it takes to convert these symbols into "fifty-seven thousand, three hundred and thirteen dollars" are enough to throw off a newscaster's pacing. Numbers pose difficulties—they must be written in the clearest possible fashion.

Some newsrooms solve the problem by spelling out all numbers. The disadvantage of this approach is that time is wasted typing long trains of words that are confusing in themselves because they are unfamiliar to us—*twenty-nine million, three hundred and seventy-four thousand.*

A few newsrooms try to get by with numerals and take their chances that their newscasters can convert *29,374,000* swiftly. But most broadcast newsrooms follow a set of rules for numbers designed to make them as easy as possible to read on the air:

1. Spell out all numbers through eleven. Three, six, ten are familiar words, while numerals like 1, 8, 11 can get lost in the copy.
2. Use numerals for all numbers from 12 to 999. They're easy to read, while writing them out—*seven-hundred and ninety-three*—takes more energy and is more confusing.
3. Spell out the words *thousand, million* and *billion,* but use numerals for the numbers that modify them—*75-thousand, 3-million, 400-billion.* Never make the newscaster count commas, as in *45,672,000.* Write—*45-million, 672-thousand.* Since the numerals 1 and 11 are so skinny that they tend to get lost or confused, always spell them out—even in combination with thousand, million or billion—*one-million, eleven-thousand.*
4. Years are an exception—practice has made us expert at reading them. Write *1988, 1492,* not *nineteen eighty-eight.*
5. Ordinal numbers under 12th can be handled either way. Both *third* and *3rd* are easy to read. From 12th to 999th, use numerals with their suffix—*22nd, 456th.*

Larger ordinals should be handled with a combination of words and numerals— *13-billionth, 2nd million.*

6. All the symbols and terms used with numbers should be spelled out. *Dollar* is the one used most frequently. Write: *3-million dollars, 48 dollars.* Never use the dollar sign (\$). This is true for cents, degrees, pounds, inches, percent, feet, miles, acres, years, minutes, seconds, hours and all metric measurements—*50 liters, five kilometers.*

7. Fractions and decimal points should always be spelled out—*three-fourths, one-half, three point two, 7 point 5 million.*

8. Numbers that are being used in the same context should be written in the same way. Don't write a score as *24 to ten.* Write: *24 to 10.* However, numbers that should be read separately can often be best understood when written in different styles: *His score was 60, twelve under par.*

These are rules that make numbers easier to read on the air, but there's one final rule about numbers that is discussed in Chapter 2—they should not be used too often.

Abbreviations

An abbreviation quiz: What do these letters stand for?

Mo.	Dec.
CST	Alta.
mm	Rep.
bros.	

If you had to hesitate for a moment over any of the answers (Missouri, Central Standard Time, millimeter, brothers, December, the Canadian province Alberta, Representative), you should be able to guess the rule for most abbreviations in broadcast news copy—don't use them. Newscasters can't afford to hesitate.

Newswriters should write a word as they want it to be read. If they want *Lieutenant Governor,* they should write *Lieutenant Governor,* not *Lt. Gov.* If they want *New Mexico,* they should not write *NM.* However, when the abbreviation is to be read by the newscaster as an abbreviation, it should be written that way, with hyphens separating the letters: *C-I-A, A-F-L-C-I-O, Y-M-C-A, I-B-M, F-C-C, p-m, A-S-P-C-A, C-B-S, A and P.* Also, *N double-A-C-P* and *N-C double-A.*

Well-known acronyms such as *NATO, NASA, UNICEF* and *OPEC* obviously don't need to be spelled out, nor do they need hyphens between their letters because the individual letters are not meant to be read.

Often in a story a writer introduces an organization by its full name, then refers to it by its initials when mentioning it again. The first time it is the *National Football League,* afterwards, *N-F-L.*

The only exceptions to this rule are titles of personal address—*Mr., Ms., Mrs., Miss, Dr.* There is no need to spell them out because newscasters can read them without hesitating.

Corrections

Amid the clutter of a broadcast newsroom some delicate work is going on. The copy those pressured men and women are slamming out of their computers must be clean enough for a newscaster, sometimes more than one newscaster, to read smoothly and surely.

The best way to correct an error is in the computer. But if the copy has been printed out, or if the writer is using a typewriter, changes will have to be made directly on the copy—neatly. Broadcast journalists cannot use complex deletion marks; they cannot add words by scribbling them in the margins; and they cannot use arrows to show that they want paragraphs flip-flopped—because the newscaster's eye should not be asked to follow arrows, glance at the margin or decipher symbols.

All corrections in broadcast news copy must be written or typed in the main body of the copy—exactly where they are supposed to be read. They must be clear and easily understood. Often corrections are handwritten—using block printing, never script. In those cases the handwriting must be neat and bold, not dainty. You will never hear a newscaster say, "I think this says . . ."

There are only four copy markings used to correct broadcast copy:

1. Deletion. To cross out a word or two, draw a bold, solid line through the words—a line that is dark enough so that there is no doubt that everything under the line is out:

    The ███████ accident was the second this month.

    Most newswriters then draw an arc over the deleted words to direct the newscaster's eye to what comes next:

    In both accidents somebody ███ was seriously injured.

2. Substitution. To switch words, cross out the old one and write the new word or words above it—neatly. Draw little lines to show exactly where the new word belongs:

    That corner ███*does not*███ have a traffic light.

Place punctuation marks next to the words they follow so that they are not overlooked:

UNACCEPTABLE

Both accidents ~~had the same cause~~ -- someone ran a stop
sign.

ACCEPTABLE

Both accidents ~~had the same cause --~~ someone ran a stop
sign.

3. Addition. To add one or more words, use a symbol that shows clearly where the additional words go:

A group of (community leaders) has petitioned the city to install a light.

4. Major deletion. To show that the end of a line of copy, or a complete line or more, has been crossed out, put a bold line through the deleted words; then draw a line to guide the newscaster's eye to the words that should be read next:

The Minnesota Pollution, ██████████████████████

████████ Control Agency is ████████████████

████████████ declaring a moratorium on the

building of large cattle and pig feedlots.

These are all the correction symbols that should be used. To change letters *in* a word, cross out the entire word and retype it or print it neatly above. Never fiddle with the letters:

UNACCEPTABLE
They'll be there to greet the

president.

Similarly, to add a whole sentence to the copy, retype the entire page. Never try to squeeze a sentence in between two other lines or connect it with arrows.

"The whole idea," explains Neil Offen, news director at WCHL in North Carolina, "is to make sure that when newscasters are at the microphone they're not going to stumble." Offen suggests that his newswriters look over their stories carefully on

Neil Offen, news director at WCHL, North Carolina. (Mitchell Stephens)

the computer screen, then print them out and edit them again—using proper correction symbols. Then, if there's time, or if they've made a lot of corrections, he wants them to make the changes on the computer and print out a new, clean copy.

Don't Split Words

The rules of grammar permit breaking a word between syllables at the end of a line if there is no room to type the complete word. In a term paper or a business report you may write "En-" at the end of one line and "glish" at the start of the next. However, broadcast style is stricter. Splitting words by syllables is not allowed because split words are difficult to read aloud without adding an unnatural pause. The newswriter doesn't want the newscaster to say "En (pause) glish." The word should be read "English," so that is how it should be written—all syllables together.

If the complete word will not fit at the end of one line, start the whole word on the next. If part of the word has already been typed, and the rest will not fit, cross it out and start again on the next line. And if your computer has a hyphenating program, don't use it.

Don't Split Sentences

This is a similar rule. Sentences should not be continued onto a second page in broadcast news because that would cause the newscaster to pause inappropriately in the middle of the sentence while flipping the page.

If the complete sentence will not fit at the end of the first page, change pages and type the whole sentence on a next page. If you find yourself running out of paper in the middle of a sentence, cross out the part of a sentence you have already typed and start it again on the next page.

Emphasis

This sentence can have four different meanings:

Then they deported him. (They had waited until that time.)

Then they deported him. (Officials of two other countries had already deported him.)

Then they deported him. (He had already been arrested and held without bail.)

Then they deported him. (His wife had been deported a week earlier.)

The meaning of the sentence depends on which of the four words is emphasized.

When words are written to be read out loud, emphasis becomes a semantic tool. Broadcast journalists often use emphasis to clarify or modify the meaning of the words they write:

He was shocked when he found HIS name on the indictment.

He was shocked when he found his name on the indictment.

There are two effective ways to indicate that a word should be emphasized by the newscaster. (Italics and boldface, while easy to produce on most computers, are too subtle for broadcast news.)

1. Underlining. This is the most common method.

The suspect was driving a car similar to the one the witness had described.

The suspect was driving a car similar to the one the witness had described.

2. All-caps. (This device is not available, of course, when the copy itself is typed in all-capital letters.)

```
Officials say ONE MATCH may have started the fire.

Officials say one match MAY have started the fire.
```

The word *not* deserves special mention. For a small word it has tremendous power—by itself it can completely reverse the meaning of a sentence.

```
The district attorney said he did do it.

The district attorney said he did not do it.
```

Not has a tendency to get confused with the word *now*. In deference to its power, underlining or typing it all-caps is usually wise. Even with this precaution, prudence dictates that the world *innocent* be used instead of *not guilty*. A libel suit could result from a newscaster omitting the *not* there (see Chapter 18, "Ethics and Law").

Pauses

Broadcast news is written to be performed. A pause is occasionally called for, and, like a stage cue, the pause should be indicated in the script.

Ensuring that the newscaster pauses a beat between sentences can help separate different thoughts:

```
The union's leader called the offer
unsatisfactory. . . . Talks will continue tomorrow.
```

A pregnant pause can add a touch of drama to broadcast news:

```
She said her major enemy is -- herself.
```

The traditional grammatical indicators of pauses are periods, commas and semicolons. The semicolon is a device for holding together long, rambling sentences. There are no long, rambling sentences in broadcast news. The semicolon is not needed. The comma and period remain valuable tools, but the broadcast journalist often looks for punctuation marks with more visual impact.

Commas and periods don't look like pauses. A dash (--) and an ellipsis (. . .), on the other hand, are graphic cues for the reader to rest a beat between words. Broadcast journalists use them frequently. For example:

```
The city council ruled that sidewalks WILL be put in
. . . in all new sub-divisions -- bar none.
                                      KCUE, Minnesota
```

Some notes on pauses:

1. Remember that on a computer a dash is typed: space, hyphen, hyphen, space (--).

2. The ellipsis is an ideal stage cue because the desired length of the pause can be shown by the number of dots in the ellipsis. The usual three dots might mean a one-beat pause. Five or six tell the newscaster to stop for one and a half or two beats.

```
The city real estate tax rate has been climbing steadily
for the past ten years . . . and today the city tax
commission said this year is no exception. . . . . The
hike will be high . . . a jump of 65 cents for each 100
dollars of assessed value.
                                          WMCA, New York City
```

3. Remember that these punctuation marks, like the periods and commas they replace, must be used in accordance with the rules of grammar.

```
UNACCEPTABLE
The town supervisor -- Paul Earl says he doesn't like
the plan.
```

```
ACCEPTABLE
The town supervisor -- Paul Earl -- says he doesn't like
the plan.
```

4. There is a subtle difference in the function of an ellipsis and a dash. An ellipsis generally is used to tack on an additional thought: "He's going to Washington . . . to finish out his term." The dash is used to qualify or clarify the previous thought: "He's going to Washington—the city where his problems started."

Spelling

Listeners will never know whether a writer spelled the name of the chairman of the Chinese Communist Party correctly in broadcast copy. They'll never find out that a newswriter doesn't know how to spell *separate* or confuses *site* with *cite*. So why worry about spelling?

Worry because faulty spelling can damage a reputation in the newsroom; worry because sloppy spelling can lead to sloppy pronunciation, which listeners *will* hear; most of all, worry because spelling errors can jar a newscaster into an error.

If *decision* is spelled *dicision*, the newscaster can read the word easily enough but, a few words later, may be wondering, "What illiterate wrote this copy?" And that thought might well interfere with the reading of the next line and cause the newscaster to stumble. If nothing else, sloppy spelling is a distraction, and distractions cannot be allowed to creep into copy.

Some people are congenitally bad spellers, but there is a cure for this disease: concentration . . . and a dictionary. Keep a concise dictionary by your desk and use it a lot (not "alot"). It takes about 25 seconds to look up a word. If a writer has any doubt about how the word is spelled, those 25 seconds are a wise investment. "You can say this is broadcast and you can get away with spelling mistakes," suggests Lee Giles, news director of WISH-TV Indianapolis. "But people are going to have to read your copy, and you're going to get caught."

Broadcast journalists do choose to differ with the dictionary in one area—the use of hyphens. The word *antiaircraft*, for instance, is easier to read with a hyphen: *anti-aircraft*. *Semitropical* reads better as *semi-tropical*. But as the stylebook used at Houston's KEYH warns, newswriters have to be careful not to hyphenate us out of the English language. For example, *master-piece* would distract, not help.

Spelling is not generally considered a creative discipline, but some broadcast journalists have come up with what they consider to be improvements on the language that go well beyond the occasional extra hyphen. They spell *says*, one of the most frequently used words in broadcast news, *sez* or shorten *night* to *nite*. And when noting the length of a story, *sex*, they find, is a shorter, and perhaps more stimulating, way to write the abbreviation for seconds. Enuf, u get the idea!

Dallas Townsend, who worked as writer and newscaster for CBS for more than three decades, developed a shorthand for typing his own copy that almost amounts to a code. *The* is *t*, *that* is *tt*, *this* is *ts*, *year* is *yr*, *service* is *svc*, etc. Other writers should wait, however, until they get a decade or two under their belts before they consider experimenting with such shortcuts. In most newsrooms alternative spellings would at the very least disorient those who weren't clued in—especially new employees. They should not be used. Except for an occasional extra hyphen, spell as the dictionary spells.

Pronunciation

Listeners can't react to spelling, but they surely would let the station manager know their feelings if the pronunciation were wrong. Incorrectly pronouncing a place name may be embarrassing. But incorrectly pronouncing a person's name can be both embarrassing and insulting.

Pronunciation is a serious problem when writing foreign news, but it is perhaps even more dangerous in local copy, especially in a small town. At a small station a beginning journalist may find it difficult to sound authoritative as the only person in town who doesn't know that Councilman McCaugh's name is pronounced Mac-COY and School Board President Finkelstein insists that it's Finkel-STEEN, not Finkel-STINE. And woe to anyone in this author's hometown who says STEFF-ens. It's pronounced STEE-fens.

There are two ways to guard against errors in pronunciation:

1. Check the pronunciation of all potentially troublesome names by asking. In a local story this must be one of the questions a writer or reporter should ask Mr. Perez: "Is it PER-ez or Per-EZ?" If necessary call someone who knows the person, or call Mr. Perez. For out-of-town names, a simple call to long-distance information can secure the correct pronunciation of a place or a person who may be well known in that area.

   Foreign names present a different problem with the same solution: ask. The late French author Simone de Beauvoir is in the news. If the wire story does not include a pronunciation guide, or if the writer is not working from wire copy, it's time to call a local French teacher. Sometimes, if the unfamiliar name is not crucial to the story, it might be better to consider writing the story without the name—if it means nothing to the journalist, it probably won't mean anything to the average listener.

2. Indicate clearly in the copy the correct pronunciation. The most effective way is to type the phonetic spelling in parentheses directly above the actual spelling:

```
                    (See-MONE duh BOH-vwahr)
French author Simone de Beauvoir

                    (EEV Sahn Loh-ROHN)
French designer Yves Saint Laurent
```

It's not necessary to master the rules of formal phonetic spelling. Any spelling that conveys the correct pronunciation will do. Just spell it as it sounds. Czech President Vaclav Havel's name sounds like VOSS-lahv HOVH-el; that's good enough. Put a hyphen between syllables and type the accented syllable all-caps.

But remember that pronunciation is a fact and, as with any fact, *almost* right is still wrong.

Timing

Newspaper copy is measured in inches. Broadcast copy is measured in seconds. A newspaper story may have to be cut to nine inches to fit the space left on a page. A broadcast story may have to be cut to 20 seconds to fit the time left in a newscast. Too short, and there may be some **dead air**—silence. Too long, and the start of the next program may be cut off.

How do newswriters calculate how long a broadcast story will run? They read it at the same speed it's going to be read on the air while timing it with a stopwatch. Most newsrooms have stopwatches. You might want to buy your own. The important thing to remember when timing copy is to read it *exactly* as it's going to be read on the air. That means reading it out loud, since we read faster when we read silently.

And read the copy at the pace used by the newscaster. If there's time, get the newscaster to read it.

Obviously, timing each story can be a time-consuming procedure, but after some practice a shortcut may be used. Writers learn how many seconds it takes their newscaster to read a line, and then, using simple arithmetic, determine the number of seconds it will take the newscaster to read a story.

On the average, a 55- to 60-character line runs 3½ to 4 seconds. But don't rely on this. The key factor is the pace of the person who will be reading the copy. Once a newswriter has that down, a whole newscast can be timed just by counting lines. Professional newscasters maintain a consistent pace. This procedure won't work as well with beginners.

The length of the tape (see Chapter 10, "Writing to Tape") used in some radio stories must also be considered when timing newscasts. Television newswriters will have to take into account videotape "packages" (see Chapter 16, "Writing to Visuals").

Some veteran radio newscasters have reached the point where, if they know how much tape they have, they can glance through the pile of copy, glance at the clock, and *know* how much they will have time to read. This sixth sense takes years to develop. Until then, time each story.

Write the time in seconds at the bottom or top of the story and circle it. Using a colon saves the trouble of writing out "seconds":

Computers can now be programmed, once a newscaster's speed is determined, to calculate the time a story will take to read and then automatically print that time on the story.

Testing

In a good broadcast newsroom people are talking to themselves. Broadcast copy is written to be read aloud, and the only safe test of how it will sound is to read it aloud. The BBC in Britain used to force its newswriters to dictate copy to secretaries to ensure that they had put their writing through this oral test.

Stories should be read aloud while they're being written—this is called talking to the computer—and then again after they are complete. A sentence that looks fine on paper may turn out to be too long to read smoothly, may be a tongue twister, may sound too stiff or may actually mislead listeners—who don't have any way of distinguishing between homonyms (words that sound the same but have different meanings). This sentence, used on CBS television, looks harmless enough on paper:

```
An Interior Department report on Teton Dam is still
pending . . . so are Congressional studies of the Bureau
of Reclamation and other dam-building agencies.
```

But when read aloud, the last three words here sound a little too much like a curse. (Better: "other agencies responsible for building dams.") "If you read your copy aloud to yourself before turning it in," Mervin Block suggested in his CBS in-house newsletter (where that sentence was flagged), "you'll catch seemingly innocent combinations of words that sound damning."

Giving your mouth a shot at what you have written can also help catch another set of problems. Certain design defects in human vocal tracts and limitations in microphones must be considered when writing broadcast copy. For example, when people read a few consecutive *s*, *sh*, *z*, or soft *c* sounds—sibilant sounds—they start hissing:

```
UNACCEPTABLE
She said small size businesses are especially
susceptible to idiosyncrasies in business cycles.
```

WAZY in Indiana changed the first wording to the second to stop the hiss:

```
No-fault car insurance is being considered . . .

No-fault car insurance being considered . . .
```

A series of popping *p* or *b* sounds can make little exploding noises in the microphone:

```
UNACCEPTABLE
Poor planning precipitated a basically perpendicular
plummet in popular products.
```

And in a sentence with too many *r* sounds, the words will be drowned out by the rumble:

```
UNACCEPTABLE
Repeated reordering errors require a corrective
response.
```

These aural annoyances shouldn't scare off all attempts at alliteration. Repeating some letters can sometimes give a sentence a pleasing sound. Notice how the repetition of *k* and *b* sounds adds flavor to this line:

```
She bakes the worms until they're crispy, and then
crumbles them into a quiche like bacon bits.
                                  Dallas Townsend, CBS
```

The only sure test of what will work is to read the sentence aloud. The ear is the best critic. Every story should be read aloud.

Wrap-Up

A list of copy style rules:

1. Computers—type upper/lower case, double or triple space.
2. Margins—leave an inch on each side of the page; center copy on the page.
3. Headings—slug, date, time of next newscast and writer's initials or last name.
4. Pages—one story per page; an arrow or *(MORE)* at the bottom if there are more pages; *FIRST ADD, SECOND ADD* instead of numbering pages 2, 3.
5. Numbers—
   up to eleven, spell out
   from 12 to 999, use numerals
   one-thousand and up, use combinations of numerals and words
   numerals for years
   spell out all symbols
   spell out fractions and decimal points
   numbers being used the same way, write the same way
6. Abbreviations—write them as they are supposed to be read, except titles of personal address.
7. Corrections—place them in the copy where they are supposed to be read; there are only four acceptable correction symbols:
   deletion (of word or words)
   substitution (of word or words)
   addition (of word or words)
   major deletion (whole or partial lines)
8. Don't split words onto different lines.
9. Don't split sentences onto different pages.
10. Emphasis—indicate by underlining or typing all-caps.
11. Pauses—dashes and ellipses effective where used properly.
12. Spelling—with the exception of conventions accepted by the entire newsroom, spelling counts.
13. Pronunciation—check; indicate difficult pronunciations in the copy.
14. Timing—time all copy.
15. Testing—read all copy aloud.

Practice Assignments

A. Edit these sentences for use in broadcast copy, using proper correction marks.

1. ¾ of a million bees are being evicted from the park at 12th St. today.
2. Police say there have been twenty-two murders in the city this year . . . 8% more than last year.

3. More than 100,000 people are expected to attend the festival named for Woodstock, NY.
4. Police say 13 lbs. of marijuana were discovered in the home of a Dedham high school student at 8:00 last night.
5. The temperature in Lansing, Mich., dropped to $-10°$ last night . . . a record low.
6. State workers in New Jersey have won a pay hike of $2.13/hr., up 5.8% from last year.
7. CORE and the NAACP will challenge the Federal Bureau of Investigation in court in Dec.
8. O-P-E-C will announce a $5/barrel price increase today.
9. County Chairwoman . . . Ellie Mays says she won't support Gov. Flannery.
10. He hopes to sail to Marseilles -- France and then drive to Cannes.
11. If they choose to negotiate seperate contracts, it could delay work at the construction sight alot longer.
12. Next he'll visit Wiesbaden, W. Germany -- then he heads home.

B. Type out this story with a heading, using proper copy style.

Two research scientists for the Centers for Disease Control are being allowed to return to work after spending 3 weeks in isolation. The two were accidentally exposed to the deadly African virus Lassa Fever, first detected in Zaire 10 years ago. Normally the incubation period for the disease is fourteen days, but medical experts kept the two men under observation for an extra week, just to make sure.

2

Words

Newspapers, books and magazines are written for the eye. The words in radio and television newscasts, however, are written to be heard, not read, by their audiences. They are written for the ear. This might seem like a mere anatomical technicality, but it is, perhaps, the key to understanding the nature of broadcast newswriting.

The eye and the ear have different tastes. More of the brain is devoted to the eyes than to any of the other senses. The eye is sharp enough to take its information straight and fast:

```
After a lengthy and politically charged battle, the
Administration and Congress today approved a compromise
civil rights bill that would reduce the proof required
of employees who take their employers to court on
charges of racial or sexual discrimination.
```

The ear, a less sophisticated instrument, gets confused, or bored, by unrelieved lists of facts. The ear prefers an easier, more clever presentation of information:

```
What do you do with a political hot potato? Washington
gave one answer today: compromise. The White House and
Congress have agreed on a civil rights bill. The bill
would make it easier for victims of racial or sexual
discrimination to sue their bosses and collect damages.
                                          Diane Sawyer, ABC
```

One effective way of determining whether broadcast writing suits the needs of the ear is to compare it to another form of communication aimed at that sense—conversation. How would a person who has heard of a major fire downtown tell a friend about it? "Four people were killed and nine others injured this morning in a fire which destroyed the Acme Packing Company." Not likely. The person would probably say, "Hey, a factory burned down this morning and four people were trapped inside and killed."

That is a more conversational way of relating the information. It works better for the listener's ear than the abrupt, fact-laden newspaper style. And that, without the "hey," is how broadcast news is written—conversationally. Not:

The vice president of the New York City branch of the
Red Cross stated in a press conference today that many
Christmas toys can inflict injury upon unsuspecting
youngsters.

That's not conversational. Instead, a broadcast journalist would write:

A Red Cross official warns that many Christmas toys can
be dangerous for kids.

A broadcast journalist generally has more to say and less time to say it than
people do in conversation; so it won't do to be merely chatty. And broadcast news
has too much power to allow guesses and opinions to spice up the copy. This is
another area in which it parts company with conversation. But the basic style of
broadcast prose is conversational:

Albuquerque could be getting an extra million dollars or
so to create jobs for young people . . . since so many
are out of work here.

KOB, New Mexico

Geoff Hammond of KYNN in Nebraska puts it this way: "Write like you talk, not
like you write." Of course, it's not quite that simple, as Andy Rooney of CBS News
has noted: "No one speaks as he writes or writes as he speaks; writing for broadcast
is a compromise between the two."

If you have been trained in newspaper journalism, broadcast newswriting is going
to require you to make some adjustments. Although newspaper style is changing (in
part due to the influence of broadcast news), newspapers still use a harder, less
conversational style. For example, the *New York Times* printed:

Dr. William J. Ronan defended yesterday the expense-paid
overseas trips he took with his wife when he was
chairman of the Port Authority of New York and New
Jersey, and he told a legislative inquiry that such
business travel by commissioners and their spouses
should be encouraged.

A broadcast journalist would write:

Former Chairman William Ronan says it wasn't a bad idea
for the Port Authority to fly him and his wife overseas.
In fact, he says, such all-expense-paid trips should be
encouraged.

In a survey of working broadcast journalists, noted in the publication of the
Radio–Television News Directors Association, 78 percent of those who responded

said that "writing competence was the most important ability prospective broadcast journalists should have." This chapter and the four that follow are about writing, starting with the basics: words.

Common Language

Broadcast news is not written to impress or uplift. Its job is to communicate information; so it must speak a language that most listeners understand. That means no stately effects, unwieldy words, strange jargon or stiff constructions . . . and slang only when it's clear. Ornamentation hinders communication.

Broadcast news must speak the common tongue. What follows are rules for writing plain English.

Informal

How often is the verb *state* used in conversation? "That man *states* that he escaped through the back." And how about the pronoun *one*? "*One* has to make a reservation to eat at that restaurant." These are not the kinds of words most of us use when we talk. They sound too formal and pretentious. Therefore, they have no place in broadcast news.

To write conversationally, broadcast journalists use a vocabulary that corresponds to the one used in conversation.

Following is a partial list of words generally too formal for broadcast news, with conversational alternatives.

FORMAL	CONVERSATIONAL
male, female	man, woman
beverage	drink
physician	doctor
attorney	lawyer
deceased	dead
passed away	died
terminate	end
commence	begin
prior to	before
subsequent to	after
endeavor	try
utilize	use
reside	live
edifice	building
residence	home
assemblage	audience

FORMAL	CONVERSATIONAL
consequently	so
transpire	happen
venture	try
cognizant	aware
youth	teenager
laceration	cut
abrasion	scrape
intoxicated	drunk
visage	face
indisposed	ill, sick

Most of the words in the "formal" column have an additional liability. They take longer to say; therefore they waste time. This example of overly formal writing was used on the air:

```
The route is a revision of the Norfolk-Cincinnati
Mountaineer, a two-year experimental route that will be
terminated in compliance with a recent directive issued
by the secretary of transportation.
```

This should read:

```
The new train route will replace the Norfolk-Cincinnati
Mountaineer. The secretary of transportation has decided
to eliminate this two-year-old experimental route.
```

Simple

In some circles an ability to toss around large, obscure words is a measure of intelligence, but not in broadcast news. Using *dissemble* instead of *lie* may impress some, but it is also likely to befuddle others. Small, common words communicate better to a mass audience than their multisyllabic synonyms. On the air this is especially important. Words that we might succeed in deciphering in a newspaper or book are much more difficult to comprehend as they fly by on the radio. For one thing, a listener cannot take the time to puzzle out an obscure word without missing the words that come after.

Here is a list of some words that broadcast journalists have removed from their copy because they are believed to be needlessly obscure, along with acceptable substitutes.

DIFFICULT	CONVERSATIONAL
eschew	avoid
oblique	indirect

DIFFICULT	CONVERSATIONAL
exacerbate	make worse
pernicious	dangerous
peruse	read
remunerate	pay
aperture	opening
imbibe	drink
obfuscate	confuse
conflagration	fire
altercation	argument
contusion	bruise
purloin	steal
prodigious	large
spurious	false

Many additional words that can confuse are in the dictionary and thesaurus. Good broadcast journalists leave them there. And don't despair that your vocabulary will be depleted—rejoice that it will be sharpened.

Journalese

Over the years journalists have developed their own vocabulary. After they had written a few fire stories, they began searching for other ways to say *fire*. So they discovered dynamic little words that had been hibernating in the dictionary—like *blaze*. From then on, the second time a fire was referred to it was called a *blaze*.

Blaze is not an unwieldy word—it weighs in at a trim one syllable. Yet it is not a word that people normally use in conversation. You don't hear mothers warning their kids not to play with matches because they might start a *blaze*.

The newsroom name for words that are used and overused almost exclusively by journalists is *journalese*. You may ask why journalists shouldn't be allowed their own language. The problem is that the more journalists sink into an exclusive vocabulary, the less contact their words have with their listeners.

UNACCEPTABLE
The chief executive scored the milk probe, saying a price hike looms in the future.

All the words above are short and informal, but this is not common language.

ACCEPTABLE
The president is predicting that milk prices will be going up. He says a congressional investigation into the price of milk has accomplished nothing.

The KCBS, San Francisco, newsroom.

JOURNALESE	CONVERSATIONAL
hit, flay, rap, blast	attack
comb	search
heist	robbery
slate	schedule
bar	prevent
nab	catch
mum	quiet

Many of these words have been popularized by newspaper headline writers looking for short, pithy words. Broadcast news must use a more conversational vocabulary.

Technical Terms

Sometimes events get technical. A vice president pleads *nolo contendere*. A *quasar* is discovered because of a dramatic *red shift*. A *capacitor* blows, cutting the sound on a presidential debate. A politician proposes *a line-item veto* or changes in the tax law on *capital gains*.

Some of the words that make news derive from the private languages of technical professions such as law, science, electronics and economics. These words are not familiar to most listeners, but broadcast journalists not only must *know* what technical terms mean, they must be able to *explain* what they mean.

Preparation for this task should begin in school and continue as a lifetime study of the major developments in human knowledge as reported in books, magazines, newspapers and the broadcast media. People who write news must be well-read. But, if a story employs a term that has escaped that lifetime study, it is necessary to get on the phone and search out the definition and explanation from a local lawyer, scientist, economist or other specialist.

Then, once the meaning of a technical term is clear to the writer, the problem is how to communicate its meaning to listeners. Here there's a hard and fast rule — translate all jargon. For better or worse, radio listeners and television viewers are not required to be well-read. Again, it is self-defeating for a newswriter to rely on words listeners may not understand. It certainly is possible to educate and explain, but only in common language.

```
UNACCEPTABLE
Astronomers at a California observatory have discovered
a quasar that demonstrates the largest red shift ever
recorded.
```

```
ACCEPTABLE
Astronomers at a California observatory have discovered
what they believe may be the most distant and fastest
moving object yet sighted in the universe.
```

If the obscure term is important enough for listeners to hear, use it *and* explain it:

```
The vice president pleaded nolo contendere. That means
he doesn't contest the charges. For all intents and
purposes it's the same as pleading guilty, except he
doesn't have to actually admit guilt.
```

A common excuse for failing to translate professional jargon is, "Well, I didn't understand it myself." Obviously that's no excuse.

Slang

Slang can be dangerous. It can exclude some listeners and annoy others. Nevertheless, slang words cannot be completely barred from broadcast news. Often they are witty, charming and pleasing to the ear. Certainly, slang is welcome in most of our conversations:

Republicans think if they can <u>pull off</u> a couple of wins
in Minnesota this fall . . . it could signal a turn-
around for the party nationwide.

WCCO, Minneapolis

Slang presents a problem—it is fun but dangerous. Here are some guidelines
for its use.

1. Don't sound dumb. There are certain slang constructions that do not sound
   clever, just unintelligent:

   ain't
   can't hardly
   you know (as an interjection)
   done up good

2. Don't offend. Obscene language, curses, derogatory names and ethnic slurs are
   out. They foul the air.
   Cops has become so comfortable in our language that it has lost its outlaw
   bite, but *cop* is still an unflattering way to refer to a police officer. Most stations
   won't use it. For one thing, they are dependent on a close working relationship
   with local police.

3. Don't ham it up. Some occasions are simply inappropriate for slang:

   UNACCEPTABLE
   The Russian leader doesn't seem to know where the
   president is at.

   And some slang terms are just flip substitutes for perfectly good words. They
   push writing beyond the conversational into the realm of the frivolous and
   affected:

   UNACCEPTABLE
   The feds are looking to chase some local politicos into
   the slammer.

4. Know your audience. On a rock-and-roll station, slang expressions such as *rad*
   or *dude* would be understood and might therefore be acceptable.

   The Supreme Court handed down a decision today that will
   make it harder for police to make drug busts.

WNDE, Indiana

You wouldn't use this terminology on a station with older listeners.

In the South, an occasional *you all* might work on a station with an informal programming format. For an extreme example, one country station supplied the following weather forecast:

```
The back side of you is gonna get kinda wet if you run
East tonight cause we is suspecting that some wawa may
fall out of the blanket in the sky and bring some of that
much needed precip. Don't worry none though -- me and
Clem will stay up all night keeping the bugger away so
you and your livestock won't get hurt. Tell man to sleep
on the couch tonight -- it's gonna be 71 for a low and
that's too much temp to mix with funning.
```

It's hard to imagine an audience for which that would be acceptable.

5. Choose your spot. A slightly unfamiliar slang term can sometimes be used if the meaning of the sentence doesn't hinge on the meaning of the term:

```
All the "good buddies" out there with a C-B radio are
facing a crackdown on violations here in Virginia and
across the nation.
```
                                                                WFIR, Virginia

Even if the listener is not really sure what *good buddies* means, this sentence makes sense.

But relatively unfamiliar slang terms cannot be used if the listener's understanding of the sentence might depend on understanding that word:

```
UNACCEPTABLE
The residents of south central Los Angeles have
apparently decided it's time to "chill."
```

6. Careful, Daddy-o. Slang is the least stable branch of the language; its fashions change rapidly. For instance, here is a selection from 40 years' worth of slang synonyms for the word *great*:

the cat's pajamas	far out
tops	right on
ducky	heavy
neat	mellow
nifty	outrageous
real gone	bad
way out	totally awesome
groovy	radical
too much	way cool
outta sight	

It's all too easy to use slang words that are either too avant-garde or too dated. Broadcast writing shouldn't be too strait-laced, but go easy on the *jive*.

Contractions

People generally *don't* say "do not," *they're* not likely to say "they are," and they usually *won't* say "will not." Contractions are part of broadcast news, just as they're part of conversation.

    WEAK
    There is a good chance.

    BETTER
    There's a good chance.

    WEAK
    It is not likely.

    BETTER
    It's not likely.

Still, there are situations where it's wise to think twice before substituting an apostrophe for one or two letters. Combining words in contractions tends to de-emphasize these words. If a word needs underlining, it's best not to contract it:

    WEAK
    The president will stay home, but his wife's going.

    BETTER
    The president will stay home, but his wife is going.

And, since it is often important to emphasize the word *not* in a sentence, it's usually best to keep it out of contractions:

    WEAK
    The president isn't going.

    BETTER
    The president is not going.

Engaging Language

A newswriter's subjects are by definition the most interesting events in a community or in the world. A serious accident does not have to be dramatized with adjectives and superlatives to capture listeners:

UNACCEPTABLE
Two fine citizens were horribly burned in a tragic fire
and explosion near the sleepy little community of Green
Castle in the wee hours of the morning.

ACCEPTABLE
A house trailer near Green Castle exploded this morning.
The Putnam County Sheriff's Department says two people
were hospitalized with burns.

WNDE, Indiana

The news can speak for itself. Yet when the rain outside is pounding on the roof as if it were a drum skin and lightning has chosen the neighborhood for target practice, a newswriter trying to get the inhabitants of that house to lend an ear to a story about a drought in another part of the country better make sure the news is speaking in its strongest and most engaging voice.

This sentence might easily have gotten bogged down in the usual tired descriptions—the sweltering Northeast, the parched Midwest, the water-starved West; instead, it grabs attention with one engaging word:

The heat wave <u>sizzles</u> on today in much of the U-S.

Dallas Townsend, CBS

The following sections distinguish words that "sizzle" from words that "sag."

Personal

Sitting alone in a small studio, staring at a microphone and a complicated mass of dials or at that mass of metal and glass called a camera, the newscaster may find it hard to imagine, but there are *people* out there listening or watching. The news must be written as if it's going to be delivered to people.

If a newscaster were suddenly to mention a listener's name, that listener's attention would naturally be engaged at once. Everyone's name cannot be mentioned, but the next best thing is to personalize the copy to the point where people think the newscaster is indeed talking to them.

A man is working in the basement when he hears on the radio:

The State Power Commission has approved the Carolina
Power and Light Company's proposed increase in electric
rates.

That might catch his attention, but there's a way of writing this story that could cause him to drop his tools and turn up the radio:

```
If you are one of Carolina Power and Light Company's
South Carolina customers, you can expect a higher bill
next month.
```

WRHI, South Carolina

The word *you* is the grabber—*you* are going to have to pay more money. The use of the second person makes the story sound as if it is being addressed directly to the listener. This sentence, which began an early morning story on coming increases in food prices, was singled out for praise in a memo Alan Walden distributed when he was at NBC. It too makes use of the second person:

```
Enjoy your breakfast. Next year the same stuff is going
to cost a lot more.
```

Walden's comment: "Terrific! Guaranteed to make the audience sit up and take notice."

Us and *we* can do the same job:

```
A Findlay man is using a unique invention to do
something that many of us take for granted.
```

WFIN, Ohio

This personalized writing usually works well with consumer stories:

```
Get ready for a shortage of natural gas again this
winter.
```

WVOK, Alabama

Of course it can be overused:

```
UNACCEPTABLE
Your roads were not that safe last night. There was a
four-car accident on Interstate 91.
```

The secret to personalizing writing is to find stories that can be related naturally to listeners' lives. It is not always necessary to use words like *you*, *us* or *we*:

```
City University students better get their checkbooks
ready for next fall.
```

WABC, New York City

Checkbooks is the sort of personal, familiar word that is guaranteed to draw attention.

Real

You've seen a *car*. Have you ever seen *automotive production*? Unless you're an economist, a car is more real to you than automotive production. Engaging writing is rooted in familiar terms:

```
WEAK
Automotive production declined last month.
```

```
BETTER
Fewer cars were produced last month.
```

```
WEAK
The people who make disposable beverage containers . . .
```

```
BETTER
The people who make throwaway bottles and cans . . .
                                          WDEE, Detroit
```

Whenever possible, write about real things rather than abstract concepts. Some examples:

ABSTRACT	REAL
precipitation	rain, snow
energy	gas, electricity
livestock	pigs
cooking utensils	pots and pans
garment	coat
educational institution	school
petroleum reserves	oil

Abstraction can make the commonplace unintelligible, as in this story about a plan for improving roads, buildings and services. It was used on the air:

```
The grant will be used to formulate a part of the
county's comprehensive development plan. This plan
includes an inventory of existing services and
facilities, identification of future needs and
development of a strategy for providing needed
improvements.
```

Make the news real:

```
UNACCEPTABLE
The mayor has introduced a proposal to cover the city's
```

recreational facilities with more vegetation and ground
cover.

ACCEPTABLE
The mayor wants to plant more trees and grass in the
city's parks.

Similarly, it often is more effective to write about the price of milk going up than
to write about inflation, or to write about a local man who has been out of work than
to write about unemployment.

Active Verbs

Good broadcast newswriting has oomph:

A man <u>burst</u> into a local diner last night, <u>shot</u> the
owner, <u>smashed</u> the cash register and <u>escaped</u> with more
than one-thousand dollars.

Verbs power sentences, give them their drive. They are the backbone of broadcast journalism.

Broadcast news is meat-and-potatoes writing—basic and direct. Adjectives and
adverbs can be out of place. They are often too rich and full of empty calories. Too
many adverbs and adjectives make writing flabby:

An <u>intimidating</u> man burst into a <u>quiet</u> local diner <u>late</u>
last night, <u>brutally</u> smashed the <u>old</u> cash register,
<u>senselessly</u> shot the owner and <u>quickly</u> escaped with over
one-thousand dollars.

With modifiers this story is almost twice as long and half as powerful. What information do the adjectives and adverbs add? Criminals are generally *intimidating*. Local
diners are usually *quiet*. There is no non*brutal* way to smash a cash register. And
how many shootings make sense? How many criminals escape slowly? The descrip-
tive words only get in the way of the story.

There are exceptions. A well-chosen adjective may sometimes be illuminating,
especially if it is unexpected:

The <u>glummest</u> summit in the 17-year history of the
European Economic Community . . .
Peter Kalischer, CBS

Glummest is an accurate yet surprising description in this context; that makes it
effective.

But adjectives and adverbs often are obvious or merely decorative. Good news-writers usually try to avoid them and tell the story with verbs:

```
WEAK
The streaking plane went through the building.


BETTER
The plane tore through the building.


WEAK
The fast-moving police officer suddenly took the gun
away.


BETTER
The police officer snatched the gun.
```

Some examples of the effective use of verbs:

```
The Decatur public transit system has been rejuvenated
by a grant from the state and federal governments.
                                         WSOY, Illinois


Citizens are scurrying to collect signatures on state
petitions by deadline-time tomorrow.
                                       KGDN, Washington


Delegates to the rich nation/poor nation economic
conference sleepwalked their way into the fourth day of
meetings . . .
                                    Peter Kalischer, CBS
```

It's important to keep the action in the verb. The active voice (the subject of the sentence does the acting) is stronger than the passive voice (the subject of the sentence is being acted upon):

```
WEAK
The building was destroyed by the fire.


BETTER
The fire destroyed the building.


WEAK
The woman was raped by the man.


BETTER
The man raped the woman.
```

Sometimes the angle from which a story is approached can be switched to strengthen the verb:

WEAK
Thunderstorms <u>brought</u> tornados and high winds to
Kentucky yesterday.

BETTER
Tornados and high winds <u>ripped</u> across Kentucky
yesterday.

WBGN, Kentucky

Verb Tenses

Newspapers take hours to print and distribute. The most up-to-the-minute sources of news are radio and television. That is where people turn when they want a quick rundown on the latest news. In broadcast news, therefore, timeliness is a dominant consideration in the selection and the writing of new stories. Our language has a vehicle for conveying timeliness: the present tense.

WEAK
Police <u>were</u> searching for clues.

BETTER
Police <u>are</u> searching for clues.

WEAK
The president <u>said</u> . . .

BETTER
The president <u>says</u> . . .

The present tense is the most engaging tense in the language. It indicates that the action is still going on.

It's more exciting to be told, "There *is* a huge fire downtown!" than, "There *was* a huge fire downtown." "The president *says* . . ."—he believes it right now! "Police *are searching* . . ."—they could come up with something any moment now!

Newspapers tend to stay away from the present tense because of the time lag between when they are written and when they are read. During the intervening hours police may have found what they were looking for or may have given up the search. "Police *were* searching . . ." is safer. Newspapers are pulled toward the past tense to protect themselves. Broadcast news doesn't have this problem. The news is aired almost instantaneously. If police stop searching, the copy can still be changed seconds before it is read on the air. The present tense is reasonably safe in broadcast newswriting. It's used often:

Former Housing and Urban Development Secretary George
Romney <u>says</u> a new political structure is developing in
the United States.

KWMS, Salt Lake City

The village of Hershey <u>is</u> still operating on emergency
power.

KODY, Nebraska

A fire official <u>believes</u> there will be no more bodies
found in the ruins of the Southgate, Kentucky, supper
club that burned Saturday night.

Ann Taylor, NBC

There are many situations, nevertheless, where the present tense doesn't work:

UNACCEPTABLE
> The bridge <u>collapses</u>.
> Two people <u>are being shot</u>.

Actions that belong to moments in the recent past cannot be forcibly dragged into
the present—that bridge is not collapsing now.

But there is a tense that maintains an air of immediacy while describing actions
that have ended—the present perfect tense. Not surprisingly, it's the most used
tense in broadcast news:

ACCEPTABLE
The bridge <u>has collapsed</u>.
Two people <u>have been shot</u>.

The present perfect is less dated than the past tense and can be used in more
situations than the present:

The holiday weekend <u>has given</u> late property taxpayers a
few hours' breathing time.

KLUC, Las Vegas

A former superintendent of schools <u>has been arrested and
charged</u> with making harassing telephone calls to 15-
year-old girls.

WKVT, Vermont

Still, the present perfect tense does not always fit. If the results of an action are
gone, or the action is explicitly pinned to the past, the present perfect tense cannot
be used:

UNACCEPTABLE
Few people <u>have shown up</u> at the meeting, so it broke up early.

Two people <u>have been shot</u> earlier today.

In these situations it's necessary to fall back on the past tense:

ACCEPTABLE
Few people <u>showed up</u> at the meeting, so it broke up early.

Two people <u>were shot</u> earlier today.

In broadcast news the present tense remains first choice. It's used where it's comfortable:

WEAK
The strike <u>has ended</u>.

BETTER
The strike <u>is</u> over.

WEAK
The governor <u>said</u> . . .

BETTER
The governor <u>says</u> . . .

The present perfect is second choice:

WEAK
The school board <u>approved</u> the plan.

BETTER
The school board <u>has approved</u> the plan.

WEAK
He <u>vetoed</u> the bill.

BETTER
He <u>has vetoed</u> the bill.

The past tense . . . ? Well, it has its uses, especially in sentences in which the time the event occurred is mentioned:

```
Former President Nixon last night had bitter words for
Washington Post reporters Woodward and Bernstein.
                                        Don Blair, NBC


Four floors of the U-S State Department were damaged
early this morning by a bomb planted in a third-floor
men's room.
                                    WINS, New York City
```

There's one major verb tense that has not been mentioned—the future. Obviously, sentences cannot be shoved into the future, but when a future angle can be found in a story, it's often the best approach to the story:

```
WEAK
The gas price increase was approved.


BETTER
Gas prices will be going up.


WEAK
The teachers voted to strike.


BETTER
It looks like teachers will be on strike in the morning.
```

Numbers

```
On February 14, 1990, a 3-month-old A-320 crashed while
preparing for landing in Bangalore, India, killing 92
people.
```

Despite its dramatic subject matter, this sentence, taken from a newspaper, has difficulty engaging our attention. The problem: too many numbers. Perhaps the newspaper reader's eye can follow this dense concentration of information. If the eye can't follow, it can always go back and reread. But the ear is confused, and probably bored, by so much data.

It takes time to figure how long ago February 14, 1990, was. It takes a second to realize that a three-month-old plane was practically new. And many of us will have to search our memories for the significance of the name "A-320." Those moments of thought are enough to cause the listener to miss the next facts, and soon the meaning of the story is lost.

Numbers can be as important as any other facts, but the weight of detail they contain makes it necessary to carefully monitor their use. In Chapter 1, "Copy," the rules for writing numbers in the copy were discussed. Here the question is which numbers should be allowed in the copy.

Avoid Numbers As a rule, the fewer numbers in broadcast writing the better.

Key numbers must survive. Listeners must be told the size of the budget increase or the amount of cash that was stolen. But in most stories there are numbers that, while perhaps interesting, are not necessary. They should be edited out. It's important to note how much larger this year's budget will be, but it's not necessary to specify the exact size of last year's. Write that this was the fifth robbery downtown this month, but it's not necessary to review how much was taken in each of the other robberies.

```
UNACCEPTABLE
The proposed budget for the '94 -- '95 fiscal year calls
for 2 point 5 million dollars in property tax relief for
the state's 250-thousand property owners.
```

```
ACCEPTABLE
The proposed budget calls for 2 point 5 million dollars
in property tax relief.
```

These sentences from a story about a killing in a jail were aired on a major New York City radio station:

```
Police say that Arthur Gomez of 111 East 145th Street,*
who would have been 17 next week, was killed shortly
before nine last night. He was being held on 2-thousand,
500 dollars bail since September 27th on a robbery
charge.
```

There is no way listeners' minds could have processed all those numbers. The solution? Leave most of them out:

```
Police say that Arthur Gomez, who lived on East 145th
Street, was killed last night. Gomez was being held on a
robbery charge. He would have turned 17 next week.
```

Another example: A story on a record-breaking art auction could easily drown in numbers—the number of paintings sold, the prices of the individual paintings, the amount taken in the latest sessions, the previous record, etc. But the secret to writing a story like this is to avoid most of these numbers. The strength of the writing that follows lies in the numbers that are not there; only two are used.

```
Some more paintings from the collection of the late
Robert Van Hirsch were sold in London last night. That
```

---

* This name and address have been changed.

```
raises the total for the record-shattering auction to
more than 28 and a half million dollars. There's still
one more session to go.
```

Bill Diehl, ABC

Round Off If a number has to be used, it should be made easy to grasp. *Almost half-a-million* is simpler than *496-thousand 578*. *More than twice as many* is clearer than *12* the first time, *25* the second.

Some of the exactness of the news is sacrificed with the use of *about* and *almost*, but exact numbers communicate little if they are too confusing to follow on the air. Unless the meaning of a story rests on the figures to the right of the decimal point, clear approximation can convey information more efficiently than befuddling specificity.

```
WEAK
The plan will cost one point five eight million dollars.


BETTER
The plan will cost more than a million and a half
dollars.


WEAK
The workers now earn 18-thousand, 985 dollars a year.


BETTER
The workers now earn just under 19-thousand dollars a
year.
```

Approximating should never mean distorting. The rounding-off process must be accurate and fair. Words like *more than*, *less than* and *almost* have definite meanings— *18-thousand 500* is not *about 20-thousand*, nor is it *almost 20-thousand*. And it is never acceptable to leave out the *about* and say *one-million* when the number is *about one-million*.

Make Them Real Numbers go down more easily if the writer predigests them for listeners.

If it's 1993 and a story talks about 1994, listeners can be saved a couple of seconds' thought if the writer writes *next year* instead of 1994. This works with most dates: 1992 would be easiest to grasp as *last year*; 1983 as *ten years ago*; November 16 becomes *later this month*, if it is later this month.

Large dollar figures can also be transformed into more comprehensible terms: 2 point 5 billion dollars becomes *about ten dollars for every person in the United States*; a point six percent General Motors price increase becomes *almost 100 dollars more for the average General Motors car.*

In election stories, stick to percentages rather than vote totals:

```
WEAK
The governor received 315-thousand votes, his opponent
220-thousand.
```

```
BETTER
The governor received 59 percent of the votes.
```

Ratios are another useful tool for making numbers more "listener friendly": *twice as many*, by a *three-to-one vote*.

Poll results are among the stories that seem to demand the most numbers. Not only do you have to indicate the size of the advantage a candidate or issue has, but—as a responsible writer—you have to say what the "margin of error" of the poll is. (See Chapter 11, "Coverage.") Yet here, too, says Richard Threlkeld, national correspondent of CBS News, the idea is to use "less numbers rather than more. If you throw a lot of numbers at people, it won't help them," Threlkeld notes. "Instead, you try to make sense of the numbers. You try to explain what the bottom line of the poll is."

```
Clinton still has a slight lead, but it's not much more
than the margin of error of the poll -- four percent.
```

Idiomatic Expressions

Idiomatic expressions are old friends. They bring warmth and color to writing:

```
He said the courts are calling all the shots on the
desegregation of Boston schools.
                                              WBUR, Boston
```

```
There were 12 hours of negotiations yesterday . . . more
on tap today.
                                           KLOS, Los Angeles
```

```
Farmers in Southwestern Minnesota are putting up a fuss
over plans for a big four-lane expressway between
Worthington and Saint James.
                                           WCCO, Minneapolis
```

But like old friends, idiomatic expressions can get too familiar and sometimes can seem so comfortable that we drop our guard. A foreign-born writer used to amuse a newsroom with his slightly distorted versions of old expressions. He'd say: "Close but no tomato." "That's second hat to me." "I just want to get my foot in the pie."

As do all words and phrases, expressions have specific meanings. They must be worded correctly and their meanings must be honored:

```
UNACCEPTABLE
A local doctor is in the big time.
```

```
ACCEPTABLE
A local doctor has hit the big time.
```

Metaphors

One of the best-known metaphors of all time is Homer's "the rosy-fingered dawn." A metaphor is a figure of speech in which one thing is spoken of as if it were another. Dawns don't really have rosy fingers. When newswriter Peggy Noonan at CBS (who went on to become a White House speechwriter) called the appearance of many conflicting wall posters in China "a wall-poster war," she was using a metaphor. Some of the idiomatic expressions mentioned in the previous section are technically metaphors. Negotiations aren't literally *on tap*.

Good metaphors can clarify or amuse. They are important tools of engaging writing—when they are kept under control. It is important not to get carried away and, for example, call a hurricane a "meteorological mastodon," as one newswriter did.

The key to using these figures of speech is to remember that they each require tiny flights of imagination. We are asked to imagine for a moment a war of wall posters. But the metaphor must paint an image that's possible to imagine.

This sentence was used on the air by a sports writer on a snowy day:

```
Let's scrape away the snow and get right to the meat of
the matter.
```

Imagine scraping away snow and finding meat! This mess is called a "mixed metaphor" because it combines two incompatible metaphors. Here are some more:

```
Fast-food operations are flooding the country, turning
small restaurants into deserts.
```

```
The stock market erupted today to a new high-water mark.
```

And, a network sportscaster once informed a World Series audience that "when you get nailed with that eraser, it really stings." This phrase was attributed to a New York politician: "The hottest gut issue ever to hit the city." And, press critic Alex Cockburn caught Louisiana's Governor Edwin Edwards saying: "You've bottled them up with a maze of red tape."

Metaphors—yes; mixed metaphors—no.

Clichés

The most common problem with using well-worn expressions is that all the meaning and charm has often been worn out of them. In that case they become those hob-goblins of people who work with the language—clichés.

A cliché is any combination of words that has been used too much. Whatever wisdom and humor was in that expression or figure of speech is gone. When we hear it we gulp and think, "Not again!"

While working on his in-house critique of newswriting on CBS, Mervin Block bumped up against this sentence:

```
Life here has not been a bed of roses for them, but
they're hanging in there.
```

"'Bed of roses' might have been vivid when it was first used, but now it's withered," Block wrote. That's the problem with clichés—we've heard them too many times before. ("Hanging in there" sounds a little old too.) Here are some other figures of speech that make news directors wince:

raining cats and dogs	in the nick of time
the cream of the crop	no holds barred
a sigh of relief	smelling like a rose
sadder but wiser	lowered the boom
making order out of chaos	a blue-ribbon panel
believe it or not	a blessing in disguise
the rules of the game	burn the midnight oil
chalked up the victory	hit the nail on the head
a slap in the face	in this day and age
ups and downs	time and time again
horse of a different color	needless to say
in the final analysis	run the gamut from A to Z
goes without saying	powers that be
it remains to be seen	long arm of the law
give the green light	once in a blue moon
dog tired	back to the wall
leave in a huff	all in a day's work
sending shock waves	a flash in the pan
more of the same	crystal clear
once in a great while	goes without saying
the light of day	pay the piper
last but not least	few and far between
cold facts	variety is the spice of life
got off with a bang	the name of the game
come home to roost	

One radio journalist was fired for writing too many weather reports that warned listeners about "the wet stuff falling from the sky" and then consoling them because "into each life some rain must fall." And, though I doubt anyone was fired for them, count how many clichés the *New York Times* used in the lead paragraph of its editorial marking the death of Mao Tse-tung:

> Mao Tse-tung's place in history is assured. When the saga of our times is written, he will be one of the towering figures . . .

Clichés make writing sound trite and unintelligent, but remember not to let them scare you away from all expressions. Just because a phrase is familiar, don't assume it's a cliché. This is the difference: Expressions have been used; clichés have been overused.

> According to one business expert . . . the president is smack dab in the middle of the biggest reason for higher prices . . . the federal government.
>
> KAKC, Oklahoma

Listeners have heard "smack dab in the middle" before, but not too often. It's still fresh enough to retain its antique charm. That one is not a cliché.

A cliché doesn't have to be a figure of speech. Any words that have been used together so often that they have lost their power are also clichés:

breathless anticipation	unmitigated gall
sure thing	ill-fated
packed house	loud and clear
no uncertain terms	checkered career
due deliberation	impressive sight
general public	action-packed
torrid pace	recent history
finishing touches	

Don't these clichés often seem apt or clever? Most do. It is because they are well-turned phrases that they have become overused phrases. The point is that whatever their original vitality, by now these phrases are exhausted. They've become obvious, "prepackaged"—with all the spice and originality of TV dinners.

Journalists have not neglected their responsibility in the prepackaging of the language. Sometimes it seems as if newsroom typewriters are programmed to punch out these phrases at regular intervals:

long holiday weekend	claimed the life of
financial circles	on the agenda

war-torn	it's official
battle-weary	hard questions
poverty-stricken	stiff opposition
up in arms	outspoken critic
mounting tension	speculation was rampant
tension is high	the incident remains under investigation
lingering illness	failing to negotiate a curve
the nation's capital	uneasy truce
police scoured the	outbreak of fighting
neighborhood	

Some journalism clichés are not only worn out, they are hollow:

tragic fire	naked aggression
senseless murder	reliable sources
innocent victims	

Somewhere there must exist a mirror universe full of comic fires, meaningful murders, guilty victims, fully attired aggression—and sources who are quoted on the news but are unreliable.

How do you avoid clichés? Lowell Thomas once drew up for his staff a list of clichés and acceptable alternatives. Soon he found the alternatives were being used so frequently that they were becoming clichés.

You can't list creative phrasings. The ability to custom tailor phrases to fit specific situations is what distinguishes good writers. For example, Dallas Townsend dodged the standard "begin deliberations" in his writing by having a jury begin "pondering" a case. And, instead of the standard "voted down" or "rejected by union members," this story employs a lively expression from America's primary image preserve—the old West.

```
A possible taxi strike by union members has been headed
off at the ballot box.
```
                                                            WBBM, Chicago

There are three guidelines for avoiding clichés in writing

1. Be creative. A description of a city under saturation bombing, for instance, could practically write itself with "panic-stricken populations," "the city in ruins," "chaos in the streets," etc. Good newswriters don't trot out clichés like these; they find their own words.
2. Be honest. Bombers are supposed to be terrifying. Are they this time? It's wrong to feed listeners' expectations with the phrases they expect to hear. Writing should accurately describe each individual situation.
3. Keep it simple. Writing doesn't have to be littered with expressions to be clever or poetic. The simplest, most direct writing can be the strongest.

Edward R. Murrow in wartime London in June 1941. In the background is the British Broadcast Corporation's Broadcast House, from which Murrow broadcast his famous "This . . . is London" reports to the U.S. audience. (CBS News Photo)

Here is Edward R. Murrow on the bombing of London during World War II— no clichés:

```
    Last night as I stood on London Bridge . . . and
watched that red glow in the sky, it was possible to
understand that that's fire, as the result of an act of
war. But the act itself, even the sound of the bomb that
started that fire, was still unreal.
    . . . Suddenly all the lights crashed off and a
blackness fell right to the ground. It grew cold. We
covered ourselves with hay. The shrapnel clicked as it
hit the concrete road nearby. And still the German
bombers came.
    . . . The bombs don't seem to make as much noise as
they should . . . the sense of danger, death and
disaster comes only when the familiar incidents occur,
the things that one has associated with tragedy since
childhood.*
```

* Robert Metz, *CBS: Reflections in a Bloodshot Eye* (New York: Signet, 1975), pp. 93–96.

Wrap-Up

The late Jim Zaillian, who was news director at KNX in Los Angeles, said good broadcast writing "shows ear." Zaillian said good newswriters "hear" the copy as they write, rather than just "see" it. They avoid difficult or unnatural phrasings that might disorient the ear; they search out lively, direct and fresh language that pleases the ear.

Practice Assignments

Rewrite the following sentences in broadcast style.

1. The Burmese government plans to repair 30 temples, generally the largest of 2-thousand 217 remaining buildings in the 30-square-mile area flooded by the seven inches of rain.
2. It was predicted by the city manager that the downtown area would have to undergo extensive renovation and modification to make it a more attractive commercial area for consumers.
3. The president of the Board of Education has stated that the citywide reading test given to all 460-thousand high school students might be invalidated for 220-thousand of them.
4. The poor overall approval rating, 32 percent, is strongly linked to how the public thinks the president is handling the economy. Seventy percent disapproved of that element of his job performance.
5. Police scoured the neighborhood yesterday for the two males and one female who are believed to have resided in the house prior to the blaze.
6. The attorney for the deceased woman said that the ill-fated star, whose face was lacerated almost beyond recognition, probably passed away while endeavoring to forcefully open the building's door.
7. Industrialist Stanley Arnold, whose copious contributions to institutions of higher learning are well known, labeled the accusations spurious.
8. A 34-year-old woman has been shot by robbers during a holdup of the Shoreham National Bank this morning.
9. It is difficult to evaluate our petroleum reserves at the moment, but some experts said that there is a possibility that many gasoline retail outlets will be closed during this long holiday weekend, causing hardship for the general public.
10. The physicians say the surgical procedures would be commenced this month.
11. An outspoken critic of the administration, who represents the poverty-stricken South Bronx, is blasting the new welfare proposal in no uncertain terms.
12. It is not certain whether there will be snow, but it is clear that there will be some precipitation this evening.
13. The mayor said he wants to submit the town's application to the federal

government immediately . . . so the city can get in on the ground floor while the iron is still hot.

14. There will be a nine point eight percent increase in the cost of lettuce to consumers in this area.

15. Black leaders say they were not allowed to enter the all-white country club, but the club's owner remains mum on the subject.

16. The entire nation breathlessly awaits the outcome of today's election, the culmination of an incredibly action-packed campaign.

17. Coach Bob Barnes says the team will be sitting pretty if it stays on its toes.

18. You would not have wanted to be standing on Eleventh Street and Fifth Avenue last night at seven-fourteen. . . . A bomb went off there, injuring three innocent bystanders and claiming the lives of two others.

19. The Supreme Court granted certiorari today in the case of Jones versus Ann Arbor School Board.

20. Mayor Andrews is expected to claim executive privilege at the extortion trial of Councilman Stanley Barker today.

Meanings

The words used in broadcast news must be easygoing and entertaining, but they must also be *exact*. This pairing of purposes is what makes writing the news for broadcast so challenging. The trick is to write conversationally without letting that relaxed style lull you into blurting out misleading information. Language is the servant of meaning; it must remember its place. If words interfere with the telling of the story or distort its meaning, they are not working.

Broadcast journalists worry about meanings. They know that *ships* are vessels that are large enough to carry *boats*, and that *prisons* are for more serious offenses than *jails*. They debate such questions as whether flags on land fly at *half-mast* or *half-staff*. Or whether *unidentified* persons can be referred to as *unnamed*. (After all, they do have names; we just don't know them.) Or whether it is clear enough that *casualties* means *dead and wounded*.

Broadcast journalists must know that William Rehnquist's title is chief justice of the *United States*, not chief justice of the *Supreme Court*; that grand jury indictments are handed *up*, court decisions handed *down*; and that the proper English usage is "equally costly," not "equally *as* costly."

Bemoaning the decline of our language skills has become popular sport. It's true; some Americans don't speak too *good*. But broadcast newswriters must rise above the fallen vernacular.

In conversation there is not that much at stake. We're prepared to take the reports of some of our acquaintances with a grain of salt, and if they use words incorrectly, if the story is distorted or exaggerated, at the most a few persons will be misinformed. But broadcast news is responsible for informing entire communities, and it must be trusted if it is to work. Misuse of words, distortion, exaggeration can be dangerous, if not fatal, for the news. Meanings must be honored.

Precision

The English language is a precise tool. With one of the richest vocabularies of any language, it has words to express even the most subtle shadings of meaning. Think of all the words we have for acts of illegally expropriating property.

steal	plunder
theft	poach
robbery	pillage
burglary	sack
larceny	extort
rip-off	blackmail
break and enter	second-story job
mug	lift
holdup	swipe
stickup	cop
piracy	rifle
embezzlement	filch
swindle	pinch
heist	snatch
pilfer	knockoff
housebreaking	purloin
shoplift	

Each of these 33 words allows us to communicate a slightly different thought: A rip-off is a minor swindle; plunderers take everything; embezzlement is a financial maneuver. The specific meaning of each word must be respected as it is used.

UNACCEPTABLE
The woman was <u>burglarized</u> on her way home. *(Burglary means that a building has been entered.)*

Someone <u>robbed</u> his desk. *(Robbery requires the use of force or fear.)*

A <u>shoplifter</u> cleaned out the cash register. *(Shoplifters just steal goods from shelves.)*

Telling a friend that a local man has been arrested for robbery, when actually it was for shoplifting, won't cause too much trouble. But that same error on the radio can cause that man serious injury. Broadcast news demands precise use of our precise language.

Usage

The language wars are fought between the "conversationalists" and the "strict grammarians." The conversationalists advocate a language that is free to outgrow the old rules. Split an infinitive! Use *like* as a conjunction! That's how people today speak. But the strict grammarians see exactness and clarity, not to mention style, being violated along with the rules. The grammatical order, they believe, is being trampled by hordes of nouns used as verbs—*prioritize*—and adverbs used without verbs—*hopefully*.

It's hard for broadcast journalists to choose sides in this dispute. Our writing is unabashedly conversational, yet we demand that it be precise. After all, Edwin Newman, author of two popular books attacking the debasement of the language, is a broadcast journalist.

Some of the new usages we accept; some we must reject. Phony words like *prioritize* have no place in broadcast news. They're stilted, certainly not conversational. But there is no real harm in the occasional split infinitive—"Congress refused *to seriously consider* the bill"—or in using *like* for *as*—"The miners may reject this contract *like* they rejected the last one."

Broadcast journalists are clearly divided on one relevant question: Is it three *persons* or three *people*? You can't spend a day working in a newsroom without being forced to take sides on this one. The grammar books are clear: a few individuals are *persons*; an anonymous group, *people*. But in conversation a few persons are often called *people*. Take your choice—the grammar books or conversational usage. CBS insists on *persons*. KFWB in Los Angeles, for instance, and a majority of broadcast stations, use *people*. For better or for worse, the future seems to belong to *people*.

Most questions of usage are simple. There are agreed-on rules for the use of our language. Violations of these rules jar the ear. There's a difference between a grammatical liberal and someone who doesn't know grammar. The partially illiterate don't last long in broadcast newsrooms. "I'm tired of playing teacher," says Carissa Howland, news director at KCWY-TV, Casper, Wyoming. "Some of the writing problems you see are so fundamental it's embarrassing. I actually had to sit somebody down and explain what a preposition was . . . and this was a person who had been through four years of college."

Here are some examples of sloppy use of the language. All of these were actually used on the air.

UNACCEPTABLE
The vote was <u>by a</u> three-to-one <u>margin</u>.

ACCEPTABLE
The vote was three to one.
The bill was passed by a three-to-one margin.

UNACCEPTABLE
The senator said the town's chances <u>are good at</u> landing the contract.

ACCEPTABLE
The senator said the town's chances of landing the contract are good.

UNACCEPTABLE
The funds would be used to turn the property into a neighborhood park, <u>according to the wishes of three surveys</u> taken in the area.

ACCEPTABLE
The funds would be used to turn the property into a
neighborhood park. That's the plan most of the community
favored when polled on the subject.

UNACCEPTABLE
Intense activity will be the <u>keyword</u> this week at the
nuclear fuel plant.

ACCEPTABLE
It will be a week of intense activity at the nuclear
fuel plant.

UNACCEPTABLE
That, of course, is quite a <u>different tune than what he
said</u> on April 11th.

ACCEPTABLE
That, of course, is a different tune from the one he
sang on April 11th.

Some must have given listeners an unintended chuckle:

He wants the junk food machines replaced with more
nutritious foods.

A local teenager was heading north on Broadway when he
was rear-ended by a car driven by another local man.

Most of these gaffes were caused by writers straining uncomfortably for effect—another reason why it pays to be simple and direct. Beyond that it's difficult to categorize these errors, just as it's impossible to ticket every possible violation of the rules of grammar—there are as many as there are words because there's a wrong way to use every word. The right way can usually be found with a dictionary and a grammar book. Newswriters have to be hard on their writing; others are going to be hard on it.

Dependent Words

Some words depend on other words for their meaning. This can cause trouble in broadcast news. As the words move by irretrievably, it is difficult for the listener to remember who *he* is, where *there* is and which one was *the former*.

The latter and *the former* should never be used—too confusing. Pronouns—*he, she, it, they*, etc.—should be treated as potentially confusing and used only when the antecedent is completely clear.

WEAK
```
He told him he had only weeks to live.
```

BETTER
```
The doctor said that the man's father had only weeks to
live.
```

And a pronoun should never be used if the antecedent that gives it its meaning isn't nearby.

WEAK
```
The mayor calls the plan a disaster. It would reduce the
number of teachers at the high schools, in some cases by
removing tenure. It would also increase class sizes and
cut extracurricular activities. He says he's committed
to fighting it.
```

BETTER
```
The mayor calls the plan a disaster. It would reduce the
number of teachers at the high schools, in some cases by
removing tenure. The plan would also increase class
sizes and cut extracurricular activities. The mayor says
he's committed to fighting the proposal.
```

In this story, the name or description of the two characters is repeated constantly to keep their identities clear in the listener's mind. Pronouns are used only three times.

```
Yesterday was just ''one of those days'' for city police
officer W-T Byers. . . . Late yesterday, Officer Byers
arrested a local man for driving under the influence and
driving without a license. The trouble began when Officer
Byers was preparing the man to take a breathalyzer test
at the Rock Hill Law Center. After the man entered the
breathalyzer room, he was asked to empty his pockets and
take off his belt. The man complied. When asked to step
into the hall for a routine frisk, the suspect
reportedly began to put up a fuss. One thing led to
another. Police say that the man took a couple of swings
at Officer Byers. They say the officer took a couple of
swings back at the man, and, police say, two other
officers had to help subdue the man. Then, much to the
dismay of all concerned, it was learned that the
breathalyzer machine was not operating properly. So the
man, now handcuffed, was taken to the County Building
```

for testing. Later <u>Officer Byers</u> and <u>his prisoner</u>
returned to the Law Center for booking. <u>The man</u> was
charged with driving without a license and assault on a
police officer. By the way, police say the prisoner
managed to get one last kick into the knee of <u>the</u>
<u>arresting officer</u> before <u>he</u> was taken away.

WRHI, South Carolina

Pronouns aren't the only words that serve as ciphers. It's also often safer to replace *here*, *there* and *then* with the specific nouns to which they refer.

WEAK
<u>He then</u> returned <u>there</u> to pick <u>it</u> up.

BETTER
<u>The suspect</u> returned <u>home</u> <u>later in the afternoon</u> to pick up <u>the gun</u>.

Precision writing for use on the air, where the listener can't backtrack, sometimes must be overly explicit.

Saying ''Says''

To say is the most used verb in broadcast news because saying is the activity that makes the most news.

Newswriters don't want to keep writing, "The president says . . . he says . . . his opponent says . . . the president says . . ." They look for alternatives to *says*, and there's no shortage of them—by one count more than 350. But each of these hundreds of verbs gives a statement a different accent.

Compare these phrases and their connotations:

the mayor claims (there's reason for disbelief)
the mayor reports (just giving the facts)
the mayor declares (a forceful statement)
the mayor mentions (offhanded)
the mayor protests (a complaint)
the mayor acknowledges (an admission)
the mayor charges (on the offensive)
the mayor observes (just a comment)
the mayor implies (didn't say it directly)
the mayor demands (forceful call for action)

These verbs are not synonyms. They have their own precise meanings and can be misused.

```
UNACCEPTABLE
```
The governor <u>asserts</u> that today will be a day of
mourning. *(''Asserts'' is for controversial statements.)*

The bill <u>reveals</u> that the companies would be forced to
sell their holdings. *(The wording of a bill is not a
revelation.)*

The candidate <u>indicates</u> that that statement is
ridiculous. *(''Indicates'' is for hints; it is too weak
for such an assertion.)*

There are two ways to correct each of these sentences: one is by finding a more appropriate substitute for *says*; the other is by using *says* itself. There's a lesson here. While all these other verbs do provide a nice change of pace, *says* remains the newswriter's most valuable verb because it is so versatile. *Says* is used almost as much as these other verbs combined.

Objectivity

When we tell stories, we tend to exaggerate. A minor scuffle can easily become a brawl since a brawl makes for a more exciting tale. Distortion? Well, our friends expect a bit of hyperbole. Similarly, in conversation we're not shy about expressing a rooting interest: "That guy deserved to get hit; he had such a mean face!"

But journalists have a different charge: to perceive and report on events for the community. They function as one of our senses, a social sense, and are entrusted with a vital political function—keeping the politicians and the people in touch. Any distortion in the reports of these community perceivers would be frightening, as a distortion in our sight or hearing would be.

In journalism, **objectivity** simply means undistorted reporting. That's a working definition for what is, strictly speaking, an unattainable ideal. Journalists are expected to write words that are not distorted by their desire to impress or by their opinions.

Superlatives

Our language has been inflated. Fires aren't serious, they're *very* serious. Elections aren't important, they're *crucial*. Events are all *special*; crimes are all *brutal*, rescues *daring*. Cold days are *frigid*, hot days *sweltering*. Words like *best, worst, awesome, largest, first, last, hottest, coldest,* and *only* are thrown around as if we were a nation of heroes. But we're not; we're a nation of *superheroes*.

Here is a not *unprecedented* misuse of a superlative from CBS television:

> The schools are expected to remain closed at least
> through tomorrow, but the critical shortage of natural
> gas here is a problem that won't go away until the
> unprecedented cold spell ends.

Mervin Block did some research for his in-house CBS newsletter and found that there had in fact been longer and colder periods in that area. The cold spell was not the *worst*, the *coldest*, the *most frigid*, nor was it *unprecedented*.

Journalism *does* want to attract attention to itself. Unique or grandiose happenings intrigue listeners. And muscular writing can help communicate the power of events. There's nothing dishonest about bringing out the drama in the news. This story, for instance, certainly doesn't mince words:

> There has apparently been some deadly confusion between
> pilots and controllers over the years . . . confusion
> that no one knew existed until it sent a plane into the
> side of a mountain . . . Now, at the National
> Transportation Safety Board hearings, the officials are
> trying to make sure it doesn't happen again. . . .
>
> WINS, New York City

A dramatic introduction to a story on a hearing? Certainly, but it's all true. The confusion did cause deaths, and the plane did hit the mountain. Powerful writing is fine if the writer has the facts to back it up.

Trouble starts when the words start creeping ahead of the facts; when 24 holiday weekend traffic accidents in the state become "blood on the streets of Georgia!"; when a store whose cash register was smashed is said to be in "shambles"; when a series of robberies becomes "fear and destruction sweeping through town!"; or when a flood downtown is written up like a disaster movie.

Words must be tightly controlled. If every fire is *very* serious, how will the really big ones be distinguished? In most parts of the country, if 80-degree days are *scorchers*, writers will be up to *fryers* and *melters* by the end of June.

Since it's virtually a sin for a journalist's language to take leave of the facts, one might call the overuse of superlatives the *worst* mistake a newswriter can make. But then there are the overgeneralizations. This clever but fallacious attempt to add emphasis to the usual Fourth of July traffic deaths story was used on the air:

> Americans did <u>not</u> have a safe and sane Fourth of July.

All Americans?

Opinion

It's easy to call dictators *evil*, and criminals *despicable*, children *lovable*, accidents *tragic*, deaths *sad*. Most listeners would agree with these characterizations, but the

Newswriter Sara Robins, WTNH, New Haven, Connecticut.

point is that it is the listener's job to come to the conclusions. The journalist's job is to present the facts.

Adding subjective adjectives to writing weakens the journalist's authority as an objective observer. And, these seemingly innocuous modifiers can easily get out of hand. It's a short distance from *evil* dictators to *noble* presidents and *foolish* mayors — clear examples of editorializing. This does not mean that journalists, deprived of the opportunity to express their opinions, cannot portray events that *do* have moral content. Journalists should not *call* a spade a spade, but they certainly should *show* that a spade is a spade. If a teacher has committed crimes or an earthquake is unusually destructive, a balanced marshaling of the facts should be able to demonstrate the immorality or the tragedy.

This story details allegations of an onerous crime, but the writer doesn't moralize. The facts speak for themselves:

```
A Chicago woman has been arrested for allegedly trying
to sell her grandson. Police say the 54-year-old woman
was arrested last night in her home after selling the
boy to undercover youth officers for 5-thousand dollars
and a 4-thousand dollar I-O-U.
```

WBBM, Chicago

In contrast, the use of the pejorative word *scabs* in the following sentence, which was used on the air, makes it subjective and unacceptable:

```
Scabs are now brewing Coors beer in Colorado.
```

A word doesn't have to be emotive to be dangerously subjective. Notice how this sentence, which was used on the air, uses two adverbs to prejudge a suspect:

```
The man was quickly charged with driving without a
license and, predictably, assault on a police officer.
```

The alleged speed and predictability of the charges implies that they were obvious and, therefore, that the man was guilty.

One word that looks harmless but can be subversive is *only*.

```
UNACCEPTABLE
Taxes will only go up six percent.
```

Let the listeners decide whether the tax increase is in fact *only* a small one.

Adverbs like *finally* or *needlessly* can also cause trouble, as can characterizations such as *hot-tempered*. Instead of writing, "The *hot-tempered* candidate *finally* answered the question," give the facts—how often the candidate raised his voice and how long it took him to answer the question.

Except when writing a commentary or an editorial (see Chapter 13, "Public Affairs"), a newswriter's opinions, value judgments or beliefs should never enter the copy. The only opinions in news copy should be those attributed to newsmakers.

```
UNACCEPTABLE
The president has lost his credibility.
```

```
ACCEPTABLE
The senator says the president has lost his credibility.
```

```
UNACCEPTABLE
The Ku Klux Klan is out to ruin America.
```

```
ACCEPTABLE
The governor has charged that the Ku Klux Klan is out to
ruin America.
```

Newsmakers' opinions can add perspective to a story. This story leads off with a police officer's characterization:

```
Sawyer County Deputy Sheriff Dick Odegar calls it ''one
of those things you thank the upstairs for.'' When the
```

car Susan Adams was driving went out of control on State
Highway 77 east of Hayward this afternoon, Mrs. Adams
and her 21-month-old son, Paul, were thrown from the
car. The car landed directly on top of the baby, but he
had landed in a snowbank and, instead of being crushed,
was pushed deeper into the snow. Mrs. Adams and a
passerby dug the baby out of the snow. Mrs. Adams was
only slightly injured in the crash, but suffered
numerous cuts and bruises trying to dig the baby out of
the snow. Both have been hospitalized for observation,
but officials say the baby appears to be uninjured.

WHSM, Wisconsin

Why are newsmakers like the deputy sheriff allowed to "thank the upstairs" when
newswriters are not? Because newsmakers are active participants in the story, but
newswriters must remain objective observers.

Maintaining objectivity becomes particularly difficult in situations where most
members of a community agree. In the 1950s the *New York Times* reported a one-
sided attack on homosexuals as dangerous "sex perverts." That seemed acceptable.
It wasn't. Whether a newswriter's audience is conservative or liberal, it's necessary
to play stories straight.

UNACCEPTABLE
Another country freed! The Communist Party has lost
Bulgaria's national elections.

The state legislature came to its senses today and voted
to decriminalize marijuana.

Opinion, even if it's in line with conventional wisdom, distorts the news.

Attribution

The fire was caused by two children playing with matches
in the basement.

Airing a charge like this is dangerous. How can the newscaster be sure that the kids
started the fire and why should listeners believe it? Two children have just been
accused of seriously negligent behavior; however, newswriters are not experts on
fires and their causes. If this story had been based on sound reporting, it was a fire
official who pinned the blame on the children. That must be clear when the story
is written. The charge must be attributed:

<u>Fire officials say</u> the fire was started by two children
playing with matches in the basement.

There are four reasons to attribute information:

Protect the Writer Clear and honest writing demands that potentially controversial statements be attributed. This protects the writer. If it is an official's theory, let that official take responsibility for it.

> UNACCEPTABLE
> The suspect had a motive for both murders.

> ACCEPTABLE
> <u>Police say</u> the suspect had a motive for both murders.

Of course this doesn't mean that newswriters can get themselves off the hook and use the theory of any crank on the street. They are always responsible for the reliability of their sources, and attributing statements does not lessen this responsibility.

> UNACCEPTABLE
> Bystanders say the suspect had a motive for both murders.

Avoid Opinion Anything that smacks of opinion must be attributed.

> UNACCEPTABLE
> The streets are no longer safe.

> ACCEPTABLE
> <u>The mayor says</u> the streets are no longer safe.

Here the newswriter is protecting a reputation as an unbiased observer.

Protect Newsmakers But perhaps the most important function of attribution is to protect the people mentioned in the news, specifically those presumed innocent. It must be clear in objective writing that charges against suspects or defendants are only allegations. Reports of potentially criminal behavior must never be treated as established fact until the judicial system has had its say.

> UNACCEPTABLE
> The suspect shot him.

> ACCEPTABLE
> The suspect <u>allegedly</u> shot him.

The word *allegedly* does this job so easily that it tends to get overused. Since it does imply that *criminal* behavior is being alleged, the word shouldn't be wasted on less serious matters.

UNACCEPTABLE
It allegedly will rain tonight.

And *allegedly*—a word that does not by itself make clear the source of an allegation—should only be used in stories where the people or documents making the charge are mentioned elsewhere in the story. It's okay to write, "He allegedly entered the store with the gun," if you wrote in the previous sentence, "According to police, a loaded revolver was found on the suspect when he was arrested." The audience should always be told who (it's usually the police) is doing the alleging. Don't forget that there are plenty of other—more precise—ways to indicate that a charge is an allegation besides using the word *allegedly*.

ACCEPTABLE
Police say the suspect shot him.

The suspect is accused of shooting him.

According to police, the suspect shot him.

The suspect is charged with shooting him.

Although peppering a story with *allegedly* and *police say* may slow down the writing a bit, this obligation to protect suspects' rights should never be overlooked.

A three-month-old Houston boy is dead. His babysitter allegedly wanted to teach the infant's mother a lesson about staying home and caring for her child. According to Houston police juvenile division officer W-C White, the baby had been sprayed with insecticide . . . in the face!
                                            KENR, Houston

According to the investigating officer, neither the cycle's driver nor his passenger was wearing a motorcycle helmet.
                                            WRKD, Maine

The other two men allegedly raped the children's mother.
                                            KGTV, San Diego

Add Authority Attribution also should be used when it's necessary to lend authority to a charge; when a writer wants to show that it's not just a radio or television journalist who has come up with this theory, but that officials, trained to make such determinations, feel this way.

```
UNACCEPTABLE
The two murders were not connected.


ACCEPTABLE
Police say the two murders were not connected.
```

Here are some examples of the use of attribution for authority.

```
Police theorize the bodies may have been dumped at the
site at 116th and Crandon by a garbage truck.
```
                                                        WBBM, Chicago


```
Bureau of Land Management spokesman Phil Jimenez says
thundershowers yesterday afternoon helped put out the
flames.
```
                                                        KREX, Colorado

Since newswriters are not inside the minds of the newsmakers, statements about people's state of mind, their feelings and beliefs, should be attributed for authority.

```
WEAK
Mayor Lincoln Upton doesn't believe the unhappy
employees represent a majority.


BETTER
Mayor Lincoln Upton says he doesn't believe the unhappy
employees represent a majority.
```
                                                        KOA, Denver

Only when people's statements or behavior make their mental state obvious can the attribution be omitted.

```
The lawyer for a group of Salvation Army employees hopes
to have a new bargaining unit formed by that group
certified by the National Labor Relations Board.
```
                                                        KOA, Denver

■ ■ ■

Most facts that make it into the news have a source; therefore it would be possible to use attribution in almost every sentence in broadcast news. Overdoing

the attribution—"according to local officials a festival was held in the park today"—
would make the copy sound pedantic. Facts that are independently verifiable—such
events as arrests, court verdicts, scores, votes—do not need attributing.

WEAK
The county clerk says voting booths will be set up in
the student union again this year.

BETTER
Voting booths will be set up in the student union again
this year.

UNACCEPTABLE
According to police, the suspect was arrested.

ACCEPTABLE
The suspect was arrested.

Of course, if the fact is not clear or is potentially a matter of debate the attribution
must return.

UNACCEPTABLE
The suspect was arrested carrying the murder weapon.

ACCEPTABLE
According to police, the suspect was arrested carrying
the murder weapon.

Broadcast writers generally use less attribution than newspaper reporters because
they don't attribute facts that aren't potentially controversial or suspect. Frequent
interjections for the sake of unnecessary attribution would destroy the conversational
flavor of the news.

WEAK
The mayor says he will hold a press conference this
afternoon.

BETTER
The mayor will hold a press conference this afternoon.

Unless the mayor has a reputation as a compulsive liar, there's nothing suspect about
this announcement; no need to protect the writer or add authority to the statement.

WEAK
According to police, the driver escaped with only minor
injuries, and fire officials say they put out the fire.

BETTER
```
The driver escaped with minor injuries, and firemen put
out the fire.
```

WPDM, New York

Sentences are clearest when the attribution is placed at the start of the sentence.

UNACCEPTABLE
```
The world will end tomorrow, according to a mystic in
the Mohave desert.
```

ACCEPTABLE
```
According to a mystic in the Mohave desert, the world
will end tomorrow.
```

Attribution prepares listeners for the statement; it tells them whose theory they are about to hear. It may confuse them to wait until the end of the sentence to find out who said it. Since broadcast news can't be reread, newswriters can't fiddle with this logical order: who is talking, then what was said—attribution, then statement. Another reason to place the attribution first is that sentences don't read smoothly when it hangs at the end.

UNACCEPTABLE
```
A cut in taxes is the only way to solve the state's
problems, the Chamber of Commerce claims.
```

Sticking attribution in the middle of a sentence doesn't work well either.

WEAK
```
A cut in taxes, the Chamber of Commerce claims, is the
only way to solve the state's problems.
```

BETTER
```
The Chamber of Commerce claims a cut in taxes is the
only way to solve the state's problems.
```

Wrap-Up

Writers must stay in control. They cannot allow every seductive phrase that comes into their heads to spill out of their computers. All potential broadcast news sentences must be evaluated. Do they mean precisely what the story means? Do they tell the story straight, without exaggeration or bias? Has controversial material been properly attributed?

Practice Assignments

A. Rewrite the following sentences in broadcast style.

1. Anarchy and chaos reign in Cambodia . . . where mounting tension followed the explosion of a bomb yesterday afternoon.
2. The Mississippi River dealt a slap in the face to Oxford, Mississippi, last night when it toppled the proud little town's dikes.
3. The mayor and the governor skipped off to Washington today, although the latter says he won't stay there too long.
4. Cambridge police finally grabbed twelve teenagers for drug possession today, but they say they won't be arraigned until tomorrow.
5. England's prime minister and France's president will come here for a ten-day tour after the European summit and then return there.
6. The Labor Department claims the Consumer Price Index shot up point one percent this month.
7. The Weather Bureau has acknowledged that this was the very hottest Labor Day since 1935.
8. Vietnam predictably charged China with border violations today and observed that it will retaliate.
9. Only 12 percent of the state's budget has been allocated for public transportation.
10. The woman's sister disappeared last week two blocks from her school and she's been searching for her ever since.
11. Cleveland residents are unhappy about a two percent rise in their real estate taxes. A group of 25 people protested the tax hike in front of City Hall yesterday.
12. Two innocent people died today in a downtown fire . . . the result of arson.
13. Anti-abortion protesters continued their campaign of terror today with sit-ins in front of two more abortion clinics.
14. New York's wishy-washy governor isn't sure if casino gambling really is such a good idea.
15. Court clerk John Houston says the Jerry Nolan murder trial will begin next Monday morning.
16. Police say there was a tiny anti-nuclear demonstration in front of the Evanstown Utility Company this morning.
17. Democratic candidate John Losey will enter the New Hampshire primary, according to his campaign manager.
18. The Independent Party supposedly more than doubled its membership last year, according to the party's chairman, Al Olsen.
19. Italy's feared Communist Party has a good chance to win a slew of seats in this month's Parliamentary elections.
20. A Newark bank official has been placed under an embezzlement charge today. He robbed his own bank by affecting the books.

B. All the information in the following story is from the police. Rewrite the story, placing proper attribution where necessary.

```
A former bank teller has been charged with the robbery
of the First National Bank yesterday. Most of the 50-
thousand dollars taken from the bank were found in his
home. The former teller -- Peter Taylor -- was fired by
the bank's president two months ago. Taylor entered the
bank armed with a shotgun yesterday and left with a
briefcase stuffed with thousand-dollar bills. One of the
bank employees recognized Taylor and notified police.
Taylor was arrested at his home at 27-27 Midlands Avenue
this afternoon.
```

Sentences

When sentences meander, so does listeners' attention. This wandering sentence was used on the air:

> The City Planning Commission met this afternoon at City
> Hall and decided . . . by unanimous vote . . . to
> recommend to the City Council an amendment to a city
> ordinance which would . . . by special exception . . .
> allow restaurants to serve liquor in areas currently
> zoned C-2.

The listeners probably got lost somewhere between the "unanimous vote" and the "special exception."

Most broadcast news stories aren't long enough to rely on paragraphs. Some writers indicate paragraphs; many don't bother. Sentences are the major unit of organization within stories, so a good deal of the responsibility for keeping the news clear and concise falls on them. Good broadcast newswriting is always characterized by tight, lucid sentences:

> Hoboken teachers came close to reaching agreement with
> the city school board last night, but apparently not
> close enough. After two and a half hours of talks, a
> near-settlement was reached, but the deal fell through.
> The union blames the board, saying it's refused to
> promise amnesty to striking teachers.
>
> WINS, New York City

Clarity

Hughes Rudd, a former CBS and ABC reporter and newscaster, once said that after reading a particularly confusing story on the air, he's often tempted to read it a second time for listeners—tempted, but he's never done it. Listeners get one chance to understand. This is one of the major differences between print and broadcast journalism. If a sentence confuses newspaper, magazine or book readers, they can simply read it again. If their attention wanders in the middle of a paragraph, they can read that paragraph again.

But broadcast news must work the first time through, and that places a number of special demands on broadcast newswriters. Perhaps the most pressing is the need to make their writing extra clear. All journalism must be clear; broadcast news must be especially clear so that it makes sense without repetition and helps listeners focus their attention.

Simplicity

This sentence from the *New York Times* would make a good reading comprehension test:

```
After nearly 18 months of difficult and slow-moving
talks, the representatives of the world's rich and poor
nations appeared to be approaching agreement early today
on a limited international program intended to help the
developing world, but a deadlock over plans to make
increases in the price of oil more difficult threatened
to sour relations between the two blocs.
```

The sentence is grammatically correct. It makes sense. The problem is that some readers would have to read it a couple of times to figure out what it says. Look at the number of ideas stuffed into one sentence:

1. The talks have lasted nearly 18 months.
2. They've been difficult and slow moving.
3. The talks include representatives of the world's rich and poor nations.
4. They appear to be approaching agreement on a limited international program to help the developing world.
5. The nations are deadlocked on a plan to make increases in the price of oil more difficult.
6. The deadlock threatens to sour relations between rich and poor countries.

Six ideas in one sentence; that's why it might take a couple of readings to understand. Sentences this complex can never be used in broadcast news. A good guideline: one, or at the most, two, ideas per sentence.

This is how the sentence might be rewritten for broadcast:

```
There was some progress and some bad feeling in Paris
today as representatives of the world's rich and poor
nations met. They are moving closer to agreement on a
plan which would provide some help to developing
```

```
countries. But a proposal to control oil price increases
is getting nowhere and causing tension. These talks have
been going on for almost a year and a half.
```

This uses only five more words than the *Times'* version but contains three more sentences—each making one or two simple points.

Simple sentences make for clear copy. Broadcast newswriters must discover simple ways to communicate the often complex occurrences that make up the news. This doesn't mean their writing has to be pedestrian. Newswriters have to be sophisticated enough to transform subtle and often involved concepts into direct, understandable language—a challenging assignment to say the least. There's nothing simple about writing simple. Here are two rules:

Divide Take a complex sentence and break it down into a few simple sentences:

```
WEAK
Strong citizen pressure against continued showing of X-
rated films at the Whitehall Drive-In has apparently
convinced Whitehall, New York, officials to consider an
ordinance to control pornography.
```

```
BETTER
Whitehall, New York, officials are considering an
ordinance to control pornography. The effort is
apparently the result of strong citizen pressure against
continued showing of X-rated films at the Whitehall
Drive-In.
                                            WSYB, Vermont
```

```
WEAK
On the fifth day of fighting between Libya and Egypt,
Libya is claiming it shot down eight Egyptian planes as
they attacked in waves across the desert, while military
spokesmen in Cairo deny that there were any raids today,
terming Libya's charges a pack of lies.
```

```
BETTER
Libya says it shot down eight Egyptian planes today
. . . as they attacked in waves across the desert.
Military spokesmen in Cairo say there were no raids
. . . and term Libya's charges . . . a pack of lies. The
conflicting reports come on the fifth day of fighting
between the two nations.
                                            KENO, Las Vegas
```

Abandon Some facts confuse more than they elucidate. To keep a sentence simple and clear, abandon these nonessential facts. Facts that might be used by a newspaper—the exact charges in an indictment, the history of an event, a description of the circumstances—must often be cut to pare down sentences. A lean sentence minus a couple of interesting but unnecessary facts is better than a plodding sentence which can't effectively communicate any facts.

```
UNACCEPTABLE
The Transport Workers Union agreed last night to ''stop
the clock'' and continue negotiations in an effort to
avert a strike, originally set for six this morning,
which would have stranded two and a half million weekday
bus and subway riders in the metropolitan area and
disrupted the life of the city.
```

```
ACCEPTABLE
No subway and bus strike yet. The Transport Workers
Union last night agreed to ''stop the clock'' and keep
negotiating.
```

Interjections and Clauses

Newspaper writers often break up their sentences with long interjections or explanatory clauses, as in this example from the *New York Times*:

```
The mediators, Josine Soumokilx, 64 years old, and Dr.
Jassaon Tan, 56, both of whom are highly regarded
members of the Moluccan community, boarded the train at
2 p.m. local time, and after nearly three hours of talks
with the kidnappers sent word that they were staying for
dinner with them.
```

Clauses and long interjections usually cause difficulty in broadcast news; they lead to complex sentence structures that listeners cannot follow. They are especially troublesome when inserted in the middle of a sentence. Notice the distance between the subject, "the mediators," and the verbs, "boarded" and "sent word," in the above example. If such a sentence were used on the air, listeners might forget the subject by the time the verbs arrived.

Never separate the subject and verb in a sentence with long interjections:

```
UNACCEPTABLE
The eleventh annual Trivia Bowl, in which 48 teams are
competing for championship T-shirts and the chance to
have their names engraved on a trophy, is underway on
the C-U campus in Boulder.
```

The WBBM-TV, Chicago, newsroom.

ACCEPTABLE
The eleventh annual Trivia Bowl is underway on the C-U
campus in Boulder. 48 teams are competing for
championship T-shirts and the chance to have their names
engraved on a trophy.

KOA, Denver

UNACCEPTABLE
In yesterday's Cherokee County election a measure <u>that
would replace the five-person county commission with a
one-man commission</u> was approved by voters.

ACCEPTABLE
Voters in Cherokee County have ousted their five-person
county commission. . . . It'll be replaced by a ONE-man
commission.

WSB, Atlanta

A clause does less damage to the clarity of a sentence when used at the beginning
or end of the sentence:

UNACCEPTABLE
The suspect, <u>after consultations with his two court-
appointed lawyers,</u> pleaded guilty.

```
ACCEPTABLE
After consultations with his two court-appointed
lawyers, the suspect pleaded guilty.

The suspect pleaded guilty after consultations with his
two court-appointed lawyers.
```

But it often is safest to give the clause a sentence of its own:

```
ACCEPTABLE
The suspect consulted with his two court-appointed
lawyers. He then pleaded guilty.
```

Broadcast newswriters must constantly monitor the distance between the subject and verb in their sentences and they must watch that the *when's*, *while's*, *who's*, explanations and descriptions aren't tangling up their sentences. Too many interruptions tend to make writing confusing. More than one per sentence is usually too many.

Names and Titles

An awkward phrasing:

```
Dr. Alvin M. Weinberg, director of the Energy Analysis
Institute of the Oak Ridge Associated Universities,
says . . .
```

Formal names and titles are rarely used in conversation and should rarely be used in broadcast news. Here are the rules for referring to people in copy:

Shorten Names Broadcast journalists start by forgetting the middle initial. With the exception of people whose first and last name are particularly common, or a few people who have become known by their initials, such as Booker T. Washington or O. J. Simpson, initials add nothing but formality to a name. It's George Mitchell, not George J. Mitchell; Alvin Weinberg, not Alvin M. Weinberg.

Other addenda to the basic name can also be chopped off. James A. Baker the Third becomes James Baker on the air. There's no chance of confusing him with James Baker the Second. *Junior* and *senior* should also be dropped except in that rare case when father and son are both making news.

Nicknames James Earl Carter Junior was kind to broadcast journalists. Not only did the former president keep his middle name and the "Junior" off the ballot, he gave himself a nice conversational nickname: "Jimmy." If a person is commonly and courteously referred to by a nickname—Mick Jagger, Bill Clinton, Magic Johnson—then it's appropriate to use the nickname on the air. But nicknames shouldn't be forced on people—Ronald Reagan should not be called "Ronnie."

First Usage   The first time a name is used it must clearly identify the person. Usually this requires presenting both the first and last name, whether the person is well known—Jesse Jackson, Paula Abdul, Arsenio Hall—or just a visitor to the news—Alvin Weinberg, Anita Hall, Joseph Cicippio.

> UNACCEPTABLE
> Shiite Muslim kidnappers pledged to release American
> hostage Cicippio by Tuesday.

> ACCEPTABLE
> Shiite Muslim kidnappers pledged to release American
> hostage Joseph Cicippio by Tuesday.
>
> Forrest Sawyer, ABC

However, if a person is very well known and has a title, often the last name and the title are sufficient to pin down the person's identity—President Clinton, former President Reagan.

But *only* if they're very well known.

> WEAK
> German Chancellor Kohl

> BETTER
> German Chancellor Helmut Kohl

The names of the singers Madonna, Prince, Hammer and Cher are exceptions. A reference to Madonna Ciccone would only confuse.

Second Usage   Once a person has been introduced in a story, the last name or the title alone is all that's needed: "Jackson also said . . ." or "The German leader plans. . . ." First names alone would be too *informal*.

> UNACCEPTABLE
> David also lost that election.

> ACCEPTABLE
> Duke also lost that election.

And titles of address—Mr., Mrs., Miss, Ms.—are too *formal*. Some stations reserve them for just one person—the president. Most stations won't even use *Mr.* for the president. *Doctor* should be used only when the person's authority as a scientist or a physician is part of the story. It's Dr. Salk, not Dr. Kissinger; and on many stations, Ms., Mrs. or Miss are used only if there's a danger of confusing the woman with a man having the same last name.

Omitting Names An unknown name is like an obscure word—it can confuse. Often a title or description is all the information needed about a person. For example, in a short item about Latin American reaction to a projected program it is sufficient to write, "Costa Rica's president attacked the plan." No need for his name. Similarly, the name of a victim or a suspect in a crime in another city is usually unnecessary. "A middle-aged woman was injured" is fine. However, in local stories names *are* important. Listeners will want to know which middle-aged woman was injured—perhaps they know her.

Titles Alvin Weinberg's title, in the example that began this section, is much too long and unwieldly for broadcast news. "Director of the Energy Analysis Institute of the Oak Ridge Associated Universities" has enough words that are irrelevant to the point of the story to cause even the most attentive mind to wander.

Long titles can be shortened. This often requires abandoning the formal title completely. It's not necessary for listeners to learn exactly how Weinberg's business card reads. It is sufficient to call him "a local energy expert" or "an energy expert at a local university" or just "a physicist" or "a scientist." Which one is chosen depends on Weinberg's role in the story.

WEAK
Undersecretary of State for Political Affairs Arnold
Kanter

BETTER
State Department official Arnold Kanter

UNACCEPTABLE
The Chairman of the New York and New Jersey Bistate
Commission to End Pollution of Coastal Waters, New
Jersey Assemblyman Anthony Villane of Long Branch

ACCEPTABLE
A New Jersey assemblyman who chairs a bistate water
commission, Anthony Villane

Also, the words in a title should be arranged so that they read smoothly.

WEAK
```
National Security Adviser to the President Brent
Scowcroft
```

BETTER
```
The president's national security adviser, Brent
Scowcroft
```

Titles First When using a title and a name in the same sentence, put the title first.

WEAK
```
Alvin Weinberg, a local energy expert, says . . .
```

BETTER
```
A local energy expert, Alvin Weinberg, says . . .
```

Why? Because a title is an explanation for a name; it tells us who Weinberg is. Were the name to come first, we might be momentarily confused by it.

Sentences also flow more smoothly with the title first.

WEAK
```
Roone Arledge, the president of ABC News, also was
there.
```

BETTER
```
ABC News President Roone Arledge also was there.
```

Quotes

Comedian Victor Borge once put together a routine in which he made a sound and a gesture for each punctuation mark in his monologue. Every time he reached quotation marks he'd say, "tswit, tswit," while waving two fingers of each hand in the air. Newscasters, however, have never been willing to do this. They will pause for a dash, comma or period and put a quizzical tone in their voices for question marks, but there is little likelihood that they will say "tswit, tswit" for every set of quotation marks.

This "timidity" on the part of newscasters leaves writers with a serious clarity problem. There is no way they can let their listeners know that there are quotation marks around that statement by the governor, even if it is important to know that those were the governor's exact words. Quotation marks lose most of their meaning on the air. All they do is encourage the newscaster to pause, which may be enough if it's not important that listeners know it's a direct quote:

```
The caller warned the clerk to ''get everybody out of
there!''
```
KODY, Nebraska

But when it must be clear that it's a direct quote, that those are the exact words, a pause is not sufficient. The governor's exact words were: "The whole bunch of them is corrupt!" How can those words best be communicated to listeners?

By far the best solution is to get the words on tape (see Chapter 9, "Tape") or videotape—but often no tape is available. Then the simplest solution is to paraphrase:

```
The governor charges that the senators who oppose her
plan are corrupt.
```

If they're not on tape, direct quotes are relatively rare on the air. Most statements are paraphrased:

```
Cook County Clerk Stanley Kusper is telling reporters
just how much more in taxes some Chicagoans will have to
pay because of a new property tax. Kusper called a news
conference this morning to say the increase will be less
than one percent.
```
WBBM, Chicago

```
Skeet appeared before the commission asking that he be
allowed to retain his job, and said that he would not
resign.
```
KLWN, Kansas

Occasionally, however, the exact wording of a statement that isn't available on tape *is* news in itself. The actual quote can be controversial, colorful or revealing. In these situations listeners must be informed that it's a direct quote, and therefore it is necessary to replace those silent quotation marks with something audible—words.

A classic example of a spot where a paraphrase just wouldn't do is when former President Richard Nixon exclaimed, "I am not a crook!" Paraphrased, the statement loses the incongruity and inappropriateness of language that makes it interesting:

```
The president says that he isn't a criminal.
```

The most obvious way to make clear that this is a quote would be to write the word *quote* at the start and *unquote* at the end:

```
The president said -- quote -- I am not a crook --
unquote.
```

Or:

```
The president said -- and we quote -- I am not a crook --
end of quotation.
```

However, while actually using the word *quote* is clear, it certainly is not conversational. This heavy-handed device has become antiquated. There are more subtle and less formal alternatives. All these more conversational phrases inform listeners that they are about to hear a direct quote:

He put it this way . . .
She used these words . . .
The governor's exact words were . . .
As he put it . . .
With this dramatic phrase . . .
. . . what she called . . .
These are the union leader's words . . .
As she expressed it . . .
To use his words . . .
In the words of . . .

So Nixon's awkward defense could be written:

```
The president's exact words were . . . ''I am not a
crook!''
```

Here are some additional examples:

```
As the principal of North High School put it, ''If on
the night we play Salisbury we have a rainy night, we've
had it.''
                                        WRBX, North Carolina

The mayor called the head of the Chamber of Commerce
. . . in his words . . . ''a professional fanny-
kisser.''
                                        WTLB, New York

The military calls it ''softening the target,'' and
today that softening took the form of 2-thousand, 500
bombing runs.
                                        Diane Sawyer, ABC
```

Even with these clarifying phrases, the use of a direct quote is uncomfortable in broadcast news. Direct quotes require that the newscaster briefly act the part of someone else.

```
NEWSCASTER AS NEWSCASTER
As the demonstration's leader expressed it . . .

NEWSCASTER IMPERSONATING LEADER
''We're not going to stand for this anymore!''
```

That switch in roles may confuse the listener. It can be especially disconcerting when the direct quote uses the first person.

```
WEAK
To use the words of the demonstration's leader . . .
''We've had enough.''
```

It almost sounds as though the newscaster has had enough. A paraphrase is, therefore, clearer.

```
BETTER
One demonstrator shouted that she had had enough.
```

Once a direct quote gets longer than a phrase or two, it can become thoroughly confusing.

```
UNACCEPTABLE
The union leader's exact words were . . . ''A breakdown
in talks has left us with no alternative but to close
the plant. I have instructed all members to stay home
tomorrow. We're on strike! And this strike could last
weeks.''
```

Placing more clarifying phrases within the quote makes it clearer but still a bit stiff.

```
WEAK
The union leader's exact words were . . . ''A breakdown
in talks has left us with no alternative but to close
the plant.'' As he put it . . . ''I have instructed all
members to stay home tomorrow. We're on strike!'' Then
he used these words . . . ''This strike could last
weeks.''
```

The solution—always paraphrase long quotes.

```
BETTER
The union leader said that a breakdown in talks has left
workers with no alternative but to close the plant. All
members have been instructed to stay home tomorrow. The
union leader says the strike could last weeks.
```

It would be useful if computers in broadcast newsrooms had red warning lights on the quotation mark keys. Quotes work so poorly in broadcast writing that newswriters should always try to talk themselves out of using them. Use a direct quote only when it's neat, compact *and* the wording is exceptional. Otherwise, paraphrase.

```
WEAK
The councilman's exact words were . . . ''I have decided
to run for re-election.''
```

```
BETTER
The councilman says that he has decided to run for re-
election.
```

Conciseness

Great writing often comes not only in simple but also in short sentences:

```
In the beginning God created the heaven and the earth.
And the earth was without form, and void; and darkness
was upon the face of the deep. And the Spirit of God
moved upon the face of the waters. And God said, Let
there be light; and there was light.
```

There are no wasted words in this passage from the King James Bible; no rambling sentences. Broadcast news may not achieve this poetry, but it must strive for something approaching this luminosity and conciseness.

We've noted that long sentences are tough for the ear to follow, but they have two other drawbacks: Wordiness wastes time and long sentences are hard to read smoothly on the air. Try reading aloud this sentence, which Mervin Block caught on CBS:

```
An attorney in the Howard Hughes will hassle says today
that the Utah gas station operator whose fingerprints
appeared on the envelope of one purported will in which
Melvin Dummar is named a major heir admits now he
delivered the will to the Morman Church headquarters,
where it was discovered.
```

The newscaster who read that one either had extraordinary lung capacity or was forced to pause for breath in the middle. The sentence is confusing enough as is. Such an unnatural pause would have made it completely unintelligible to listeners.

How long should a broadcast news sentence be? It depends on how many pauses there are in it and how good the newscaster's lungs are. But most broadcast journalists warn that when a sentence stretches more than two, or at the most three, lines of copy—it's trouble. A sentence that long will probably be difficult to say and difficult to understand.

Pauses

Newscasters have different lung capacities, but all of them need to take a breath once in a while. So a newscaster reading copy that lacks a place for a natural pause is either going to add an unnatural pause or turn blue. Here's what can happen to writing that leaves no room for breathing:

> Groundbreaking and dedication ceremonies were held in the rain earlier today for a new theater (pause) to house works produced by the County Art and Dramatic Society's (pause) summer stock resident company.

Such inappropriate pauses interfere with the flow of words and, therefore, can confuse.

Most newscasters get hungry for air every 20 syllables or so. If a sentence is that short, the period or question mark will provide the opportunity to inhale. Otherwise a dash, ellipsis or comma should be written into the copy to make sure that the newscaster pauses where it suits the sentence construction, not in the middle of a phrase.

This story never goes longer than 19 syllables without giving the newscaster a break:

> Could it be? Is it possible? Right here in Virginia? Well, Rupert Williamson thinks so. . . . Williamson has found footprints in his strawberry patch in Dinwiddie County . . . Size 25 triple-D footprints to be exact. The sheriff's department thinks it's a prank. . . . Williamson says one of his neighbors is so scared he can't sleep. The bigfoot has been seen all over the world. . . . Some places it's called Sasquatch, Yetti, and in Arkansas the Boggy Creek Monster. Maybe it's just a case of Kilroy was here, updated. Convince Rupert Williamson.
>
> WROV, Virginia

And notice how clearly the pauses are indicated in this story. The newscaster is never asked to read more than 20 syllables between commas or ellipses:

> Another one of those smoking-in-bed tragedies. . . . The victim this time a 75-year-old woman. . . . . Firemen were able to rescue Edith Mordey's 85-year-old husband,

and he was hospitalized with smoke inhalation and chest
pains . . . but it was too late for the woman. . . . The
fire was confined to the first-floor bedroom of the two-
story home. . . . The second floor apartment was
vacant. . . . . The building's located at 91-06
143rd Street . . . in Jamaica, Queens.

WINS, New York City

Not all broadcast news is quite this terse, but it can never be much more longwinded, because newscasters do not have that much wind.

The Point

Broadcast journalists should never have to be told to get to the point; they should already be there. Their sentences should provide the shortest possible route to the meaning of a story.

Earlier in this chapter the need to divide sentences and abandon ideas of little import was discussed, but there's another method for keeping sentences trim— conserving words.

Some linguists maintain that less than 50 percent of the words we use actually convey meaning. The rest, they say, are merely used for style or to satisfy conventions. The broadcast journalist's goal should be to make the percentage of words that make the point in a sentence as high as possible.

UNACCEPTABLE
There are about 30 <u>different</u> states that have <u>inserted</u>
provisions in their <u>state</u> constitutions allowing
initiative, recall and referenda. Indiana <u>is one of the</u>
<u>states that</u> does not <u>have such a provision in its</u>
<u>constitution.</u>

ACCEPTABLE
Some 30 states have provisions in their constitutions
allowing for initiative, recall and referenda. Indiana
does not.

WNAP, Indiana

This phrase, used on the air, says in five words what could have been said just as accurately in three:

A rate increase in rents . . .

Every word that doesn't help make the point should be pruned. And some words must be watched particularly closely. They have a reputation for leading sentences astray:

Detours These words detour sentences because they are so imprecise. *Involved*, for example, merely hints at a relationship. Other words must be wasted to tie down the loose ends this word leaves:

```
UNACCEPTABLE
They were involved in a move to unseat him.
```

```
ACCEPTABLE
They tried to unseat him.
```

Involved is often an ambiguous substitute for clearer phrasings. This suggestive sentence, used on the air, provides an exaggerated example of the problem:

```
He was taken to a local hospital for treatment of head
and facial injuries after his vehicle was involved with
another car. . . . .
```

Here are some other examples of detour words and phrases:

```
WEAK
The expressway is experiencing a delay.
```

```
BETTER
Traffic is delayed on the expressway.
```

```
WEAK
The money represents one quarter of the funding they
will need.
```

```
BETTER
That's one quarter of the money they'll need.
```

```
WEAK
He succeeded in escaping.
```

```
BETTER
He escaped.
```

```
WEAK
The bill was delayed due to the opposition of one of the
council members.
```

```
BETTER
One of the council members delayed the bill.
```

WEAK
That was the first proposal <u>concerning</u> a health center.

BETTER
That was the first proposal for a health center.

Redundancy Overstating also clogs sentences with useless words. It's not enough to set a record; people are said to have set *new* records, as if it were possible to set an old record. Similarly, surprises have become *unexpected* surprises, though you have to be pretty sharp to expect your surprises.

Mervin Block spotted this sentence on CBS television:

Four tons of fireworks lit up the skies around the
Washington Monument for a full 30 minutes.

To be distinguished from a *partial* 30 minutes? In his in-house newsletter, Block also criticized CBS writers who talked of "true facts" (a journalist who thinks there might be such a thing as a *false* fact might be dangerous), "grocery store" (*grocery* says it well enough) and "human beings" (*humans* handles this job alone). In addition, Block objected to this sentence, which was used on CBS television presumably to describe a frozen or blocked body of water:

Boats literally cannot move.

"If they can't move, they can't move," Block wrote. "'Literally' adds only bulk."

Redundancy blunts writing and wastes time on the air. See if all these words don't get the point across just as clearly without their modifiers:

over-exaggerate	quite depressing
completely destroy	final conclusion
general consensus	complete stop
total annihilation	honest truth
personal feelings	positively identify
brief minute	strictly prohibit

Obvious adjectives or adverbs are not the only form of redundancy. Often words seduce us into believing that they are adding meaning when in fact they are only wasting time. For example, "this nation's Greek-Americans" is just as clear without the "this nation's."

Wasteful Phrases Our language is full of phrases that substitute a few words for one word. Newswriters try to avoid them.

WORDY	CONCISE
in an effort to	to
in order to	to
for the purpose of	to
at the present time	now
at this point in time	now
in the near future	soon
having to do with	about
with reference to	about
due to the fact that	because
along the lines of	like
in the event that	if
with the exception of	except
was the recipient of	received
is of the opinion that	believes
venture a suggestion	suggest
take action	act

There may be occasions when it is desirable to elaborate somewhat, to use a longer phrase. Succinctness is not the only goal, and a longer phrase may improve the pacing of a sentence or help emphasize a point. But it's important not to fall into these phrases ignorantly. First look for the concise way to make the point.

Grammar This statement is concise:

No abortion clinic for Melbourne.

WMEL, Florida

But is it a sentence? It doesn't even have a verb.

Sentence or not, such shorthand constructions are used frequently in broadcast news, in stories as well as in headlines (see Chapter 12, "Newscasts"):

Some disagreement at the city council meeting last night.

WADA, North Carolina

Winter in May. The area received four inches of snow today.

WARA, Massachusetts

Two dead in weekend traffic accidents.

KWTX, Texas

Another highjacking in progress at this hour.

WKVT, Vermont

Broadcast newswriters choose to violate the rules of formal grammar and use these technically incomplete sentences because they save words, and their staccato rhythm gives writing punch:

```
Tanks in the streets . . . Shots in the night . . .
Soviet politicians involved in the coup against
President Gorbachev now allegedly in their sickbeds.
There isn't much that's clear in the Soviet Union
tonight. . . .
                                    Peter Jennings, ABC
```

Beginners have a tendency to overuse this style. An incomplete sentence or two may pick up the pace of a newscast, but a whole newscast full of these punchy partial sentences may leave listeners or viewers reeling. As Lynn Woolley at KRLD, Dallas, says, "It's still nice to have a noun, verb and the whole works." Some news directors won't accept any fudging at all with the rules of grammar, but most will buy it occasionally—if the result is clear and conversational.

Beginners also have a tendency to exaggerate this style and write so concisely that their writing sounds like newspaper headlines:

```
UNACCEPTABLE
Intellectuals appeal to Chinese to free
dissidents. . . . Administration silent.
```

This is so compact that it isn't remotely conversational. Even if a sentence is not complete, it must flow and be understandable.

```
UNACCEPTABLE
Four percent police, fire and city employee raise
approved last night.
```

```
ACCEPTABLE
Final approval given last night to a four percent raise
for police, firemen and other city employees.
                                          WAZY, Indiana
```

Another danger is that newswriters will use the license occasionally to stretch the rules of grammar as an excuse for sloppiness or revenge on high school English teachers.

Misuse of the language is never acceptable in broadcast news. These unfortunate examples found their way onto the air:

```
The pronoun that doesn't agree: Quite a number of Ohio
farmers are plowing up strands of winter wheat and
planting soybeans in its place.
```

The verb that doesn't agree: Ford's <u>finding</u> of bombs in a county mine <u>were</u> at first taken as an act of heroism.

The dangling modifier, or worse:
Extortion notes have been sent to two companies in addition to the three that received the letter bombs in the mail, demanding money or else more bombs will be sent.

The Cinema X theater has been convicted of shipping obscene films across state lines, stemming from the showing of Deep Throat in 1973.

The lesson? Know the language. Grammar *can* be learned after high school. If there's a problem, a good grammar book is the place to start. Marching naively into the realms of grammatical freedom in search of conciseness can lead to convoluted sentences and embarrassment.

Wrap-Up

The late novelist Isaac Bashevis Singer once said that the wastepaper basket is the writer's best friend. Broadcast writers may not always have time to crumple pages (or the computer equivalent) and start again, but in their search for effective sentences they discard a lot of useless words and awkward phrasings. Broadcast sentences must be cleaned, trimmed and polished until they are clear and to the point.

Practice Assignments

Rewrite the following sentences in broadcast style.

1. Israel's prime minister said today that if an Arab administrative council to be set up in the West Bank and the Gaza Strip under a proposed autonomy plan proclaimed a Palestinian state, its members would be promptly arrested and the Israeli military government brought back.
2. Voters in the state will decide whether to approve a proposition that would involve a drastic cut in property taxes.
3. A campaign contribution by Roland S. Savoy to a member of the State Senate panel that for the past seven weeks has been considering his nomination as correctional services commissioner appeared today to put his already-troubled nomination in jeopardy.

4. Responding to attacks and criticism by the Administration, the oil industry insisted today that their profits are *not* overly excessive.

5. The mayor went to Washington for the purpose of fighting the proposal and told the committee, "We don't like the idea one bit."

6. John Stark, Democratic senator from Wisconsin, says that, before introducing his tax-cut bill onto the floor of the House of Representatives next Monday afternoon, he will consult privately with the Republican leadership.

7. Federal Reserve Board cuts interest rates in move to boost economy.

8. France says it will cooperate "in economics, in culture and in education" with other European countries, "but militarily, no."

9. He began initiating the senior citizens program in an effort to improve and upgrade their lives.

10. Auto makers say profits *not* too high.

11. The 15-year-old boy, who was a sophomore at Oak Ridge High School, said he spent most of his time practicing for the homecoming game, which would have been held next weekend.

12. The decision to establish a senate is a concession to the king's critics, but it's not certain just how the senate will be chosen to assure participation from representatives of the many groups which make up the country's opposition.

13. Jane Rose, associate commissioner of the State Energy Commission, has called for a halt to the building of nuclear reactors.

14. Assistant Commissioner of General Social Services and Income Maintenance Eric Falk says the welfare rolls are increasing.

15. Mrs. Jane Adamson, Ridgedale's town alderman for the last 13 years, says she won't run for re-election.

16. In the words of a leading communications expert—Dr. Henry Green—"TV is the new industrial-corporate religion . . . seizing the minds of today's youth and creating an entire generation obsessed with violence."

17. The Fire Department says that the severity of Wednesday's fire at Lamston's Department Store in which four shoppers and two firemen died has been traced to a broken sprinkler system on the store's fourth floor.

18. An extremely serious car accident involving two cars and three trucks which collided while traveling on Interstate 61 has resulted in six people dead and two people injured.

19. The City Council failed again to approve the school budget for the third time this year in an attempt to hold down costs.

20. Terrorist bullets killed two people in Italy today: Angela Lombardi, a 15-year-old high school student, and Gianninni Mordi, a 23-year-old factory worker at a Fiat plant in Turin.

21. Former Mayor Arthur S. Dorf has retracted his charges against Governor David W. Chalk . . . saying it was prompted by his drinking problem.

5

Leads

In broadcast news the **lead** is the first sentence, or occasionally the first two sentences, of a story:

> Another time-out has been called in the Los Angeles
> school integration proceedings. Superior Court Judge
> Paul Egly has given the Board of Education a month to
> let him know in writing exactly how the plan's going to
> work. Specifically, Egly wants to learn which schools and
> students will be participating in the integration plan
> submitted by the board. Egly says he hopes to rule on
> the plan within a month.
>
> KNX, Los Angeles

The lead doesn't sound any different from the other sentences in a story—listeners won't know they're hearing a lead. Yet writing a good lead is often the key to writing a good story.

Broadcast news stories are so short that it is imperative to get off on the right foot. It's also necessary to grab listeners' attention with that first sentence. Newswriters put their best sentence forward:

> Inflation, it seems, is hitting everyone these days, even
> those who traffic in and use heroin. A federal drug
> enforcement agent says the cost of an ounce of heroin on
> the illegal market has jumped from 600 dollars a year
> ago to 900 dollars today in the Houston area.
>
> WARU, Indiana

Like any other sentence, the lead must follow the rules for broadcast newswriting outlined in the previous chapters, but, since this first sentence has more responsibilities, it has to meet additional standards.

This chapter devotes quite a few words to the story's first few words and the job they have to do.

Intriguing

The news wants attention. The lead has to get it. Listeners are driving in traffic or doing the dishes. Viewers are chatting with friends or sprawled, exhausted, on the couch. A newswriter has a complex story to relate about some technical changes in the format of the venerable *New York Times*. What's the best way to break through the road noises, the daydreams, the fatigue or the conversation to get that story across? The obvious strategy would be to weigh in immediately with the facts:

```
The New York Times will switch from an eight-column to a
six-column format on September 7th.
```

Will that catch their attention? Doubtful. Except for that familiar name, the *New York Times*, this is just a jumble of facts. What is needed is something that will make the story sound more interesting—a lead that will bring out whatever is arresting about this story. Here is a lead that did just that:

```
The New York Times is getting a face lift.
```

                                                    WOR, New York City

The basic fact is still here, but what's been added is a touch of irony: the staid *New York Times* acting appearance-conscious.

A lead doesn't have to be clever to be intriguing. Often all it takes is an unadorned presentation of what's happening:

```
A month-old baby is lost.
```

                                                    WBLG, Kentucky

```
In New York, one of the worst subway accidents in the
city's history.
```

                                                    Ted Koppel, ABC

A lead is a "hook." It may be cute, it may be straightforward, but it must be sharp, to the point and baited with something fresh.

Newsworthiness

The surest way to get attention is to lead a story with whatever in the story carries the most wallop. Newsworthiness is a measure of wallop.

Broadcast journalists have to calculate newsworthiness at every stage in the production of a newscast. They must decide what questions to ask at a news conference; what facts to include in a story; what aspect of each story to use as the lead; what taped quotes to play on the air; and, finally, what stories to use in the newscast.

Many journalists maintain that news judgment is exclusively a product of experience and, therefore, cannot be taught. But the ability to decide what is newsworthy is really just a matter of common sense plus knowledge of current events and basic journalism principles. Perhaps common sense can't be taught—although learning to concentrate and think carefully can help people reach conclusions that make sense. But current events are easy to learn; the standard textbooks are newspapers, news magazines and the broadcast media. And the guidelines for evaluating newsworthiness can definitely be taught. The news judgment that the already initiated possess is a composite of a bunch of basic rules they know too well to have to verbalize, but these rules can be spelled out.

There are six criteria for determining what is newsworthy: *importance, interest, controversy, the unusual, timeliness, proximity.* They are introduced here in terms of choosing a story's lead, but since these six standards are employed in many other broadcast news activities, they will be referred to frequently in future chapters.

Importance If historians wrote the news, this would be their standard. It's unconcerned with gossip, free of parochialism and not obsessed with the fleeting or freakish. Importance is the measure of the significance of an event, the magnitude of its effect on the world or community and the power of the people and positions involved.

A new tax on gasoline isn't historic, but it is more important, in most cases, than approval of an agency's budget—it affects more lives.

> The R-T-A board has approved a five percent gasoline tax
> for the metropolitan area . . . a move that will boost
> gas prices by at least two-and-a-half cents a gallon.
>
> WBBM, Chicago

That's the lead. Later in the story the budget increase is mentioned.

> At yesterday's meeting the board also approved a 237-
> million-dollar budget for fiscal 1978.

A death is more important than a serious injury and it belongs in the lead:

> A 17-year-old from Bowling Green is dead as the result
> of a head-on collision around midnight last night.
>
> WBGN, Kentucky

Later in the story listeners are told what happened to one of the other passengers:

> A passenger, 18-year-old Danny Miller, received multiple
> injuries in that accident.

News 1080 KRLD, Dallas, Texas, Managing Editor Jo Interrante. (HBJ Photo/Annette Coolidge)

All other things being equal, the president's behavior is more important than that of his aides. The president goes in the lead:

```
President Bush collapsed at a state dinner in his honor
early this morning in Tokyo.
```

KGTV, San Diego

Had any of the other members of the president's party on that trip taken ill, their plight would have been mentioned much later in the videotape report that followed (see Chapter 14, "Visuals"), if it were mentioned at all.

The opening of the baseball season is a more important event than an average basketball game. It's the lead:

```
The baseball season officially underway. . . . Seattle
beating Minnesota last night three to two.
```

WSB, Atlanta

We learn that the Atlanta Hawks won that evening later in the sports news.

And the apparent end of the Persian Gulf War on February 27, 1991, was more important than the results of a final, one-sided battle:

```
The war in the Gulf is virtually over.
```

Peter Jennings, ABC

A report on the day's fighting was held for later in the story:

```
The last great battle was being fought today -- U-S
tanks and air power overwhelming what used to be called
''the elite Republican Guard.''
```

Randy Renshaw of KLGA, Iowa, provides this example of a lead with a mixed-up sense of importance:

```
Damage is estimated at 3-thousand dollars following an
explosion at a local factory that claimed two lives.
```

Loss of life is more important than property damage. Failure to emphasize the two deaths is a mistake in news judgment.

Interest   People are *not* always interested in that which is most important. Sometimes they just want to know what the president's wife is up to or what happened to that cute four-year-old who was hurt in the crash. This is the gate through which gossip gets into the news. If Princess Anne finished third in a horse show, that goes in the lead—ahead of the name of the person who finished first. Famous people interest, sometimes fascinate, us:

```
You don't need to be a sports fan to know who Magic
Johnson is. . . . You also don't have to be a sports fan
to be saddened by the news that Magic Johnson has the
virus that causes AIDS.
/
                                      WTAE-TV, Pittsburgh
```

Fortunately, interest, as the Magic Johnson story demonstrates, can take us beyond mere social notes. In fact, if novelists wrote the news, they probably would measure events in terms of the characteristics that make them revealing . . . interesting.

The president's plan to build a tree house on the White House lawn isn't important, but it is interesting and therefore newsworthy. The fact that the fire went out during a presidential "fireside chat" is also insignificant—but amusing. Often these items will make for a more intriguing lead than a straightforward recounting of the president's latest pronouncement. Similarly, a movie company's choice of locale isn't important, but . . .

```
Does Texas look like Wyoming? A movie company hopes so.
                                            KVOC, Wyoming
```

And there is one minor detail in this story about gas seeping into a city's sewer system that forces itself into the lead . . . because it's interesting:

```
It all started when a man's toilet blew up.
```

WSOY, Illinois

WEAK
```
A 19-year-old woman from Dallas has been missing for the
past week.
```

BETTER
```
One week ago tomorrow a 19-year-old woman from Dallas
went on her lunch break. Everyone thought Sarah Hawkins*
would return in about an hour, but so far there has been
no sign of her.
```

KEX, Oregon

Interest is where news judgment becomes most human.

Controversy   The news looks for controversy. The governor's approval of the highway environmental groups have been fighting for the past year is more newsworthy than his okay of the reconstruction of an old parkway everyone agreed had become a safety hazard.

Broadcast journalists must know what the issues are and look for new issues. If sometime in the mayor's press conference she mentions a decision not to build that low-income housing project in the city's most fashionable district, that's the lead. If the mayor announces the appointment of a local builder as recreation director, it's the journalist's job to find out how many health clubs the builder owns and how much he gave to the mayor's campaign. That could be the lead to this story. When a key ballplayer says the coach can't even keep score, let alone motivate the team, and the story starts with a quote on pregame strategy, that's the wrong lead. It isn't as newsworthy.

UNACCEPTABLE
```
A young woman has been arrested on a charge of keeping a
bawdy house in Botetourt County. She had once run for
mayor in Roanoke City.
```

ACCEPTABLE
```
A former candidate for mayor in Roanoke City has been
arrested on a charge of keeping a bawdy house in
Botetourt County.
```

WFIR, Virginia

* This name has been changed.

Exposing controversy and corruption is called muckraking—an important political function of journalism.

The Unusual News is often news because it is out of the ordinary. If a teenager steals an elderly woman's purse, on most big-city stations that is not even a story, and certainly isn't the lead. But, if an elderly woman steals a teenager's purse, that has to be in the lead. Similarly, politicians who say they are going to do their best to represent the people of their district are not news. If a politician says he is going to vote for a certain bill no matter what the folks back home think, that's the lead. Perhaps buried somewhere in the information about a fire downtown is the fact that this was the city's first solar-heated building. That's unusual—it should be in the lead.

> UNACCEPTABLE
> The number of rapes was up five percent during the first quarter of this year, while the number of serious crimes overall declined.

> ACCEPTABLE
> For the first time in 19 years, a drop in the rate of serious crimes.
>
> KLOL, Houston

Of course, this bias toward the unusual, as well as the controversial, is why the news is so often attacked for being too negative. Bad news is usually more unusual than good news. It's not news that the plane arrives safely; it's news if it crashes. It's not news that politicians are honest (although some might disagree here); it's news when they're caught with their hands in the till.

Timeliness News, like food, spoils after it's been out for a while. News turns stale quickly on television. It perishes even more quickly on the radio, where people expect up-to-the-minute briefings. Jim Farley, now with ABC News, calls radio the medium of the "hear and now." So the lead of a broadcast story must take advantage of the freshest element of the story.

> UNACCEPTABLE
> Two forest fires in northwest Colorado were declared under control last night after they burned more than 18-hundred acres.

> ACCEPTABLE
> Mop-up operations are underway at the site of two forest fires in northwest Colorado, which burned more than 18-hundred acres.
>
> KREX, Colorado

If the secretary of state said something controversial at the airport before flying to Europe last night, the lead—this morning—is that the secretary *is* in Europe *this morning* where he will be discussing that controversial issue with European leaders.

If suspects were captured last night, the lead this morning is that they're in jail. If the accident happened this morning, the lead tonight is that the injured are in the hospital, with a report on their condition.

```
The mayor of Sioux City is in the hospital today . . .
thinking of things he should have done instead of taking
a ride on his son's motorcycle.
                                              KWSL, Iowa
```

```
Richard Goodwin remains in jail in Pueblo this morning
after he was denied bail by Pueblo Judge Phillip Cabibi
yesterday.
                                              KVOR, Colorado
```

In journalism this is called looking for the **second-day angle**—an updated slant on the story. Yesterday the story was that the airplane crashed, but today that's old news. The second-day angle is the condition of the survivors or theories about the cause of the crash.

In radio, where the news is aired every hour or so, it's almost a question of looking for a "second-hour" angle:

```
The body of Indiana helicopter pilot Joseph Miles is
being flown home at this hour.
                                              WAZY, Indiana
```

Neil Nelkin of KODY in Nebraska calls this "accenting the speed of radio." Many television stations now present the news almost as frequently. So television news-writers now also have to worry about updating their stories—presenting not only a fresher angle than viewers read about in the newspapers that morning but a fresher angle than they witnessed on a newscast earlier that evening:

```
Operation Desert Storm is now 24 hours old, and the
White House says do not be lulled into thinking it will
all be quick or easy.
                                              Peter Jennings, ABC
```

Some smaller stations, where the news is less insistent, may still use yesterday evening's angle as this morning's lead. They don't always struggle to discover a second-day angle, but there are limits. This lead, used on the air, clearly fails the test of timeliness:

```
A small safe, containing money, jewelry and important
papers, was taken from the home of Robert Sklar last
week.
```

There *was* an up-to-date angle in this story—Sklar had told the station that day that he was offering a thousand-dollar reward. That should have been in the lead.

Proximity If the government is shutting down eleven military bases and one of them is five miles outside of town, the lead is that the local base is closing. People tend to be interested in what affects them, and local events have more effect. This means that a robbery in a neighbor's house will, for better or worse, be more newsworthy to most of us than a massacre in Pakistan.

A 19th-century newspaper editor, Horace Greeley, put it this way: "The subject of deepest interest to an average human being is himself; next to that he is most concerned with his neighbors. Asia and the Tonga Islands stand a long way off after these in his regard."

International stories often contain national angles that newswriters will want to exploit.

WEAK
Sixty-four men and women have now advanced to the third round of the Australian Open tennis championships.

BETTER
A good day for Americans at the Australian Open tennis championships. Thirteen U-S players advanced to the third round.

> WFAN, New York

Still, local news is the bread and butter of most radio and television stations. Whenever possible, leads must include the local angle. For example, if the Centers for Disease Control is reporting an increase in measles cases nationwide, the writer should check with local health authorities to see if there have been many cases in the area. If there have been, that's the lead.

WEAK
A group of investors has put together a plan to buy the UNISYS Corporation.

BETTER
A group of investors has put together a plan to buy the UNISYS Corporation -- which has a division in Great Neck.

> Channel 12, Cablevision, Long Island

WEAK
The federal government is pushing states that have vast areas of wetlands in the region of the Gulf of Mexico to develop coastal management areas.

BETTER
```
The federal government is pushing states like Louisiana,
which have vast areas of wetlands in the region of the
Gulf of Mexico, to develop coastal management areas.
```
KWKH, Louisiana

This can be overdone. Newswriters should not get so parochial that they miss larger stories. An American may have been runner-up in a tennis tournament—to return to that international example—but the lead is still the person who won.

■ ■ ■

The reason these guidelines cannot provide neat solutions to all problems is that they constantly overlap, and it becomes necessary to weigh importance against interest or an unusual angle against a more timely angle—this is where common sense comes into play.

War has broken out in Israel. That's important. It started on a Jewish holiday. That's interesting. There are many Americans in Israel—that's a local angle. Both sides are accusing each other of starting the war—that's controversy. All these facts belong in the account of such a major event, but what's the lead? The war. That is very important and has to be the heart of the lead. One of the other facts might be thrown in to flesh it out:

```
War in Israel . . . and it started today on the most
solemn Jewish holiday.
```

Newswriters have to look over all the facts they have on a story and determine which are the most newsworthy and will make the most intriguing lead. These lists of some of the available facts on a story are followed by the lead the newswriter chose.

1. Two light planes have collided in the air.
2. It happened four miles off the coast at Laguna Beach.
3. One of the planes had a third of one wing sheared off.
4. That plane landed safely at the Orange County Airport.
5. Neither of the two people on board that plane was injured.
6. The other plane crashed into the ocean.
7. A search is underway.

Forget the plane that landed safely for the lead. The news here is the unusual collision and the important fact that one of the planes crashed into the ocean, but the timely angle—the search—also has to be in the lead:

```
A search is underway off Laguna Beach for a light plane
that plunged into the ocean after an in-flight collision.
```
KNX, Los Angeles

1. A truck rammed into a section of the Alaska pipeline at eleven o'clock last night.
2. The pipeline was shut down.
3. Eighty-four gallons of oil leaked out after the truck hit.
4. Repairs were made and oil started moving again at two o'clock this morning.
5. Officials are putting the blame on human error.
6. This was the third shutdown on the pipeline in the past 16 days.

An 84-gallon leak isn't very important. The news here is the interesting fact that these shutdowns are becoming a habit, and the timely angle is that everything is now okay:

```
Oil is moving again through the Alaska pipeline after
the third shutdown in 16 days.
                              WMAL, Washington, D.C.
```

1. A gang of South Moluccan terrorists is still holding 59 hostages in a northern Holland school and in a train.
2. It's been a week since they took over the school and train.
3. The terrorists have been negotiating with Dutch officials.
4. They're insisting that the Dutch force the Moluccan government to give the South Moluccans independence.
5. Many of the hostages are children.
6. The gunmen have just said they'll release all the hostages in return for a safe flight out of the country.
7. They won't say where they want to go.
8. Dutch officials don't know whether to believe that the terrorists are serious about the new deal.

This has been going on for a week. The news is the timely element—whatever has changed since listeners last heard the story—and the answer to the important question: What's going to happen to those hostages?

```
There appears to be some movement in the negotiations
between Dutch government officials and South Moluccan
terrorists holding some 60 hostages.
                                      Ann Taylor, NBC
```

There isn't only one answer to these problems. Here's a different version of the lead written a bit later, but based on the same facts:

```
The gang of the South Moluccan terrorists holding 59
hostages in a northern Holland school and in a train
have made a settlement offer to Dutch authorities . . .
but the authorities don't know whether to take it
seriously.
                                      Steve Porter, NBC
```

Details

A foolproof method for encouraging the members of the audience to concentrate on something besides their radio or television is to use a "kitchen-sink" lead. Chris Gardner of WFMW in Kentucky suggested this example:

```
28-year-old John Jones and 37-year-old Fred Wallace were
killed at seven-twenty last night in a one-car crash on
Madisonville's West Side near the L and N rail crossing
on Highway 70.
```

Most of these facts don't even belong in the story. Pressing them forward into the lead means forcing a mass of uninteresting and virtually unintelligible information on listeners.

Important details can be saved for later in the story. This is all the lead should include:

```
Two men were killed when their car hit a pole on Highway
70 last night.
```

There's no action in names, addresses, ages, times, etc. Details anchor a story; they don't move it forward. Few details deserve a place in the lead, where the writer is trying to build momentum. Here are some guidelines for choosing which details to include:

Names Few names mean anything to us—the famous, our neighbors, some others. Since the lead must capture attention, starting with a name that means nothing to most listeners is an error. Mary Kellan of WAXC, New York, demonstrates with this example:

```
A change in Robert Silver's condition.
```

Who, besides Silver's friends, would care? The correct lead:

```
The man shot in last night's holdup is now in serious
condition.
```

Silver's name should probably be in the story somewhere (see Chapter 6, "Stories"), not in the most important sentence—the lead. Familiar names, on the other hand, do attract attention. They work in a lead:

```
Former President Nixon went to a ballgame last night in
Anaheim.
```
Bill Diehl, ABC

In a small town, every local name may qualify as familiar. And there are rare occasions when a writer uses an unfamiliar name in the lead to tease the listener. This lead works because it exploits the listeners' curiosity about who this man is and what he's doing in the news:

> A year ago, says Thomas Tetro, he wanted to die. He
> learned he had cancer of the face. . . .
>
> Liz Shanov, WCBS, New York City

Who is Thomas Tetro?—the man who just won the Jersey Jackpot lottery.

Ages We all have one of the 90 or 100 possible ages. The particular one that made someone uncomfortable on his or her last birthday is not of great interest to viewers or listeners. Maybe it's nice to know the age of a person who was injured in a nearby accident or arrested for armed robbery, but that detail can be dropped into the body of the story. There's no reason to slow down the lead with it. The only ages that find their way into leads are ages that are particularly interesting or affecting:

> A nine-year-old boy is undergoing emergency treatment at
> Nashville General Hospital after being struck by a train
> this afternoon.
>
> WMAK, Tennessee

Addresses In a traffic accident or a fire on a major thoroughfare, the name of the road may be interesting enough for the lead:

> A skateboarding accident yesterday on State Route 113
> left a Wakeman boy hospitalized.
>
> WLEC, Ohio

But most addresses are just dull strings of anonymous numbers. Notice how the address slows down this lead, which was used on the air:

> A representative of Phil Simpson, Incorporated, 4-21
> East 8th, reported to the police that someone struck a
> company vehicle early this morning. . . .

This should read:

> The Phil Simpson company complains that someone crashed
> into a company car early this morning.

The address, if it needs to be mentioned at all, can be held for the body of the story.

■   ■   ■

Other candidates for demotion to the body of the story or complete banishment: hours of the day—*at 1:18 p-m*; exact dollar figure—*the damage was estimated at one point eight three million dollars*; car makes—*driving a Honda Accord*. Of course, there are times when each of these details may be newsworthy—perhaps this was the 16th Honda Accord stolen in the last two weeks—but usually these details are mere technicalities.

The lead is no place for fine points. Notice how this lead, which was used on the air, is dragged down by the weight of its details:

```
Sheriff Arnold George reported this morning that Bob
Watkins, age 20, of 5-43 Maple Street, was drowned
yesterday afternoon around 5 p-m in Logan's Creek in the
upper end of the county near the Randolph County line.
```

The Ordinary

Some facts say nothing:

```
The Coalition of Organizations for Mass Transit held a
meeting this afternoon.
```

This lead, intercepted by Stan Zimmerman of WSPB, Florida, merely notes that a meeting took place. Where's the news here? The same lead could have been written, in a different tense, even before the meeting took place. The fact that a group met is rarely news and rarely does it inspire listeners to listen to the rest of the story. What happened at the meeting—that's the news.

Bill Quehrn of KGMI, Washington, supplies the ultimate example of a lead filled with empty facts:

```
The City Council met last night at City Hall in regular
session.
```

Lead with whatever distinguishes an event from the ordinary:

```
The City Council lowered city utility charges for most
homeowners last night.
```
```
                                        KGMI, Washington
```

```
UNACCEPTABLE
The United Nations met today to act on an important
question.
```

ACCEPTABLE
Vietnam finally became a member of the United Nations
today after the United States dropped its
opposition. . . .

                                        WMAL, Washington, D.C.

Some words and phrases are so commonplace in broadcast news that they can easily bring a yawn. They are best kept out of the lead, or at least out of the first few words of the lead—what might be called the "lead's lead." *Yesterday* and *today* are prime examples. Practically every story used in broadcast news happened either yesterday or today. Since every lead could begin with one of these two words, it's wise not to start any leads this way. News is what is special about a story, not what is common to every story.

UNACCEPTABLE
Today Colorado House Republicans voted not to fund the
state Civil Rights Commission next year.

ACCEPTABLE
Colorado House Republicans have voted not to fund the
state Civil Rights Commission next year.

                                        KOA, Denver

UNACCEPTABLE
Today representatives of the U-S, Russia and Britain
open talks in Geneva on a total ban on nuclear test
explosions.

ACCEPTABLE
Representatives of the U-S, Russia and Britain open
talks in Geneva today on a total ban on nuclear test
explosions.

                                        CBS

The phrase *police say*, and its variations, is another news regular. It's unavoidable in broadcast newswriting because attribution is indispensable, but there's no need always to start the lead with the obligatory.

WEAK
Riley County police say a family's escape from a burning
car yesterday on Highway K-19 was ''miraculous.''

BETTER
''Miraculous'' is the way one Riley County police officer
described a family's escape from a burning car yesterday
on Highway K-19.

And there are other run-of-the-mill constructions that are not quite clichés but are not intriguing either. WIFF in Indiana avoids leads that start with this dull phrase—"Meeting in executive session this afternoon in Kendallville. . ."—because it wastes eight words, says nothing and is boring.

```
WEAK
Assistant Agriculture Secretary Carol Foreman says the
department is working on an information campaign that
would encourage children to make the switch to healthier
foods.
```

```
BETTER
It may take some doing -- persuading the nation's kids
that a fresh carrot or a juicy peach is better for them
than a grape popsicle or a double fudge delight.
```
                                                    KNX, Los Angeles

And how about this insipid lead? It was used on the air:

```
This morning the county commissioners met at their
regular weekly meeting and Sheriff John Parklin started
out the meeting with his report about a Cambridge County
selective traffic enforcement program.
```

Punch

The lead must contain the most intriguing news and must be written in the most intriguing style possible—a style that unleashes the power of the facts. The lead should have *punch*.

In broadcast news, the short sentence is king. Short sentences are easy to read, easy to follow, powerful. So leads are often most effective when they are short and sharp:

```
The Red Cross says that the cost of blood is too high to
give it away anymore.
```
                                                        KBWD, Texas

At times an incomplete sentence works best:

```
Robbery by telephone. That's what someone tried to pull
off at the Seven-Eleven store on West Cook Street last
night.
```
                                                    KSMA, California

```
The price of gasoline going up this weekend across the
nation.
```
KGO, San Francisco

And, if there's irony or paradox in a story, a well-written lead can get attention by bringing it out:

```
About 400 workers at Hammell Manufacturing Company no
longer have to raise their hands . . . to go to the
bathroom. The recently imposed rule requiring the
supervisor's permission to leave the work area was
rescinded yesterday.
```
KLOL, Houston

```
One government agency -- the Environmental Protection
Agency -- has decided to join lawsuits against another
government agency -- the Tennessee Valley Authority.
```
Dallas Townsend, CBS

The lead demands a broadcast journalist's most conversational, most engaging writing.

```
Maybe . . . just maybe . . . your car insurance rates
won't be increased as much as first thought when the
State Insurance Board began its latest hearings.
```
WARU, Indiana

```
The magazine sales people are here . . . and the Chamber
of Commerce and police agencies say they have been
flooded with complaints.
```
WGHN, Michigan

Bob Walker of WRVQ-FM in Virginia says a lead is bad when "it could have touched more people's lives, been simpler and cleaner, and done it all in a five-word, seventh-grade sentence."

Preparing

Listeners and viewers are easy to confuse. They can be overwhelmed with a barrage of facts; the key facts can be slipped by them; and they can be disoriented by clever but misleading lines. To avoid this, listeners or viewers must be carefully guided into a story. So leads have a second job. They not only have to catch the audience's attention; they must prepare the audience to receive the facts to come.

Soft Leads

In a memo to NBC staffers, Alan Walden compared two leads that had been broadcast on the network's newscasts. One is full of facts:

> The administration is changing its anti-inflation
> program, easing slightly the limit on wages and
> tightening restriction on price increases.

The second takes a gentler approach:

> The administration has done a little tinkering with its
> anti-inflation machinery.

Which is most effective? For Walden the answer is obvious—the gentler lead.

In broadcast news too many facts can drive listeners away. A lead should not come on too strong. Jerry Godby of WLOG, West Virginia, provided this example of one that does:

> A 17-year-old Logan resident was injured yesterday when
> he attempted to remove a baseball from a drain pipe
> while construction workers were moving the drain from
> the boy's front yard.

That makes sense, but its meaning would be lost on the air. All the major facts in the story are hurled at the listeners at once with no preparation.

> ACCEPTABLE
> A Logan teenager was injured yesterday after chasing a
> baseball . . . into an unlikely place.

Compare this with newspaper style. The traditional newspaper lead paragraph contains most of the "five Ws"—who, what, when, where and why. While many papers are moving away from this style, it is still common to find—in the lead to a story about a demonstration, for example—information on *who* was demonstrating, *what* they were doing, *where* the demonstration took place, *when* it took place and *why* they were demonstrating:

> While the Interior Department held hearings in Fresno
> today on a federal government proposal to limit the size
> of farms using water from federal reclamation projects,
> farmers from across the state staged a parade to protest
> the plan.

This is the classic "hard" news lead, and for our purposes it's too hard—too hard for listeners to grasp. "Some reporters still try to apply newspaper style leads to broadcast writing," notes Carissa Howland, news director of KCWY-TV, Casper, Wyoming. "It never works."

Broadcast news employs *soft leads,* often similar to the leads used in newspaper features:

```
The band wore cover-alls and the ''floats'' were more
than 100 farm tractors. The event was a noon-time parade
in Fresno to protest government efforts to limit the
size of farms using water from federal reclamation
projects.
                                          KNX, Los Angeles


UNACCEPTABLE
West Lafayette police began issuing more speeding
tickets last night to protest an ordinance passed Monday
by the City Council that would penalize them for staging
slowdowns.

ACCEPTABLE
Speeding in West Lafayette may be risky this morning.
                                          WAZY, Indiana
```

It's not always necessary to shy this far away from the basic facts. There is nothing wrong with building the lead around a hard fact, as long as the facts are spread out enough to be easily digestible:

```
Marion County property owners have less than six hours
to pay their tax bills.
                                      WISH-TV, Indianapolis


The winter cloud-seeding program is still going . . .
and officials are already debating the need for another
program next winter.
                                          KOA, Denver
```

The five Ws? The complete story should usually include all these facts (see Chapter 6, "Stories"), but there's no room for them in the lead. This lead, used on the air and picked up by one of the wires, shows what can happen when all five Ws are stuffed into a broadcast lead. It is too "hard":

```
The New Jersey State Police underwater recovery unit is
readying a six-man search team to begin operations at
nine o'clock tomorrow morning in an effort to recover
the body of 20-year-old Fred Morrison of Oxford.
```

The Set-Up

An old saw in broadcast news says that for a story to be clear it should tell listeners what it is going to say—*then* say it. This is an exaggeration, but listeners and viewers do need help in concentrating on the news. It's often wise to prepare the audience for what it is about to learn, and that is the lead's job. This lead tells listeners what the story is going to say:

> Trouble today for President Bush's already controversial
> Supreme Court nominee Clarence Thomas.
>
> Carole Simpson, ABC

Viewers are now ready to find out what the trouble is.

Here's another lead that "sets up" the information that follows:

> A major step today to aid the republics of the former
> Soviet Union.
>
> Tom Brokaw, NBC

Not every lead has to be a *set-up*. Often the facts are easy enough to grasp by themselves:

> Convicted killer Robert Sullivan died in Florida's
> electric chair this morning.
>
> WINK-TV, Florida

There are two situations, however, where a set-up is necessary:

Complicated Stories

When the story is complicated, the lead should ease listeners or viewers into the intricacies. Here is a story about a tax reform plan that called for 40 different changes in tax laws. Instead of attempting to describe the changes, the lead simply prepares listeners to hear about them:

> During a floor speech today, Senator Edward Kennedy will
> outline a tax reform proposal.
>
> WBBM, Chicago

Some of the intricacies can be discussed in the story that follows. Had they been stuffed into the lead, listeners might have been swamped:

> Senator Edward Kennedy will introduce a proposal today
> to close tax loopholes, emphasize tax credits and make
> more than 40 changes in the tax laws.

"Yes or No" Stories Compare these two leads supplied by Chris Gardner of WFMW in Kentucky. The first has the basic fact:

```
Former Owensboro policeman James Stallings has been
found guilty of murdering his wife.
```

The danger here is that by the time listeners have focused their attention on the story, the key fact may be gone; they may miss the verdict. Gardner's second version sets up this fact. It alerts listeners to listen for the verdict:

```
After two days of deliberations, a Hopkins County
Circuit Court jury has finally reached a verdict:
```

When the news is yes or no, guilty or not guilty, victory or defeat, listeners usually deserve a warning that the answer is on its way. Here the question is who will get to bury a man's body—his parents or the motorcycle gang to which he belonged:

```
A disagreement over who would get the body of that slain
member of the outlaw motorcycle club has been resolved.
                                              WLOD, Florida
```

In the next sentence listeners learn that his parents got the body. The lead set up that fact.

The Angle

In a broadcast story there's rarely room for more than one **angle** or approach to the story. The lead must announce that angle. It can't stray too far from the point to be made.

A judge has issued a temporary restraining order preventing the destruction of some mangrove trees a county wants saved. *Small victory in county effort to save mangrove trees*—that's the angle. The lead can't wander off into irrelevant jokes:

```
Perhaps they should be called ''persongrove trees.''
```

That is not the story. Nor can the lead flirt with irrelevant facts:

```
Mangrove trees are most abundant in tropical Asia, in
Africa and on the islands of the southwest Pacific.
```

The news here is *not* where mangrove trees are most at home. The lead has to prepare listeners or viewers for the story; it must introduce the angle of the story:

```
Lee County has won what officials say they consider a
small victory in their battle to save area mangrove
trees.
```

WINK-TV, Florida

There are many ways to introduce the angle of a story, not all of them straightforward:

```
Strike -- the workers say no . . . the buses won't go.
```

WBRG, Virginia

```
Title fight tonight. . . . The champ: Marvin Hagler. The
challenger: Roberto Duran. At stake: the undisputed
middleweight championship.
```

WISH-TV, Indianapolis

The lead doesn't literally have to state the angle; it can play off or set up the angle, as in this July Fourth story about the American Revolution:

```
Sometimes a revolution is a slow thing . . . not an
overnight smash.
```

WINS, New York City

Or this about machines capable of performing household chores on command:

```
So you thought those robots in the movie ''Sleeper''
were just science fiction?
```

WCBS, New York City

But the lead must aim in the direction of the main point of the story. It must never *mislead*.

A story about an OPEC conference in Sweden is going to be about oil and oil prices. Opening with a comment about Sweden would mislead. And if the story is about oil prices, the lead should also stay away from a discussion of the safety of the oil ministers—that's another story. The lead must establish the angle:

```
Oil prices are not on the agenda, but oil prices are
much discussed, at the OPEC conference now underway in
Sweden.
```

CBS

In choosing the lead the writer is looking for the most newsworthy approach to the story—and the story will have to conform to the decision represented by the lead.

Types of Leads

All leads have the twin responsibilities of intriguing listeners and getting them ready for the information to follow. As the previous sections have made clear, there are numerous ways to accomplish this, but there are a few broad categories into which most leads fall.

The Main Point

Most leads are members of this family, and all leads are at least related, since a lead can never lose sight of the main point of a story.

An example of this type of lead:

```
In Albany . . . there's some hope that the City
University system may be able to reopen . . . thanks to
a compromise package of bills which comes up for a vote
today.
```

WABC, New York City

The main point—a prospective solution to the financial troubles that have closed the university—is in the lead. Here's a lead that finds a different way to communicate this same point:

```
The City University may get some cold cash today . . .
enough to get it open again.
```

WABC, New York City

Another station used three different leads for the same story, in different newscasts; all of them include the main point:

```
A collision between a truck and a skateboard has landed
a youngster in the hospital in fair condition.

A 12-year-old boy -- whose skateboard collided with a
truck yesterday -- is hospitalized this morning in fair
condition.

A 12-year-old skateboarder is hospitalized in fair
condition after he was hit by a truck.
```

WSOY, Illinois

This type of lead works well when the central point of the story is dramatic:

A Poughkeepsie man charged with robbery has escaped from
the Dutchess County Jail.

WWLE, New York

Gary Gilmore was shot to death today by a Utah firing
squad.

WBUR, Boston

Still, there are situations where a main-point lead doesn't fit or a writer can do
better.

Umbrellas

Sometimes a story has more than one main point. In these cases, a lead is needed
that can cover all the points—an **umbrella lead.**

For instance, when the Supreme Court announced a decision on busing, there
were two completely different reactions in Boston. Choosing one of the reactions for
the lead would leave it incomplete:

WEAK
A leader of Boston's anti-busing protests says the
Supreme Court's decision on school busing leaves the
people without hope.

WEAK
The president of the N-double-A-C-P in Boston says the
Supreme Court's decision on school busing means that
desegregation is here to stay.

The solution is an umbrella lead setting up both points of view; however, such a
"dual" lead can't merely throw both opinions into one overstuffed sentence:

UNACCEPTABLE
While the president of the N-double-A-C-P in Boston
calls the Supreme Court decision on school busing a sign
that desegregation is here to stay, a leader of Boston's
anti-busing protests says the decision leaves the people
without hope.

The umbrella lead has to simplify as it combines:

BETTER
Two different reactions today to the Supreme Court's
decision on school busing.

WOR, New York City

Of course, if one of these reactions stood out, it would be best to fall back on a simple main-point lead.

Umbrella leads are not only used when a story has more than one main point; they also can be used to tie together more than one story. Newswriters often find themselves with little time and lots of stories to tell. The solution is often to combine related stories (see Chapter 6, "Stories"). An umbrella lead is usually given much of the responsibility for pulling the stories together.

Sometimes the lead will simply state what the stories have in common:

```
A couple of marijuana stories in the news. . . .
                                         WINS, New York City


Some very expensive burglaries in Santa Maria over the
weekend.
                                         KSMA, California
```

The secret to writing any kind of umbrella lead is to find the common thread that can tie the points, or the stories, together. This one is easy—two Supreme Court decisions:

```
The Supreme Court has said yes to lawyers and no to
abortions.
                                         WFFV, Virginia
```

Sometimes stories can be tied together by their obvious contrasts:

```
While the governor is in Washington to talk with the
president about farm prices, commodity prices dropped in
Chicago.
                                         KCUE, Minnesota


Gasoline rationing and oil import quotas are under study
in the White House, but in Detroit they're saying our
love affair with the big car hasn't cooled.
                                         WSOY, Illinois
```

If there isn't a common theme for an umbrella lead to exploit, the stories don't belong together.

Delays

Sometimes it's better not to jump right into a story, but to delay the main point and take another tack. One method: Begin at the chronological beginning of the story:

> It started raining in Johnstown, Pennsylvania, at ten
> o'clock last night. By the time it stopped . . . eight
> hours later . . . there was a waist-high torrent in the
> city.
>
> > WMAL, Washington, D.C.

This is especially effective with feature stories:

> Six years ago, Larry Cox of San Diego was denied
> admission to a sailing class because he's blind. But Cox
> was determined to learn to sail, just as he had
> conquered water skiing.
>
> > KNX, Los Angeles

Another type of delayed lead steps back from the breaking events and puts them in perspective:

> Congressman Thomas Downey, the young liberal Democrat
> from Long Island, considers himself a good friend of
> Israel.
>
> > WSOY, Illinois

> It has happened again. A man with a gun -- an automatic
> handgun in this case -- has killed a great many people.
>
> > Peter Jennings, ABC

Essentially these delayed leads are exaggerated set-ups. They may add a touch of drama to a story by building anticipation, but if overused they just waste time and sound pretentious.

UNACCEPTABLE
Teenage vandalism remains a major problem in our
society.

ACCEPTABLE
A young man jumped from an overpass onto a transit
authority train in Brooklyn tonight.

> WABC, New York City

And delayed leads must still point toward the main point of the story. They must introduce the angle of the story or else they are misleading. A story about defense witnesses at a major trial should not start with a discussion of the prosecution.

UNACCEPTABLE
Some questions about prosecution strategy at the Mandel
corruption trial.

ABC's Peter Jennings reporting in New York harbor. (© 1986 copyright Capitol Cities/ABC, Inc.)

```
ACCEPTABLE
More defense testimony at the Mandel corruption trial.
                                WMAL, Washington, D.C.
```

Statements

```
''I have sent a letter to the secretary of state
announcing my resignation as President of the United
States.'' The words of Richard Nixon resigning the
presidency tonight.
```
```
                                            WBUR, Boston
```

Sometimes a statement by a newsmaker is so powerful that it is a ready-made lead in itself. But this is rare. Statements that aren't on tape are too often confusing, and usually the writer can develop a more efficient lead (see Chapter 4, "Sentences"). But if a statement is *unusually* compelling, a writer might take advantage of it:

```
''All I could think of was that I was going to hit bottom
and die -- but the bottom never came.'' Two days after
she fell five stories down an air shaft, Linda Dalianis,
feeling much better and relieved.
```
WJDA, Massachusetts

It's not necessary that the statement be a direct quote:

```
Adolf Hitler had sinus trouble and only four of his own
teeth. That according to an X-ray of the dictator's head
sold at an auction Thursday night for 375 dollars.
```
UPI

Statement leads don't include attribution in the first sentence—all the responsibility for explaining who is being quoted and what is going on falls on the second sentence. This example was written the day before the Persian Gulf War began:

```
''There is a fatal moment where one must act, and this
moment has, alas, arrived.'' That's what the prime
minister of France said today . . . when it became clear
that Saddam Hussein was not even going to comment on the
last minute French effort to avoid war.
```
Peter Jennings, ABC

There are a number of different phrasings that enable the second sentence to carry out this responsibility:

```
Those were the words of Fourth District Congressman Jim
Weaver.
```

```
The words of Fourth District Congressman Jim Weaver.
```

```
That's the way Fourth District Congressman Jim Weaver
kicked off his speech. . . .
```

```
Fourth District Congressman Jim Weaver . . . speaking
to . . .
```

```
At least that's what Fourth District Congressman Jim
Weaver told. . . .
```

Never leave the listener confused about whose words those were.

Remember, statement leads should be reserved for particularly powerful statements. Here's another historic example:

```
''He's an S-O-B!'' That was President Truman's reaction
to the critic who attacked the singing of his daughter
Margaret.
```
WSOY, Illinois

Most quotes are *not* strong enough to justify such special treatment. This statement lead, built around a standard piece of political rhetoric, was used on the air:

```
''It's time to turn the city around. . . .'' That's the
word from Democratic mayoral hopeful George Loeb.
```

And if a statement is too unusual and shocking, a statement lead can cause more serious problems:

```
UNACCEPTABLE
''The whole human race will be wiped out by AIDS if a
cure isn't found soon!'' That's the prediction of one of
the gay activists protesting at City Hall today.
```

A nervous listener's heartbeat might speed up considerably before that gloomy prediction is attributed in the second sentence. Never lead with a *startling* statement. The audience deserves advance warning. It must at least be told who is talking *beforehand*:

```
ACCEPTABLE
Gay activists marched in front of City Hall today. One
of the protesters predicted that, if a cure isn't found
soon, the virus will eventually wipe out the whole human
race.
```

Too many beginners pounce on the statement lead as an easy formula for getting into a story. The result, more often than not, is some confusion. These leads violate a basic principle of broadcast newswriting: that the identity of the speaker (the attribution) should be introduced *before* the statement (see Chapter 3, "Meanings"). That principle should be violated only in exceptional circumstances.

Questions

Questions perform the set-up function superbly:

```
Should a man be executed for rape?
```
WBUR, Boston

Ask that question and listeners are automatically prepared for the "answer"—a Supreme Court decision. This lead gets listeners ready to hear about an announcement from General Motors:

> How much will that new car cost? G-M had at least part of the answer today.
>
> WSOY, Illinois

Question leads also can bring out the irony in a story:

> By most accounts California has the country's toughest campaign against smoking . . . and it seems to be working. So why is the tobacco industry smiling?
>
> Connie Chung, CBS

> Lightning never strikes twice, right?
>
> WRVQ, Virginia

But there are two serious drawbacks to question leads. First, they sound too much like commercials, which many newscasters also read:

> AD: Which pain reliever do four out of five doctors recommend?

> LEAD: What's the result of the latest study on cigarettes?

Newswriters prefer to maximize the difference between their copy and advertising.

The second problem with question leads is more profound. Many newswriters avoid them because they believe journalists are in the business of telling, not asking, and that the news should be composed of answers, not questions. Still, there are situations where question leads efficiently direct listeners or viewers to information, usually by reflecting a question actually on the minds of the newsmakers or the audience:

> Does the city of Merrill need an ordinance to control business signs?
>
> WSAU, Wisconsin

But these leads should be used sparingly, and they should never be used as guessing games or to rub in the fact that journalists know something listeners don't know.

> UNACCEPTABLE
> Did you know your gas bill may be going down?

```
ACCEPTABLE
Your gas bill may be going down if the Senate has its way
today.
```
```
                                          WZZM-FM, Michigan
```

Humor

The news is generally so grim that occasional moments of levity, when appropriate, are welcome. The lead is a good place for humor because humor is an attention-getter. Often a cleverly worded lead can *tease* listeners into concentrating on the story. This is what one station did with a Girl Scout convention:

```
Altos is being invaded by little green people today.
```
```
                                             KWHW, Oklahoma
```

Good writers look for humor. You don't have to be Woody Allen to write a light lead. The trick is to think, mull the words over and look for puns or phrases to twist:

```
Abuse of the litter control program may result in the
program itself being tossed out of the city budget.
```
```
                                           KGMI, Washington
```

```
Industry and some cities are pressuring Congress to
water down the clean water act of 1972.
```
```
                                            WNOR-FM, Virginia
```

And here's John Harding of WRVA, Virginia, opening a story on a late winter blizzard:

```
Here in Virginia, where the principal means of snow
removal is the month of July. . . .
```

Unlike a David Letterman monologue, where a bad line can get as big a response as a clever one, a bad joke in broadcast news is a disaster. It's embarrassing and demeaning to the station's news operation. If a pun or witticism may not work, leave it out. And never force a joke into a story it doesn't fit.

```
UNACCEPTABLE
The ball was in the other court today. The trial of the
hockey player accused of assault during a game
continues.
```

First problem: hockey is played with a puck, not a ball; on a rink, not a court. And no "other court" is involved—the trial is merely continuing.

Never tack a funny lead onto a sad story. A major network once began a story on the death of an actress with this horrible lead:

```
Rosalind Russell's performances will endure, but she
won't.
```

No humor in obituaries, disasters, serious crime, accidents . . . or even injuries to pets. There are a lot of people listening. Humor can't be allowed to insult or offend. Here is a story about the second suicide in a jail in three months:

```
You've heard of a hanging judge? Well, Sarasota County
has a hanging jail.
```
WSPB, Florida

Apparently the sheriff was listening, and according to news director Stan Zimmerman, the sheriff saw this as an example of inappropriate use of humor in a lead.

Wrap-Up

Newswriters must remember that listeners and viewers have other things on their minds. For a news story to work, it has to get those people to pay attention and then carefully point the way to what is newsworthy in that story. Most of the responsibility for this falls on the *lead*.

Practice Assignments

A. Write a lead for each of the following five stories, based on the facts given.

1.

1. The Department of Labor released last month's consumer price index this morning.
2. Nationwide, prices on the items measured in the list were up .5%.
3. The previous month's increase was .6%; the month before that—.4%.
4. In the metropolitan area, the consumer price index was up by 1% last month, according to the Department of Labor.
5. The Department of Labor said that that is the largest increase in the index in the metropolitan area in 18 months.
6. The Department of Labor said increased food costs were primarily responsible for the increase in the metropolitan area.

2.

1. The state attorney general, Louis Stoppard, held a news conference at 11 a.m.
2. Stoppard announced some changes in his staff.
3. Staff lawyer Howard Conway will become assistant attorney general for criminal affairs.
4. Conway has worked in the state attorney general's office for two years.
5. Conway graduated from Harvard Law School in 1978.
6. Stoppard: "Howard Conway is a first-rate lawyer, and I'm confident he'll do a first-rate job."
7. The present assistant attorney general for criminal affairs, Robert O'Brien, will leave that position in two weeks, Stoppard announced.
8. O'Brien has been an assistant attorney general for five years.
9. O'Brien's brother Albert was indicted two weeks ago for conspiring to fix milk prices.
10. News reports over the last two weeks have questioned whether the attorney general's office had tried to cover up the alleged milk price-fixing plan.
11. Robert O'Brien's name had been mentioned frequently in connection with the alleged coverup.
12. Stoppard: "Robert O'Brien is resigning to return to private practice. We are sorry to lose him, and we want to emphasize that his departure has nothing to do with scurrilous accusations in the news media over recent weeks."

3.

1. A spokesman for Japanese Motors announced today that the company will be closing two factories in the United States.
2. The spokesman cited high labor costs as the primary reason for the shutdown.
3. According to the spokesman, Japanese Motors plans to retain its other two U.S. plants—in Toledo, Ohio, and Austin, Texas.
4. The remainder of the company's automobile production, the spokesman said, will return to Japan.
5. The factories to be closed are in Tulsa, Oklahoma, and here in the city.
6. The Tulsa plant employs 6,000 employees.
7. The Japanese Motors factory here employs 4,000 people.
8. Japanese Motors is the second largest employer in this city.
9. The two factories will be closed on the first of the year.
10. The company spokesman said there are no plans for placing any of the laid-off employees at other plants.

4.

1. A 15-foot boat capsized in rough waters off Point Lookout yesterday evening.
2. Two men—Terry Reston, 23, and Will Bendix, 25—were in the boat.
3. The men said offshore winds increased wave heights and capsized their boat.

4. The men were picked up by a Coast Guard boat after an hour in the water.
5. Both were hospitalized for observation, but the hospital lists their condition today as good.
6. The men say they were hunting sharks about 200 yards offshore.

5.

1. The City Council met last night in executive session.
2. Last week's minutes were approved.
3. The Council approved, by a vote of 11–0, a plan to send flowers to Mayor Cheryl Boutin's husband, George, who is in Hasbrook Hospital.
4. The Council approved, by a vote of 11–0, the Housing Commission's budget request.
5. The Housing Commission asked for $4,000 for the second half of the fiscal year—the same amount as it spent in the first half.
6. The Council approved, by a vote of 8–3, a plan to make three downtown avenues—Merchant Street, South Street and Reed Avenue—one-way.
7. Merchant and Reed will go north; South Street—south.
8. Councilman Walter McCreary, who proposed the plan, said it will ease traffic congestion in the downtown area.
9. Councilwoman Martha Rigoli said the plan will inconvience residents and hurt business downtown.
10. The plan called for police to begin changing traffic signs and rerouting traffic today.

B. Rewrite the following leads to make them more effective.

1. After negotiations with the school board broke off, local teachers voted yesterday evening to begin striking the city's schools this morning.
2. A two-car accident at the corner of Fourth Street and Blaine Avenue in town this morning killed Elliot Ford, a lawyer from Hillsdale, and Lieutenant Governor Richard Coburn of East Orange.
3. The president's national security adviser, Frederick Adams, left for Israel yesterday to discuss the latest Mideast proposals with Israeli leaders today.
4. Fourteen-year-old Jeremy Sikes, from Alabama, was killed at 9 this morning when the car his mother, Margaret Sikes, was driving hit a telephone pole on East Brunswick Street.
5. Police Officer Paul Adler said this morning that Joseph's Hardware Incorporated, of 309 Straight Street, lost $500 to burglars between 3 and 4 this morning.
6. Today a parade in honor of the city's victorious high school football team is scheduled for Broadway.
7. Meeting in its regular weekly session at City Hall today, the City Council debated the future of the Harris Housing Project.
8. A group of over 100 chanting demonstrators, opposed to a plan to raise rents at a government-owned housing project on the West Side, marched in front of Housing Commissioner Frank Stern's office this afternoon.

9. State Senator Mary Ruggles introduced a bill today which would ban discrimination against homosexuals in jobs and housing, repeal state laws making homosexual behavior among consenting adults a crime and ensure homosexuals the right to maintain custody of their children.

10. Sunlight streamed through the window of the courtroom as the jury returned from its deliberations with a verdict in the case of the teacher suspended for spanking a student.

11. A fire in Newtown left three families homeless tonight and one fireman in the hospital suffering from smoke inhalation, while in Summerset—two families lost their homes to a fire that took firemen three hours to control.

12. "I will do my best to represent the people of this district in Congress." Those words from newly elected Congresswoman Elizabeth Franks today as she began preparing to move from the state legislature to Washington.

13. Do you know how much the consumer price index rose this month? Three tenths of one percent—the smallest increase in six months.

14. The chips were down for a gambling operation in Marketville. Police raided the place for the second time in a week this morning.

Stories

The *New York Times*'s story about a survey of public attitudes toward the New York Stock Exchange used 508 words. The Mutual Information Radio Network reported on the same survey in 69 words. The *Times* employed 21 long sentences to communicate all the information. Mutual had to make do with four short sentences:

> The chairman of the New York Stock Exchange wanted to find out why five and a half million investors had deserted the market in the past decade. Now, after a study, he knows. Small investors are so worried about inflation that they won't take a chance on investments with any more than a small risk. . . . Instead, they put money in savings accounts and certificates . . . life insurance and real estate.

A 439-word handicap is par for the course in broadcast news. Many more words can be fit on a page of newsprint than in a 5-, 10- or even a 20-minute newscast. Walter Cronkite has noted that all the words used in the half-hour CBS Evening News, which he anchored, would fill only two-thirds of the front page of the *New York Times*.

This is an important part of the challenge of broadcast newswriting. Broadcast stories must report on some of the most important goings-on in the world in a handful of short sentences. This chapter explains how that trick is performed.

Efficiency

Tight is a word heard often in broadcast newsrooms—"Write it tight!" It's clear why: There isn't room in a broadcast story for anything that doesn't move the story forward. Every sentence must serve a purpose and must accomplish that purpose efficiently . . . no extraneous information, no wandering, no loose ends—tight.

Length

How long should a broadcast story be? It would be nice to be able to give a simple answer such as "Long enough to tell the story." But it isn't that neat. Consider this example: NBC Radio has 5-minute newscasts on the hour, but after commercials are subtracted, that leaves only 3½ minutes for news. Much of that time is usually devoted to the top two or three stories, which include taped reports. The other three or four stories considered newsworthy at that hour must split the remaining minute or less. So how long should a story be on a turn for the better in an area where a drought has been hurting farmers? Eleven seconds. That's all the time left for it. Were this story any longer, another story would have to be cut:

> Areas of Montana, Wyoming and the Dakotas got some long-
> awaited rainfall today. . . . Crop production in those
> states has been severely hurt by a year-long drought.
>
> Don Alexander, NBC

The length of most broadcast stories is determined, in large part, by the length of the newscast and the demands of competing stories. There is some flexibility, but if a story *needs* an additional sentence, the extra seconds will require cutting a few words somewhere else.

How short can a broadcast story be? It is hard to say much about anything in less than 10 seconds. Can you think of a shorter way to write this 10-second story?

> Three of the nation's largest tire companies will raise
> prices next month. Goodyear . . . Firestone . . . and
> Goodrich . . . plan increases of between three and six
> percent.
>
> WDEE, Detroit

And the maximum length? That's tougher. One or two public radio or television stations will go on for pages, but most news directors believe that a story without tape, or videotape on television, gets dull after 45 seconds. Actually, it's rare for a story without tape or videotape to run more than 35 seconds. The average broadcast story, to the extent that it's possible to generalize for thousands of stations, would be 20 to 25 seconds long—that leaves time for four or five sentences; 55 to 70 words. Time is tight. Stories must be tight.

Is there something lost in this incessant drive for brevity? Undoubtedly. That's why most stations try to work in some programs where stories can be discussed in more detail (see Chapter 13, "Public Affairs"). It's also a good reason to encourage people to turn to newspapers, books and magazines to supplement the information they receive on the air.

Form

Most newspaper stories peter out. They use the inverted pyramid style—important information first and less important information toward the end. This is great for skimming a page, but how can a listener or viewer skim a newscast?

In conversation, stories are not supposed to decline in interest. In fact, they often build to a punch line or climax. The same is true of broadcast news. Forget the inverted pyramid. Broadcast newswriters must sustain the information level throughout a story. There's no time for the less newsworthy material that's added on to the end of a newspaper story, anyway. There is no drop in the information level here:

> A rather unusual march scheduled for Atlanta
> tomorrow. . . . It's billed as Atlanta's first annual
> Marijuana March and Smoke-In. Pro-marijuana
> demonstrators will rally at Hurt Park and then march to
> the steps of the capital. . . . Mayor Jackson's office
> warns that the protestors had better leave their
> marijuana cigarettes at home or be prepared to go to
> jail.
>
> WSB, Atlanta

Broadcast news stories have to sustain the listener's interest in the information—they can't be allowed to sag or fade.

Supporting the Lead

The lead has responsibilities to the story—it must interest the listener or viewer in the story and direct the listener or viewer toward the heart of the story. But the story also has responsibilities to the lead. All the promises made in the lead must be delivered in the story. The story must include the information that supports the claims made by the lead.

Some leads are nearly self-sufficient. They make their point:

> The Manhattan District Attorney's office has cleared
> former school's Chancellor Anthony Alvarado of any
> criminal wrongdoing.

The rest of the story need only expand on the point or add additional information:

> Alvarado resigned last year under fire, but investigators
> looking into his tangled finances say they haven't found
> anything warranting prosecution.
>
> WPIX-TV, New York City

But other leads can't stand on their own and require more support from their stories:

> It was the forces of sweetness and light . . . versus
> the rowdies at Yankee Stadium last night.

The story that follows has to explain this celestial battle, and it has to justify the use of such charged terms:

> Police say a couple of dozen incidents erupted in the ballpark bleachers last night when street gangs and opponents of the Unification Church romped through corridors and started fights. Nine people were arrested. 35-thousand people came to see the million-dollar extravaganza with the New York Symphony and Korean Folk Ballet. When the Reverend Moon began to speak, however, many of the people began to leave. Moon is revered by his thousands of followers . . . but damned by some parents who believe his methods of conversion include brainwashing.
>
> WABC, New York City

The rowdies are certainly there, and the Reverend Moon and his followers pass for the forces of sweetness and light—perhaps with tongue in cheek. The story explains and supports the lead.

> UNACCEPTABLE
> The fate of Loring Air Base in Maine could be decided today. Residents are deadset against the closing of the base . . . as is Maine Senator Bill Hathaway. He says Loring is the closest SAC base to Russia. . . and that makes it more important than ever.

The lead here states that a decision on the base is imminent. But the body of the story gives no evidence to support that claim. There is room in the story for the opinions of the residents and the senator, but there needs to be a sentence that at least tells listeners what event justifies the supposition that a decision could come today.

> ACCEPTABLE
> The fate of Loring Air Base in Maine could be decided today. <u>Public hearings are going on up there now on the closing of the base.</u> Residents are dead-set against it . . . as is Maine Senator Bill Hathaway. He says Loring is the closest SAC base to Russia . . . and that makes it more important than ever.

There's only one chance to choose the angle of a story—in the lead. So, the body of the story also must support that decision on what to emphasize.

UNACCEPTABLE
```
Several letter bombs were found in Manhattan
today. . . . F-B-I experts note that the letter bomb has
been a favorite weapon of terrorist groups since World
War II. Recent developments in explosives technology
have made them even more dangerous -- a letter bomb
using the latest plastic explosives can be hidden in a
letter no more than a few inches thick.
```

Interesting, but the lead promises a story about the letter bombs found in Manhattan today—the story doesn't deliver.

ACCEPTABLE
```
Several letter bombs were found in Manhattan
today. . . . One of them exploded in the offices of the
Merrill Lynch brokerage firm at One Liberty Place. . . .
Four women were slightly injured. The other bombs were
deactivated without incident.
```
WMCA, New York City

Incidentally, since the lead mentions several letter bombs, this story needed the last sentence to account for all of them and support its lead.

It's a mistake in broadcast newswriting to let the lead get too far ahead of the story. It's also a mistake for the story to lag too far behind the lead. The lead blazes the trail; the story must follow along in that same direction.

Information Selection

Fortunately, broadcast newswriters are almost never in the position of having to pad a story. There's usually an abundance of information to choose from. Unfortunately, however, broadcast newswriters must often leave out newsworthy information.

By the time a story has been gathered in the newsroom it's usually full of facts. There is the name of the victim, the time his body was found, how it was found, the clothes he was wearing, the location of the body, the date he was reported missing, the town he's from, information on his family, the apparent cause of death, information about the autopsy, the names of the person who found him and the person who will perform the autopsy, statistics on the number of people who have died in this area in the past year, etc. And this isn't even a particularly important story. There's time in the newscast for maybe 15 to 20 seconds on it. What to include? Before beginning, you must brace yourself. A newswriter has to be ruthless with facts. When you have only 15 or 20 seconds, you have no time for any but the most pressing facts. The rest, no matter how difficult they were to uncover or how much they seem to excite the police, must simply be cut—listeners will never hear them.

```
The Humbolt County Coroner's Office says a man found dead
near French's Resort apparently died of natural causes.
The Oakland man was found dead in his sleeping bag
. . . . . after being reported missing. The Coroner's
Office says an autopsy is being performed this
afternoon. . . .
                                        KRED, California
```

Nothing on his family, no statistics, not even his name.

And here are 14 seconds taken from the information available on an effort to locate and photograph the Titanic:

```
Rough seas prevented a research ship from taking
underwater television pictures of what scientists think
may be the wreck of the Titanic. . . . The research ship
is now running short of food and fuel . . . and may have
to return to port without any photographic evidence.
                                        Wally Robinson, NBC
```

Obviously this is where broadcast news gets its reputation for superficiality. There's a limit to the depth a writer can reach in 14 seconds. Still, if those seconds are used efficiently, listeners can be presented with the heart of a story. Many of the extra facts a newspaper can present are relatively trivial.

For a final example, here is a report—from the news summary that begins the MacNeil-Lehrer NewsHour—on a significant battle in the trade wars. The *New York Times* was able to devote half a page to this story. This version takes 22 seconds:

```
Los Angeles officials have cancelled a 122-million dollar
contract with a Japanese company to build rail cars for
a new mass transit system. Public protest arose when the
county's Transportation Commission awarded the contract
to the Sumitomo Corporation -- in spite of a lower bid
by an American firm. Local citizens complained that
county tax dollars should be used to create American
jobs . . . not Japanese ones.
                                        Roger Mudd, PBS
```

The broadcast newswriter must choose the facts that mean the most. Two guidelines:

Points How many points can be communicated in a broadcast news story? There is the main point—either established or indicated by the lead. Then there are the facts which support that main point. Beyond that it usually is difficult to make more than one or perhaps two other major points in an average-length broadcast story.

The main point:

> The man who pioneered the coronary by-pass operation
> takes issue with those who say the surgical technique
> may be of little value.

Supporting facts:

> Doctor Michael DeBakey has told a Houston news
> conference a Veterans Administration study on the
> procedure is preliminary and limited.

Other point (the other side of the argument):

> The V-A report claims non-surgical treatment of heart
> patients can usually achieve the same results as the
> coronary by-pass operation.
>
> KNX, Los Angeles

Another example. Main point:

> The first attempt to add the heart of a baboon to the
> heart of a human has ended with the patient's death.

Supporting facts:

> Transplant pioneer Doctor Christiaan Barnard said the
> 26-year-old woman would have died without a transplant,
> and no human heart was available.

Other point:

> Barnard told a news conference that he will try to use
> the heart of a chimpanzee next time.
>
> WNDE, Indianapolis

Most stories won't fit this pattern exactly—there are many different ways to write a story. But this does demonstrate how few points can be made in the average broadcast story. No matter how the story is written, it is difficult to make more than two or three points.

Since there may be many possible points to make about a story, one of the newswriter's first decisions is which of these to include and which to eliminate. That determination is based on newsworthiness. In the story about the heart transplant, the facts that it was the first attempt to add a baboon's heart and that it ended unsuccessfully were the most newsworthy and therefore deserving of a place in the lead (see Chapter 5, "Leads"). The decision on what other point to include in the story must be based on the same standards: importance, interest, the unusual, controversy, timeliness and proximity. Barnard's statement that he intends to try a chimpanzee's heart next time is unusual and interesting. It is more newsworthy than the name of the woman who died or the specifics of the operation.

There is certainly an element of subjectivity in these decisions. Different newswriters may play a story differently, and one newswriter may select different points when writing different versions of a story (see Chapter 12, "Newscasts"). But there are moves that most newswriters would label as errors. For example, if somebody dies and the story dwells on the injured—that's a mistake in news judgment. If the verdict in a controversial rape case has just come in and the story focuses on the background of one of the attorneys—that's also choosing the wrong point.

Sometimes it takes so much effort to get a piece of information that writers can develop an attachment to it. This affection for a point can obscure news judgment. So newswriters must fight such feelings. The audience doesn't care whether information took two hours and thirty phone calls to get. Since they're just going to hear a couple of points, they want them to be the most newsworthy.

The Basics Listeners or viewers have certain basic questions about a story. The newswriter must include the answers. Here it's not a matter of selecting the points that stand out; it's a matter of filling in all the holes with facts.

What are the basic questions about a story? Who? What? When? Where? and Why? Here's where these five fit into broadcast news. The story should answer most of these questions. For instance, the answer to all five Ws in 15 seconds:

```
One person was killed by the storms that hit Illinois
yesterday. He was a construction worker in the Kankakee
area -- who was crushed when an unfinished house
collapsed. Seven tornadoes struck the state yesterday.
                                           WSOY, Illinois
```

How specific the answers to the five Ws get depends on the time available and the audience. In a local story in smaller towns listeners want to know exactly who it was, where the person lived and perhaps even what time of day it happened. They may know the person and the place and may have been nearby at that very hour. In larger cities, however, these details lose significance and can be sacrificed for time considerations. And, in out-of-town stories, laborious details should be actively avoided. It's enough to say, "A construction worker in the Kankakee area . . . yesterday."

But whether or not the answers are detailed, listeners should not be left with major questions about the basic facts of a story. What's missing here?

```
UNACCEPTABLE
Passenger aircraft at northern Virginia's National and
Dulles airports are once again being sprayed with D-D-T
```

before leaving on flights to California. The pesticide,
which may cause cancer, has been banned for years by the
Environmental Protection Agency, and airline employees
did not want to have to begin using it again. But the
Department of Agriculture says the concentration of
D-D-T is too low to cause trouble. The pesticide remains
the strongest tool available to control destructive
bugs.

Why? Why spray planes? And why only planes to California? The last sentence can
be sacrificed in favor of a sentence that provides this basic fact.

ACCEPTABLE
Passenger aircraft at northern Virginia's National and
Dulles airports are once again being sprayed with D-D-T
before leaving on flights to California. The pesticide,
which may cause cancer, has been banned for years by the
Environmental Protection Agency, and airline employees
did not want to begin using it again. But the Department
of Agriculture says the concentration of D-D-T is too
low to cause trouble. The spray is being used to prevent
East Coast Japanese beetles from reaching California and
destroying crops.

WRVQ, Virginia

■ ■ ■

So there are two considerations in selecting the information to include in a story:
What are the two or three most newsworthy points? And what basic facts must be
provided?

Here is a list of facts from a story supplied by the Associated Press:

1. Italian feminists with support ranging from the Communist Party on the left to
    the Liberal Party on the right wanted abortion legalized in Italy.
2. A law legalizing abortion was enacted two weeks ago.
3. It's one of the most liberal abortion laws in western Europe—permitting free
    abortions on demand for women over 18 in the first 90 days of pregnancy.
4. The measure was denounced by the Catholic Church.
5. Under the law doctors who don't want to perform abortions for moral or religious
    reasons may sign up as "conscientious objectors."
6. The doctors have 30 days to apply for objector status.
7. Scores of doctors are registering as concientious objectors.
8. The Rome Medical Association predicts that 90 percent of the doctors in the
    metropolitan area will eventually register.
9. The abortion law took effect today.
10. It still faces the possibility of a repeal referendum.

A newswriter for Mutual worked from a similar collection of information. Mutual had 20 seconds on the story. Most of the points from the AP story were not particularly newsworthy because they were not timely. The law had been passed weeks before. . . . Mutual could not just recap that story. The timely and newsworthy elements are the law taking effect and a new development—the doctors counting themselves out. Mutual's writer decided that no other points were compelling enough to squeeze in. The basic facts were filled in, and this was the story:

```
The new Italian law permitting abortion on demand went
into effect today. But women seeking the operation may
still have trouble. The law allows doctors to register
as conscientious objectors -- and not be required to
perform abortions. Many are doing so in predominantly
Roman Catholic Italy.
                                                  Mutual
```

Making Sense

The information that does pass muster is still worthless if its meaning is not communicated clearly.

A writer obtains some important but confusing information. Why did the mayor say this? What does it mean for the town? Who'll benefit? And what does "tax abatement" mean, anyway? Such befuddlement should start red lights flashing. Stop! Do not write anything. A writer should never write a story before figuring out what it's about. Unfortunately, that is done all too often. The mayor's words will be dropped into the story undeciphered, confusing listeners or viewers as they confused the writer. If the writer doesn't understand the story, it is unlikely the audience will.

The correct move? Reaching for the phone and calling half the government, if necessary, to find out what the mayor's proposal means. The next story this writer handles on tax relief will be easier.

There's another way newswriters can go wrong. Sometimes a story is so obvious to them that they forget it still must be explained to their listeners or viewers.

Newsrooms are inhabited by news experts. They spend their working hours studying current events. Most of the stories they deal with are stories they have been following for days or years or similar to the stories they've done for years. A writer facing the fifth story of the day on a successful flight to Mars can easily forget that most members of the audience didn't hear the other four, that listeners or viewers have not been privy to all the wire copy on the Mars mission and that they haven't been on the phone all day with local scientists and professors who are commenting on it. It is easy to forget that what makes sense to the writer may not make sense to the audience. Retrorockets, orbiters and the first picture sent back cannot just be tossed hastily into a story. Writers must slow down and make sure they are being clear.

Stories start losing listeners as they pick up speed. Try to ride this roller coaster of a story. It was used on the air:

A letter will be mailed today to the governor
petitioning him to make two appointments to the Hightown
City Council, following the recall of the mayor and
another councilman last week. Only two of the five
members are officially on the governing body, and no
business may be conducted until the temporary
appointments. Anyone from the second or third wards
should submit his or her names by May eleventh to the
office of the city clerk. The last Council session could
not be held due to a lack of a quorum. Consequently the
seasonal and overtime payrolls are in limbo until the
council is back in action.

While typing this up, some guilty writer was probably mumbling, "They'll get the idea." That's the weak writer's justification for every phrase, sentence or story that didn't turn out quite right: "They'll understand." But in these short, ephemeral stories, most listeners won't understand.

How to make sense:

1. Apportion facts. It's always better to clearly communicate a couple of facts than to do an incomplete job on a bunch of facts. So, it's foolish to include too many. A fact shouldn't be in the story unless there's time to make it clear.

   In the above example, it's best to forget the plea for volunteers for appointment to the Council seats. Second and third ward would-be politicians will have to find out somewhere else. There isn't time to explain the procedure fully here, and this hazy reference just serves to make the entire story foggier. The deadline date and the fact that the appointments are temporary can also be omitted. The extra time must be used to clarify the central points. Dense writing isn't efficient.

2. Explain. Clarify anything that might possibly confuse. This story mentions two Council vacancies, but then says only two of the five Council members are now "official." What happened to the others? And, what does "official" mean here? These are loose ends. No loose ends are allowed. Also, what's meant by "governing body"? And whose "seasonal and overtime payrolls" are being discussed?

3. One idea at a time. The story discusses disruptions in the Council's business in the second sentence, then gets back to the subject again in the fourth and fifth sentences. But listeners' minds function best when they're presented with one idea at a time. When everything that has to be said about disruptions is said, then the story can move on.

A slower and clearer version of the same story:

This is the procedure: A letter will be mailed to the
governor today. It will petition him to fill the two
vacancies on the Hightown City Council. Those vacancies
were created when the mayor and another councilman were

```
recalled by the voters last week. Since another Council
member is out sick, that left only two of the five
councilmen at the last session. That's not a quorum --
meeting cancelled. So, such Council business as
approving city workers' seasonal and overtime payrolls
may have to wait until the governor gets the official
letter . . . and appoints the two new people.
```

Even the cleverest phrasings and the most interesting stories are a waste of air time if they don't make sense to listeners or viewers.

Flow

Like a play or a poem or a piece of music, a broadcast story's construction must satisfy certain aesthetic imperatives. The news doesn't have to be pretty or showy, but it has to move gracefully. A story should flow from the first sentence to the last, not just because that makes it more attractive. It should flow because that will help it convey meaning most effectively.

Organization

Broadcast stories are not constructed from blueprints. They are so brief that writers rarely even resort to an outline. But there are a few principles that can guide the sentences into place and make for a smoother, more understandable story:

Related Ideas The facts should be laid out in the order that takes best advantage of their natural connections. The goal is to minimize the cracks between thoughts in a story by fitting the pieces of the puzzle together properly—in other words, proceeding from idea to related idea.

```
WEAK
Those Japanese fishermen who threw back the carcass of a
supposed sea monster are now wishing they hadn't.
Russian scientific vessels are on their way to the area
off New Zealand where the creature was caught and
photographed. The Japanese trawler's owners have
suddenly become aware that one smelly prehistoric beast
is worth more than a whole fleet load of fresh tuna.
Scientists used to think that particular species had
been extinct for millions of years. Now they're not so
sure.
```

The CNN newsroom in Atlanta. (© CNN, Inc. All Rights Reserved)

Sentences are not interchangeable. The lead here flows naturally into the discussion of the trawler owners' sudden awareness. Following it with the sentence about the Russian vessels needlessly interrupts the natural progression of thoughts.

BETTER
Those Japanese fishermen who threw back the carcass of a supposed sea monster are now wishing they hadn't. The trawler's owners have suddenly become aware that one smelly prehistoric beast is worth more than a whole fleet load of fresh tuna. Russian scientific vessels are on their way to the area off New Zealand where the creature was caught and photographed. Scientists used to think that particular species had been extinct for millions of years. Now they're not so sure.

                                            WNOR, Virginia

WEAK
Maryland Governor Marvin Mandel may take the stand today at his Baltimore Federal Court trial. Mandel's defense attorney says that the governor may be called. The first witness today is former House Speaker Thomas Hunter Lowe. Federal Judge Robert Taylor already has agreed to a limited schedule for the ailing governor's testimony . . . no more than three-and-a-half hours on the stand on any day.

The fact that the governor may be called is connected more directly to the limit in the time he'll be on the stand than it is to Lowe. The direct connection must be exploited.

> BETTER
> Maryland Governor Marvin Mandel may take the stand today
> at his Baltimore Federal Court trial. Mandel's defense
> attorney says that the governor may be called. Federal
> Judge Robert Taylor already has agreed to a limited
> schedule for the ailing governor . . . no more than
> three-and-a-half hours any day. The first witness today
> is former House Speaker Thomas Hunter Lowe.
>
> WMAL, Washington, D.C.

Sequence Many elements in stories can be organized chronologically—earlier event, then later event, then still later event.

> At a quarter to two yesterday Jersey City police got a
> call on the emergency line from a woman who they say was
> hysterical. . . . In a heavy Spanish accent she seemed
> to be talking about her child getting hurt . . . his
> head. . . . then she hung up without giving an address.
> She called back in about five minutes and this time the
> officers were able to get the address . . . but they say
> it is doubtful if the extra time made any great
> difference. The injured boy, three-year-old Amos Rivera,*
> had been shot through the head. The bullet came from his
> father's service revolver. Jorge Rivera* is a member of
> the Hudson County police. . . . The mother, who could
> barely answer questions, indicated the boy had found the
> gun while playing. . . . but police are still
> investigating. The child is alive but doctors say he's
> not expected to survive.
>
> WINS, New York City

Sometimes the sequence begins after the lead:

> A Rock Hill car dealer has found out that you can't
> always trust a pretty face -- or in this case, three of
> them. According to the Rock Hill Police Department,
> three young women, described only as being attractive
> and in their early twenties, drove into Pendleton Motors
> on Saluda Street around ten yesterday morning. The three

---

* These names have been changed.

reportedly told salesman A-G Waters they wanted to try
out a car on the lot. At least one of the women drove off
in a used Plymouth valued at one-thousand dollars, and,
as of this morning, Waters hasn't seen the women or his
Plymouth again. City police are still investigating the
apparent auto theft.

WRHI, South Carolina

There are a lot of facts in this story. If they hadn't been told chronologically, they
could easily have confused the audience.

UNACCEPTABLE
A Rock Hill car dealer has found out that you can't
always trust a pretty face -- or in this case, three of
them. A woman drove off with one of Pendleton Motors
salesman A-G Water's cars yesterday. City police are
still investigating the apparent auto theft. Waters
hasn't seen the woman or the used Plymouth she was
driving, valued at one-thousand dollars, again. She was
one of three women in their early twenties who drove
into the dealer's on Saluda Street around ten yesterday.
The other two women also disappeared.

This story also uses a chronological organization, although it is a little harder to
spot:

Fred Wimple* of Saint Cloud has been found guilty of
assault. His wife testified that he had tried to strangle
her, then had told her that he always wanted to kill
someone, and that he was going to stuff her into a
trunk. Stearns County Attorney Roger Van Heel wanted a
first-degree attempted murder conviction . . . but the
jury returned the simple assault verdict after
deliberating for an hour and a half. Wimple gets a
year's probation. . . . He'll spend another 30 days in
jail and have a checkup at a mental health center before
his release.

KCLD, Minnesota

After the lead, events are described in the order in which they happened at the
trial—right through the verdict and the sentencing.

Indexing The final method of organization is the most heavy-handed, and
therefore the least common. It explicitly states that a series of thoughts is being

---

* This name has been changed.

presented, using numbers or names to separate and therefore organize the material. The organization is written in.

```
The magazine sales people are here . . . and the Chamber
of Commerce and police agencies say they have been
flooded with complaints. A team of solicitors is
apparently working in the community this week.
Authorities have two suggestions for all local
residents: The first is that solicitors be asked to prove
that they have registered with the Chamber of Commerce.
If they have registered, they should be carrying proof
with them. The second suggestion is that solicitors not
be paid with cash or with checks made out to cash.
                                              WGHN, Michigan
```

The words *first* and *second* help order this story. In the next example the key is the names of the different towns.

```
Police and fire protests over salary continue spreading
around Indiana. In Elwood, police and firemen walked off
the job early this morning after being offered a seven
percent wage increase. The Elwood officers want 20
percent. In Franklin, police began a slowdown to demand
a 12 percent hike. In Kokomo, a state of emergency
declared by the mayor continued as Kokomo police and
firemen remain off the job. Sheriff's deputies are
patrolling the city. And police in Peru and Jefferson
are continuing their job action for higher pay.
                                                WAZY, Indiana
```

The town names hold the story together. A story this complex—making so many points—needs some form of "indexing" to control them all.

■　■　■

These types of story organization are not mutually exclusive. Many stories use more than one. After the lead, most accident or crime stories, for instance, go back to the chronological beginning; then they simply connect related ideas rather than sticking strictly to the sequence of events:

```
A national pathology lab will attempt to determine the
cause of death of a nine-year-old Shreveport boy who
```

* This name has been changed.

authorities think was a murder victim. The nude and
decomposed body of Jack Gruber* was found near his home
last Friday, and local tests have failed to turn up any
substantial information. Detectives say they have little
to go on, although they assume the boy was the victim of
a sexual attack.

KWKH, Louisiana

The writer's job is to choose the method of organization that organizes the elements of the story most logically and therefore enables the story to flow smoothly.

Transitions

Our conversation is studded with words and phrases whose only job is to help thoughts and sentences relate to each other. These **transitions** play an important role. Without them, conversation is stiff and unfriendly: "Fred bought a car. His wife, Susan, doesn't think cars are a good idea in the city. She's angry." With transitions: "Fred bought a new car, *but* his wife Susan doesn't think cars are a good idea in the city. So, she's angry."

Transitions are just as important in broadcast news:

It was all finally too much for Suzy Harris of London,
England. Her husband had just finished watching two weeks
of World Cup soccer matches, <u>and</u> he was getting ready
for another two weeks of tennis from Wimbledon . . .
<u>when</u> the yearly tax bill on the television arrived from
the government. Suzy fumed. . . . ''I don't pay the tax
just to watch sport and nothing but sport!'' she yelled,
<u>and with that</u> she snatched up the telly, ran out to the
yard, got a sledgehammer, <u>and</u> . . . <u>well</u> to quote
her . . . ''There was an almighty bang <u>and</u> that was the
end of it.''

Gil Fox, ABC

Notice what happens to a few of these sentences with the transitions removed:

Her husband had just finished watching two weeks of World
Cup soccer matches. He was getting ready for another two
weeks of tennis from Wimbledon. The yearly tax bill on
the television arrived from the government.

Without these words the story is choppy and harder to understand.

A list of transitional words and phrases:

and	while
also	when
too	meantime
in addition	meanwhile
well	now
plus	again
just as	then
furthermore	so far
but	incidentally
however	so
yet	therefore
only	that's why
on the other hand	thereby

Sometimes a sentence can also be joined to the sentence preceding it by a phrase that simply looks back, such as the "with that" in the "telly" story.

Transitional words, phrases or constructions may also be given larger assignments. Often newswriters face this problem: two stories, related theme, not enough time for both. Solution—combine them.

Two stories can be pulled together by an umbrella lead (see Chapter 5, "Leads"), or they can be connected by a transitional phrase. Here are three stories merged into one by two strong transitional phrases:

```
The House Ways and Means Committee might be able to put
the finishing touches on a tax cut by the end of the
week. . . . It would include a one-time-only tax rebate,
and a long-range tax cut, with the emphasis on middle-
and low-income groups. . . . . . . . . . . . In the
meantime, the president and Congress seem to be trying
to find a way to compromise on his oil tariff
plan. . . . . . . . . . . All this against a backdrop of
the first encouraging signs that the recession . . .
depression . . . whatever . . . is getting ready to
bottom -- heavy action on the stock market . . . some
pickup in car sales, and so on.
                                        WINS, New York City
```

Transitions are the oil that enables stories, or combinations of stories, to work smoothly. Without them ideas grind against each other. The story sputters and stalls. But transitional words have their own specific meanings which must not be ignored. *But*, for example, has to connect ideas that contradict.

```
UNACCEPTABLE
The president opposed the bill, but he vetoed it.
```

And *and* must connect related thoughts. Otherwise it creates non sequiturs.

```
UNACCEPTABLE
The president opposed the bill, and he left today on
vacation.
```

Transitions must also be used judiciously.

```
UNACCEPTABLE
Your state income tax could go down a notch at midnight,
and the Legislature will have to do something in the
next 16 hours . . . or it automatically drops. So, a
family of four -- for example -- making 20 thousand a
year, under this plan, would save 28 dollars a year.
```

```
ACCEPTABLE
Your state income tax could go down a notch at midnight.
The Legislature will have to do something in the next 16
hours . . . or it automatically drops. A family of four
-- for example -- making 20 thousand a year . . . would
save 28 dollars a year.
                                            WDEE, Detroit
```

Snappers

The final sentence in a broadcast story, called the **snapper,** is second in importance only to the lead. This last line takes the tight little package that is a broadcast story and wraps it up. The snapper should be crisp and clean, and when appropriate, it can end the story with a little snap:

```
A magazine column in Washington recently labeled Senator
John Melcher of Montana a vegetarian. Since he comes
from cow country . . . it brought some nasty mail from
back home. Melcher also says he may no longer be invited
to barbecues and weenie roasts. Melcher says he is NOT a
vegetarian. He IS a veterinarian.
                                    WMAL, Washington, D.C.
```

There are five different types of snappers:

The Main Point It's a little late in the story to be introducing the main point, but sometimes the snapper can shoulder part of the responsibility for making that point and supporting the lead:

> The consumer price index in the Los Angeles-Long Beach
> area went up three-tenths of a percent last month . . .
> due mainly to higher prices for coffee, hamburger and
> cars. Don't feel too bad, though . . . the Department of
> Labor says that's exactly half the national increase.
> <u>What it all boils down to is that we paid 17-dollars and</u>
> <u>85-cents last month for what cost us 10 dollars ten</u>
> <u>years ago.</u>
>
> KNAC, California

While there is no room in a broadcast story for a sentence that merely restates the main point, the snapper *is* the logical place to conclude the story. The trick is to wrap up without wasting time repeating:

> WEAK
> The country last month BOUGHT 2 point 6 billion dollars
> more in goods and services from overseas than it sold.
> <u>In other words we're paying out a lot more than we're</u>
> <u>taking in.</u>

> BETTER
> The country last month BOUGHT 2 point 6 billion dollars
> more in goods and services from overseas than it sold.
> <u>That is another all-time high trade deficit.</u>
>
> Bob Cain, NBC

Another Fact Often the snapper is saved for one additional fact. This works only if the new piece of information helps place the story in perspective. The end of the story is no place to open up a new can of worms.

> UNACCEPTABLE
> A spur of the Washington Metro Commuter Rail system in
> northern Virginia is to be officially opened today.
> Governor Godwin is scheduled to attend the Fourth of
> July Metro dedication ceremony along with the mayor of
> Washington and the acting governor of Maryland. <u>There's</u>
> <u>some question whether the new spur is too little and too</u>
> <u>late to handle the growing transportation needs of this</u>
> <u>area.</u>

The new fact must be self-sufficient; it can't leave loose ends. And the new fact must be relevant enough to tie the story together.

ACCEPTABLE
A spur of the Washington Metro Commuter Rail system in
northern Virginia is to be officially opened today.
Governor Godwin is scheduled to attend the Fourth of
July Metro dedication ceremony along with the mayor of
Washington and the acting governor of Maryland. Metro
will eventually extend from Washington deep into the
Virginia and Maryland suburbs.

WRVQ, Virginia

Meanwhile is a calling card of another-fact snapper:

The cost of the proposed building, meanwhile, continues
to rise, while county politicians continue their
squabbles.

WCEM, Maryland

Another example of a story with this type of snapper:

Back to square one in the investigation of the shooting
of porn publisher Larry Flynt. A New York judge has
released a man who tried to sell Flynt's family
information on the shooting . . . turns out he didn't
have anything to sell. Flynt is still in serious
condition.

KGO, San Francisco

This type of snapper is so common that some versions have become clichés. How
often do stories end with this additional fact?

Police are continuing their investigation into the
incident.

The Other Side In a controversial story the snapper can be reserved for the
other side of the argument. This has a certain justice—the point of view that is
making the news gets most of the story, but, for balance, its opponents get the last
word:

In what's considered a victory for the administration,
the Supreme Court has ruled that abortions may be legal
-- but that the government does not have to pay for
them. The court ruled that states aren't required to pay
for the abortions of Medicaid patients just because

```
they're legal. In a dissenting view, Justice Brennan
said the majority opinion showed what he called ''a
distressing insensitivity to the plight of impoverished
pregnant women.''
```
KNAC, California

The Future Ramification What happens next? What are the bill's chances of passing? What is the candidate's next stop? How long before the price increase is felt in the stores? Answering these questions—looking toward the future— is a natural way of ending the story:

```
The Council is expected to take up the budget
considerations tomorrow.
```
WRHI, South Carolina

```
Burns says he will appeal the judge's ruling to the
State Supreme Court.
```
KCLD, Minnesota

Here is a story that ends with a somewhat more subtle look to the future:

```
Some Japanese investors now have their eyes on our
national pastime. Officials of the videogame company
Nintendo offered to buy a majority interest in the
Seattle Mariners baseball team -- in a deal worth 100-
million dollars. Other club owners, however, must first
approve.
```
Tom Brokaw, NBC

This future-ramification snapper should not have been used—probably too subjective—but it's clever:

```
The Council will meet again next week . . . to get some
work done.
```

The Punch Line Some of the best snappers are the ones with the most snap:

```
With his wife in the hospital expecting their first
child, New Kensington's mayor cancelled an appearance
before the Rotary Club today. His prepared speech: how
to act in an emergency.
```
WKPA, Pennsylvania

Rhythm

Most broadcast newswriters will tell you they don't fool with anything as elevated as "prose rhythm," but if they're good, they're wrong. All good writing has rhythm, and broadcast writing—written to be performed—is certainly no exception. Subconsciously at least, a newswriter should hear a beat. Nothing fancy or syncopated—but without it the words and sentences, no matter how carefully turned out, will sound flat.

Fortunately, the rhythm of broadcast news is simple enough so even those who can't dance a lick can be taught it. There are four steps:

Sentence Length   The dominant percussion instrument in broadcast stories is the short sentence, or incomplete sentence. It can add dramatic power:

> Letter bombs . . . the F-B-I says extortion messages
> have been sent to several corporations demanding money
> or else more bombs will be sent.
>
> WOR, New York City

> A phony documentary on British television last night
> said that American and Soviet scientists plan to set up
> a colony on Mars to escape the possible end of the
> Earth. Many viewers believed it.
>
> WNDE, Indianapolis

But too many very short sentences in a row will make the rhythm too choppy:

UNACCEPTABLE
A new organization has been formed. It's for all you
folks who are opposed to adopting the metric system. A
columnist for the Chicago Sun Times . . . Bob Greene
. . . formed the group. He calls it ''WAM.'' That means
''We Ain't Metric!'' Greene says he needed an idea for a
column. So he came up with this . . . and it caught on.
Now it has millions of members. Greene says the U-S
shouldn't change to the metric system. That would
accommodate the other nations of the world. He says they
should adopt our system.

On the other hand, too many relatively long sentences will make the rhythm sluggish:

UNACCEPTABLE
A columnist for the Chicago Sun Times . . . Bob Greene
. . . has formed an organization for all you folks who

are opposed to adopting the metric system. Greene says
he came up with the idea for the group -- called
''WAM,'' which means ''We Aint't Metric!'' -- one day
when he didn't have any material for a column. The group
now has millions of members who believe that, instead of
the U-S changing to the metric system to accommodate the
other nations of the world, <u>they</u> should change to <u>our</u>
system.

To keep the rhythm lively, writers try to mix one or two short sentences and
short independent clauses with medium-length sentences.

ACCEPTABLE
There is now an organization for all you folks who are
opposed to adopting the metric system. A columnist for
the Chicago Sun Times . . . Bob Greene . . . has formed
a group called ''WAM'' . . . which means ''We Ain't
Metric!'' Greene says he came up with the idea one day
when he didn't have any material for a column . . . but
it caught on and now has millions of members. Greene
says the U-S shouldn't change to the metric system to
accommodate the other nations of the world . . . <u>They</u>
should adopt <u>our</u> system.

WSB, Atlanta

Sentence Structure The straight subject-verb sentence works fine in
broadcast news, but if too many are strung together or the same subject and verb
are repeated too frequently, the sentence will fall flat. This was used on the air:

<u>The New York Police Department says</u> it's recovered about
100-thousand dollars in blackout loot. <u>Police raided</u> an
abandoned apartment on West 108th Street. <u>They said</u> it
had been converted into a warehouse of stolen goods.
<u>Five people were arrested.</u> <u>They were said to be</u> fences
buying goods from looters for resale. <u>The law was tipped</u>
by phone.

Good writers vary their subjects, verbs and sentence structure—sometimes doing
that requires a clause at the start of some sentences:

<u>When New York Police raided an abandoned apartment on
West 108th Street</u> . . . they say they found 100-thousand
dollars in blackout loot. <u>According to the police,</u> the
place had been converted into a warehouse of stolen
goods. Five people were arrested . . . said to be fences
buying goods from looters for resale. The law was tipped
by phone.

Strong Words Some words have the power to punctuate a story. Put a strong word at the end of a sentence and it will usually pick up the rhythm:

> The Black Panther founder is returning to the U-S . . .
> after hiding out the past two-and-a-half years . . . in
> <u>Cuba</u>.
>
> WDEE, Detroit

> A story about a baseball player tonight who is capable
> and suddenly very <u>rich</u>.
>
> Peter Jennings, ABC

> The conviction <u>stands</u> . . . William Weeks is guilty of
> <u>manslaughter</u>.
>
> KCLD, Minnesota

Repetition Writers are usually hunting down synonyms to avoid repeating words too often and sounding stiff—as in this sentence, which Mervin Block caught on CBS television:

> We'll have a report on current White House thinking when
> it comes to our current energy problems.

As Block wrote: "Apparently, there's no shortage of current." That sentence would have sounded better if the word "current" had been left out one of the two times it was used. More frequently the solution is to substitute another word: "officer" the second time a policewoman is mentioned, for example.

Falling into unnecessary and awkward repetition is a mistake, but there are times when conscious repetition of words can be used to enhance a story. This was written by Morton Dean, then with CBS television:

> The Federal Trade Commission charges that the dental
> profession not only fixes teeth, it fixes prices.

In the hands of a good writer, repetition can also clarify:

> It will be noon before a decision can be reached. Noon
> because more members of the board can be in attendance
> at that time.
>
> KPNW, Oregon

■ ■ ■

These tricks should help writers keep stories lively. Reading and listening to other good writers also helps. A writer has to *hear* words and sentences, get a feel for the story's sound.

"Some days are beautiful," George Brooks of KCUE in Minnesota writes. "Some days, words are music."

Wrap-Up

The main job of the story is to communicate. This requires a smooth and selective presentation of information. A bit of an ear for the music in words doesn't hurt.

Practice Assignments

A. Write a 20- to 25-second story based on the following facts.

1. Lt. Gov. Michael Mars has completed state tour.
2. Mars says the drought is already severe in southern half of state.
3. Southern half contains ¾ of state's population.
4. Mars describes tour as "eye-opening experience."
5. Says situation in south more serious than many people and officials realize.
6. Says Sturbridge is within 30 days of running out of water.
7. Mars is coordinating state drought assistance.
8. Says federal aid possible.
9. Sturbridge pop.: 15,768.
10. State submitted application for federal drought relief funds last week.
11. Federal decision regarding funds will be released tomorrow.
12. Drought began 2 months ago—worsening since then.

B. Combine the following information into one 20- to 25-second story.

1. Prison guards in Montana are on strike.
2. Started 4 days ago.
3. National Guardsmen on duty in prisons today.
4. There are 1600 Nat. Guards on duty.
5. NGs sent to the state today.
6. About 5000 prison guards on strike.
7. 38,000 copper workers were on strike.
8. Their strike has ended today.
9. 2 largest copper companies agreed to relatively quick settlement. Strike ended sooner than some labor mediators had expected.
10. Copper workers won extra $1.00 per hour.
11. Had demanded: $1.25/hr.
12. Walked off job 3 days ago.
13. Many wildcat copper strikes last year.

C. Write a 25- to 30-second story based on the following facts.

1. Alfred Lewis, county maintenance supervisor, appeared before County Commission last night asking to be allowed to keep his job.
2. He said he wouldn't resign.
3. Charged that media had "killed" him.
4. Commission last night reviewed and released an investigation, which was conducted by County Attorney David Malone's office.
5. The investigation charged that Lewis misused county vehicles.
6. It also revealed that he had granted personal favors involving the use of various pieces of county equipment during the last 2½ years.
7. Following the review, Commissioner Bob Newhouse moved that Lewis be fired, with no severance pay.
8. The motion was approved, unanimously, by the 11-member commission.
9. Pete White, the commission's chairman, said the Malone investigation also revealed that Lewis misused his office to better his position.
10. Lewis said: "All charges against me are totally, completely erroneous and false. My enemies are trying to ruin me and my family."

D. Write a 20- to 25-second story based on the following facts.

1. City Council meeting last night.
2. Lasted 2 hours.
3. Second meeting of month.
4. Last month's appointments approved: Sue Murphy as public relations supervisor; John Katz as assistant liaison for city affairs.
5. School Board appropriations for playground approved.
6. 12 members of Council present; 2 absent.
7. Chaired by Evan Jones, acting council president.
8. 2 percent hike in real estate tax approved.
9. Vote: 7-5.
10. Council member Jane Andrews says: "This will drive people—constructive people—away from town, people whom our town needs."
11. Jones: Hike needed for balanced budget.
12. Closing of all town parks after 10 p.m. approved.

E. Write a 15-second or shorter story based on the following facts.

1. Rick Peters, high school student.
2. Lost 2 toes when foot run over by school bus last year.
3. Sued school district for ½ million dollars.
4. 2 months ago: jury finds school district not negligent.
5. Attorney Betty Burns requested new trial last month.
6. Called previous decision "perverse."
7. District Court Judge Robert Penn denied request this afternoon.

8. Penn: "The case was properly put before a jury and decided. The proper legal process was carried through."
9. Burns says will appeal to State Supreme Court.

F. Write a 20- to 25-second story based on the following facts.

1. Man found dead in boat around noon yesterday.
2. Boat docked at marina.
3. Police identified him as Evan Rows.
4. Local police are continuing their investigation.
5. Autopsy performed last night.
6. Performed by Dr. Sybil Jones.
7. Apparent cause of death: stab wounds.
8. Rows was 32.
9. Police arrested a teenager today.
10. Charge: theft on property where the murder allegedly occurred.
11. He's 18.
12. Name: Robert Ray.
13. Will be arraigned today.
14. Presently in county jail.
15. Policy say Ray is suspect in murder.
16. He was picked up in Concord at app. 2:00 this aft.
17. With him was female juvenile, name undisclosed.

G. Write a 15- to 20-second story based on the following information released by the police.

1. Auto accident yesterday evening, app. 5 p.m.
2. Location: Highway 14.
3. Rained yesterday.
4. Car skidded on wet pavement.
5. Left highway, rolled over on top.
6. 6 in car.
7. Were driving through town—all from out-of-state.
8. Driver of car: Gerald Smith.
9. 1 adult, 1 child seriously injured: Meredith Smith of Santa Clara, Cal., age 31, and Janey Smith, same town, age 4.
10. Gerald Smith, 33, and Jacob Smith, 6, also of Santa Clara, both killed instantly.
11. Janet Simon, 44, of San Francisco, and Joseph Shields, 14, also from SF, injured: listed good condition.
12. Meredith and Gerald Smith parents of Janey and Jacob Smith. Simon and Shields not related.

II

Reporting

Sources

The best way to cover a news story is to go there. The second best way is to call up a bunch of people who were there. Many radio stations and most television stations have reporters out in the field chasing down news, but a reporter can only cover one story at a time, and only a story that's within reach. All stations should have their news people on the phone getting the low-down on those out-of-reach stories, but even with a telephone the number of stories a station's news staff can get a bead on is limited. Yet most radio newsrooms are putting together reports every hour on perhaps a half-dozen breaking events taking place around the world. Television newsrooms report less frequently, but on more stories at a time. How does information on all those stories reach these newsrooms?

Some news arrives by mail; some by telephone. A never-ending stream of information about the day's events pours out of computer printers—at the rate of 1,200 words per minute. It is prepared by **wire services** and arrives in newsrooms via satellite. Similar transmissions from **audio and video news services** bring in sounds and pictures captured at news events. Books and other publications help. And radio **scanners** draw the internal communication of police and fire departments into newsrooms.

Along with reporters and their contacts, which will be discussed in the following chapters, these are the sources of broadcast news. Broadcast journalists have to know how to work with them.

The Wires

WXTA in Rockford, Illinois, has two reporters. Neither is ever sent to Washington, let alone Tel Aviv. But WXTA supplements its reporting staff with the more than 300 reporters United Press International has sprinkled around the planet. By subscribing to UPI's broadcast wire, the station can avail itself of the work of UPI's journalists in Washington or its bureaus in Africa or Europe or the Middle East or the reporter UPI has stationed in the state capital—Springfield. The wires cover the world for newspapers and television and radio stations like WXTA.

Certainly these are among the most powerful tools a news operation has. When a presidential news conference ends, UPI's Helen Thomas, as one of the senior

White House correspondents, may say, "Thank you, Mr. President"; then she dashes to her phone in the White House pressroom to call in her story. Shortly it will be relayed to WXTA and thousands of other UPI customers. But UPI wasn't waiting for Helen Thomas's detailed report in order to begin its coverage. Other UPI reporters were monitoring the news conference on television and writing stories based on the earlier questions. WXTA will have a story, even if the station does a newscast before the news conference ends. At the networks and the larger stations wire stories are now routed right into newsroom computers, so newswriters can call up the latest facts on a breaking news story as they write. Even smaller stations like WXTA now get reams of pages of information at phenomenal speeds from the wires, thanks to satellite hook-ups and computer printers.

The wires are fast. UPI still proudly recalls beating the Associated Press by four minutes in reporting that shots had been fired at President John Kennedy in Dallas. UPI also beat the AP by four days in announcing the end of World War I. Unfortunately, it scooped the politicians and generals, too. The war didn't end for another four days.

The wires are also comprehensive. "There are only two forces that can carry light to all corners of the globe," Mark Twain once observed, "the sun in the heavens and the Associated Press down here." The AP has reporters stationed in more than 83 bureaus around the world and more than 136 in the United States. When the Communists were taking South Vietnam, for instance, the AP was covering the story with three staffers in Saigon, two near the demilitarized zone, two in Laos, two in Thailand, four in the Philippines, three on Guam, one on Wake Island and two staffers aboard a carrier in the South China Sea.

For many years newspapers, rightly viewing radio as a dangerous competitor in the news business, tried to prevent stations from using the Associated Press, but today there are more broadcast stations hooked up to AP wires than newspapers. Only a handful of radio and television stations can survive without at least one computer printer, churning out the news of the region, world and nation.

Only three wire services attempt complete coverage of the United States and the world. One, Reuters, is known primarily for the quality of its foreign news. In larger newsrooms Reuters might be used to supplement the other wires. Most stations rely primarily on the Associated Press; others still use United Press International.

The AP is older (founded in 1848), healthier and larger than its rival, but UPI has been catering to radio stations longer (since 1935—when it was called United Press). The AP now serves about 6,000 broadcast stations, UPI many fewer. The AP is a cooperative—owned by its domestic newspaper subscribers—while UPI is a private company, which has experienced severe financial difficulties in recent years.

Some larger stations still use both AP and UPI. Smaller stations can generally afford only one. Which one they choose might depend on the deal each wire is willing to offer or which wire the competition has, or the station might base its decision on preference for the writing or services one provides. Years of cutbacks at UPI have certainly hurt its position in these competitions.

The wire services' services have multiplied over the years. They have developed specialized wires designed to satisfy specific news needs. Radio and television newsrooms have found uses for many of these wires, some of which place special demands on the broadcast journalists who use them.

Broadcast Wires

Radio and television stations have different news needs than newspapers. The **broadcast wires** are designed to satisfy these needs.

Most radio stations cover the top news every hour, so the broadcast wires repeat and update all the top stories every hour. Broadcast newscasters need to know facts such as the correct pronunciation of difficult names, so the broadcast wires include pronunciation guides. And news written for broadcast must follow the rules outlined in the previous chapters; the broadcast wire is written in broadcast style:

```
(PINEVILLE) -- TWO MEN ESCAPED FROM THE MCDONALD COUNTY
JAIL IN PINEVILLE, MISSOURI, LAST NIGHT . . . APPARENTLY
SIMPLY BY WALKING OUT THE FRONT DOOR. THE SHERIFF'S
OFFICE IS INVESTIGATING THE ESCAPE. THE MEN ARE BELIEVED
TO HAVE LEFT THE JAIL ABOUT 11 P-M . . . BUT THEIR
ESCAPE WASN'T NOTICED UNTIL AFTER MIDNIGHT WHEN
AUTHORITIES DISCOVERED AN EVIDENCE CABINET HAD BEEN
BURGLARIZED.
     UPI 07-27 12:17 PCD
```

This story opens with a **dateline,** the name of the city where it was written— *PINEVILLE*—but most stations won't read this on the air; the location is mentioned again in the lead. The line at the end of the story, or at the end of a complete newscast, gives the date (*July 27*) and the time ("PCD" is *p.m., Central Daylight* time).

The broadcast wires have a staff of newswriters turning information, mostly taken from the wires intended for newspapers, into copy suitable for broadcast. UPI and AP also ensure that the copy is regionalized. UPI, for instance, has 52 separate, regional broadcast wires—almost every state has a regional wire and a few states are divided into two regions. Each regional wire mixes about 30 minutes of state or regional news with the 30 minutes of national and international news everybody gets. The broadcast wires also supply stations with complete newscast scripts. Here's UPI's schedule of national newscasts:

```
World in Brief Summaries -- 3½ minutes of the top
stories for use in a 5-minute newscast; sent almost
every hour before the half-hour.
World News Roundups -- 7 minutes of news for use in a 10-
minute newscast; sent before 5 a.m., 4 p.m. and 9 p.m.
on weekdays.
```

In addition, UPI sends out a minute of sports before the half-hour eight times a day; a sports roundup five times a day; as well as regular weather, business news, features, commentaries and farm news—all ready to read on the air. The AP's schedule is similar.

Essentially, all a station has to do is rip stories, or even complete newscasts, off the printer and read them on the air. There's no need for a news staff; a disk jockey can do it. This method, called **rip and read** journalism, is used by many stations to present the news. Rip and read has two major advantages: It is easy and it is cheap.

Rip and read has many disadvantages. Good newsrooms develop a style. Their copy has a characteristic "feel" to it, determined by pacing, language and news selection. Listeners won't hear this in stories ripped off a wire. The wires are certainly not known for the quality of their writing—churned out in large volumes under intense deadline pressure, it often sounds hurried. And the wires cannot risk style, even if they have the time to develop it. They have to please hundreds of stations. Turning on a little style might mean turning off some subscribers.

Still another of the basic strategies of broadcast journalism is denied to the wires—they can't localize a story for a town or a county; they have to write for whole states or regions.

Here's a lead off one of the wires; it is awkward and dense:

```
FIRE FROM AN UNDETERMINED CAUSE GUTTED A TURN-OF-THE-
CENTURY STONE CHURCH IN KANSAS CITY, MISSOURI, EARLY
TODAY AND SLIGHTLY INJURED FOUR FIREMEN.
```

Sitting in a somewhat less hectic newsroom, aware of the local listeners' interests and able to add whatever style suits their station, most radio and television newswriters can do a better job on a story than the wires. For example, here is the church story as rewritten for a Kansas City station:

```
Saint Andrew's Methodist Church on Troost Street was
built at the turn of the century. A fire started in the
basement there this morning . . . and it burned all the
way through to the sanctuary and roof of the old stone
church.
```

Wire copy should be rewritten. If there isn't time or staff for that, it should at least be edited. Wordings can often be improved.

```
WIRE
THE PRESIDENT HAS DECLARED 26 DROUGHT-STRICKEN ALABAMA
COUNTIES ARE NOW ELIGIBLE FOR FEDERAL AID.

STATION
The president has declared that 26 drought-stricken
Alabama counties are now eligible for federal aid.
```

WIRE
THE HOUSE HAS OKAYED A 12-BILLION, 700-MILLION DOLLAR
FUNDING BILL THAT PROVIDES 5 POINT 6 BILLION DOLLARS FOR
FOOD STAMPS.

STATION
The House has okayed a funding bill that provides more
than 5-billion dollars for food stamps.

The story sometimes can be localized.

WIRE
PATRICK HENRY'S ''GIVE ME LIBERTY OR GIVE ME DEATH''
SPEECH WAS REENACTED AT HISTORIC SAINT JOHN'S CHURCH
NEAR THE STATE CAPITOL.

STATION
Patrick Henry's ''Give me liberty or give me death''
speech was reenacted at historic Saint John's Church
here on Church Hill.

WRVQ, Virginia

To localize a wire story it is sometimes necessary to do some additional research.
This was a story about 80 Illinois communities and factories accused of missing a
pollution clean-up deadline. WSOY added a sentence about the local violators:

Included among the violators are the municipalities
of Bloomington-Normal and Champaign-Urbana, as well as
the Revere Copper and Brass Company in Clinton, and
several Peoria-area plants of the Caterpillar Tractor
Company.

Operating at such high speed also forces the wires into errors. The Associated
Press broadcast wire once killed Marshall Tito of Yugoslavia when he was still very
much alive. ABC and CBS led with the story on their newscasts. The editor on duty
at NBC, however, was puzzled that the story hadn't appeared on any other wire,
including other AP wires. He held the story and called AP. AP admitted that it was
a mistake. CBS and ABC had to air embarrassing corrections after the wire carried
a correction.

In fact, the wires conscientiously spend much time correcting themselves and
updating their work. This means newswriters have to be alert for an item that refutes
something they are about to put on the air. This should also make newswriters
anxious to check facts on their own when possible. This version of a wire service
story, for example, corrects the number of months mentioned in the first version.
The original had talked of the "smallest trade deficit in ten months":

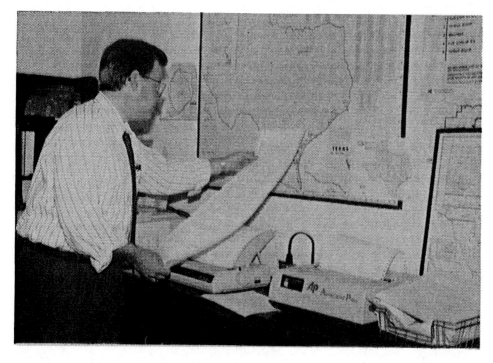

Newscaster Brad Barton reviews wire copy at News 1080 KRLD, Dallas, Texas. (HBJ photo/ Annette Coolidge)

CORRECTION
THE UNITED STATES RECORDED ITS SMALLEST TRADE DEFICIT IN
EIGHT MONTHS IN MAY.

Stations that missed this revision, or used the story before it was corrected, were led into an error. It may not be feasible for a station to call Washington to check the facts on a story like this, but the frequency of errors of this sort points to the need to confirm the facts in wire stories when possible—and it should be possible on all local stories.

All this is not intended to imply that every broadcast wire story is poorly written or inaccurate—just that most can use some rewriting and checking to make them more effective. Of course, stations have also been known to make wire copy worse. One added this unfortunate sentence to an AP story:

It is believed, however, that the damage will not amount
to as great a cost as that of a similar fire in November.

Because broadcast wire stories enter the newsroom with all the appearances of finished broadcast copy, it is tempting to rip and read or "tack them up"—staple them into the script and read them on the air. Good newswriters fight that temptation and treat the broadcast wires as no more than a first draft.

If the wires are looked on primarily as source material, it becomes obvious that the broadcast wires have a serious disadvantage—they don't contain much information. These wires are already one step removed from the facts. They are composed of stories that have been rewritten in broadcast style from print sources. Since broadcast stories must be short, they can't squeeze in too much information. Working with the broadcast wires, a writer is limited to the few facts selected by the wire service writers. A broadcast story is a poor place to look for the information on which to base an original version of that story. While the larger radio and television news organizations may rely on the broadcast wires for breaking stories that must be quickly edited, then thrown on the air, they base most of their writing on wires actually intended for newspapers.

Print Wires

The wire services used to send two wires to the nation's newspapers—the A and B wires. Both contained national and international news. The *A wire* had the more important stories; the *B wire* had whatever was left over. Broadcast stations—with no back pages to fill with secondary news—would only be interested in the A wire.

The AP and UPI still provide national A wires, but they now offer subscribers a chance to take a mix of national news and regional stories, similar to the mix available on the broadcast wires. Separate regional-only wires are also available. Broadcast stations that choose to use a major *print wire* will select from this grab bag.

The first problem a broadcast newswriter has with these print wires is their schedule. The newspaper world is divided into two groups—morning and afternoon papers. Print wires reflect this split and are designed to produce a complete run-through of the day's news every twelve hours—from noon to midnight for the morning papers and from midnight to noon for the afternoon dailies. A television station usually needs to recount the news a few times a day, a radio station every hour, so this is inconvenient. But fortunately, the print wires constantly update the major stories—the stories in which the broadcast journalist is most interested. Although it isn't organized into neat one-hour blocks, the news is kept fresh enough for broadcast.

Another problem with the print wires is that, because there are no Sunday afternoon papers, the print wires do not send out a regular cycle of news on Sunday mornings. Sunday tends to be the slowest news day anyway; so newswriters will squirrel away some *evergreens*—feature or background stories that can be held a couple of days—for use on Sunday.

The advantage of the print wires is the wide selection of information they offer newswriters looking to carve out their own stories. The print wire's version of a story will use many more words than the broadcast wire's. It is likely, therefore, to carry many more facts. In another step to maximize the available information, most newsrooms collect different versions of a story off the wires and file them together. Newsrooms have set procedures for ripping and filing wire copy. Usually the first step is to break it down into national, international, state and local news; then to separate the individual stories. A newswriter may then look at the whole day's file on a story.

Larger newsrooms have versions of the story off a few different wires in the file because frequently one wire will miss a fact another has. In a grisly story about a Moscow man who attacked three tourists with an axe, for instance, UPI, AP and Reuters all had substantial reports on the story on their wires for 7:30 a.m.; but the AP was missing a witness's report that one of the tourists was decapitated, UPI was missing the age of the Moscow man, and both the AP and Reuters missed a description of the man as "husky." Any of these facts could have made it into the story. Only a writer with a chance to look over all three versions would have had them all to choose from.

The first step in turning print wire copy into broadcast stories is reading all those plentiful facts carefully. Writers wait until they understand a story thoroughly before they hazard skimming later updates.

Working from more than one wire requires that the newswriters or editor, if there is one, take responsibility for **copy control**—ensuring that the station's version of events is consistent and based on the best available information. It won't do to say "27 are dead in a plane crash" in one newscast based on the AP, then have someone go on the air an hour later saying "22 dead" based on UPI. When reports conflict, someone in the newsroom must carefully evaluate the different reports and choose from them a set of the timeliest and most consistent facts. Then all the newswriters must stick to that version—until the facts change again. Incidentally, when in doubt, use the lower number of casualties. It's always better to add a few dead later on than to have to resurrect people you've already announced as having been killed.

Once a set of facts has been compiled, the writing begins. Here the story must of necessity undergo a total transformation—newspaper and broadcast styles are different enough so that it's a rare sentence that meets the requirements of both. Sentences off the print wires must be minced, thinned, seasoned and molded. When the stories are done, only the facts will be the same. As a rule, most broadcast writers do not allow any sentences from print wires into their copy. Not because that would be unethical—the wires are written to be "plagiarized"—it's just foolish to use newspaper sentences on the air.

Here's an example of a story off an AP print wire—written when the much-reviled Idi Amin was in power in Uganda.

```
PM-UNIVERSE, 120
    NEW YORK (AP) -- JANELLE COMMISSIONG SAID TODAY THAT
SHE WANTS TO MEET UGANDAN PRESIDENT IDI AMIN DURING HER
REIGN AS THE FIRST BLACK WOMAN CHOSEN MISS UNIVERSE.
    ASKED WHOM SHE WOULD LIKE TO MEET, THE BEAUTY QUEEN
FROM TRINIDAD, TOBAGO, MENTIONED AMIN AND SAID SHE WANTS
TO SEE ''WHAT HE'S REALLY LIKE.''
```

```
      ''I WOULD LIKE TO SIT DOWN AND HAVE A CHAT WITH HIM,''
SHE SAID. ''I'D LIKE TO ASK HIM WHY HE DOES THE THINGS HE
DOES AND WHY HE HAS TO HAVE THE WORLD IN AWE.''
      THE NEW MISS UNIVERSE WAS ALSO ASKED WHETHER SHE
STILL CONSIDERS MARLON BRANDO THE GREATEST LIVING
AMERICAN.
      ''WELL, HE WAS THE FIRST NAME THAT CAME TO MIND, BUT I
CAN COME UP WITH 10 OTHER ANSWERS,'' SHE SAID,
MENTIONING TWO: BOB HOPE AND MOHAMMAD ALI.
1148AED 07-21
```

First, what do those codes mean? *PM* denotes a story written for afternoon or PM papers; actually it means the story was transmitted during AM hours—midnight to noon. *UNIVERSE* is the slug (see Chapter 1, "Copy") the AP is using for the story. *120* says the story is 120 words long—a fact that is of no interest to a broadcast writer who must make it much shorter. The story begins with a type of dateline and the initials of the wire service. The line at the end of the story tells what time it was transmitted—*11:48 a.m., Eastern Daylight* time—and the date—*July 21st.* The time is important—it measures freshness.

What's the news in this story? For a New York City station, the most newsworthy element is hidden in the dateline—the first black Miss Universe is in town today. Beyond that, some of her statements are unusual and perhaps controversial, though they're much too long for use on the air and must be chopped and paraphrased. The story that was written from this piece of print wire copy employs a completely different lead from the wire copy and uses a fresh set of sentences.

```
      The new Miss Universe is visiting New York. Janelle
Commissiong, Miss Trinidad, is the first black woman
chosen Miss Universe.
      When reporters asked her who in the world she would
most like to meet, she said . . . Idi Amin.
      Miss Universe says she wants to sit and chat with the
Ugandan president and ask him why he does the things he
does.
      Miss Universe also added to her list of greatest
living Americans. She had mentioned Marlon Brando. Today
she put Bob Hope and Mohammad Ali on the list.
                                        WCBS, New York City
```

Rewriting from print wire copy is basic broadcast newswriting. It involves taking long compilations of facts and whittling them down into short, smooth broadcast stories.

Bulletins

The wire services are organized to move breaking news to clients with dispatch. When one of their reporters comes upon a major story, the routine news is interrupted. Once upon a time, bells would ring in subscribers' newsrooms. Now, in some places, electronic alarms on printers sound off. In addition, words often start flashing on computer screens, giving new meaning to the wire service heading "flash" described below. The breaking story follows immediately. Broadcast journalists are also in the business of instant news, so they have to be on their toes for these bulletins on the wire.

There are three standard headings used by the major wires for breaking news:

Flash This is reserved for stories that are of immediate interest to absolutely everybody: men landing on the moon, the result of a presidential election, a major assassination, the beginning or end of a major war. The *flash* was introduced at the AP after the San Francisco earthquake in 1906. Sometimes years will go by without a flash. When something this momentous does move on the wire, ten bells will ring on the teletype, and most radio and television stations will shortly be interrupting their programming to air the story.

Bulletin This is news of immediate interest to *almost* everybody: plane crashes, presidential primary results, earthquakes abroad. Five bells ring, and stations will consider interrupting programming. The AP calls this "prime news." *Bulletins* are also used when the wires want to instruct subscribers that it is mandatory that they *kill* a story. The wires will send out a "bulletin kill" after sending out a story that they now believe to be dangerously inaccurate or possibly libelous.

Urgent Breaking news that's unusually important but not that gripping gets this treatment. Major Washington developments are usually labeled *urgent*. The wires also use this designation for their important corrections. Four bells ring. Rarely will radio or television programming be interrupted.

Other Wires

WBBM in Chicago, one of the largest radio news operations in the country, has the AP broadcast wire as well as the AP, UPI and Reuters A wires. But WBBM also has AP and UPI sports wires, the CQI SportsTicker, the NOAA weather wire, the Dow Jones business wire, a service called City News, which covers Chicago news, and something called Custom News from UPI, which sends subscribers reams of information at high speeds. Obviously, there is no shortage of information available to a broadcast news operation that can afford it. Here's a rundown of some of the possibilities:

Weather   Weather news is a staple of all radio stations, probably because no other medium can compete with radio in keeping up with changing forecasts, conditions and storm warnings. And television newscasts almost always feature a segment on the weather. If a small station, especially in a farm area, is going to supplement its UPI or AP broadcast wire, it will usually get a weather wire.

This is one area in which the journalist's traditional adversary—the government—gets into the news business. The National Weather Service, a branch of the National Oceanic and Atmospheric Administration, supplies weather wires tailored to different regions throughout the country. These wires are full of charts and short notations. They give nationwide and area forecasts, warnings of hazardous weather and current weather observations. Actually UPI and AP get their weather information from National Weather Service wires. By subscribing, a radio station just gets the information faster—by cutting out the middleman—and in a more complete form.

Some radio executives maintain that more people died in a tornado a number of years ago than should have, because the area's radio stations did not have National Weather Service wires and therefore had to wait crucial minutes before the tornado warning appeared on the broadcast wires.

Sports   Sports news is important enough to some listeners, and therefore to some stations, that the information provided by the major news wires isn't sufficient.

Western Union started its sports *ticker,* or wire, in 1909 to provide complete play-by-play accounts of baseball games. Announcers in the studio (Ronald Reagan once held this job) could simulate live coverage just by reading the wire. Western Union's wire has changed hands—it is now called the CQI SportsTicker—and it no longer simulates live coverage now that games can be broadcast live. Instead, the ticker provides detailed coverage of all the major team sports—scores every half-inning for major league and triple-A baseball games, for instance. This wire is used for scores at the ballpark by sportscasters, as well as in radio and television newsrooms.

AP and UPI also have separate sports wires and no shortage of information to fill them. The Associated Press says it has enough sports news to operate a 1,050-word-an-hour sports wire around the clock. All these words are arranged in newspaper style.

Business   Broadcast news can also capture listeners through comprehensive coverage of business and financial news; so some stations pay for special business and financial wires. AP and UPI provide such wires as does Dow Jones. The Dow Jones News Service uses *Wall Street Journal* reporters to keep up with such matters as annual reports, earnings, the price of gold and the performance of the stock markets. Then the Dow Jones broadcast unit rewrites this information for use on the radio.

Farm   Farm Radio News, headquartered in Kansas City, Kansas, provides about 100 radio stations with "ready-to-read" news about livestock futures, grain futures, harvest information, etc. Reuters also has a wire that reports on farm commodities.

Local   Some large cities and some states have special wires filled with local or regional news. In New York City, the Greater New York wire, operated by UPI, provides this service; in Los Angeles it's City News Service; in Houston it's News One Houston. These wires are written for newspapers, and, like the A wires, they must be completely rewritten for broadcast.

Custom   The old-fashioned **teletype** machines that used to rumble away in the corners of broadcast newsrooms printed 66 words a minute. Now that they use 1,200-word-per-minute computer printers, or inject their stories directly into newsroom computers, the wires can send stations many, many more words.

So news directors now customize the packages they receive. One high-speed printer can transmit the broadcast wire plus the A wire, the sports wire and a regional wire. You want the business wire instead of the A wire? No problem. WPOR in Maine has a lot of listeners in Massachusetts and New Hampshire, so in its arrangement with the Associated Press, WPOR asks to have the regional wires for those states thrown in, too.

And, since all this is organized by computer, these arrangements remain flexible. Ed Walsh, news director of WRKO in Boston, says that, when the station gets particularly interested in a subject, he can phone the local wire bureau and ask them to route everything they have on the subject to him on the high-speed wire.

Fax   These computerized services can be expensive. But new technologies keep appearing all the time, and an entrepreneur has been able to use one to devise a cheaper way to transmit news to stations. The trick: sending a much more limited selection of news not by satellite but through long-distance telephone services—by fax. Zap News—with a seven-person news staff in Fairfax, Virginia, stringers around the country and the right to use information off some of the wires—now has more than 400 broadcast clients.

Other Sources

The wires dominate broadcast news. They are such busy producers of information that it's hard to look beyond them. But the wires have limitations. There are holes in the services they provide that are filled by other news sources.

Audio News Services

The wires omit a factor that is vital in radio news—sound. They can explain what the president said, but the wires can't provide listeners with the president's voice saying it. Reporters capture such sounds on tape for local stories (see Chapter 9, "Tape"). *Audio news services* bring in the sound of the news from the rest of the world.

The two major wire services also run the major audio news services. The Associated Press and United Press International each uses a satellite to transmit newsmakers' voices and reporters' on-the-scene reports to clients who are willing to pay for these *inserts*—ready to insert in a newscast. About 1,000 stations use UPI's audio service, which, like the AP's, also gives subscribers a ready-to-broadcast, hourly national and international news program.

The taped inserts are fed to UPI subscribers hourly at 10 minutes after the hour. Each *feed* includes anywhere from four to 40 different reports. Inserts are repeated; on the average UPI sends out 125 different reports each day. Both UPI and AP index or *billboard* these reports on their broadcast wires:

```
AUDIO-HOURLY NEWSFEED
63 :19 SANTA BARBARA -- (BLAZE) -- (ED WALDAPFEL, U-S
FOREST SERVICE) CURRENT STATUS OF FIRE (AT THIS TIME)
64 :43 SB -- (BLAZE) -- (WALDAPFEL) ANS Q: HOW BIG AN
AREA BURNED -- WHAT ABOUT DAMAGE AND INJURIES (VERY,
VERY FORTUNATE)
65 :28 SB -- (BLAZE) -- (WALDAPFEL) ANS Q: WHERE ARE THE
EVACUEES, WHEN DO YOU EXPECT FIRE TO BE CONTAINED
(CRITICAL FIRE WEATHER)
66 :41 CAP HILL -- (FARM) -- (GENE GIBBONS) HOUSE
REJECTS EFFORTS TO LIMIT USE OF FOOD STAMPS
67 :27 CH -- (KOREAN) -- (REP MILLICENT FENWICK, R-NJ,
MBR HOUSE ETHICS CMTE) NOT SATISFIED WITH JUSTICE DEPT
BRIEFING ON KOREA PROBE (CLOUD OVER CONGRESS)
68 :34 CH -- (KOREAN) -- (REP JOHN FLYNT, D-GA, ETHICS
CMTE CHAIRMAN) JUSTICE DEPT OFFICIALS WENT AS FAR AS
THEY COULD IN EXPLAINING PROGRESS OF KOREA INVESTIGATION
(OF IT)
```

The billboard for a UPI hourly feed is above. The inserts are numbered each day (63–68 in this feed), and their length follows the number. They never run longer than 45 seconds. Notice the three inserts on the afternoon's top story—a fire in Santa Barbara; all three are taken from an interview with a forest service official. The last few words for most inserts are noted, in parentheses, as a cue for newscasters using the insert. These words tell them when the tape is ending.

The four major networks are also in the audio news service business. A few times a day they transmit tapes of newsmakers or reporters—items that are not going to be used in their network newscasts—to local stations for use in the station's own newscasts. NBC calls this service "Newsline," CBS—"Newsfeed," ABC—"News Call," and Mutual—"Operation News Line."

These audio news services basically cover national and international news. The AP sends two regional feeds a day out of Washington to stations in each of the four time zones, but with this exception, the national networks have not found it practical to set up localized or specialized audio services. Into this gap have stepped a number of regional operations. For example, the Texas State Network sends four feeds a day of reports on Texas news to 150 to 175 stations throughout the state. There are audio news services in many other states. The National Black Network provides a similar service for stations interested in minority news, and the Spanish Information Service does the same thing in Spanish.

The stations that receive these audio reports still have to write copy to go with them. This requires the same skills as writing to tape collected by the stations' reporters and is discussed in Chapter 10, "Writing to Tape."

Video News Services

Television news requires pictures—moving pictures, video. The four main television news networks—ABC, CBS, NBC and Fox—all supply their affiliates with *video feeds,* similar to the audio feeds radio affiliates get—one or more times each day. In addition, television stations can subscribe—for a fee—to special video news services like Conus, Viznews and Newsfeed.

Conus, for example (the name is an old military acronym for "continental United States"), takes stories produced by individual stations and distributes them to all members via satellite. It operates as something of a cooperative. An example of how such video news services are used is provided in Chapter 17, "Television Newscasts."

Police Radio

The police must talk to each other, sometimes over long distances, often in a hurry. They use two-way radios and it is perfectly legal for citizens to listen in. Many radio and television stations eavesdrop on police and fire frequencies—that way they find out about major stories as soon as the police do.

If police were to switch these conversations to cellular telephones, that would be bad news for broadcast journalists. It is *not* legal to eavesdrop on cellular phone conversations. So far, fortunately, most police departments seem still to be using their radios, which are often quicker and easier than the telephone, to transmit their initial reports on potential crimes—the reports reporters want to hear.

Other radio frequencies may also be good sources, although they are used less frequently. The networks do their best, for example, to monitor Secret Service conversations when following the president. Some stations listen in on citizens' band channels for traffic information.

In the Boston area there are 73 cities and towns, so it would be impossible to keep a radio tuned to the communication of each police and fire department. Instead, WRKO uses radios with *scanners,* designed to jump back and forth between a set of frequencies, pausing every time someone is talking. At WRKO one such radio is tuned to 50 different police channels; another to fire and airport frequencies. With half an ear WRKO's news staff monitors these internal communications, listening for key words such as "homicide" or special code numbers.

Police initiate conversations on the radio with codes that provide clues to the nature and seriousness of the incidents they're investigating. With a knowledge of the codes employed by a police department, journalists can quickly, almost subconsciously, begin to separate the newsworthy from the routine on the police radio.

A *ten code* is used by many police departments, though the meaning of the numbers that follow the obligatory "ten" — *10-4, 10-30, 10-40* — differs from city to city. "In Houston *10-40* means there is a four-alarm fire," explains Steve Ramsey of KWCH-TV in Wichita. "In Oklahoma City *10-40* means the fire is out." Broadcast journalists eavesdropping on the New York City police, who use their own ten code, won't waste much attention on calls such as a *10-63* — that means the officer is going to take time off to eat. But if they hear a *10-70* — a call for a rapid mobilization of 56 police officers — a reporter will soon be sent to the scene or someone will be dialing police headquarters . . . or both.

In larger cities, the police may also provide news organizations with a teletype which reproduces police reports. An item off such a teletype:

MAN SHOT TWICE IN THE FACE AT 1655 MADISON AVE -- A BAR.
DOA AT SCENE. PERP FLED THE SCENE.

DOA, in this case, is used to mean the man was dead when the police arrived. *PERP*, of course, is short for that standard of police jargon — "the perpetrator." The teletype will also print the name of the precinct that is handling the case and the officer to contact for further details. Such a report off the teletype would seem to have the makings of an up-to-the-minute story, but airing it would be a serious mistake. The important thing to remember about the police radio or teletype is that they give *preliminary* reports, often just rumors, not established facts.

If someone tells St. Louis police that an airplane has hit the Gateway Arch, police headquarters might send squad cars to investigate. The radio or television station that hears these calls to the squad cars and jumps on the air with "An airplane has crashed into the Gateway Arch" is going to look awfully foolish when the airplane turns out to have been a large kite.

The police radio and teletype are for tips, not facts. Broadcast journalists must always confirm information off the police radio, either on the phone or in person, before airing it. And it should be noted that the FCC specifically prohibits rebroadcast of items actually recorded off police, fire, FAA, citizens' band or ham radio broadcasts.

Press Releases

Press releases are the cheapest source of news. They come free; they come in droves; and they are often followed by calls from public relations people who are anxious to assist. In the larger cities, press releases also conveniently arrive on a special public relations teletype.

Yet press releases—**handouts** as they are called—are not one of the more respected news sources. People in the business world don't give away anything without a purpose. In this case the free information and assistance is designed to snare some publicity. It's the rare handout that doesn't place its author, or its author's boss, in a favorable light. Press releases are advertisements as much as information. An example from the North Carolina Department of Crime Control and Public Safety:

```
CONTACT: Linda Blake, Special Assistant
         for Information Services
         Telephone: 919/733-1234

Highway Patrol Geared Up for July 4th

    The State Highway Patrol is preparing for a record
volume of traffic during the long July 4th weekend,
according to Patrol Commander John T. Jenkins. He said
that traffic usually increases on any given weekend, but
with the activities normally associated with July 4th,
the highways this year are expected to be very crowded.
Traffic is expected to be heaviest on Friday night and
the evening of the 4th, Jenkins said.
    The Patrol is not planning any special programs to
cope with the traffic except that every available man
will be on duty. Jenkins said the Patrol is going to
make travel as safe as possible during the holiday by
strictly enforcing all motor vehicle laws. Special
attention will be given to speeding motorists and
drinking drivers.
    According to J. Phil Carlton, Secretary of the
Department of Crime Control and Public Safety, 19
persons lost their lives on the highways during the July
4th weekend last year. ''I am confident the Patrol will
do everything possible to make this a safer holiday and
that motorists will assist the Patrol by obeying all
traffic laws and driving as safely as possible,'' he
said.
```

This handout is not big news, nor is it the place to turn for a balanced appraisal of the performance of the Highway Patrol. But if these public relations people want to maintain any sort of reputation for reliability, the noncontroversial facts can be trusted.

There are four things that can be done with such a press release:

Garbage File This is how self-serving statements from minor politicians on minor issues are handled—they are thrown out. This is also the fate that awaits announcements of award ceremonies that are of little interest outside the lucky person's immediate family, or reports on esoteric or insignificant new programs.

Journalists have to ask themselves whether the information contained in a hand-out deserves time on the air. That judgment hinges in part on the size of the town in which the station is located (see Chapter 19, "Programming"). In large cities, where the volume of handouts tends to drown the usable information in them, the answer is usually "No." At WRKO in Boston News Director Ed Walsh estimates that 90 percent of the press releases the station receives are thrown out. Small-town stations consider releases more carefully.

Certainly there's nothing shocking or urgent about this standard holiday preparation by the Highway Patrol. It would be no crime to ignore it.

Future File Most stations establish a file that will remind them of future events (see Chapter 8, "Gathering News"). Press releases that arrive with announcements of interesting events will be filed under the date the event will occur, so the station can arrange coverage. Most of the press releases WRKO saves will end up in such a file. The Highway Patrol release might be filed for the day after the holiday so that someone can check and see what kind of job the police did and how high the fatality total was this year.

Follow-up Most handouts, if they have any value, are used as tips. Someone will call the number listed on the release and get some additional information—in this case, how many patrolmen will be on duty and how does that number compare with last year when there were so many accidents. Other points of view, if there are any, should also be given a chance. But, unless the performance of the Highway Patrol has become an issue, there's no "other side" to the point of view expressed in this press release.

Follow-up reporting is the only method of transforming a press release into a substantial story.

Short Write-up Sometimes there are a few facts in a handout that may be allowed on the air by themselves. But since press releases are often poorly written and are written for print, the facts must be completely rewritten:

```
The State Highway Patrol says it's going to have every
available person on duty to cope with this weekend's
holiday traffic. Officials are predicting that Friday
```

night will be their busiest. Last year 19 people died in
traffic accidents over the July 4th weekend in North
Carolina.

There's nothing wrong with using handouts as leads to stories, guides to upcoming events or for a few facts. However, they should never just be swallowed whole. Journalists should not have to be accused of a lack of cynicism.

Audio and Video Releases

If your goal is to get a client's point of view onto a broadcast newscast, why just send out a piece of paper? Why not send out some audio (for radio) or some video (for television)? Public relations people catch on pretty fast. Station mailboxes have, consequently, been filling with piles of unrequested audiotapes or videotapes.

Want some tape of Governor Ernest saying something patriotic on July Fourth? No need to send a reporter. Ernest's press people will send it to you. Or you can call this simple toll-free number and take your pick of any of a number of heartfelt, prerecorded statements from the governor.

Having trouble getting some videotape to use in your story on those pollution charges that have been made against Skuzzy Chemical Inc.? Well, Skuzzy's PR people have been kind enough to supply you with their own carefully produced shots of birds and bunnies playing around their innocuous plant.

The best place for these **audio or video handouts** is the garbage file. (See Chapter 11, "Coverage.") The audience will learn little from take seven of the governor's attempt to read through a July Fourth message his speech writer has prepared. And videotape supplied by one side in a dispute can hardly be trusted—those birds and bunnies could easily have been borrowed from Paula's Petting Zoo.

If a station decides there is some compelling reason to use an audio or video handout on the air, its source should be clearly identified to the audience: "Here's a July Fourth tape produced by the governor's public relations people." "This is what Skuzzy Chemical says it looks like around its plant."

Tips

Most newsrooms encourage listeners to call in tips. For every five people who just want the opportunity to talk with a minor celebrity, there may be one with something important to relate. In a competitive business like this, that's worth the inconvenience of taking such calls.

"They're usually not all that useful," suggests Walsh of WRKO. "Still, when somebody calls up, you want to hear what they have to say." Walsh recalls at least one instance when a tip paid off: A small plane had crashed north of Boston; a listener called in with a tip; and WRKO had the story first.

And now that many listeners and viewers are armed with cellular telephones and their own video cameras, the chance that they'll have something—an eyewitness account, some home video (see Chapter 14, "Visuals")—to contribute to a newscast have increased.

However, tips are like amateur press releases, and they must be looked at with at least as much suspicion as a press release. A phone call about a fire or accident can lead to the station getting a jump on the story, but first the report must be checked out with a call to the authorities or with a visit to the scene. Listeners are not trained observers. The "huge smoky fire" can turn out to be an unusually obnoxious factory chimney.

Unsolicited accusations of corruption or other malfeasance must travel an even longer route before they come close to being allowed on the air. They reek with the danger of libel (see Chapter 18, "Ethics and Law"). Such charges should not be ignored, but they must be confirmed independently in their entirety before they can be turned into hot investigative scoops. In other words, the tip is, at best, just the cue to start the investigation.

Newspapers

In the first years of radio journalism, too often there was a striking similarity between the news people read in their papers and the news they heard a short time later on the radio. Early radio stations, in some cases, were guilty of borrowing a little news from their well-stocked print competitors. This made the newspapers understandably annoyed—occasionally annoyed enough to go to court—and it didn't do much for the reputation of radio journalists.

Radio and television journalism has matured to the point where this little crutch is no longer necessary. With help from the wires, networks and their reporters, most stations pride themselves in beating the local print media to the news. Newspapers are so used to be scooped by now that they've pretty much abandoned the "extra" edition and have begun to feature more analysis and less of the breaking news their readers have already heard on radio or television.

Yet, even with this background in mind, it's neither a waste of time nor a sin for a broadcast journalist to read a newspaper. Most newsrooms subscribe to a broad selection of local periodicals and often the major, nationally read publications such as the *New York Times, Washington Post, Wall Street Journal, Time* and *Newsweek.* If nothing else, print media help keep journalists up to date in their field—current events.

"It is imperative that each of us read and watch and listen as closely when we are away from the newsroom as when we are on duty," Alan Walden wrote in a memo distributed to the staff at NBC Radio. "Without information gathered from newspapers and magazines and television, we'd be flying blind much of the time, deprived of some of our most important reference sources."

There is a clear line between stealing from a newspaper and using it as a source of information. If a newspaper develops a story on its own, the broadcast station must give the paper credit for the story:

```
The Daily News reports this morning that some 55-
thousand jobless workers in New Jersey exhausted their
```

unemployment benefits over the past 13 weeks. That's
unprecedented in the history of the state. Most of the
workers reportedly were drawing 90 dollars a week. They
will now have to seek welfare or loans if they cannot
find jobs.

WINS, New York City

Similarly, if the paper gets a good quote on a story, or gets a fact that no one else has, it must be given credit or else the broadcast station is in the position of having stolen that paper's news. Radio and television stations expect the same courtesy on stories they break.

However, newspapers can be used, without credit, as one source to check information—such as the spelling of a victim's name or the number dead. Stories in newspapers also can be used to brief reporters on background information—at WRKO the local papers are clipped and filed, and those files are given to reporters assigned to particular stories. Finally, newspaper stories can be used as leads. The station's reporters can now get in touch with some of those New Jerseyites the *Daily News* says will be losing their benefits and do their own story.

Certainly newspapers are too important an information source for broadcast journalists to ignore.

Research Tools

Term papers aren't being written in a newsroom, but facts are being compiled. These facts are going to have roots and ramifications that need pursuing, and gaps and rough spots that need to be examined. Journalism requires research. The newsroom must be properly equipped.

A good supply of newspapers and periodicals is a start—perhaps with important local articles clipped and filed. Then there are the basic books: a good unabridged dictionary—"What is the exact meaning of 'coup d'état'?"; a concise encyclopedia—"When was the last coup d'état in El Salvador?"; an almanac—"How does the population of El Salvador compare with that of the other countries in Central America?"; an atlas—"How far from the capital is that town they're fighting for?"; who's who books—"What's the background of that American ambassador who was shot?"

Telephone books are free. All current local and regional books should be there—to check names and addresses as well as to find numbers. In addition, many newsrooms purchase "reverse directories"—organized by address, not name. With such a directory a reporter can easily call the people who are along the route of a proposed highway, or who live next door to a house where a murder occurred, for quick comment.

The newsroom needs a detailed local street map for pinpointing locations and directing reporters. It should also have a map that indicates the station's coverage area—the area in which its signal can be heard clearly—to help determine whether a given story is local or not. A batch of road maps of surrounding regions—still free at some gas stations—may come in handy.

A file should also be kept of the station's own news stories for the past couple of years—to use as a research tool should an old issue flare up again. These files of old stories can now usually be kept on computer, where they are easy to search through.

Data Banks

Many newspaper and magazine journalists have gotten into the habit of looking up the subjects they're writing about in computer "data banks," like NEXUS—which maintains an electronic file cabinet full of all the stories that have appeared in a selection of the country's top publications. Type in the words "heavy metal," and you can obtain a list of all the articles that used these two words together this year, last year or back in 1985 . . . then you can call up any of those articles.

Broadcast newsrooms have been slower to subscribe to these services. Broadcast stories, after all, tend to be shorter and require fewer details. And station budgets are often tighter. But as the cost of hooking up to these data banks comes down, there's no reason why they won't find a home in broadcast newsrooms—increasing the supply of information newswriters have to choose from, decreasing their dependence on the wire services.

Writers at KGTV in San Diego, for example, already can search through local newspaper coverage just by pressing a few keys on their computers. Writers at the larger networks can access everything from recent television or radio scripts on a subject to the notes filed by network bureaus in Washington or Tel Aviv.

It also won't be long before newsrooms routinely have encyclopedias and other reference works plugged into their computers. Those metal boxes that now sit on newswriters' desks, in other words, are not only marvelous word processors, they have the capacity to transform themselves into small, easily accessed libraries.

Satellites

A congressional committee in Washington was holding a hearing on the basing of a Navy task force. For most Americans that hearing was of limited interest, but for the citizens of Everett, Washington, it was a major story—Everett was being considered as a possible site for that task force. So, KWYZ in Everett asked its network, NBC, if it would be possible to feed that hearing to the station live so that it could monitor the hearing and pull tape from it for use in the station's newscasts. NBC agreed. "It cost us nothing," then NBC Radio News President Jim Farley said.

Before satellites, networks and audio news services transmitted their materials over land lines rented from the telephone company. As anyone who has ever made a long-distance call knows, telephone company lines are expensive to use. Each network used one line, and the idea of interrupting network programming to send a congressional hearing to a small station in Everett, Washington, would have been absurd. The idea of KWYZ paying for its own line from Washington would have been equally absurd.

With satellites, however, NBC can now transmit four different things at once to its affiliates, probably for less than that one land line used to cost. There's usually a line free for a congressional hearing, if an affiliate wants it. In fact, any number of national events can now be transmitted live to affiliates—candidates' speeches during campaigns, victory and concession speeches when the campaigns end, news conferences, trials, sports events, live reports on breaking stories. The station can monitor these transmissions, if it's interested, and find tape for use in newscasts.

At the major networks there's even a satellite channel reserved for network news people to communicate directly to the newsrooms of their affiliates. Speakers hooked up to this channel are called *squawk boxes*. A newswriter rushing to finish an update on the president's speech might hear a network editor announce—over the squawk box—"The president's motorcade has just left the United Nations."

And some stations, particularly television stations, are beginning to use satellite hook-ups of their own to transmit live reports from their reporters in neighboring cities or neighboring states.

Newsrooms are always hungry for information, and the point is that new technological developments are going a long way toward satisfying that hunger.

Wrap-Up

Most newsrooms get the same basic information from the wires and other standard sources. What distinguishes the top news operations is the job they do with this raw material, and how they supplement it with whatever their own reporters are able to secure.

Practice Assignments

A. Write a 20- to 25-second story based on the following wire copy.

ALPINE, N.J. -- THE 400-FOOT RADIO AND MICROWAVE TOWER IN ALPINE, N.J., FROM WHICH THE FIRST FM RADIO SIGNALS WERE BROADCAST IN 1939 CRASHED TO THE GROUND TODAY IN WHAT POLICE SAY "MAY HAVE BEEN A CASE OF SABOTAGE."

ACCORDING TO SGT. SETH NOAH OF THE ALPINE POLICE, NO ONE WAS HURT AS THE TOWER, NOW USED FOR CABLE TELEVISION, CORPORATE AND GOVERNMENT COMMUNICATION, TUMBLED TO THE GROUND AT 9:11 A.M. IN A WOODED AREA NEAR ROUTE 9W IN ALPINE.

THE TOWER IS OWNED BY LAUREN COMMUNICATION. THREE EMPLOYEES WERE WORKING IN THE VICINITY OF THE TOWER WHEN IT FELL, SGT. NOAH SAID.

"OUR INITIAL INVESTIGATION INDICATES THAT THE SUPPORTS UPON WHICH THE TOWER RESTED MAY HAVE EXPLODED," SGT. NOAH SAID. "THIS MAY HAVE BEEN A CASE OF SABOTAGE." SGT. NOAH SAID THERE WERE NOT YET ANY SUSPECTS IN THE CASE BUT THAT POLICE WERE CONTINUING THEIR INVESTIGATION.

ACCORDING TO ALPINE MAYOR ARIELA FRYMAN, SOME COMMUNITY MEMBERS HAD COMPLAINED THAT RADIATION FROM THE TOWER WAS POSING A HEALTH HAZARD. "BUT I CAN'T IMAGINE ANYONE AROUND HERE DOING ANYTHING LIKE THIS," SHE SAID. "I'M SHOCKED."

THE ALPINE TOWER WAS BUILT IN 1939, AT A COST OF $300,000, BY RADIO PIONEER EDWIN H. ARMSTRONG TO DEMONSTRATE HIS PLAN FOR A NEW REDUCED STATIC BROADCAST SYSTEM -- FREQUENCY MODULATION OR FM. ARMSTRONG'S STATION, W2XMN -- THE WORLD'S FIRST FM RADIO STATION -- FIRST WENT ON THE AIR, BROADCASTING FROM THE TOWER, ON JULY 18, 1939.

THE HUGE RED AND WHITE TOWER HAS LONG BEEN A FAMILIAR SIGHT ON THE PALISADES, NEAR THE HUDSON RIVER, IN NORTHEASTERN NEW JERSEY, SEVEN MILES NORTH OF THE GEORGE WASHINGTON BRIDGE.

SGT. NOAH SAID THE TOWER'S CRASH HAS STOPPED CABLE SERVICE TO ALPINE AND NEARBY CRESSKILL, N.J. OFFICIALS OF LAUREN COMMUNICATION COULD NOT BE REACHED FOR COMMENT, AND NO INFORMATION ON THE AMOUNT OF PROPERTY DAMAGE WAS AVAILABLE.

B. Write a 15- to 20-second story based on the following wire copy.

ATLANTIC CITY -- MISS WESTERN WORLD YESTERDAY ACCUSED PAGEANT PROMOTERS OF CHEATING HER OUT OF MONEY, VACATIONS, A SCREEN TEST IN HOLLYWOOD AND A DIET COLA PROMOTION CONTRACT IN HAWAII.

JANE DAVIES, 23, OF LIVERPOOL, ENGLAND, SAID SHE WILL ATTEND NEXT WEEK'S FINALS IN AUSTIN, TEXAS, TO EITHER COLLECT HER PRIZES OR CLOSE DOWN THE CONTEST.

"I'VE BEEN PATIENT. I'VE WAITED. BUT I'M BEING RIPPED OFF AND I'M TIRED OF IT AND I WANT TO LET OTHER WOMEN KNOW WHAT THEY'RE LETTING THEMSELVES IN FOR."

DICK O'NEILL OF LONG SPRINGS, CAL., THE PAGEANT'S PROMOTER, SAID, "SHE WILL GET EVERYTHING WE PROMISED HER, BUT WE NEVER PROMISED HER SOME OF THE THINGS SHE SAID."

MISS DAVIES SAID SHE PAID $150 TO ENTER THE PAGEANT AND SOLD OVER $200 WORTH OF TICKETS TO THE PAGEANT. SHE

SAID SHE WAS PROMISED $2,000 AS WINNER AND A $15,000
COLA PROMOTION CONTRACT, PLUS ROYALTIES.

SO FAR, SHE SAID, SHE HAS RECEIVED $200, A TIN
TROPHY, TWO SWIMSUITS AND AN IMITATION-EMERALD CROWN.

MISS DAVIES WAS CROWNED ALMOST ONE YEAR AGO IN
MADRID. HER SUCCESSOR AS MISS WESTERN WORLD WILL BE
SELECTED NEXT WEEK IN AUSTIN.

C. Write a 20- to 25-second story based on the following press release from City
Councilwoman Helene Green.

City Councilwoman Helene Green charged today that the
Board of Education overpaid for products by nearly
$500,000 last year because of improper purchasing
practices.

"This is a disgraceful situation -- a blatant flouting
of opportunities, abundant opportunities, to buy at the
lowest possible price," Mrs. Green said.

She cited the purchase of garbage cans from two
sources for prices ranging from $11.42 to $15.43 per
half-dozen, when the same item can be obtained for
$10.02. She also charged that some staples -- such as
paper napkins -- could be bought at local supermarkets
for lower prices than those which the Board of Education
paid.

"My independent audit has shown that a complete lack
of internal controls exists at the Board of Education's
Food Purchasing Department. The question now is whether
these overpayments are due to dishonesty or stupidity."

The Councilwoman, who has represented the Northside
district for over eight years, has urged other Council
members as well as the mayor and the comptroller to
scrutinize her findings and to conduct their own
investigations. She said she will forward her findings to
the District Attorney.

The Board of Education supplies lunch to 23,000 and
breakfast to 15,700 children per day. Last year it spent
more than $7.4 million on meals.

Councilwoman Green's audit began last spring, when a
random voucher check turned up certain irregularities.
The audit was expanded in August, when the Board of
Education reported a $175,000 deficit in its Meals
Program Division.

Councilwoman Green's report states in part: "This
outrageous situation can only shortchange our children
in the end. The Board of Education has tried to cover up

rather than solve the problem. But who will protect the interests of our children, if not the Board?"

In the last year, Mrs. Green has been responsible for the passage by the City Council of the Air Standards Act and the second Consumer Protection Act.

D. Write a 15- to 20-second story for a Macon station based on the following press release from the Stanhide Corporation.

Macon's newest industrial plant, dedicated to the craft of yesterday and the technology of tomorrow, will be unveiled by the Stanhide Corporation at a ceremony on Friday at 12 noon.

Stanhide's new lumber mill is located two miles north of Macon's city limits, just off Route 19.

The public is cordially invited to the dedication ceremonies. A tour of the plant will be conducted. Refreshments will be served. Charles Hopewell, President and Chairman of Stanhide, will deliver the opening remarks. Miss Macon County, Terry Sharp, will also attend the ceremony.

Other special guests will include Macon officials, representatives of the State and County governments, Jack Shell, President of the Chamber of Commerce, and representatives of the U.S. Forest Service and the Agricultural Extension Service.

Stanhide is a major producer of lumber and chemicals. Annual sales for the last fiscal year exceeded $16 million. The company is located in Austin, Texas.

Stanhide's new mill represents a capital investment of over $3.2 million. The new mill will increase utilization of raw materials through the use of newly developed electronic saws and by the use of high-speed sanders instead of planers. The mill is expected to produce over two hundred tons of lumber per month.

The establishment of the Macon mill is part of Stanhide's "Southern Region Development Program." Within the last two years we have opened mills in Savannah, Ga., Mobile, Ala., and Tallahassee, Fla. Stanhide recently closed its Chicago, Ill. plant.

The Macon mill will generate over 6,000 jobs in its first year of operation and 8,000 by the second year.

Gathering News

Reporters at WNEW in New York City got the first hint that something was up from the police radio: "We have a rotor on Madison Avenue." Nine minutes later, WNEW had the story—a helicopter had crashed on top of the Pan Am Building. In those nine minutes the station also got a tape of an eyewitness. That's effective reporting.

It takes a nose for news—or at least ability to sense that when a rotor blade lands on Madison Avenue something is very wrong. Then it takes an aggressive and efficient search for facts, and behind it all, solid preparation.

A WNEW reporter had been doing a story on the opening of the helicopter service a couple of months earlier and, conscientiously, had taken down several phone numbers in the small control tower atop the Pan Am Building. The station's reporters tried those numbers until they were able to get through to someone who had seen the crash.

Broadcast reporters must be fast. At a news event, the only journalists who are more conscious of their watches are those working for the wire services. Newspaper reporters have one deadline, or at the most two or three, a day. Most radio reporters, however, have a deadline every hour, and television reporters—because of the increasing number of television newscasts—are beginning to catch up. KCNC-TV in Denver, for example, now has newscasts at 6 a.m., noon, 4:30 p.m., 5 p.m., 6:30 p.m. and 10 p.m. That keeps its reporters hopping.

However, gathering news for radio or television is more than just a race. Being first means nothing if there are holes in the story or if it's erroneous. The community relies on reporters. Speed gathering the facts must be tempered by responsibility in handling them.

Facts are the quarry of all reporters. This chapter lays out some strategies for stalking them. Chapter 9, "Tape," discusses how news is trapped on tape. Specific types of reporting assignments are outlined in Chapter 11, "Coverage." Responsibilities specific to television reporting are presented in Chapter 15, "Television Reporting."

Preparation

Digging

To have a nose for news a reporter has to be nosey—curious, willing to pry into things. Blake Hooper of WNPT in Alabama notes that some people will drive past a construction site every day without thinking twice about it. But a good reporter, says Hooper, will immediately start wondering what's being built, how much it's costing, who's paying, who's getting the jobs and what this will mean for the local economy and environment. There are stories everywhere. Reporters have to sniff around and smell them out.

Reporting is not easy. A lot of drudgery goes into producing glamorous scoops. Bill Lynch, who now works for CBS, was reading a voluminous report prepared by the controller of the currency on Bert Lance—who was then budget director in the Carter administration. Lynch took the time to read through it all—including the appendix. There he stumbled on the fact that Lance had continued to write overdraft checks *after* becoming budget director. Lynch mentioned that disquieting fact at a news conference held by the president that day, and his diligence produced an additional shocker. As Lynch tells it, the president looked "genuinely startled" for a moment and then confessed that he too had been writing checks for more than his balance.

Stories have to be dug out of reticent people as well as out of dense volumes. People don't always realize that that strange tale they've been telling friends qualifies as news, and when they realize they have a story, they sometimes prefer to keep it quiet. The reporter's job is to share these tales with the community and to ensure that controversial stories are heard. To accomplish this, shyness must be left at home. Reporters don't have to be outgoing. In fact, some journalists are said to have chosen the profession to compensate for a retiring nature, but they must be industrious and aggressive enough to pull a story out of its protagonists.

Assignments

Radio stations rarely have more than a couple of reporters in the field at any one time; television stations perhaps a half dozen. Even when these reporters are assigned specific **beats**—police news or political news, for instance—they still must be prepared to move should a hot story break elsewhere. Some broadcast reporters may have such special assignments but most will also have to be prepared for **general assignment** reporting, prepared to follow the news. That pursuit will sometimes take reporters no further than the telephone, where they might track down a quote from the detective in charge of investigating last night's murder or another candidate's reaction to the governor's statement. But often news is pursued directly to its lairs—the room where the health commissioner is holding the news conference, the scene of the holdup, the street where the parade is.

Just where reporters are sent is determined by a combination of their own news judgment and that of their superiors (with their superiors getting the last word, of course; a newsroom is not a democracy). The raw materials for that determination are news sources such as the wires, tips, police radio, along with the station's future file and schedules produced by the wires.

Preplanned Events
Although it belies the news's reputation for spontaneity, most news events are preplanned. The news media are warned, usually well

Assignment Editor Julius Graw of News 1080 KRLD, Dallas, Texas, works on the station's assignment board. (HBJ photo/ Annette Coolidge)

in advance, that an announcement, demonstration, speech, meeting, news conference, even a police raid, is scheduled. If the station itself is notified, it files the notice under that date in the future file (see Chapter 7, "Sources"). The evening before or that morning someone in the newsroom checks through the file, sees that an announcement is scheduled and, if warranted, arranges for coverage. In big cities the local wire transmits a list of the day's major events. Those listings are called *daybooks.*

At WNEW in New York City, reporter Mike Eisgrau doubles as assignment editor. (Television assignment editors are discussed in Chapter 17, "Television Newscasts.") Each morning, based on the future file and daybook, he makes up a tentative schedule for the station's two other reporters and himself. The three reporters' hours are staggered somewhat to ensure that someone is in the field throughout the business day. At some stations, like KRLD in Dallas, this schedule is written on a large board in the newsroom. At most stations it's typed, as it is at WNEW:

```
REPORTERS' RUNDOWN FOR FRIDAY, JUNE 3
PEGGY STOCKTON:
1. 11 A.M.    --Newark, N.J. -- Ferrara Catering --
              Verona Ave. Newark PBA rank and file meet
              to vote on proposed new contract
              agreement.
```

2. Noon   --also: NJ residents talk about the
               upcoming state primaries for Governor.
               Democratic and Republican primary voting
               is next Tuesday.
               --also: NJ residents talk about effects of
               casino gambling in Atlantic City.

MIKE EISGRAU:
1. 9 A.M.   --Emergency Financial Control Board meets
               to discuss next year's budget for NYC,
               amid warnings over possible extra deficits
               in years to come. 2 World Trade Ctr, 58th
               fl.
2. 10 A.M.   --270 Bway. State Assembly Task Force on
               Crime Victims compensation holds hearings
               on increasing such payments.
3. 11 A.M.   --40 W. 8th St. -- drummer Tracy Burrows
               tries to break world marathon record by
               playing for 21 days.
4. 1 P.M.   --News Closeup -- Bella Abzug.

DAVID FEINBERG:
1. 1:30 P.M.   --Campbell Funeral Chapel, 81st &
                   Mad. -- funeral services for Ben
                   Grauer -- many radio/TV
                   personalities expected to attend.
2. 2:30-3:00 P.M. --Fox Movietone Studio, 54th St. &
                   10th Ave. -- Channel 13 opens its
                   yearly Auction -- to raise funds
                   for public TV.
3. 4:30 P.M.   --Hotel Americana -- United
                   Federation of Teachers opens its
                   Spring conference -- honors Sen.
                   Moynihan -- reaction of union
                   leaders like Shanker to Board of
                   Education losses in next year's
                   budget. . . . -- conference can
                   provide several angles for weekend
                   use.

Preplanned events are too often merely *media events*—staged strictly for publicity—such as the mayor's election-year pornography raid or, at the other extreme, a stripper's ride down Broadway dressed, or undressed, as Lady Godiva to plug her burlesque show. Reporters may have one of these performances on their schedule. Hunger for news sometimes leads the news media to swallow baloney. If the event is really nothing more than an uninteresting advertisement for its sponsors, reporters should finish their Danish, then call the newsroom and ask to move to another assignment. If they're instructed to stay on, reporters should keep in mind this newsroom saying: "There's no such thing as a bad assignment, just a bad reporter." A good reporter should be able to pull a decent story out of almost any assignment.

Preplanned news certainly can't be ignored. Much of it is important, and all of it has the value of predictability—an important factor when trying to plan assignments and organize reporters' movements.

Breaking News Still, reporters are always prepared and anxious to toss out their schedules to track the unexpected event that gives news its reputation as a live wire. The unpredictable communicates with the newsroom through a number of channels. Most breaking events fall within the province of the police, so they'll often break on the police radio. Sometimes a tip will be the source; sometimes those stories arrive labeled "URGENT" on one of the wires. It might be a national bulletin with a local angle: How will the sharp rise in oil prices affect the local economy? Were there any local people on board that plane?

Reporters can uncover the unexpected through calls to regular news sources. Occasionally a reporter will actually be on the scene when it happens. More frequently, the *newsroom* learns of breaking developments first. That's why it's so important for reporters to check in regularly.

Story Origination Most good reporters are also capable of coming up with their own stories, their own assignments. They accomplish that, in part, just by keeping up with the stories they have been covering. "If you're following a bill through the city council, you have to make sure you know when that bill is going to come up for a vote," explains Mitch Lebe, who reports for WCBS in New York City. "You listen for the date or you ask your sources on the council when it will be, and you mark it down in your own schedule." That upcoming vote may not be announced in the daybook or the wires, but good reporters will be there.

In addition, good reporters are always alert for leads to new stories. Sometimes the trick is *localizing* a national story. For example, Pam Burke of WTNH, a television station in Connecticut, noticed an article in *USA Today* pointing out that college radio stations are among the few places on the dial where listeners can hear "new" music. Burke found a college station in Connecticut that played that music, and WTNH had an interesting feature—a local angle on a national story.

Story ideas sometimes move in the other direction, too. It may not be big news if one school district is having trouble hiring science teachers. But if, upon investigation, it turns out that other area school districts are also experiencing this problem, the story grows more important . . . it can be *regionalized.*

The ability to come up with story ideas depends on a reporter's news sense (see Chapter 5, "Leads") and on the breadth of that reporter's experience. That is to say, first you have to know how to recognize a good story; then the more things you see, the more likely you are to spot one. Reporters can "see" more by reading more. Some reporters will pick up publications they don't normally read for the specific purpose of finding story ideas. A glance through a computer magazine, for example, may lead to this intriguing question: How have the new, much more powerful, desktop computers changed the working environment at local businesses? A health magazine this: Have local gourmet restaurants made any significant changes in their recipes in response to reports that Americans eat too much fat? Travel is another way of seeing more. Sometimes all it takes is another route home: Why aren't there any kids using that playground? Or simply a trip to an unfamiliar aisle in the supermarket: Who is buying all this "gourmet" pet food?

There is never any shortage of story ideas floating around. Alert reporters grab them.

Background Information

With or without advance notice, reporters have to try to approach a story with as much of the background information as possible already in their heads, or in their notes. "You have to cover more than one story in a single day," notes Mitch Lebe, "so there's not always the opportunity to do the digging that you would like to do. But it is always important to be knowledgeable, to be well read and, if you know what your assignment is going to be, to do some research beforehand."

On a planned story there's no excuse for failure to do the homework. For a start, that means studying the press release or wire copy that brought the story to the newsroom's attention. With the basic facts already digested, there'll be more time for the news; and without good comprehension of these basic facts, it may not even be possible to locate the news.

An event sponsor's conception of what is news should not always be trusted. That is why preparation for covering an event should, if possible, go beyond the initial press release or wire copy. What other stories on the subject have moved on the wire today?— the newsroom should have them filed. What other stories has the station done on this subject?—those should be available in files. And what have the local papers been writing?—if the station doesn't have a comprehensive file by subject, recent issues should at least be available.

If the press release was a straightforward announcement of the dedication of a new hospital, without a look through the files it may not be apparent that this was the hospital that environmental groups had battled three years ago because it was built on scarce inner-city parkland. Failure to call these groups for their reactions would be a mistake.

Phone calls can be an important element in a reporter's preparation. Calls to the opposition or other affected parties can arm reporters with probing questions.

Encyclopedias may answer such questions as, "What's a breeder reactor?" If there's time, a visit to a library may be called for on a major story. When the USA's Olympic winners were due to arrive in New York for a ticker-tape parade, Lebe, then working for an NBC affiliate, headed over to the NBC library to read through newspaper clippings on their exploits. "I wanted some background on them so that I could have it ready at hand when I had to speak about them," he explains. Lebe has also used a public library on occasion to brief himself. If a news organization has access to data banks, a computer can substitute for the library.

On breaking stories there may be no time for detailed research, but an abbreviated form of that information hunt is still worth the moment or two it requires. Reporters should at least grab whatever is around. The wires may have something on the story; it can be read on the run.

If reporters are given a story while still in the field, or if they have to dash off before looking through the files, background information should be secured by others in the newsroom and communicated by phone at the first opportunity. Preparation pays. It's necessary to be informed before proceeding to become well informed.

Methods

On the Phone

Two pieces of equipment dominate the decor of all newsrooms: telephones and computers. Between them, they sum up the journalist's job—getting and writing the news.

For a communications center, a newsroom can seem an isolated place. Instead of the world passing through, all you get are a few wandering disk jockeys and someone with the coffee. But people who presume to inform the community can't cut themselves off from the community. Some stations delegate some people to go outside and find news, but every journalist is a reporter even if trapped behind a computer. Everyone can at least get information—report—by phone.

Telephones are powerful devices. By dialing numbers, most of which are listed, journalists—if they sound important enough to get by the secretary—can question anyone. The White House phone number is listed, and there are people there whose job is to help the press get facts. Local officials are usually anxious to talk. The telephone is the all-purpose reporting instrument. It fills holes in stories, finds local angles, determines exact spellings, pursues leads.

A story enters the newsroom on a regional wire saying that the state highway commissioner is about to propose a new six-lane highway that will bisect the center of town. Within minutes someone in the newsroom is talking to the commissioner, asking where he got an idea like that. Meanwhile on another line, someone gets the mayor to carry on. Soon city council members, the head of the local Chamber of Commerce and some of the people who live along the prospective right of way have been contacted. It turns out to be a little more difficult to get through to the commissioner's brother. One of the calls has turned up the fact that he owns many acres along the proposed route.

Cleverness helps here. On hearing a report of a fire on the scanner, the obvious call is to the fire department. But to get additional information, how about dialing the police—they put in an appearance at fires—or the water, power and gas companies—they will be at the scene to ensure that their pipes and wires are not going to explode or burn. If there were injuries, the obvious call is to the hospital, but how about the ambulance service—perhaps one of the drivers can come to the phone for a quick eyewitness description of the victims.

A listener tipped KABC's Rick Wallace to the fact that a DC-10 had crashed on takeoff at Los Angeles Airport. The obvious place to confirm this would be the airline. Instead, Wallace called the information office at the airport. He remembered that the office is located in the tower—overlooking the runways. If there was a crash, that office would know about it first.

The telephone is also used to fish for stories. Journalists establish a series of regular **beat calls**—numbers they dial at specific times during the day to keep tabs on developments. Local police and fire departments should be rung up several times a day. Hospitals in the area should be contacted regularly. If there wasn't a reporter at a government meeting, someone who was there should be called to find out what happened.

A list is prepared of these key contacts and their phone numbers—home and office—along with the best time to call. The best time to call a hospital or police station is *before* a shift goes off duty. The new shift won't have a firm fix on what has been happening.

KOEL in Iowa has a card file filled with hundreds of numbers. Reporter Karen Crow arrives in the newsroom at 5:55 a.m. and immediately begins to dial. By the time she has made her way through the file box, she has turned up a robbery in which the robbers wore Halloween masks, a dispute at a school board meeting and an automobile accident. Then it's time to start the next round of calls.

When reporters start getting lazy, the beat calls are the first to go. It's frustrating to call a sheriff three times a day for weeks and turn up nothing more exciting than a lost dog. And it's easy to lose confidence that there are stories waiting in a place so small that when you ask for the police department, someone responds, "I'll get *him*." But without these calls a radio or television station just cannot properly cover an area. Beat calls ensure against missing that armed robbery, serious accident or murder that some official out there knows about.

Sometimes these regular calls pay unexpected dividends. Blake Hooper of WNPT in Alabama had been calling one county sheriff's department for months without learning of anything more serious than a traffic accident. Still, Hooper kept calling. One morning he talked to a radio operator who had just had breakfast with a state trooper, a trooper who was telling an exciting tale about the emergency landing of an airplane at a nearby field. Hooper called the field and had a scoop.

Good reporters keep little black books, or fat Rolodexes, filled with useful phone numbers. WNEW's Mike Eisgrau has collected more than 500 special numbers ranging from Norman Mailer's—in case Eisgrau needs Mailer's reaction to a story— to the number of the phone booth just outside Madison Square Garden—in case something goes wrong inside. Eisgrau says he learned the hard way that his black book must be photocopied—should it be lost, some record will exist. He puts time and effort into his number collection. He gets news out of it.

On the Scene

Of course, the best place to be when covering a news event is at that event. The telephone restricts reporters to one person at a time and one sense—their hearing—at a time. "Most of the time I like to go there in person," Lebe explains. "You're more able to get the flavor of an event when you're there, when you can see and feel what's going on." And while there, a reporter also gets a chance to meet people and make contacts that can be useful on future stories. Developing contacts is much more difficult on the telephone.

Reporters usually arrive by car; though in some clogged cities taxis or even subways are more efficient. The car might be equipped with something fancy like a two-way radio or a portable computer, but it must have something as basic as a good street map. There's no time for getting lost. Travel time is used to think through the story—to anticipate developments and reporting strategies, perhaps even to play with some preliminary ideas for communicating the information. Many journalists will talk the story through in advance. In other words, they try to explain it to themselves.

Park where the car won't get boxed in. It may be necessary to move on in a hurry.

Once there, often the first thing a reporter must establish is not what the story is, but where the telephone is. Big scoops perish rapidly while searching the streets for a functioning pay phone. A direct line of communication to the newsroom is invaluable.

Increasingly, the solution to this problem is for reporters to carry their own portable cellular telephones. These phones broadcast their signals to nearby towers, which then route calls through normal phone lines. The quality is often as good as that of an ordinary telephone. (Portable cellular phones have limited battery life, so reporters must always remain aware of how much time they have left.) Cellular phones, adds Wendy Rieger of WRC-TV in Washington, D.C., also allow reporters to continue reporting stories while driving to them.

If it is going to be necessary to depend on public phones, reporters will often locate more than one . . . just in case someone else decides to make a call. And all journalists carry small change to work the phones, although calls are usually made collect or charged to credit card numbers. Jim Farley, now with ABC, tells the story of the time he forgot to call collect and was live on-the-air when the operator came on and asked for "five cents please for the next five minutes."

Pay phones are not the only alternative. Regular phones—in liquor stores, dry cleaners, pharmacies, lawyers' offices—are easier to work with and in quieter locations. Reporters walk in, introduce themselves and make arrangements to come back and use the phone later.

Next step: Call the newsroom and check in. The people at the station want to know exactly where the reporter is and what the situation looks like there. They may also have additional information relevant to the story. Occasionally the newsroom will order the reporter to pack up and leave for a new and hotter story.

Now it's time to get the news.

At a news event, many good reporters are masters of the art of making small talk, getting friendly. They don't just walk into city hall—they joke with the guard, exchange greetings with the television news crews and ask everybody, "What's up?" This isn't required behavior, but it can be a valuable shortcut to information. The guard can aim the reporter in the direction of the breaking news; the television crews might advise that nothing's happening in there yet—cluing the reporter that there's time to make some calls. Reporters also talk to the people with whom many of them spend most of their time in the field—other reporters.

Major news events in larger towns attract representatives of several different media. When they are not competing for scoops, these reporters tend to get along and even help each other. They talk out their thoughts on a story and sometimes share information. But when the union leader announces the strike vote and starts walking through the lobby, they push to the front of the pack and then race each other to the phones. Friendly competition.

In competitive situations, the good story usually goes to the aggressive. The reporter who is too gentle to push to the front, too timid to approach the mayor, too polite to impose on the victims will not be a reporter for long.

News events can be tame affairs with prepared statements—transcript provided—and publicity-hungry newsmakers willing to answer everybody's questions in turn. But news events can also be madhouse scenes of police, spectators, ambulances, crazies, sometimes blood. These are the times when a reporter has to function like a quarterback after the snap. Quick thinking: "Where's the telephone? What's the story? Who's going to tell it to me?" Then quick, decisive action: ducking around police lines, press card waving in the air; quick dash for the person in charge; not finding any witnesses to interview, yelling out, "Okay, who was here when it happened?"

Radio reporters have to get tape and file reports from the scene of news events—skills to be discussed in Chapter 9, "Tape." Television reporters need videotape (see Chapter 15, "Television Reporting"). When those jobs are done, and before leaving, all reporters should always check back with the newsroom to make sure the folks back there have gotten what they wanted from this story and to clarify plans for the next story.

Questioning

Once reporters have been set on the trail of some news, the trick is to find the story—better yet, to find a bunch of stories. Stories may be conspicuous—sitting there in the first controversial words of the statement—or stories may be hiding in the questions that aren't being asked or behind an optimistic smile.

Many reporters had the news that someone had tried to wiretap Democratic headquarters at the Watergate, but for a while only two reporters went out and got the story. They got the story by digging, using the same tools a reporter might use on a good police story: industriousness, aggressiveness and much, much questioning.

Reporting is the search for answers, and they're usually uncovered by intensive questioning. To do it well, reporters need the right questions. Questions should always be to the point.

UNACCEPTABLE
So I hear you, and some of your friends over here, were
around when he started to shoot. I might be interested,
I mean I'd really like to know, what your thoughts, at
that time during the shooting, were and, while I got you
here, what, considering the time element, you thought
really occurred?

Reporters must stick to the subject—one subject at a time.

ACCEPTABLE
What happened?

Later:

ACCEPTABLE
How did you react?

And phrasing can be all-important. Politicians sometimes find it entertaining to answer questions such as, "But I asked you about the *payment*, didn't I?" with the word, "Yes." A question that sounds ignorant sometimes may be dismissed with a joke; sometimes it simply inspires the newsmaker to treat the reporter less seriously. Questions should reflect the reporter's intelligence and understanding.

UNACCEPTABLE
When are you gonna start work on that new hospital?
Where is it? Over on Fourth Street?

ACCEPTABLE
When will work begin on the new hospital at the corner
of Fifth Street and Lydecker?

The right question sometimes requires research. It may take a whole afternoon pouring through zoning records to come up with the question, "How were you able to build that office building *there*?"

If there's time, it's wise to write the questions out beforehand. Even if the reporter doesn't refer to them, the act of writing questions down can help focus thoughts; and written questions are a hedge against forgetting under pressure.

With all this in mind, it's still important to remember that the job of a question is to get information, not to prove how much a reporter knows. It is better for a reporter to ask and sound uninformed in an interview than not to ask and sound uninformed on the air.

Choosing questions is an exercise in news judgment. The right questions aim for newsworthy answers. They don't ask the mayor if he believes his new plan will be good for the town. Of course the mayor will say "Yes." They ask how he plans to pay for the plan.

Frequently the news is not what the newsmaker says, or thinks, it is. The governor may speak as if the news is an attack on the state legislature, but the real story might be her concessions to the state liquor lobby.

Sometimes questions cause discomfort—that's usually a sign that they're newsworthy. Reporters have to be firm—and press on. When the person a reporter is interrogating starts coughing, frowning and looking at her watch, the reporter must have the courage to continue until the story is out.

Tough and unfriendly questions have a way of drying up a source of information. That's a risk reporters have to be willing to take, but there's a strategy for minimizing the risk: Save the tough questions for last. "Isn't your ownership of the sewer company a conflict of interest?" as the first question is going to make it difficult to get that person to fill in the background details. Instead start with, "When will the sewer replacement project get started?" Set the trap. The pointed questions should come when there's nothing left to lose by alienating the newsmaker. Rick Wallace of KABC in Los Angeles calls this "mending the fence before breaking it."

At times reporters are faced with the imposing task of getting people to say something that they don't intend to say. This requires not only all the common sense, news sense and firmness a reporter can muster; it may also require an element of stealth.

Dick Petrik of KOEL in Iowa gets a tip that a car has hit a pole on a nearby highway. Petrik calls up the local police. "What crash?" The person on duty says he knows nothing about it. Next try—the nearest hospital. Petrik doesn't know the name of the person in the car. He doesn't know the nature of the injuries. He doesn't know if police are charging that the person was drunk. This is called "fishing."

The hospital doesn't have to respond to a completely unfocused request for information, but Petrik tries an old reporter's trick: "I want to make sure I have the name spelled right on that person whose car hit a pole last night," he says, hopefully. It works. The receptionist spells out the name, and he's got it. Petrik asks for the first name, then gets the nature of the injuries and is ready to confront the local police with hard facts. He's got the story.

Overused or used inappropriately, such tactics can easily become obnoxious and counterproductive. But there are times when reporters' questions should get bold, and even cunning.

Once the angle has appeared, the questions must be aimed at getting the facts. Here radio and television reporters have a slight advantage: They don't need the minor details that fill up newspaper columns. There will be no room in their report for detailed background—everybody's exact address or the names of the police and fire personnel at the scene. A broadcast reporter needs enough of the background information to understand the story, then just the facts—plus a little spice if it's there to be gotten.

The basic, necessary facts are, not coincidentally, the same who, what, when, where and why that it takes to write the story. The questioning can't stop until all those questions have been dealt with. The spice—the nugget that makes the story special—can be harder to locate. This may require attention to some of those seemingly insignificant details.

A group of reporters in New Jersey interrogated police after the discovery of a dismembered body the week before Christmas. All the reporters left with the basic facts, but one asked an extra question and got a grim extra detail: "How was the body wrapped?" The answer: "In Christmas boxes." One extra question . . . a better story.

The final question: "Is there anything else I should know about this?" There may be something else. Sometimes the source will supply it.

Preparing a Beat

All reporters have areas for which they are responsible. Since most radio and television reporters are on general assignment, the area could be as large as the City of New York or as small as Oelwein, Iowa, and surrounding towns, or it could be the police department in Oakland, California.

When assigned to an area, reporters have to plan on some intense getting acquainted. They will want to read through back issues of local newspapers to familiarize themselves with the major ongoing issues. It won't do to be one of the only people in town not to know that *Democratic* Mayor Hazel Bloom has a reputation as the most conservative politician in the state.

New reporters will want to sit down with well-informed citizens for informal briefing sessions (tape recorder turned off) on local issues: How did Bloom end up in the Democratic Party? When was she first elected? Who runs her campaigns? Where did she make her money? Have there been any moves to unseat her within the party? and so on.

Reporters preparing a beat will also want to find out where the relevant public records can be found. If they're covering the courts those records would include, for example, the *calendar* of scheduled cases, *transcripts* of hearings and trials, *indictments* (formal charges by a grand jury) or *depositions* (sworn statements by witnesses). When covering politics, reporters would want to know, for example, where to find *ordinances* (the laws on the books in a town), *zoning regulations* (rules on what can be built where), *property tax records* and the *minutes of governmental bodies* (see Chapter 11, "Coverage"). The logical place to start such searches would be with the court clerk or the city clerk—part of their jobs is minding the files.

Of course, most stories will be about people, not papers. A reporter starting out in an area must get to know the characters most likely to be performing in upcoming stories. Who wields power in the town? Who leads the different political factions? Who are the major business leaders? The major labor leaders? Who is active in citizens' groups? Who is in charge of transit? Of the schools? Of housing? Who heads the police and fire departments? Names and titles will start pouring out of those newspaper clippings and those discussions with the well-informed. Then it's time to get to know the people behind the names and titles.

Contacts

Some things don't get mentioned in press releases or announced at press conferences. Some news—the arrest on drunk driving charges of a college's football coach, the vandalism problem at a high school—is supposed to be kept secret; some just isn't supposed to be discussed too loudly. It is impossible for reporters to do their jobs, to go beyond the official pronouncements, without hearing some of what they're not *supposed* to hear. They need **contacts**, **sources**, people who are willing to blab.

Contacts also help reporters get to stories faster. If a congressman's car smashes into a guard rail on the interstate, a friendly police officer might decide to give a reporter a call. If the zoning board suddenly decides to allow industrial development in the wealthiest neighborhood in town, a councilwoman might pick up the phone and suggest that a reporter come on down.

Why do news sources talk with reporters? Some do it because they like and respect that journalist; others because they get a thrill from being part of the "glamorous" world of broadcast news; others talk to reporters to gain personal publicity, to grind axes, push programs, test plans, attack enemies, or sometimes even to keep the public informed. This is often a symbiotic relationship. Reporters cultivate some newsmakers as contacts to stay on top of the news, and some of these contacts are cultivating reporters to gain access to air time. But the crucial point is that reporters need people who are occasionally willing to fill them in.

When CBS's Bill Lynch, then covering the White House, heard an official statement on economic policy, he might have gotten in touch with an assistant secretary of the treasury, a White House domestic policy adviser, a staffer on a congressional committee responsible for economic policy and perhaps labor or Chamber of Commerce leaders. It was important for Lynch to have people who were willing to expand and explain.

News travels through people, so reporters benefit from establishing a personal relationship with as many people as possible. "I always make a special effort to seek people out at a story and introduce myself," says Mitch Lebe. "So, the next time when I call them up, it's, 'Oh yeah, Mitch . . . How you doing? What can I do for you?' I also try, particularly on telephone interviews, to get to know the secretaries, to get their names and jot them down in my book. Then, the next time I call I can say, 'Hi, Pam' or 'Hi, Frank.' It helps get you through to their bosses."

Contacts can be found by hanging around with newsmakers, acting friendly, asking questions and listening. Reporters have been known to buy a politician a glass of lemonade, or whatever they drink, to establish a friendship. Phone numbers are exchanged, and the next time the reporter has a complex story to puzzle out, this new friend might get a call. When the politician hears of a story, he might call this reporter first.

The danger here is cronyism. A certain quid pro quo aspect to a reporter-source relationship is inevitable. Reporters might get their friend's name on the air once in a while as a way of saying thanks for the scoop, but when the demands of friendship start interfering with news judgment, the relationship becomes an ethical problem. Reporters can't allow their affection for newsmakers, or their desire not to lose them as sources, to put them in the position of hiding news. Police are important sources for reporters. A reporter who is not on good terms with the police may have to struggle to keep up with stories. Still, if a reporter catches the police roughing up a suspect, that's news, and it must be aired, whatever the repercussions.

There is, for example, a limit to Mitch Lebe's friendliness: "I don't believe in becoming pals with news sources. I think you can become too close."

A reporter without contacts is handicapped; but so is a reporter who gets too close to newsmakers.

Ground Rules

Newsmakers sometimes give reporters information ahead of the time they want to release it. They expect that reporters will *embargo*—hold—the information until the agreed-on release time. Information is often sent over the wires with such provisions. Any reporter who violates such an agreement risks losing sources and risks the wrath of other journalists. It just isn't done.

There are other ground rules by which newsmakers and reporters are supposed to play. Everything a newsmaker says to a reporter *can* be used in a story unless the newsmaker indicates in advance that it is confidential. There are a number of phrases a newsmaker can use, in advance, to limit how reporters will make use of their comments:

Background When a newsmaker says information will be *on background* or *not for attribution*, reporters may use what that person says, but they can't attribute it directly to that person. So, on the air they might say, "According to a source close to the governor. . . ." Henry Kissinger, while secretary of state, was a master of the background briefing. He was referred to in stories by titles such as "a high State Department source."

Deep Background If this is invoked, reporters can still use the information, but they can't attribute it to the source in any way. If they air the information, they must do it on their own authority. Woodward and Bernstein's "Deep Throat" was a contact who gave all his information on *deep background*.

Off the Record This is the most sweeping. It binds reporters to a pledge not to use whatever the source says in a story—unless someone else says it on the record. In other words, the information is just for the reporter's benefit. Some reporters won't accept information on these terms; however, most believe it's better than nothing. "I've had many people tell me things *off the record*," explains Mitch Lebe. "I would never use their information, but it gives me an idea of where to look on my own. It's led me to new angles on stories."

■ ■ ■

There are times when background or deep background are invaluable reporting tools. How else could an employee of the school board be convinced to reveal what he knows about the kickback allegations? In recent years, however, some news organizations have grown suspicious of newsmakers who seem too quick to place information on background or deep background. Public officials, particularly in Washington, appear sometimes to be using these ground rules as camouflage as they attempt to manipulate public opinion. Sometimes it seems that only the public is being fooled. Everyone else—from other officials to other nations—has a pretty good idea of who is saying what. There have been efforts to persuade Washington officials to stay *on the record* more frequently, and some reporters have walked out of large White House briefings when administration officials suddenly choose to hide behind titles such as "an administration official."

Nevertheless, once the ground rules for an interview have been established, if reporters choose to stick around, they must abide by those rules.

Wrap-Up

Good reporters, no matter what medium they are working in, have some things in common. They're aggressive; they're curious; they're thorough; they're informed; and they know whom to talk to.

Practice Assignments

You're in the newsroom and . . .

1. The mayor announces a 25 percent cut in the police force. List the people you would call and the questions you would ask.
2. A report from the police radio comes in, saying the town's largest bank has just been held up . . . for the second time in a month. List the people you would call about the robbery and the questions you would ask.

3. The local university has just received a 100-thousand dollar grant from an unknown philanthropist to establish an affirmative action/minorities recruitment program. List the people you would call and the questions you would ask.

4. The mayor declares July National Brotherhood Month. Local civil rights organizations issue a joint statement opposing the mayor, charging that such symbolic gestures obscure the real problems of the town's minority groups. List the people you would call and the questions you would ask.

5. In Washington the Senate has voted down a proposal to allocate more gasoline to urban areas and less to farmers. List the people you would call and the questions you would ask.

9

Tape

All reporters carry a pencil and pad. Radio reporters also carry a cassette tape recorder. (Some even take it when they are off duty—if something comes up, they are prepared.) On that tape recorder reporters can capture the sounds of events for listeners—the voice of the survivors, an interview right after the verdict, the sound of the guns or their own descriptions of the rubble. Besides getting information, radio reporters' primary responsibility is feeding that tape recorder. (Television reporters work with more equipment, discussed in Chapter 15, "Television Reporting.")

Types of Tape

Short sections of tape are played in a newscast as part of the presentation of some stories. They are called *cuts.* With rare exceptions, the sounds that dominate these cuts are of people talking. Newsrooms divide the possible combinations of voices that may be heard on a cut into four categories—*actualities, Q and As, voicers* and *wraps*—distinguished from each other by who is doing the talking.

Actualities

Rioting in Matamoros, Mexico; an ABC reporter tapes interviews with a fire chief from a nearby town in Texas and an English-speaking intern at the hospital where the injured are being taken. Then the reporter selects the best quotes from these interviews and puts them on separate tapes. Soon they are ready to be used in stories on the rioting. The first cut gives the fire chief's reaction upon arriving at what he thought was a fire:

```
When we got to the scene of the fire, then I saw that it
was more than a fire . . . it was a riot.
```

202

The next cut gives the chief's more detailed description of the rioters:

> Some of them were still in the furniture store, and they
> were putting cars together on the street and blocking it
> off and setting them on fire.

Finally, the intern's recap of events:

> They started out with violence . . . started some fires
> in front of the mayor's office, and trying to blow up a
> car and things like that. The local police answered with
> guns. Then they went to the jail and tried to get out
> some of the people who were there. And everybody with
> guns and knives, and we had about 22, 23 hurt.

Newsmakers or eyewitnesses are talking in these tapes. Often their language is not grammatically correct, nor is it always perfectly clear, but their statements convey the excitement of being there and participating. These tapes are called **actualities** because they consist only of the *actual* voices of newsmakers.

Actualities are the most basic kind of tape. Radio news is at its best when they are used since they give listeners a chance to hear voices—their tone, inflection, pacing and emotion. Mere quotes in a newspaper can never bring the people who are making or witnessing the news this close.

How long should an actuality be? That decision is based on the length of the newscast, the significance of the story and the importance of the taped quote. Actualities must be long enough, however, to establish that someone is speaking—one lonely phrase floating in the middle of the story would likely confuse listeners. Few actualities are shorter than 5 or 10 seconds, but the newscaster doesn't want to surrender the air for too long to another voice either. Long actualities break the flow of a newscast and may become boring. A statement must be electrifying to warrant more than 30 seconds. Most actualities run between 10 and 25 seconds.

Of course these are guidelines, not rules. One station obtained the tape of the pilot's radio conversations just before a major air crash. That tape made a gripping actuality—5 minutes long.

Incidentally, some politicians have learned to phrase their comments in neat 20-second packages that are perfect for use on the air. These experts in media probably get more air time than those who speak in convoluted, rambling sentences that are difficult to edit into 10- or 25-second actualities.

What sort of comment does a reporter look for in an actuality? Something the newsmaker can say better than the reporter:

Eyewitness Reports Reporters can state the facts, but unless they were present, they cannot describe what it was like to watch the event develop. Eyewitnesses should be given a chance to do that on tape. However, it would be a waste of time to have an eyewitness discuss background details such as where Matamoros, Mexico, is. Reporters or newscasters can do that.

Here's an actuality in which an eyewitness, one of the first rescue workers to arrive, describes the scene of a flood in Brady's Bend, Pennsylvania:

```
We had a state of extreme flooding . . . vehicles were
strewn over the area. . . . It put your mind to somebody
using a giant bowling ball and knocking cars and trucks
around like there was no tomorrow. We had water on the
highway in several places as high as four feet deep.
Really and truly it was unbelievable.
```
NBC

Expert Knowledge Reporters can explain the extent of the damage, for example, but they're not trained in matters such as what causes fires. They'll let a fire department official speculate in that on tape.

A local official explains the cause of that flood in Brady's Bend:

```
You had in the neighborhood of about five to five and a
half inches of rain in about 30 minutes. Due to the
amount of rain we've had this year, the ground is
saturated with water . . . everything was runoff. You
just got too much, too quick.
```
NBC

Subjective Comments Reporters can cover the details of a plan. But the proponents of the plan can do a better job of explaining why they believe in it. Newsmakers' feelings and beliefs make effective tape. For example, here's a representative of the National Women's Health Network speaking at a Food and Drug Administration advisory panel hearing on a new form of birth control—a female condom called Reality:

```
We ask the panel to recommend approval of Reality now.
Reality appears to be as effective as the other barrier
methods currently in use.
```

■   ■   ■

Reporters don't write the words in an actuality. They are not responsible for the grammatical errors in what the newsmaker is saying, but reporters are responsible for ensuring that the actuality adds something to the story. The actuality must be clear and limited in scope—rarely more than one or two ideas per cut. It must make sense and be newsworthy.

This comment on the less appealing characteristics of the participants in the Buck and Nanny Goat Race in Jasper, Minnesota, is hardly of earth-shaking import, but it is newsworthy because the event is unusual and, in its way, interesting. The organizer of the race is speaking:

```
I'd say the most offensive is the odor of the goats.
They stink pretty bad, and some of them are pretty mean-
tempered . . . and they'll chew on just about anything.
```
NBC

Reporters are also responsible for seeing to it that actualities are factual. In stories that are still developing, it is often wise to avoid actualities that include changeable facts—such as the number dead. The actuality would have to be thrown out if the death toll were to rise.

Also, no tape should ever be used unless it is audible. Anything that reporters have difficulty in understanding, listeners probably would find completely unintelligible after it has passed through the transmitter, the atmosphere and their radios. But while all tape must be clear, the quality that is demanded depends on the importance of the comment and the situation in which it was recorded.

Actualities are recorded in two types of situations: The first is an interview in which reporters have **control** over the dialogue, can comfortably position their microphones and can steer the conversation into potentially useful areas. The second is an **uncontrolled** situation such as a speech, comment made over a bullhorn at a demonstration or an argument between two newsmakers. Here the tape recorder is merely eavesdropping, and reporters are at the mercy of events. In uncontrolled situations, a little more leeway might be given for poor quality tape. In controlled interviews, there's no excuse for lapses in quality.

Q and As

The meeting of the Policemen's Benevolent Association delegates is finished. They've decided to postpone a decision on the city's new contract offer for a week. Mike Eisgrau of WNEW in New York City files this tape of the head of the PBA explaining, with Eisgrau himself asking questions:

```
PBA President:   Well actually, we recessed the meeting
                 on the issue of this offer that was
                 made by the city to have the delegate
                 body go back to their membership, poll
                 their membership for their feelings. We
                 want the membership to have input into
                 whatever we're doing. We want them to
                 have a say.
```

Eisgrau:	One week from now you come back here?
PBA President:	One week from now we will come back.
Eisgrau:	And what are you going to do then?
PBA President:	At that time, whatever the delegate body dictates, that's what we're going to do.
Eisgrau:	If they find out from the rank and file that the rank and file is not happy with this proposal, are we talking about the next step -- a job action of some kind?
PBA President:	If the delegates so state, that's what we will do.

In a *Q and A,* the question makes it onto the tape along with the answer. Some stations are pleased to have their reporters' voices on tape—it shows that their people were there. But most stations feel that a reporter's voice is not particularly exciting. Reporters are on the air frequently and are not newsworthy in and of themselves. From this perspective, an actuality is preferable to a Q and A. Q and As have another drawback: mixing two voices—the reporter asking the questions and the person giving the answers on one tape—may confuse listeners. Listeners may not be sure where the answer ends and the question begins.

For these reasons, many news directors insist that reporters use a Q and A instead of an actuality only when there is justification for it. Here are the possible justifications:

Can't Edit A reporter in the field cannot edit tape. So if there's a good cut with an unnecessary question in the middle of it, the reporter has two choices: throw out the actuality or use it with the superfluous question. Mike Eisgrau's question, "One week from now you come back here?" wasn't necessary, but he was not in a position to edit it out, and the material around it was worth using.

Important Question A question can be newsworthy. The PBA president was not going to mention a possible job action, but that's what was on listeners' minds. Eisgrau's question gets it onto tape: ". . . are we talking about the next step—a job action of some kind?" The very discussion of a job action by police is newsworthy.

Sometimes a question is needed to understand an answer. The PBA president's statement, "If the delegates so state, that's what we'll do," doesn't make any sense without the question it follows. That statement is newsworthy; the question has to be included to support it. (Another solution is to leave out the question on the tape and let the newscaster's lead-in to the story set up the answer. See Chapter 10, "Writing to Tape.")

Sometimes newsmakers refuse to comment; occasionally this nonresponse is news in itself. But "No comment" alone doesn't make for a very informative actuality. Again, the reporter's questions must add the substance missing from the answer. A smart reporter turns "No comment" into a usable Q and A by putting solid information into the questions.

Although the PBA delegates, who were filing out of the meeting, had been instructed not to talk with reporters, Eisgrau chased them anyway to get this Q and A:

> Eisgrau: What about the one-man patrol cars?
>
> Policeman: No comment.
>
> Eisgrau: What was your reaction to the deferral of the six percent wage increase?
>
> 2nd Policman: No comment.

The story is in the questions. Actually, Eisgrau never filed this last Q and A. The PBA president's revealing answers made a better cut than various delegates saying, "No comment," no matter how informative the questions they were ducking.

Explaining Newsmakers are liable to slip into jargon or talk about issues that the public does not understand. When the words get dense, reporters must often interrupt with a question that clarifies and, thus, saves the tape.

> PBA President: The new schedule would have 16 six to two's.
>
> Eisgrau: Six p-m to two a-m shifts?
>
> PBA President: Right. . . .

■ ■ ■

These are the situations where the questions rightly claim a place on the tape. Reporters should not include their own questions just because they were proud of their phrasing or impressed with their tone of voice. Eisgrau also got this exchange on tape:

> Eisgrau: And what about the one-man patrol cars?

> PBA President: Well, the one-man patrol cars, we still
>   don't like it, and they want to imple-
>   ment that. What they stated was they
>   would put it in on a trial basis, but
>   it's still a bad pill to swallow.

Here Eisgrau simply began the tape after the question and used this as a straight actuality.

Since Q and As have more than one person talking, they can hold interest longer than an actuality—up to 40 seconds without pressing it.

Voicers

Rick Wallace of KABC in Los Angeles is driving toward the airport where a DC-10 has just crashed on takeoff. There's a huge traffic jam on the outskirts of the field. Wallace triple parks and climbs on top of his car to look over the fence that surrounds the airport. He can see the plane lying on its side; so he starts his tape recorder and begins describing the scene. He's recording a *voicer.*

The Russian president has just finished a meeting with the American president at Camp David. ABC's Ann Compton listens to the official statements and press briefings, and talks to some administration officials, then she phones in a report on the meeting. Compton is also doing a voicer.

Voicers are reporters' monologues. They do not contain anything as special as a newsmaker's voice, but they provide an alternative when there is no newsmaker to interview. Fire department officials sometimes prefer to wait until they've put out the fire before explaining themselves to reporters, and survivors may be in no shape for an interview. But it is always possible to arrange an interview with yourself.

Voicers also supplement actualities and Q and As. A reporter can walk to the back of an auditorium and record some background on the press conference; a White House reporter can summarize the decision-making process behind the president's proposal; a reporter can describe the scene of the disaster. From the scene of that disaster the reporter might also be expected to send back a few actualities.

A voicer is a kind of broadcast story. Unlike actualities or Q and As, the reporter is totally responsible for the words on tape. Voicers generally run from 20 to 50 seconds. NBC and some of the other networks ask that they come in at about 35 seconds.

When all a reporter has to do is describe the scene, it may be possible to produce a voicer extemporaneously. Nevertheless, most voicers are written out in advance. Not too far in advance, however—there isn't time for that—and not under the best circumstances—no computers, dictionaries or neat stacks of papers are available at most disasters. Most voicers are written on small pads while leaning against the hood of a car, a fence or a folding chair. Still, voicers must meet all the standards of good broadcast writing, plus some more.

Voicers have to justify themselves. They must answer a basic question: Why are we listening to a report from the field? Is the reporter saying anything that could not be said by the newscaster? The answer should be that the reporter is providing us with an element that only a trained observer on the scene can present. The writing, therefore, must emphasize that special element.

There are two types of voicers—*ROSRs* and **reports**. Both take advantage of the reporter's proximity to the action:

ROSRs **ROSR** (pronounced "rozer"), along with a half dozen other radio news acronyms, is a name invented by the people at ABC News. It stands for *Radio On Scene Report*; the key words are the middle two: "on scene." The reporter is *there*, and what that reporter can provide that the newscaster cannot is the feeling of what it's like to be *there*.

At the Palace of Versailles in France after a bomb exploded:

```
Standing in the garden of the palace I can see on
the first floor a line of tall French windows, about
12 or 13 feet high. A whole line of them has been
smashed in. . . . In one of them the mouldings have
been blown out, and stacked up against the bottom of
it are piles of wood, either bits or pieces of the
window or of the wooden shade. Everywhere you look,
furniture, decorated with gold, heavy wallpaper, ripped,
torn, blown apart. -- Jack Smith, ABC
```

A newscaster in the studio can give the facts on the bombing. Only a reporter on the scene can provide this vivid description.

ROSRs are the most personal form of radio news. The first person, which is excluded from other copy, is welcomed here:

```
I'm sitting on the front lawn of a house. What remains
of a single-story house is across the street from me
. . . there's nothing there but burned-out timbers. The
house next door is gone, the house is down the street is
gone, the house on the corner -- just a small portion of
it is left standing. Directly across the street from me
-- about 50 feet away -- appears to be the fuselage and
one of the engines of the plane. There is a car across
the street from me totally demolished and burnt up.
                                    WINS, New York City
```

This is radio news at its most evocative. Peter Flannery, former president of ABC Radio News, says he likes to see ROSRs call into play as many of the senses as possible—the smell of the smoke, the feel of standing in the snowdrifts. "After hearing a good ROSR," Flannery says, "a listener should open the paper the next morning and say, 'I heard that picture on the radio yesterday.'"

Clearly, however, the degree of evocation must suit the story.

UNACCEPTABLE
```
The car's fenders are distorted, jagged metal jutting
out. Clouds of steam billow up from the radiator. On the
street a lonely hubcap, jarred loose in the accident.
Another car has wrapped itself around a utility pole.
This time on Interstate 80. The driver, Art Smothers,
was not hurt. . . .
```

ACCEPTABLE
```
A car hit a utility pole here on Interstate 80, and
while the driver, Art Smothers, was not hurt, his car's
taken quite a beating. The front end is bashed in and
steam is pouring out of the radiator. . . .
```

And trite subjectivity should not be allowed to sneak in with the first person, as in this phrase used on the air in a ROSR about a terrorist attack:

```
A senseless act of terrorism . . .
```

Reporters can perceive for listeners in ROSRs, but they should still let the listeners draw the conclusions.

ROSRs are rare. They can only be used when a situation's sights, sounds, smells and feelings are newsworthy: the scenes at crashes, fires and floods, for example; or historic meetings, important trials and colorful events. At run-of-the-mill news events the sight is usually of people in business attire talking to each other or perhaps a police officer giving out information; the sound is of voices questioning and quipping; the smell is of doughnuts, coffee and smoke. These less picturesque events get a different kind of voicer.

Reports   Being on the scene gives reporters another advantage over writers in the newsroom: Not only can they describe events but also they are in a position to develop a sophisticated understanding of their meaning. Reporters with the news-makers are in a position to question, observe and analyze:

```
This Saturday summit will go down in history as the
moment that Moscow and Washington declared: they are
friends. Boris Yeltsin said, after his half-day visit to
Camp David, Russia no longer considers the U-S a
potential adversary. President Bush called it ''the real
end of the cold war and the dawn of a new era.'' In
private meetings the two presidents discussed drastic
nuclear cuts. But no formal agreement can be expected
until at least a Washington summit early this summer.
```

Both men say their countries need to retain some nuclear
capability to restrain what Yeltsin called ''adventurers
and terrorists in the world.'' -- Ann Compton, ABC News,
Camp David

Reports are voicers that tell the story with the understanding of one who was
there. They are used much more frequently than ROSRs because any story complex
enough to deserve explanation can support a report. Reports are filed from serious
fires, court hearings, candidates' headquarters, picket lines and ribbon cuttings. At
the scene of a crash, a reporter may file a few ROSRs and a report.

Reports do not resort to the intimate description used in ROSRs. But reporters
are *there* and it doesn't hurt to remind listeners of that fact with at least a "here":

The feeling among Arab observers <u>here</u> in Cairo is that
the Saudis have lost a round.

> John Cooley, ABC

To emphasize the reporter's presence at an event, it may also help to include some
first-person references, as in a ROSR:

A museum curator here told <u>me</u> that some statues inside
have been blasted into a thousand pieces.

> Bill Dowell, ABC

Of course, this too can be overdone.

UNACCEPTABLE
Yes, your reporter was right there on the spot as a
museum curator looked me in the eye and said, ''Some
statues have been blasted into a thousand pieces.''

Often reports offer analysis or perspective, occasionally even some well-founded
interpretation:

Energy and inflation problems are deemed so overwhelming
that no solution to them is seriously expected to emerge
from the 24-hour get-together. What is at stake is the
very existence of the organization.

> Peter Kalischer, CBS

Reports can also discuss the feelings of newsmakers—if the reporter has information
to back up the discussion:

Auto executives feel a general economic recovery will
lift the industry out of its most prolonged slump in
sales since the Great Depression.

> Bill Curnow, CBS

However, reports are not excuses to let guesswork into the news, and they are not editorials. They must remain objective. This report on one of the networks, about a conference in Libya directed against Egyptian peace moves, fails the test of objectivity:

> Libya's supreme ruler, Muammar el-Quadafi, complete with
> swagger stick, is the host for this conference . . . and
> he can be expected to indulge his penchant for flaming
> rhetoric, even though it may be doubted this meeting
> will produce anything else. . . . With the exceptions of
> the Syrians, all these leaders here have at least one
> thing in common: In every Arab war with Israel, they
> have contributed almost nothing but strident speeches.
> They are, as the saying goes out here, ready to fight to
> the last Egyptian. . . . There is almost a holiday mood
> here, until you remember that these people are shouting
> not for peace and understanding, but for hatred and
> revenge. . . .

This is not analysis; it is undisguised abhorrence.

■   ■   ■

When filing either kind of voicer, it is wise to leave out changeable facts. In an ongoing news event, the number of casualties or the cost of the damage may change within hours or minutes. Stating those numbers in a voicer may make that voicer obsolete in those hours or minutes. It's better to leave such facts to the writer responsible for the lead-in to the voicer (see Chapter 10 "Writing to Tape"). The voicer is frozen on tape, but the lead-in can be changed at any time to update facts.

In general, also leave out the time element in a voicer. If a reporter filing a story at 10 p.m. says, "The city council *tonight* decided . . . ," that tape is useless after midnight. It is also important to leave something to be said in the lead-in. Every taped report must be introduced in the newscast; that introduction should include some facts. A voicer that says everything of significance almost is "lead-in proof." Often it's best to leave the basic introduction to the situation for the lead-in and begin the voicer as if the scene has already been set. This voicer talks about "the crash," leaving the lead-in a chance to explain what crash:

> Aviation experts from Canada and the United States are
> trying to pinpoint the cause of the crash, American
> officials joining in the search because the Air Canada
> jet and its engines were built in the United States.
> Investigators are looking at two possible causes --
> engine failure and a tire blowout. Whichever, they do
> agree that the pilot's action in maneuvering his
> aircraft away from landing lights may have averted an
> even greater tragedy. -- James Walker, ABC News, Toronto

Voicers often start with the word *the—the* fire, *the* meeting, *the* arrest—to allow the lead-in to introduce the subject:

```
The general said in a statement issued today that his
troops vacated the town of Mapai yesterday
afternoon. . . .
```
CBS

The lead-in can now introduce *the* general.

Even with these special requirements to satisfy in writing voicers, reporters most often go wrong by violating one of the most basic newswriting rules—clarity. Perhaps *being there* makes it harder to remember that listeners are not there and may know nothing about the story. This voicer, which was used on the air, would make complete sense only to an expert on the issues. It concerns a plan for a county to buy control of its electric supply from the present electric company, Consolidated Edison.

```
Con Ed Chairman Charles Luce has a lot of disagreements
with the report received by the Westchester County
Legislature on the possible takeover of the utility by
the county, but basically he says the bottom line is the
rate structure and how much it would cost the people of
Westchester to take over the utility. The basic
difference he says is that, in Con Ed's computation, it
would actually wind up costing Westchester County more
money for electricity after the takeover than it does
now. The issue is how much the Con Ed assets are worth in
Westchester County and the difference is in the range of
hundreds of millions of dollars.
```

This violates basic rules. It contains abstract terms—"rate structure"—unexplained issues—"Con Ed assets"—and it doesn't slow down long enough to make points clear. That this voicer was probably scribbled on a note pad outside the room where Luce spoke, just before the reporter dashed to the telephone, is no excuse. In fact, the difficult situations under which most voicers are written should make reporters more inclined to write simply and clearly. This is the last place to hazard a complex wording.

Voicers, like other broadcast stories, can't afford to make more than a couple of points. However profound the analysis, the writing must be direct:

```
Con Ed Chairman Charles Luce disagrees with a report
received today by the Westchester County Legislature
. . . a report which suggests that the county might save
money by taking over Con Ed's operations. ''Not so,''
says Luce. According to his calculations, a county
takeover would actually increase electric rates. The
difference between Con Ed's arithmetic and the report's
```

```
arithmetic seems to hinge on the price the county would
have to pay to buy Con Ed's assets in Westchester. Luce
believes buying those assets would cost the county
hundreds of millions of dollars more than projected in
the report. Those hundreds of millions of dollars, Luce
says, would have to be paid by consumers . . . in higher
electric rates.
```

Most voicers end with an *ID*—identification of the reporter and the station:

```
-- Greg Adams, WERC News.
-- I'm Duane Gray, 12-10 News.
```

Some news organizations ask the reporter to add the location to the ID. This seems more impressive on networks when the locales mentioned stretch around the world, not just across town:

```
-- Bill Redeker, ABC News, Tokyo.
-- David Dow, CBS News, Quito, Ecuador.
```

One or two stations have fiddled with this standard close, which is now so much of a cliché that Kermit the Frog uses it on Sesame Street. WNEW in New York City, for instance, has tried having reporters identify themselves and their locations at the beginning of a voicer:

```
This is Mike Eisgrau at City Hall . . .
```

When they have finished sending in their voicers, reporters are asked at some news organizations to answer a few questions on the event from someone in the newsroom—with tape rolling. The idea is to get some additional, often shorter and more conversational, cuts. Just to confuse matters, these voicer-like cuts are sometimes also called "Q and As."

Wraps

Wraps are hybrids—part voicer, part actuality. First the reporter tells the story; then a newsmaker makes a comment; then the reporter returns to conclude:

```
Reporter:   Arrest orders have now been issued for
            striking Dayton, Ohio, school teachers --
            many of whom today defied a county judge's
            order to quit picketing and return to the
            classroom. Teachers have rejected a six
            point five percent wage increase here, and
```

> while many say they are troubled by the threat of jail or a fine, most agree with teacher Bob Bruggeman that now striking employees have very little choice but to defy the court order.

Newsmaker: I have had my share of dedication that everybody calls for . . . and sacrifice that everybody calls for, and they've left me no other avenue, so here I am.

Reporter: The judge who issued the back-to-work order says he expects arrests will start this afternoon, and each teacher arrested could get up to ten days in jail. -- Bob Faw, CBS News, Dayton, Ohio

To produce a wrap, the reporter selects an actuality, or in some cases a Q and A, and then writes a voicer that fills out the story. The voicer is *wrapped* around the actuality. The challenge is writing a report that does its part in telling the story, while smoothly introducing and setting up the actuality. This requires the same writing skills as writing copy to go with an actuality in the newsroom. The first part of the wrap (the "lead-in"; see Chapter 10, "Writing to Tape") must answer any questions that may be raised by the actuality and tell listeners whose voice they'll be hearing in the actuality. After the actuality plays, the reporter has to wrap up the story (the "write-out"; also see Chapter 10).

The only difference between writing a wrap and writing to an actuality in the newsroom is that wraps, like voicers, should take advantage of the reporter's proximity to the action.

Wraps are the most sophisticated type of tape a reporter can send back. Essentially they are self-contained stories.

Guidelines on the length of wraps? Generally they run between 30 and 60 seconds. They are the longest of the four types of tapes because they are the most varied.

Techniques

Interviewing

The previous chapter discussed how to get *information* by questioning. Working with tape gives reporters an added responsibility when interrogating newsmakers: They have to get newsmakers to say what they have to say on tape.

Reporter Eric Eskola of WCCO Radio, Minneapolis, conducting an interview. (WCCO)

Newspaper reporters need only the facts. Radio reporters need a cogent 20-second version of the facts, spoken while their tape recorders are on and no airplane or loud truck is rude enough to roar by. There are no guidelines for warding off trucks and airplanes, but there are ways to encourage newsmakers to supply good actualities:

Preparation The frantic pace of breaking events necessarily limits preparation time, but any extra moments—on the way to the scene, during a lull, during a boring speech—should be snatched for this purpose.

Reporters should arrive at an interview as familiar as possible with the interviewee and the issues surrounding the interviewee. That takes reading—clips, newspaper articles, press releases—and talking—with contacts, opponents, even other reporters.

Reporters should begin an interview with a clear idea of what they want to ask. As noted in Chapter 8, "Gathering News," writing questions out in advance helps to order thoughts, even if the reporter is never able to refer to the written questions. At least reporters should take a few moments to think through the line of questioning.

Short Essay Questions If reporters ask: "Isn't it true that you oppose the construction of those new apartments downtown because they'll break up the community there?" they can expect the following response: "Yes." And one word makes a poor actuality.

Reporters want "short essay" responses to their questions, so they shouldn't ask true/false, yes/no or multiple-choice questions. Questions should be phrased so that newsmakers do the talking, not reporters: "What's your reaction to the plan to build those new apartments downtown?" "What do you think they'll mean for the community?" This way the newsmaker has to do some explaining.

UNACCEPTABLE
I hear that this was the worst accident ever on this
stretch of highway and that both cars were on fire when
you arrived. Right?

ACCEPTABLE
What did you see when you arrived? Has there ever been
an accident this bad on this stretch of highway?

The job demands that reporters get impressive answers, not that they ask impressive questions.

Reporters' questions may be open and general if all they need is a basic rundown of the situation: "Why are you demonstrating?" More often time and tape are tight, so reporters rely on specific questions that get to the heart of the matter: "What will you do if the school board doesn't change the policy?"

Repeating What if a candidate delivers a broadside while a reporter is still in transit or before the tape recorder is ready? Or while the television camera people are yelling for room? Simply ask the candidate to say it again. A reporter might say, "I didn't catch that, would you mind repeating it?" Or, "Could you please explain that again?"

Most newsmakers are understanding. Usually they have as much desire to get their statement on tape as the reporter does. Reporters cannot be afraid to repeat a question or ask a newsmaker to repeat a statement for the second, third or fourth time. One advantage of repeating questions is that the newsmaker often perfects the answer—which makes for a tighter actuality.

Guiding Before most reporters interview someone, they have a good idea of what they need from that person, what they want that person to say. They want survivors to say it was horrible; they want demonstrators to state their complaints. Without putting words in people's mouths, reporters' questions should lead newsmakers in the direction of usable tape.

Interviews are rarely fishing expeditions. They are designed to obtain specific pieces of the story. They should be tightly controlled. Newsmakers must be guided through the interview—given a chance to repeat and clarify confused answers and reminded to keep their statements concise. The quality of the answers can be a serious problem. Some newsmakers, especially amateurs, are too wordy and unclear. A reporter's question to an eyewitness might elicit an answer like this:

I was standing here when I saw this plane, you know,
flying real low. I, ah, stand here a lot, you know. You
see I work at night, at that Exxon station. So, you
know, I ah, like to come here and watch the planes. So
anyways, I was here, where I am a lot, and this plane

with fire coming out of an engine, you know, I don't see
that too much you can bet, this plane is flying real low,
you know. I almost jumped out of my pants. But I saw the
whole crash. Anything more you want me to tell you 'bout
it?

It's perfectly appropriate, and sometimes imperative, that reporters suggest to persons being interviewed that their comments will be more effective if they keep them short and to the point. Frequently it is necessary to interrupt a filibuster to bring the interview back on course:

Sir, could you simply describe what you saw the plane
do?

Interviewing, like many other interpersonal activities, requires firmness and friendliness, in various combinations. "There are two schools of reporting," says Mitch Lebe who reports for WCBS in New York. "In one, you beat them over the head [figuratively speaking, of course] into telling you something. In the other, you ask nicely. Asking nicely has worked much better for me." It is likely that someone treated with compassion will be more forthcoming than someone who feels stepped on. At times a little hand-holding may even be needed to calm microphone fright. "You might make a joke to settle someone down if they're nervous," explains Richard Threlkeld of CBS News. But reporters can't waste much time or tape on friendly chitchat. Getting good tape fast—that's the goal.

Clarifying Reporters are the listeners' representatives. They must remain conscious of their responsibility to raise any questions the listeners might have. Answers full of jargon or obscurities are useless as actualities. Reporters have to be ready to interrupt for the definitions and explanations that listeners need:

Wait a second. What zoning laws are you talking about?

Without this law could they build the shopping center?

What would this shopping center mean for the community?

Conducting an interview with a tape recorder is like writing a story. The end product must be just as lucid. The interviewer has to steer the interviewee into statements that are understandable enough to be used on the air. That may mean asking questions that both of them can easily answer. Again, there's more going on here than information gathering.

Listening When the tape is rolling and a harried newsmaker is staring at that microphone, the pressure is on the reporter. Fortunately, we are born with multitrack minds. Reporters must be thinking up questions, guiding the interview and clarifying statements . . . all at once. They also have to listen.

There is a danger that reporters become so sure of what the newsmaker is going to say that they forget to listen to what that person is saying. Once in a while a bombshell explodes in the middle of the standard answers: "No, I'm not worried what the voters will think. In fact, I've just decided not to seek reelection." More frequently, a remark is made that at least requires a follow-up question.

Reporters also listen to determine if they've got "it"—that tight, substantive statement that makes a solid actuality. When WCAU's reporter got this on tape from a woman whose apartment house in Atlantic City was going to be turned into a gambling casino, it was clear that this was the actuality:

```
I lived here now for over nine years and this is my home.
We've sold a business, and we've retired. My husband is
over 70, and at this time in our lives it's not fair to
uproot us and make us move.
```

When they've got "it," reporters should make mental, or written, notes of what has been said, so they can find it quickly on tape. Then, if they only need one good actuality from that person, reporters can bring the interview to a close. If they haven't gotten the statement they need, reporters must be plotting their route to it.

Microphones In the field you'll usually have an **omni-directional microphone,** which picks up sound from all directions at once. But there are also **uni-directional microphones** that pick up sound from one direction and "**shotgun microphones**" that are especially good at isolating a particular sound source from a distance (like the president speaking to reporters from a golf cart or under the blades of a helicopter). **Lavalieres**—tiny microphones that will clip onto a shirt or blouse—are often used in television. Television reporters also sometimes use **wireless microphones.**

Omni-directional mikes, the most common, work best when they are four or five inches from the speaker's mouth, not when they're a polite distance away or a few bodies back in a crowd. Radio and television reporters armed with these mikes have to get to the front of the pack and can't be shy about sticking their microphone into a newsmaker's face.

At organized news conferences, all reporters set up their recorders at the front of the room, so that the speaker talks directly into their mikes. At times it's possible to plug the recorders directly into the room's PA system.

Microphones are sensitive enough to pick up all sorts of sounds. The hand that holds the mike mustn't fidget; papers shouldn't be rustled on a desk that supports a mike. And a microphone picks up the "yeahs" and "uh-huhs" that we use to assure people that we are listening. These sounds may be effective tools in interpersonal communication, but "yeah . . . uh-huh" sounds awfully funny in the background on an actuality. Reporters can nod their heads to demonstrate the requisite interest; some won't even nod—believing it to be a form of editorializing on what they are hearing.

Tape and Batteries Interviews are too valuable to risk losing. Since weak batteries in the cassette recorder can threaten an interview, check and change or charge them regularly. A faulty tape cassette can also ruin an interview. Cassettes should not be overused and should be checked to see that they are wound tightly and not ripped. Always carry spare cassettes.

Under the pressure of a breaking event, reporters have been known to start recording one interview over the end of another—wiping out some material. Again, check.

Reporters record the name of the person being interviewed at the beginning and again at the end of the interview; that way, if they forget who is talking when filing, the answer is never too far away.

Phoners

Phoners are telephone interviews. They used to be called *beepers* because of the beep every 15 seconds that the FCC required to warn people they were being recorded. The beep no longer is necessary, but the first thing to learn about telephone interviews is that a warning *is* necessary. The FCC still requires that people be told in advance that their comments on the phone may be used on the air. The only exceptions are the station's reporters—they don't need to be warned—and people who call telephone call-in shows, who should know what they're getting into.

The governor is asking for a city tax cut; the mayor says it isn't feasible yet. Reporter Bob Parlante of WHDH in Boston calls the president of the City Council for his opinion. The City Council president is apparently in the mood to be controversial. Parlante tells him that he is being taped, starts recording and selects this phoner from that tape:

```
I think the mayor would like to hold onto a bit of a
surplus that we might generate this year and sit on it
for a while, and lower the tax rate next year when he
runs for reelection.
```

This phoner, of course, has another name. It's also an actuality. A phoner can also be a Q and A that is recorded on the telephone.

There is no simpler way to get sound for the newscast. Instead of hustling from event to event, reporters can let their fingers do the walking and get comments from newsmakers all over the area. There is no substitute for being on the scene to report on events. There's no excuse, however, for failing to take advantage of the telephone's ability to get speedy actualities and Q and As when a reporter is confined to the newsroom.

Here is an example of telephone reporting: An NBC staffer, in a *tape operations room* off to the side of the newsroom in New York, was given the assignment of getting some actualities on a tornado that had touched down in the

At KGW, Portland, Oregon, a reporter records a phoner. (Frankie Jenkins/ KGW Radio 62)

evening near St. Paul, Minnesota. First call: to police in the area. Busy signal. Second call: to a local fire department. (These numbers were all from an information operator.) Busy signal. A dozen or so calls to the same or other police and firehouse numbers followed in quick succession. Busy, busy, busy. . . . Then a call to a local hospital. It's ringing. "Hello, can I have the emergency room?

"Hi, I'm with NBC Radio News. Is there anybody there who saw the tornado and is in a position to come to the phone?" There was—an employee of a local department store—and he told, on tape, a dramatic tale of how he had to run through the store trying to get customers down on the ground when store officials heard the tornado was about to hit. That store employee, being treated for minor injuries at the hospital, also described how at the last minute he ran out after a young child he had spotted walking just outside the store, how he grabbed the child, pulled him in and threw himself on top of the child as the tornado hit. The child was unhurt. The store employee was cut on the arm by flying glass. NBC had four powerful phoners, and calls to a gas station, 7-Eleven store and a Denny's restaurant in the area (reporters always keep in mind what places will be open if they call at night) produced more eyewitness reports on the tornado.

Natural Sound

A reporter was sent down to a railroad station to get commuter reaction to a change in service. With his actualities recorded, the reporter dashed back to the newsroom to record a voicer. But his news director sent him dashing right back out again to the railroad station—that voicer had to have the sound of trains and commuters in the background. Former NBC Radio News President Jim Farley, for another example, still recalls with frustration the time an NBC reporter covering the Indianapolis 500 auto race recorded all his pieces in a hotel room. Farley responded with an angry memo.

Natural sound does for radio news what pictures do for newspapers. NBC reporters covering battles over the landing of the supersonic Concorde jet were specifically instructed to raise their microphones to the sky to record the sound of the landings. One WNEW reporter traveled across the Brooklyn Bridge to find a supermarket in which to record a voicer on the closing of a supermarket chain. He wanted the sound of cash registers in the background.

War reports benefit from the sound of shooting in the background—although bullets whistling may be going a bit too far. A farm story could use a couple of moos, clucks or baaas. A piece on the garment center should have some hustle and bustle in the background. One NBC reporter recorded a voicer on the death of a foreign leader with the sound of church bells behind him.

Of course, the natural sound should not be so loud or intrusive as to obscure the reporter's words, and it always must be clear what that noise is. If the natural sound is people yelling, the story must explain who is yelling and why.

The neatest way to handle natural sound is to record it alone on some tape; then bring it back to the newsroom to edit into the story. This way it can be kept at just the right volume and faded in and out if necessary. WNEW's Mike Eisgrau recorded the sound of the rifles at a local gun club, then mixed that sound into a report on gun control. He started the shots at full volume, then faded them to a *bed*—quiet enough to read over.

With the latest generation of cassette recorders these effects can now be produced from the field. Some reporters carry a small, extra cassette recorder with which they record natural sound. Then they plug this second recorder into an extra audio imput on their main cassette recorder to play the natural sound under their report. A rougher version of this effect can also be produced when a cut is first recorded. Reporters aim their microphones at the sound they want . . . to establish it. Then they turn away from the sound and bring the mike closer than usual to their mouth to keep the sound unobtrusive in the background while they talk. At the end of the report they might aim their mike at the sound again to reestablish it for a second or two.

If it's available, natural sound is compulsory in ROSRs. For example, an NBC reporter describing bomb destruction on Manhattan's Park Avenue opened his voicer by aiming his mike at a man with a broom sweeping up the broken glass. Reporters must describe the look, smell or feel of events in ROSRs. The sound, at least, they can allow the listeners to experience directly.

One day, reporters were handed an assignment that presented an opportunity to get some natural sound without leaving the newsroom—the death of the inventor of the teletype.

Filing

Different stations look for different mixes of tape from their reporters. Many expect their reporters to send back at least one voicer or wrap from each news event to "establish their presence" at the event. In addition, these reporters try to get a few usable actualities or Q and As. Other stations are primarily interested in the actualities. Large metropolitan stations often are more wrap-oriented, while small stations and the networks stick to shorter voicers and actualities.

If there's no hurry, reporters can carry all the tape back to the newsroom to edit. But there usually is a hurry. An hourly newscast is always approaching, and the station will want to include something timely on that story in that newscast. Reporters have to *file*—send in their story from the field—as soon as possible.

Tim Lennox of WERC in Birmingham, Alabama, once covered a story that had to be handled in quite a hurry. That day the National Weather Service wire had been warning of possible severe thunderstorms—par for the course in that area at that time of year. Suddenly the station heard a report of unusually high winds causing destruction in a suburb. Lennox was already in a station car driving to the scene when the newsroom informed him over his two-way radio that the weather wire was calling those high winds "a tornado."

Arriving in the area, Lennox tackled his first job: to find out exactly where the tornado had struck. His method: Ask everybody he saw on the street until he was directed to the destruction. He knew when he was there—13 houses had been virtually leveled. Lennox described what he saw in three ROSRs, filed by dictating them directly into the two-way radio in his car. (Most stations now use cellular phones in cars.) Normally they would have been recorded in the newsroom and put on tape cartridges—*carts*—for use in the next newscasts. This time those voicers went on the air live.

As rescue workers and relatives dug through the rubble searching for bodies, Lennox began looking for tape. First target: someone with the facts. Lennox asked a fireman, who directed him to the fire chief, who directed him to a civil defense official. Lennox recorded a brief interview with him on his cassette recorder. (The Marantz PMD 200 is now widely used as a remote recorder in radio news.) Then the mayor arrived and Lennox got his comments on tape; time to file again.

The tape could have been sent to the newsroom by plugging his cassette recorder into the two-way radio, but transmitting the tape over the air tends to reduce the quality of the sound. As a rule, telephones—cellular or the old–fashioned wired kind—carry sound with less distortion, so Lennox needed a phone. While the tornado had tossed about houses on one side of the street, it had ignored those on the other side. He walked up to one of those houses—where residents were still in shock over the death of neighbors and friends. Although he felt insensitive, Lennox did what he had to do . . . as gently as possible. He got permission to use the telephone, and he also got an interview with one of the women in the house—an eye-witness: "All of a sudden there was this big explosion. . . ." Having secured access to a phone, the process of filing the story began. There were eleven main steps:

Select Quickly, Lennox had to choose cuts from his tape of the interviews. He moved back and forth on the tape, searching for usable sections, and chose this Q and A with the mayor:

Mayor: I think we've got it under control at the moment. However, they're still looking for several more missing persons. They've found four bodies and there are two that they can't account for at this time. I believe Birmingham fire and police have it under control at the moment.

Lennox: The four, were they children? I had an unconfirmed report . . .

Mayor: There was a mother and two children over here . . . about two doors down. I haven't gotten a report on who the other person is. There are two children missing and they have found another person off by the side of the hill. Apparently about eight houses on this side of the road were simply picked up and blown off the hill . . . down into a ravine and there's water at the bottom. There could be bodies down in the water.

Note The cassette recorder has a counter, so the exact place where a cut ends or begins can be noted. In his note pad Lennox jotted down these numbers along with the first few words of the cut—the *in-cue:* "I think we've got . . ."—and the last few words—the *out-cue:* ". . . in the water." Looking at his watch, he noted the length of each cut, which he also scribbled in the pad.

Cue Up Pushing the rewind button, Lennox returned to the place on the tape where his first cut began, as indicated by the numbers on the counter. That cut was then **cued up.**

Call In   The next problem? Getting through to the newsroom. The storm had knocked down some phone lines, and those that remained were in demand; but Lennox was able to get a dial tone and place his call. After warning the reporter in the newsroom who took the call that he had three cuts ready to go, Lennox said, "Stand by."

Hook Up   He then proceeded to dismantle part of the telephone. First, he unscrewed the round plastic mouthpiece of the receiver (some reporters carry a wrench for this, but usually it can be done by hand) and removed the round microphone from under the mouthpiece. (Other reporters have taken to carrying modular telephone headsets to get around those fancy telephones you can't unscrew.) The inexpensive microphone inside telephones is what gives phone conversations their tinny sound. Reporters substitute their 100-dollar microphones for the telephone company's.

Removing the mouthpiece and the microphone from the receiver exposes two metal strips. Lennox took out a wire with a small plug on one end which he placed in the "monitor" output of his recorder. The other end of the wire had two clips with jagged teeth. He attached these **alligator clips** to the two metal strips.

Portable cellular telephones have made telephone dissections like the one Lennox performed less common. The increasing number of radio reporters who carry one can usually plug their tape recorders right into a jack on the portable telephone unit. Lennox was still operating the old-fashioned way, but it worked just fine. By plugging his microphone into the recorder and pushing the red "record" button, he was able to talk through the microphone into the telephone.

Fill In   Back in touch with the reporter in the newsroom, Lennox provided a quick run-down on the first cut—that Q and A with the mayor. The newsroom would use this information to write a lead-in for the tape (see Chapter 10, "Writing to Tape"). Then Lennox passed on the needed details: the in- and out-cues and the length of this Q and A.

Countdown   The reporter in the newsroom flipped a switch so the phone line Lennox was on was **patched in**—connected—to a reel-to-reel tape recorder. Lennox played a couple of seconds of his first cut to allow the newsroom to **take a level**—adjust the volume on the reel-to-reel. Then he re-cued the Q and A; the reporter in the newsroom started recording on the reel-to-reel; and Lennox said, "Five, four, three, two, one. . . ." This countdown would be used later to help re-record the cut onto a tape cartridge.

Play   At "zero," Lennox pushed the forward button on his cassette recorder. The Q and A played through the phone and was recorded in the newsroom.

Stop Through the telephone receiver's earpiece, Lennox monitored the tape as it played. Listening for the out-cue, and double-checking by glancing at the counter, he figured out when to press the "stop" button. Next, using the counter, Lennox cued up the actuality of the civil defense official, summarized it, read off the cues and time, counted down and played it. Then he cued up the eyewitness actuality.

A Voicer With the "record" button depressed, Lennox was then able to read a ROSR through his mike over the phone wires and into the reel-to-reel recorder. He counted down and started reading at "zero":

```
The damage, it's just hard to believe. As the mayor
said, there were houses that were completely ripped up
from their foundations and thrown off this hill and
thrown into a valley. What's making it worse -- if
anything could make this situation worse -- the rain has
continued here. The rain is pouring. It's pouring on
rescue workers and the survivors. There are people in
the house across the street, and one of the residents of
the house -- one of the houses where the children are
missing -- was there. She was uncontrollably crying
. . . hoping that the children will turn up safe. -- Tim
Lennox, WERC News, in Smithfield
```

Confirm Before saying "goodbye," Lennox checked with the reporter in the newsroom to make sure he had gotten all the cuts on the reel-to-reel.

In the newsroom, Lennox's three cuts were *dubbed*—re-recorded—onto carts; then they were walked into the studio and used on the air (see Chapter 20, "Careers").

If Lennox had recorded a wrap, he would have sent it the same way. While the newsroom recorded, he would have read his introduction into the microphone with the "record" button down, hit the "forward" button to play the actuality then "record" again to read the conclusion. Or the pieces of the wrap could have been sent separately with separate countdowns and edited together in the newsroom. But there was no time for any of this.

Tim Lennox spent the remainder of the afternoon and evening in the pouring rain, getting new tape and filing it. Twenty-three bodies were eventually found in the rubble, WERC's coverage of the tornado won a state Associated Press award.

Stories are not usually filed under such trying circumstances, but the same basic procedures are used.

Editing

In the field, editing tape means selecting from a tape. All a reporter can do is select whole sections of that tape to file. But if that tape is carried back to the newsroom or gathered by phone from the newsroom, it can be *cut and spliced*—rearranged in the form that turns it into the most effective cuts.

Bob Parlante of WHDH in Boston conducted a telephone interview with the president of the State Police Association, Fred Guerrero:

Reporter: Listen Fred, I know what you're going to be talking about tonight. Why don't you run it down very briefly for us. Okay? We're rolling.

Guerrero: The meeting tonight will be to inform the membership of the current status of negotiations between the state police and the governor's Office of Employee Relations. At this meeting tonight, will be all members of the State Police Association, the Association numbering approximately 900, and at this particular time, uh . . . at this particular time the members will be voting on options that they would like to take in light of the latest delay by the fact finder, Mr. Howard of Michigan, in rendering a fact finder's report in the current state police negotiations hiatus.

Reporter: And those options are what, Fred, quickly?

Guerrero: Quickly, well the options will be anything that the membership mandates from waiting, continuing to wait -- we've been waiting five years now -- up to and including a full-scale strike.

Parlante edited the two underlined sections together into one actuality for use on WHDH.

With the tape on a reel-to-reel tape recorder (tape recorded on a cassette machine has to be dubbed to reel-to-reel before it can be edited), Parlante found the places where he wanted to make cuts—between "negotiations hiatus" and "And those options," for example. He marked the exact spot on the tape itself with a grease pencil, then pulled the tape away from the machine and placed it on an *editing block*—a piece of metal designed to hold the tape firmly in place.

Using a razor blade he cut the tape—separating the section he wanted to use from the answer after it. Then he made a similar cut between "Quickly, well . . ." and ". . . the options will" and threw out the section of tape with his question and Guerrero's "Quickly, well." Parlente placed the tape that ended with "negotiation

hiatus'' on the editing block next to ''the options will'' and connected them—
spliced them together with a piece of adhesive tape. They now could be played
back as if they were one smooth statement.

Using this method, coughs or deep breaths can be cut out of the tape, ''uh-
huhs'' or ''you knows'' excised and, more significantly, dull sections removed from
the middle of an actuality—***internal editing***, that's called—or a couple of related
answers merged into one actuality.

It should be noted that electronic editing devices, now used in television reporting to edit videotape (see Chapter 15, ''Television Reporting''), are beginning to be
heard from in radio news. They promise to speed up the process of editing cuts by,
among other things, removing the necessity of actually cutting the tape.

Editing guidelines:

1. Edit out: anything on the tape that is not relevant, newsworthy or understand-
    able. Meaningless pauses longer than three seconds and reporters' questions that
    add nothing should be cut. Cut sections that are of poor technical quality or are
    marred by extraneous noises. Leave out facts that can be told more clearly by
    the newscaster or a section where a newsmaker stammers annoyingly.

    If there is sufficient time to edit this tape, only the underlined sections will
    be used:

    > You know <u>this is the first time, that</u> we, I mean . . . I
    > mean not we but the, <u>the school board has voted to,</u> you
    > know, voted to, <u>negotiate with a union.</u>

2. Leave in: substantive or revealing comments, particularly (as outlined earlier in
    this chapter) expert knowledge, eyewitness reports and subjective comments.
    Leave in reporters' questions if they are important or needed. Leave in mean-
    ingful pauses or sighs:

    > Yes . . . . . . I guess you guys are right . . . . . .
    > I'm finished.

A wily tape editor can easily reverse the meaning of a talk by cutting and flipping
the words and phrases. A simple splice and the State Police Association is ready
to strike:

> The members will be voting on *[splice]* a full-scale
> strike.

Clever, but it couldn't be more unfair and unacceptable. Reporters have an ethical
responsibility to ensure that their editing *never changes the meaning of a quote*. Editing
cannot be allowed to make a statement stronger or weaker, or to change its connotations. A statement by a police chief:

```
If the mayor gives the order, we're going to go in there
and get those hostages out. If the mayor gives the
order, my men are all in position . . . their guns are
loaded . . . we're ready as we can be.
```

The opening clause *cannot* be edited out of the first half of this actuality.

```
If the mayor gives the order, we're going to go in there
and get those hostages out.
```

But the second qualifying statement—"If the mayor gives the order"—can be edited out of the second section without distorting its meaning:

```
My men are all in position . . . their guns are loaded
. . . we're ready as we can be.
```

Editing must preserve the integrity of a statement.

Sometimes two pieces of tape sound choppy when spliced together. The tone or volume of the speaker's voice may differ in the two sections. This can often be corrected if a second of *air*—tape with background noise, but no talking—is left in or added between the two sections.

One other consideration: Voices get lower at the end of a thought. A cut that ends with a rising inflection sounds awkward and may momentarily confuse listeners. When editing, try to end the cut with the inflection falling.

Carts

Tape cartridges—*carts*—are the final version of a cut, ready to be used in a newscast. These rectangular plastic containers, filled with a continuous loop of tape, are designed, when used properly, to cue up automatically to the start of a cut. All the newscaster or engineer has to do is push a button, and the cart immediately starts playing at the beginning of the cut. If more than one cut is recorded on a cart, the second cut is cued up immediately after the first has stopped playing.

Cuts are usually dubbed onto carts from reel-to-reel tapes after they have been edited or directly after a feed from a reporter in the field has been recorded. If a station has a few cart machines, each cart has one cut on it. If the station has a limited number of playback machines in the studio, it may be necessary to place a few cuts on a cart so they can all be used in one newscast.

After they're recorded, carts must be labeled. Stations usually paste a removable label directly on each cart which lists the slug, the name of the person or persons speaking on it, the out-cue and how long it runs. Many stations supplement this label with sheets that include a description of the contents of each cart. A newswriter can use these sheets when writing lead-ins to the cuts, although most still want to listen to the cart before they begin writing.

Radio News
Tape Information

NBC
News

Name and title
  Lt. Robert Slater, Sugarcreek fire dept

Location
  Brady's Bend, PA

Taken by
  ms esr

Time and date taken
  4a   8/16

Quality
Good [☒]   Fair [ ]   Marginal [ ]

Wraparound [ ]   Voicer [ ]   Actuality [☒]   ·On-Scene [ ]

Q&A [ ]

Opens: "Her father....

Closes: ...off the road.

Runs: :26

Summary:
  ...and her mother and her were trapped in a pickup truck and the
  current was strong enough to start tumbling the pickup off the road...
  they were thrown off the pickup...the father and the mother were
  found down river...the little girl was found down the road about three
  quarters of a mile from where the truck was swept off the road.....

Other info (Background, suggested intro, writeout. release/kill time, additional payment information, etc.)

  Slater was one of the first rescue workers on the scene...

  He saw the ~~battered~~ body of a four-year-old girl who died

  in the flash floods along with her parents....

Cart number

  B-22

Time used: [| |]

NS 353 (7/79)

Shown here is a **cart sheet** from NBC. ("On-scener" is another name for a ROSR; "quality" refers to the sound, not the journalism.) Because wire copy was available on this story, the background information on this sheet is not extensive.

The newsroom may have a playback device for carts that makes it possible to stop them at any point while a newswriter is working with them. If so, those newswriters must remember to recue the carts before they are filed or handed to a newscaster. One of the most common problems in radio news is a cart that starts somewhere in the middle of the newsmaker's or reporter's statement because that's where it was left.

Cuts lose their news value after a day or so. Carts then are erased by passing them over a magnetic device called a **bulk eraser** so they can be used again.

Wrap-Up

A balance must be established when reporting with tape recorders. Reporters cannot devote so much energy to their search for sound that they fail to fulfill their basic responsibility for gathering information. But good tape is so important, and can be so elusive, that reporters must always be conscious of where their next cut is coming from.

Practice Assignments

A. Select two actualities and one Q and A from this interview at City Hall with Mayor Judy Douglas. Then write two voicers based on the interview.

Q. Mayor Douglas, it's taken the city over five months to award the school lunch contract. Why?

A. Well, uh, it's been a very delicate issue, a very sensitive issue. As you know, there were, uh . . . many interested parties, and we felt that, uh . . . we couldn't make any hasty decisions. We had to study all sides of the question.

Q. You awarded the contract to the Strawn Company today? Is that correct?

A. Yes.

Q. The Strawn bid was significantly higher . . . at least $25,000 per year . . . than that of the Jackson Food Corporation, the nearest competitor. Why has Strawn been awarded the contract?

A. Well . . . price is not the only consideration in a matter such as this . . . especially when we're dealing with our children. Quality and service are also considerations. After all, we're dealing with an issue in which the health of our children is involved.

Q. You felt that Strawn would ensure the health of our children more than Jackson?

A. Well, uh . . . yes, that was a factor, health was a factor. We felt that

Strawn's menus were, on the whole, more nutritionally balanced. This was no off-the-cuff judgment. We consulted with several nutritional experts in this matter.

Q. So the nutritional content of the menus was the decisive factor?

A. Well, it's hard to pinpoint one factor in such an important decision, but . . .

Q. What were the others?

A. Well, yes, I guess you could say health was the most important thing.

Q. As you know, Mayor Douglas, this station broadcast a story last week charging that the president of Strawn is your husband's uncle. Does that have anything to do with today's announcement?

A. I said last week that I, and my husband, have no personal or financial connection with either Strawn or Jackson. I stick by that statement. I have no idea how the media will react to today's announcement. I can't worry about that.

Q. But the story has generated a lot of controversy in town. Do you foresee today's announcement creating any political problems for you?

A. Well, political problems are a funny thing. I mean, they're always there. Some people might choose to believe that the contract was awarded on some basis other than, uh . . . well, than merit, I suppose you could say. But all I can say is the health of our children is what's behind this contract.

Q. It's been reported that, no matter who wins the contract, an investigation of the whole matter will be conducted by an independent audit committee. Is this so?

A. Citizens of the community have the right to investigate anything they want.

Q. Will you cooperate with such an investigation?

A. Absolutely! I don't think it's necessary . . . but if that's what people here want, I would welcome it.

Q. Mayor Douglas, are you still planning to run for reelection this year?

A. Well, I never said I definitely would . . . I'll make my decision on that soon.

Q. Some people . . . such as Council President Marrero . . . have said their support for you would hinge on the outcome of the school lunch contract. Are you waiting until the controversy over this blows over before deciding on your candidacy?

A. I'm not waiting for anyone. I just haven't decided yet. And I'm sure everyone involved . . . including my good friend Jim Marrero . . . will agree that the Strawn contract is the best possible decision.

Q. So when can we expect an announcement on your candidacy?

A. Soon. Soon.

Q. Thank you, Mayor Douglas.

B. A bill that's being called an "anti-quota bill" will be voted on by the state legislature tomorrow. The bill would make it illegal for any employer in the state to favor any racial or ethnic group—including minority groups—in its hiring practices. A group called Fairness in the Workplace has organized a demonstration in support of the bill. About 35 people are marching in front of the State Capitol chanting: "Equal rights!" and "Fairness!" The following is an interview with the president of FIW, Kristen Sussman, at the demonstration. Select two actualities from the interview and write two voicers about the interview and demonstration.

Q. I'm here with Kristen Sussman. Kris, let me just get some facts here. You're the president of the Sussman Secretarial Service—is that right?

A. Yes, it is.

Q. And you started this organization—Fairness in the Workplace?

A. Yes, I did. Now I'm president of the group. We have about 100 members.

Q. Okay, Kris, why are you here today?

A. Well, you see, we're here to, you know, show our support for Senator Garrett Roper's fine bill, which we think will begin to put this state . . . and this country . . . back on the right track.

Q. Why are you opposed to quotas?

A. First, let me say that this isn't a racial issue. We just, you know, think equal rights should mean what it says. Equal rights means everyone should get an equal chance. No one—and this is my point here—should get more of a chance than anyone else, I believe, at a job. You know, we've got to put some sense of fairness back into the workplace.

Q. But, opponents of the bill argue that the issue here isn't quotas, it's affirmative action—making sure minorities get a little extra consideration to break down old patterns of discrimination.

A. We've certainly heard that line before. It's bunk. Affirmative action means quotas.

Q. You don't think there have been historical injustices against blacks that might need rectifying in the workplace?

A. Hey, you know, they've been doing these quotas for years now. Enough is enough! Now it's time for everyone to have an equal shot at a job. It shouldn't help me get a job if I'm white. It shouldn't help me to get a job if I'm black. That's our point.

Q. Shouldn't a company be able to make ensuring ethnic or racial diversity a goal—just like, say, ensuring geographical diversity. Opponents of the Roper bill say it would make such efforts illegal.

A. This racial diversity business is just another way of saying they're gonna have a quota to fill with blacks. We say, that's not fair.

Q. How many employees do you have in your Sussman Secretarial Services?

A. Let's see, we have about 53 full- and part-time employees.

Q. Critics of Fairness in the Workplace say that all of those employees are white.

A. We don't keep a count of who is what race.

Q. Are you denying the charge that your entire workforce is white?

A. I'm not going to comment on that.

Q. Okay, thank you very much, Kristen Sussman.

10

Writing to Tape

Joe Templeton of ABC has this actuality to include in the newscast he's writing:

> This incident in my judgment raises a fundamental
> question about whether criminal law enforcement in this
> country is doing an adequate job. My own sense is that
> it is not.

Who is talking? What incident is he talking about? Obviously, the cut makes no sense by itself. Templeton has to write a story around it that answers these questions. He writes the following copy on this well-publicized story to be used *before* the cut is played:

> A New York grand jury is weighing whether to indict
> Bernard Goetz for four attempted murders in a subway
> shooting incident. Goetz says he was protecting himself,
> and he's won the support of many people. At a
> congressional hearing in Washington this morning,
> Senator Arlen Spector of Pennsylvania said it's clear
> the Goetz situation has touched a sore spot . . .

Templeton also has to write something to be read *after* the cut has played to wrap up the story:

> Spector said he is not surprised at the way people have
> reacted to the subway shooting.

Tape isn't self-sufficient. When newswriters get a cart for use in a newscast, they have to get the facts on that story—either from the wires, their own reporters or their own research—and write a story around that piece of tape. Even the voicers and wraps that reporters produce need introductions to integrate them into the newscast. And similar introductions are used in television news before videotape stories are shown (see Chapter 16, "Writing to Visuals").

Lead-Ins

Listeners are rarely thrown into a cart cold. They are led in by the newscaster:

```
We're riding the buses more often. Chapel Hill Transport
reports that ridership throughout the system is up by 38
percent from the same time last year. Transportation
Director Bob Godding says there are several reasons for
the increase. . . .
```
WCHL, North Carolina

Then the tape of Godding plays. The introductory copy a newswriter must write could be called the introduction. It's usually called the **lead-in.**

Lead-ins have two functions: First, they have to do their part in telling the story. In fact, the lead-in may be responsible for carrying much of the necessary information:

```
The advertising for Mick-or-Mack stores says ''Come on
down!'' . . . but someone went a little too far late
this morning. A car crashed through the front window of
the Tower's Mick-or-Mack store shortly before noon.
Police on the scene say 57-year-old John Wysong of
Roanoke was apparently ill when he lost control of his
car. It hopped the sidewalk and smashed into the front
of the store. As passers-by ogled at the late-model
Buick parked in the middle of the produce section, 96
newsman John Kessling talked to this eyewitness. . . .
```
WFIR, Virginia

The other function of the lead-in is setting the scene, preparing listeners for the tape.

Preparing

If the tape records a complaint about the possible elimination of the state Civil Rights Commission, the lead-in must prepare listeners by explaining why the Commission might go and by introducing the person speaking on the tape:

```
Colorado House Republicans have voted not to fund the
state Civil Rights Commission next year, thereby
eliminating the agency that investigates cases of sexual
and racial discrimination. The Reverend Milton Proby is
chairman of the commission. . . .
```
KOA, Denver

If the tape has the governor talking about "House Bill 21-97," the lead-in has to explain what that is:

```
Governor Straub today urged the legislature to . . . as
he put it . . . ''Get off its duff'' and move on some key
issues. The governor was particularly interested in
passage of House Bill 21-97 . . . the city revenue
sharing plan. He talked about why that bill is a top
priority . . .
                                              KROW, Oregon
```

When writing to a cart, newswriters must ask themselves not only what needs to be said about this story but also what needs to be said for this cart to make sense.

Voicers and wraps should have fewer holes to fill than actualities and Q and As because they feature professional storytellers. Reporters won't leave many loose ends in their tape. In writing a lead-in to a voicer or wrap, newswriters just have to figure out what facts the reporter left them. Usually the lead-in gives only a bare-bones description of the event:

```
A train hit a van-camper last night near Columbus,
Georgia, killing two members of an Arlington, Texas,
family. More on that from KRLD newsman Russ
Rossman. . . .
```

Actualities and Q and As, on the other hand, can be awfully skimpy:

```
What was burning was City Hall, in Matamoros, a
furniture store right next to it, and from what I could
tell, part of a bank.
```

This gives the lead-in a lot of work to do:

```
Mexican troops, armed with submachine guns, are
patrolling the streets of Matamoros, Mexico . . . across
the Rio Grande from Brownsville, Texas . . . following a
night of rioting. Rioting students burned City Hall
. . . and battled with police last night to protest
alleged Mexican police brutality. Brownsville Fire Chief
Mario Guyaygos says he was called in to help Matamoros
firefighters battle the fires set by rioters. . . .
```

Now that actuality will make sense.

Something Different

The "parroting," "echo-chamber" or "heckle-jeckle" effect:

Lead-in:　Fireman Robert Blarney called it one of the hottest and most violent fires he's ever seen . . .

Cut:　That was one of the hottest and most violent fires I've ever seen.

This milder example of **parroting,** used on network radio, involved the author of this book . . . as a newsmaker:

Lead-in:　New York University journalism professor and author Mitchell Stephens puts it simply -- sex and crime bring in ratings and sell papers . . .

Cut:　Sex and crime have sold since the days when criers were walking through primitive villages yelling out the news.

Lead-ins have to find something different to say. They must set up the tape, but they can't repeat the wording or the ideas used in the tape:

Lead-in:　A huge fire swept through two garden apartments on Glover Avenue this afternoon. Fireman Robert Blarney helped put it out . . .

If the cut is specific, the lead-in may want to confine itself to a general description:

The City of Orlando has yet another convention center proposal to look over. This one was presented by the Orlando Development Consortium. Consortium spokesman Gerald Simons made the presentation to a city commission. . . .

WKIS, Florida

Metro Fire's Jim Sallee says the cause of yesterday morning's Continental Inn fire has been found. . . .

WVLK, Kentucky

If the cut is vague, the lead-in should pin things down:

> The holiday weekend has given late property taxpayers a
> few hours breathing time. Clark County Treasurer Bill
> Galloway says, though, if the property tax bill is not
> paid by tomorrow . . . a four percent penalty is added.
> Galloway says the county has no grace period. . . .
>
> KLUC, Las Vegas

If the cut spells things out, the lead-in might give the background:

> Manhattan Chamber of Commerce officials say they're
> taking advantage of the American Institute of Banking's
> move of its headquarters from Chicago to Manhattan.
> Director of Economic Development James Rothchild tells
> us how. . . .
>
> KMAN, Kansas

If the tape covers one point thoroughly, the lead-in can concentrate on other points. The cut this lead-in introduces has the mayor explaining his reasons for opposing a tax cut; so the lead-in, after introducing the issue, gives someone else's reasons:

> Should Councilman Bill McPherson get the 20-thousand
> signatures required to have his sales tax repeal measure
> placed on the November ballot . . . it's going to be
> quite a fight. The Metro School Board is against it . . .
> claiming they'll lose 38-million dollars from their
> operating budget, and Mayor Dick Fulton tells WLAC's
> Eddie Parker that he'll fight passage too. . . .

Even while dodging redundancy, the best lead-ins stay close to the most important facts in a story. That isn't difficult when writing to actualities and Q and As—newsmakers leave plenty unsaid. But because voicers and wraps are more thorough, they may force the newswriter to scrounge for additional morsels of information to relate. That is why lead-ins to voicers and wraps are often only a couple of sentences long:

> In Rome . . . a mass treason trial is underway. . . .
> David Willey reports that among the 200 people expected
> to testify is the Italian prime minister. . . .
>
> Ann Taylor, NBC

The newswriter's struggle to avoid redundancy is also why good reporters try to leave out one or two basic facts in their reports (see Chapter 9, "Tape")—to leave room for a lead-in. A voicer:

> The purchase which cost about 800-million dollars, was
> made because the three airlines want to supplement and
> upgrade their air fleets. But the government is touting
> the sale as proof that it is trying to reduce the huge
> balance of trade surplus with the United States. It is,
> however, only a small contribution. The U-S trade deficit
> with Japan has grown to a huge three point two billion
> dollars, depressing the value of the dollar overseas
> . . . and forcing up prices of imported Japanese goods
> in America. -- Bill Redeker, ABC News, Tokyo

What's left for the newswriter? Redeker consciously left out the most basic facts of the purchase:

> Three Japanese airlines say they are planning to buy 28
> U-S jets. More from Bill Redeker in Tokyo . . .
>   Don Fisher, ABC

One network newswriter developed a method for writing to those voicers and wraps that seemed to be "lead-in proof" because they said too much. He'd steal the reporter's first sentence for his lead-in, and just edit that sentence off the start of the cut. That worked . . . until one day he forgot to do the edit. The story went on the air with the voicer repeating the lead-in word for word . . . an unusually faithful echo.

Actually, no cart is lead-in proof. There is always something different to say in the lead-in even if the reporter seems to have said it all—if only a sentence stating the purpose of the cut:

> Dean Johnson reports on Mayor Freund's plans for
> renovating City Hall. . . .

Throws

The last sentence of the lead-in turns over—*throws*—the air to the person on tape:

> . . . Brenda Hancock says bankers are beginning to
> realize the importance of dealing with women. . . .
>   KWMS, Salt Lake City

Then we hear Brenda Hancock's voice.

> . . . Arv Johnson reports from the Independent-
> Republican state convention. . . .
>
> WCCO, Minneapolis

Then Arv Johnson's report plays.

As the last sentence before a new voice comes on, these *throw lines* have an important job. It is worth distinguishing them from the rest of the lead-in and spending some time looking at them. The simplest method of introducing a new voice would be with an incomplete sentence:

> . . . Mayor Kucinich's reaction . . .
> . . . Mayor Kucinich says . . .
> . . . As the mayor explains it . . .

But most stations avoid these incomplete throw lines. There is a danger in using them: Too often in radio news some technical problem delays a cart or keeps it off the air completely. The newscaster who has just read an incomplete throw line can look pretty foolish in these situations:

> . . . Mayor Kucinich's reaction . . . ah . . . was . . .
> ah . . .

Incomplete throw lines leave the newscaster hanging in the middle of a sentence and therefore vulnerable to technical slip-ups. It's always safer to use a complete thought as a throw line:

> . . . The whole thing doesn't seem to bother Mayor
> Kucinich. . . .
>
> WCCO, Minneapolis

Now if the tape doesn't play, the newscaster can simply read the rest of the story. Even if the tape plays smoothly, a completed thought as the throw line sounds more polished.

> WEAK
> . . . Metro narcotics officer Dan Stopka comments . . .

> BETTER
> . . . Metro narcotics official Dan Stopka says it's the
> first such operation ever uncovered in southern
> Nevada. . . .
>
> KLUC, Las Vegas

WEAK
. . . City Commissioner George Stewart says . . .

BETTER
. . . City Commissioner George Stewart says he was
impressed. . . .

WKIS, Florida

Only two kinds of people speak on carts—newsmakers and reporters; and they require different introductions. Since the four types of tape (actualities, Q and As, voicers and wraps) feature different combinations of reporters and newsmakers, they get slightly different throw lines:

To Actualities Only one voice is heard—a newsmaker's; the throw line must tell listeners to whom this unfamiliar voice belongs. That means the name of the newsmaker *must* be mentioned in the throw line:

. . . The city's new railroad consolidation coordinator,
Don Weisbaum, explains what happens next. . . .

WKNR, Michigan

. . . From Wakarusa Manor Governor Bennett went to
Valley View and gave us this assessment. . . .

KLWN, Kansas

If the speaker has been introduced earlier in the lead-in, the throw line may contain nothing more than the person's name and a hint at the content of the actuality:

. . . Dr. McAnulty says the installation of the
pacemaker is a very expensive proposition. . . .

WCAU, Philadelphia

But if the rest of the lead-in doesn't give the necessary information on the speaker, the throw has to do the job:

. . . One of those parents filing suit is Cherokee P-T-A
President Peg Harrison. . . .

WHOO, Florida

. . . The superintendent of operations for the bus
lines, Robert Truscott, suggests some other ways of
getting to work. . . .

WBBM, Chicago

Sometimes throws to actualities use verbs such as *says* or *explains* to indicate that listeners are about to hear the person talking:

> . . . Oneida County Humane Officer Toni Hanna says ''dog-napping'' is getting to be big business here. . . .
>
> WTLB, New York

Some stations use phrases like *tells us* or *we talked to* in their throw lines; some go further and mention their call letters:

> . . . KWHW News talked with Booker about his decision to withdraw. . . .
>
> KWHW, Oklahoma

But the throw line does not have to be too explicit. As long as an actuality is preceded by a sentence that includes the newsmaker's name, listeners understand that the name belongs to the next voice they hear:

> . . . Her bloodstained body was found in the trunk of her parents' car by State Police Trooper Jim Wyner. . . .
>
> WSJM, Michigan

Then Wyner speaks.

To Voicers There is also only one voice on these cuts—but this time it's the reporter's. A few stations don't even bother to mention the reporter in a throw line to a voicer. They rely on the reporter's own final ID—"Paul Parker, WINS, at the New York Hilton"—to take care of the identification.

Most stations *do* tell listeners who they are going to hear before the voicer plays, but they don't waste many words introducing their reporters. No description or title is needed; all that's necessary is the name:

> . . . Patti Berman has the report on their report. . . .
>
> WJET, Pennsylvania

> . . . Linda Ashley reports that you can get relatively cheap burglary insurance. . . .
>
> WDEE, Detroit

The throw line might also mention location, especially if it's exotic:

> . . . David Dow in Quito tells us about it. . . .
>
> Dallas Townsend, CBS

The pitfall in writing throw lines to voicers is repetition. It's too easy to get stuck using the same words over and over:

```
. . . Neil Curry has that report. . . .

. . . Leonard Pratt has the story. . . .

. . . Bernard Redmont reports. . . .

. . . John Given has the story. . . .
```

Writers must vary their throw lines. Here are some from one newscast:

```
. . . Neil Curry handled that part of the Ullman
plan. . . .

. . . A backgrounder now from Group W's Leonard
Pratt. . . .

. . . Bernard Redmont filed a report on a revolution
which accomplished its major goals more than 200 years
ago, but is still wrapping up details. . . .

. . . Overseas to John Given in Tokyo. . . .

. . . Let's get an update from Matt Cooney. . . .
                                  WINS, New York City
```

Here's another clever throw line:

```
The National Urban League releases its annual report on
Black Americans. Barry Bagnato has read it. . . .
                                  Bill Lynch, CBS
```

To Q and As Throw lines to these cuts are more tricky. There are two voices to introduce—the newsmaker's and the reporter's. Both names must be mentioned in the throw:

```
. . . Butler told Jerry Bohnen he was inspired because
the convention brought together the top blacks in the
country. . . .
                                  KMAN, Kansas
```

One obvious strategy is to mention that the reporter was questioning the newsmaker:

> . . . WLAC's Eddie Parker had a talk with Mayor Dick
> Fulton about that today. . . .
>
> WLAC, Nashville

To Wraps In a wrap the reporter introduces the newsmaker on tape, so the throw line's chief responsibility is to mention the reporter. For instance, this throw line could have been used for a voicer; it was used to introduce a wrap that contained a tape of the fire commissioner:

> . . . News 88's Irene Cornell has the details. . . .
>
> WCBS, New York City

Then on the tape Cornell uses her own throw line:

> . . . Fire Commissioner Augustus Beekman says they never
> had a chance. . . .

However, the throw in the lead-in to the wrap could have hinted that an interview with the fire commissioner was coming:

> . . . Fire Commissioner Augustus Beekman was on the
> scene, and News 88's Irene Cornell filed this
> report. . . .

Since a wrap is a prepackaged story, the throw line has less responsibility. It must mention the reporter, but the newsmaker's name is optional.

Lead-ins to wraps are the most susceptible to redundancy, since there are so many elements to the wrap. How's this for a parroting effect?

Lead-in:	Reporter Marv Johnson reports on the mayor's call for a cutback in the city sales tax. . . .
Reporter in Wrap:	The mayor discussed with me his call for a cutback in the city sales tax. . . .
The Mayor in Wrap:	I'm calling for a cutback in the city sales tax.

Write-Outs

What's left to say after a voicer or wrap has been played? The lead-in and reporter's story should have covered all points, and the reporter has signed off:

```
. . . Richard Threlkeld, CBS News, New Hampshire.
```

Rarely will the newscaster return after a voicer or wrap with more information. But actualities and Q and As are a different story. Even with their lead-ins, these cuts leave loose ends.

```
Lead-in:   T-V-A's generating plant at Brown's Ferry is
           out, and spokeswoman Brenda Carnes says the
           agency is asking us to cut back on the use of
           electricity. . . .

Cut:       The T-V-A today did issue an urgent appeal to
           all consumers to temporarily curtail their
           use of electric appliances during the peak
           hours of three p-m to nine p-m today. It's
           very unlikely that the emergency will deteri-
           orate to the stages of a black-out, but we
           would like to point out that if you're not
           conserving electricity, it is costing us
           dearly because we're having to buy power to
           cover these peak periods.
```

That's not enough. A newsmaker cannot wrap up a story—for one thing, many listeners may still not be clear on whose voice they've been hearing. The newscaster has to conclude:

```
Spokeswoman Carnes tells us the T-V-A doesn't know how
long the problem will last.
```

This final section of a tape story is called the "tag line," the "close" or the **write-out.**

Renaming

Who was that talking? Listening with partial attention or tuning in after the lead-in, many listeners do not catch the name of the person they were just listening to in an actuality or Q and A. So most newswriters take a second to remind them. The first few words of the write-out should include the name of the newsmaker who was talking on the tape. Some writers simply state the name:

```
The Commission's chairman, Reverend Proby.
```

Or they mention the name again in a quick recap of the content of the tape:

```
Reverend Proby defending the Civil Rights Commission.
```

There is, however, a more conversational and informative alternative. The name can be restated as part of a sentence that communicates additional information.

```
Proby says his agency handles about 2-thousand cases
each year, and most can be solved locally.
                                            KOA, Denver
```

The name is there. Another version of the same write-out:

```
Proby says there is now the chance that the federal
government will step in and run the Colorado civil
rights program.
                                            KOA, Denver
```

If the speaker in an actuality is not an important participant in a story, it may be hard to come up with a smooth way of mentioning that person again in the beginning of the write-out. There are news organizations that will waive the obligation to mention that name again in those stories. However, it's a good idea to get in the habit of finding a way to repeat the name of the newsmaker after every actuality. Renaming the speaker adds clarity, which is always a welcome addition to a broadcast story.

Concluding

Along with repeating the name, the write-out must bring the story to a close. This may require adding new information. The write-out after a tape of a city official discussing bus shelters:

```
Bradley says the Council Transportation Committee will
review an ordinance allowing such shelters to go up, but
that the city doesn't have the money available to build
them if private industry won't. The Regional
Transportation District says it wants to build another
100 shelters, but the bulk of them will have to be paid
for by private companies.
                                            KOA, Denver
```

Or the write-out may conclude with one short sentence. The editor of a local journal has analyzed the president's energy plan on tape. Here is the write-out:

```
And Lawrence promises that . . . in the next issue . . .
the Oil and Gas Journal will have plenty to say about
the president's proposals.
                                              KAKC, Oklahoma
```

Write-outs for actualities and Q and As can use the same approaches to conclude stories as do snappers (see Chapter 6, "Stories"): supporting the main point, giving the other side of the issue, giving the punch line. The two most common, however, are adding another point and discussing future ramifications.

The cart contains Smathers' attack on the state's education system; the write-out is making another point:

```
Smathers says he is running a strong second in the
Democratic race for governor. That despite figures
released yesterday which show him with about one-million
dollars less in contributions than front-runner Robert
Shevin.
                                               WHOO, Florida
```

The cart has an FDA spokesman reevaluating the ban on saccharin; this write-out speculates on the future:

```
That F-D-A man guesses the sweetener will be sold as a
non-prescription drug, carrying a warning about what
happened to those rats in Canada.
                                              KAKC, Oklahoma
```

Beware! Write-outs can parrot just as easily as lead-ins.

```
UNACCEPTABLE
     Cut:    That's the craziest plan I've ever heard.

Write-Out:   Gentry called the plan the craziest he's
             ever heard.
```

There are generally enough points to be made about a story to fill the write-out with something besides an instant replay of the tape or the lead-in. But, if a story is so painfully thin that it is impossible to squeeze out another fact or even future ramification, then it might be necessary to fall back on the most primitive form of close:

```
City Council President Gentry.
```

It's better to be terse than redundant.

Tape Copy

How should a story with tape appear on the page or pages that will be used in the script for the newscast? Writing out a verbatim transcript for the cut would be time consuming and of little value. Newscasters just need the copy they are going to read—the lead-in and the write-out—plus enough information so they know when the cart is over and it's time for them to read again.

Cues

First, a bookkeeping matter. There are usually a few carts in a newscast. To ensure that the newscaster or engineer plays the right cart with the right story, most stations ask writers to include the number of the cart in the copy. After the lead-in they type the word *Cart*, then a colon and that number:

`Cart: 409`

Newscasters know when the cart is supposed to begin—right after the lead-in. But how do they know when it's over and time to read the write-out? Waiting for silence at the end of the cart would allow that silence to go out over the air—that is unacceptable. So newswriters add two important pieces of information on the copy for the story:

The Time Noting how long the cut runs gives newscasters an idea of how long they have—10 seconds? a minute?—before they are "on" again. The time in seconds is usually written after the word *Runs* and a colon:

`Runs: 15`

The Out-Cue The real secret to bringing newscasters back at exactly the right moment is giving them a cue. Newswriters jot down the final words said on the cart. Those final two or three words are called the ***out-cue*** (see Chapter 9, "Tape"). Newscasters hear those words and then begin talking again. They're usually written after "Out" and a colon:

`Out: within the state`

Out-cues are simple except when those final words are also said earlier in the cut. This is called a ***double out***. In a Q and A, for example, the newsmaker's last words may be "Yes, that's correct," but he may also have said the same thing— "Yes, that's correct,"—in response to an earlier question in the cut. Merely writing the out-cue here could lead the newscaster or engineer to stop the tape too early.

To solve this problem newswriters write *Double out* next to the out-cue. Then whoever is playing the cut knows that it must be allowed to play until that out-cue has been said twice:

```
             Out: Yes, that's correct.
                   (Double out)
```

The number, time and out-cue of a cart are placed after the lead-in and before the write-out, if there is one. They are separated from the copy by a few lines and often indented—you don't want these cues accidentally read on the air as part of the story.

Some stations add one more item: an *in-cue*—the *first* few words on the cart (see Chapter 9, "Tape"). This may help ensure that the right cart is playing, but otherwise the in-cue doesn't tell newscasters anything they need to read the story. Most stations leave it out:

```
CIVIL RIGHTS
3/31
gat


Colorado House Republicans have voted not to fund the
state Civil Rights Commission next year, thereby
eliminating the agency that investigates cases of sexual
and racial discrimination. The Reverend Milton Proby is
chairman of the Commission. . . .


                 Cart: 409
                 Runs: 15
                 Out: within the state


Proby says there is now the chance that the federal
government will step in and run the Colorado civil
rights program.
                                              KOA, Denver
```

Voicers and wraps end with the standard reporter IDs—usually called "direct closes," "standard closes" or *"standard out-cues."* Instead of the actual out-cut— "12-10 News"—many stations simply type the word *direct* or *standard* after *Out;* or they use abbreviations like *std* or *soc*:

```
SPANK 3 August amn


An elementary school teacher in the Chester-Upland
school district has been acquitted of charges stemming
```

```
from her spanking of a nine-year-old student. WCAU's
suburban reporter Duane Gray has more. . . .
```

```
                        Cart: 9
                        Runs: 39
                        Out: soc
                                        WCAU, Philadelphia
```

More Than One Cart

All the examples considered in this chapter so far use only one cart per story. Radio stories sometimes use more:

```
AIR RESCUE
27 April
felice
```

```
A 21-year-old motorcyclist from Roy is recovering from
accident injuries. He was rescued yesterday by a
helicopter crew from Hill Air Force Base. Air Force
Information Specialist John Loflin says the helicopter
was on a routine training flight west of Ogden when crew
members spotted Ned Patterson. . . .
```

```
                        Cart: 28
                        Runs: 10
                        Out: that did it
```

```
Loflin says the helicopter crew didn't have to call in
any support services. . . .
```

```
                        Cart: 28
                        Runs: 20
                        Out: him into Ogden
```

```
Air Force Information Specialist Loflin says Patterson
was suffering from a broken jaw and head injuries when
the chopper crew arrived. Patterson was taken to McKay
Dee Hospital, where he is reported in serious condition.
                                        KWMS, Salt Lake City
```

The lead-in and write-outs in this example follow the same rules as the others discussed in this chapter. But the copy in between the two cuts is something new— a combination lead-in and write-out. It leads into the second cart and writes out of the first. These **bridges** between carts must contain enough information to prepare listeners for the second cart, while also mentioning the name of the newsmaker in the first cart. KWMS did this in one sentence:

```
Loflin says the helicopter crew didn't have to call in
any support services. . . .
```

Bridging carts that feature *different* newsmakers is trickier. If the first cart has the union president, the second, the company's president, the copy in between them could read:

```
Mullaney called the company's offer completely
unacceptable . . . but company President Larry Jameson
says that's all he can afford to pay. . . .
```

Writing copy to bridge two voicers or wraps in one story is easier since these cuts are more self-sufficient. If the story includes reports on the two candidates for an office, they can be bridged with:

```
Meanwhile at Stanton headquarters on the West Side,
reporter John Hendley found the mood more subdued. . . .
```

Stories can include more than two carts, although a story with many cuts is more of a short documentary (see Chapter 13, "Public Affairs") than a news story. Most news stories with tape use one tape; a few use two or three.

Wrap-Up

Lead-ins and write-outs have double responsibilities. They have to meet the same standards as other broadcast writing, while at the same time they have to make the tape comfortable in the newscast.

Practice Assignments

A. Write lead-ins and, where necessary, write-outs for the actualities, Q and As and voicers produced in the assignments on pages 231–233, at the end of Chapter 9, "Tape."

B. Write a 35- to 40-second story based on the facts below and including the actuality that follows.

1. San Antonio, Texas, experienced a bad snowfall which began yesterday and ended this morning.
2. Past record snowfalls in San Antonio: 6.4 inches, 1926; 4.7 inches, 1949; and 4.2 inches, 1895.
3. Total this storm, according to National Weather Service: 13.5 inches.
4. City emergency, declared by Mayor Henry Cisneros, required that all city offices close today and that it be strongly suggested that people stay off streets of city.
5. Closings in city today included: all schools, all banks, all airports and most businesses.
6. Mayor Cisneros said today the city was not equipped with any snowplows and did not plan to purchase any.
7. A snowman was built by some children in front of the Alamo.
8. A number of people were seen skiing on streets that have palm trees.
9. The worst damage caused by collapse of roof at luxury car dealership. Nine luxury foreign cars, each valued at more than $35,000, were damaged by roof collapse.

ACTUALITY: Cart number A5; 14 seconds long; from an interview with Cisneros today in San Antonio:

```
We had to jury-rig some snowplows -- we used road
graders -- and there was some damage to the streets
because of that. But as a test of our emergency
procedures it was good. Not a single police officer
failed to show up.
```

C. Write a 35- to 40-second story based on the facts below and including the actuality that follows.

1. Bill calling for equal rights for homosexuals defeated tonight in City Council vote.
2. Bill would have outlawed discrimination against homosexuals in city.
3. Vote was 5–2.
4. Councilwoman Wilma Sheer, who voted against: "Hey, we're just not ready for this. The majority of the people of this city believe homosexuality is wrong. There are a number of places we believe discrimination against homosexuals might be okay, starting with the schools."
5. Councilman George Winston, who introduced bill: "I think it's sad that these people can't respect the basic human rights of this group of citizens who happen to have a different sexual preference than we do. Obviously, this bill wouldn't have condoned homosexual proselytizing in our schools, any more than any other type of proselytizing is condoned."
6. 15 members of Gay Rights Coalition in audience. Booed after vote.
7. Sheila Ruiz, president of Gay Rights Coalition here: "We'll be back again

next year to try to get this bill passed, and before that we'll make our feelings known about some of these council members at the voting booth. There are many, many gay people in this city, and we are prepared to make our political impact felt.''

8. The bill specifically said that it did not "protect homosexuals or anyone else who would attempt to impose their preferences on school children."

ACTUALITY: Cart number A6; 15 seconds long; from an interview after the meeting with Ruiz:

This is a sad day for the gay people of this city. We're only asking for the same right to keep a job and find a place to live everyone else has. We don't want to impose our life style on anyone. We just don't want to be persecuted for it.

D. Write a 45- to 50-second story for Ransey station WOE, based on the wire copy below and including the voicer that follows.

RANSEY -- A TWO-ALARM FIRE TONIGHT COMPLETELY DESTROYED JANE'S FURNITURE WORLD, ON FOREST STREET HERE, INJURING THE STORE'S NIGHTWATCHMAN.

ACCORDING TO SGT. RODNEY FIELDS OF THE RANSEY FIRE DEPARTMENT, NIGHTWATCHMAN PAUL OFFEN, THE ONLY PERSON INSIDE THE STORE AT 16 FOREST STREET WHEN THE FIRE BROKE OUT, SUFFERED MINOR BURNS. OFFEN WAS TAKEN TO MEMORIAL HOSPITAL.

''WHEN WE ARRIVED AT 8:45, MOST OF THE BUILDING WAS ALREADY ON FIRE,'' SGT. FIELDS SAID. ''BY 10:30 IT WAS GONE.''

A SPOKESWOMAN FOR JANE'S, PAMELA VICTOR, ESTIMATED THE DAMAGE AT $450,000. SHE SAID SHE DID NOT KNOW IF THE OWNERS WOULD REBUILD THE STORE.

JANE'S IS THE LARGEST FURNITURE STORE IN RANSEY.

SGT. FIELDS SAID HE COULD NOT SPECULATE AT THIS POINT ON THE CAUSE OF THE FIRE.

VOICER: Cart number A7; 37 seconds long; from reporter Ellen Michaels at the fire:

The flames are out now . . . and most of Jane's is gone. All that's left where the furniture store used to stand is a pile of smoking rubble. Sergeant Rodney Fields of the Ransey Fire Department told me that the fire was first spotted by nightwatchman Offen at eight thirty in the

bedroom furniture area of the store. According to
Sergeant Field, Offen was burned when he tried to
extinguish the flames by himself. Fields says the
nightwatchman then fled from the building and called the
fire department. The store burned quickly, too quickly
for firefighters to save Jane's. Offen was treated and
released for minor burns at Memorial Hospital. -- Ellen
Michaels, WOE News

11

Coverage

Each story is different. The best part of a story is often that which makes it unique, and the best reporters are often those who can find a unique approach to a story. There is no formula that works for every fire story or demonstration. News is news because it's full of surprises.

That said, it must also be acknowledged that reporters do have certain standard strategies in mind when they cover particular types of stories—priorities on whom to interview, information on what facts and opinions they can expect to get; guidelines.

It would be foolish to follow these guidelines slavishly—reporting remains a creative profession. But it would be equally unwise to venture out in search of news without the benefit of the tricks, techniques and theories other reporters have developed. This chapter introduces the basic procedures radio reporters should at least have in their repertoires. With the techniques discussed in Chapter 15, "Television Reporting," these procedures should also be of value to television reporters.

Tragedies

A call to police, a tip or a conversation overheard on the police radio usually provides the first clue. Then a reporter is on the way. Whether it's a fire, accident or disaster, the first rule is: Keep your eyes open. How high are the flames? How far is traffic backed up? How widely is the wreckage scattered? How many fire trucks are here? How many cars were involved? What are the weather conditions? Before they have had a chance to question anybody, reporters already should have secured a collection of basic facts.

Officials

The first person to talk to after arriving on the scene is usually whoever knows the most about what's going on—the fire, police or civil defense officer in charge. In many areas, the chief wears a white hat. When reporters arrive they walk toward that white hat; otherwise, they stop the first person in uniform they see and ask,

"Who's in charge?" ("I try to be careful not to interrupt a key person who might be involved in something more important than my interview," says Mitch Lebe of WCBS, New York City. "I make my presence known, so it's clear I'm waiting, but I try not to interrupt.")

When the person in command is ready to talk, at least part of that interview should be recorded. Simple, direct questions should produce the first couple of usable actualities. A good opening question: "What did you see when you arrived?" That gets them to set the scene on tape. Then: "What happened?" "Anybody hurt?"

At a fire in New York City in which six firemen were killed, the person in charge was the fire commissioner, Augustus Beekman. WCBS in New York City used this actuality of Beekman discussing why the men couldn't be saved:

```
There were men inside and men on the roof. . . .
The men who were inside we were able to get out.
The men who were on the roof, unfortunately, went down
at a point in the building at which the fire erupted, in
other words in full flame.
```

From this initial interview with an official, reporters must start to assemble a clear picture of the event which they can then communicate in a voicer or wrap. Perhaps it will be necessary to catch up with a couple of other officials, without recording, to fill in the holes.

Experience and even advance preparation make for speed here. Rick Wallace of KABC in Los Angeles works in an area that is plagued by brush fires; so, he has made it his business to study brush fires. He spent a night with firefighters at a small fire, just to learn. Now when he arrives at a fire and hears talk of "back fires," "chimney effects" and "pre-ignition," Wallace doesn't have to waste time seeking translations and explanations—he's an expert of sorts himself. The voicers come quickly.

In interviews with officials, reporters must be on the lookout for facts that measure the scale of the tragedy—obviously the number of dead and injured, the number of alarms, the number of houses or cars destroyed, comparisons with other local disasters. These facts should then be allowed to speak for themselves without the aid of trite and subjective descriptions like *senseless* or even *tragic* (see Chapter 3, "Meanings").

After talking with officials, a radio reporter in New York City filed this report from the scene of that fire in which the six firemen died:

```
A corner supermarket in a middle-class neighborhood in
Sheepshead Bay on Avenue I and Ocean Avenue became a
tomb today for six firemen -- the worst toll in the Fire
Department since 1966. These firemen were on the roof of
a Waldbaum's supermarket here when it collapsed under
them without warning, plunging them into the flaming
wreckage below . . . and apparently they had no chance.
```

The other firefighters rushed in, went to the rescue of
some of their fellow officers, managed to drag out some.
But, the flaming wreckage, the smoke, the flames, kept
them from seeing the others and finding the others. There
were no screams for help. And so by the time they got to
the other men, it was too late. -- Stan Brooks, WINS,
New York City

With a couple of actualities on tape and a voicer or wrap written out, reporters
should check their watches. If a newscast is approaching, first priority is filing these
first reports.

The next interview at the scene of a tragedy is often with the most disheveled
rescue worker there—someone who appears to have been close to the action. Questions: "Could you describe what it was like in there?" "What were you thinking?"

Witnesses

Officials, police, firemen are professionals—trained to react with a certain detachment, a stance that doesn't make for particularly gripping actualities. The extraordinary is best communicated through amateurs—survivors, relatives, eyewitnesses.
So amateurs, rather than professionals, are the next interview targets.

Survivors and relatives must be treated tactfully. Approaching them is difficult,
but it must be done . . . delicately. "How does it feel to lose all you own?" is of
course unconscionable; but, "Would you mind talking with us for a moment?" . . .
then, "Could you describe what you saw when you came home?" is acceptable.

Eyewitnesses make the best actualities. If necessary, reporters have to walk up
to a crowd of bystanders and yell forcefully, "Okay, who was here when it happened?" Then: "Could you describe what *you* saw?" Never, however, should these
witnesses be relied on for such crucial information as the cause of a fire, accident or
disaster.

Speculation about arson must be left to fire officials. Disposition of blame in an
accident should be left, properly attributed, to the police. And the nature and severity of injuries is a determination only doctors and nurses can make. Even the police
or ambulance drivers can only give the number hurt and a description of what the
victims said and how they looked. They are not in a position to say who is near
death and who is just in shock.

Questions should be directed only to those qualified to answer. Just as eyewitnesses are not qualified to speculate on the cause of the accident, police, who arrived
later, are in no position to describe what the crash looked like—that's a question for
the witnesses. And don't ask neighbors what the firemen are saying or the firefighters
how the neighbors are reacting. Ask officials officials' questions and witnesses witnesses' questions.

Frequently bystanders complain that it took too long for firefighters or rescue
workers to arrive. Walter Dibble, news director at WTIC in Connecticut, warns

against airing such charges of tardiness. Bystanders usually are not aware of exactly when officials were notified, nor are they expert on how long is "too long."

Witnesses and rescue workers must be interviewed promptly — before they wander off or are sent home. Then the reporter can record ROSRs while strolling around the scene and work on additional voicers or wraps.

Hospitals

If there were casualties, attention shifts to the hospital. The seriousness of what goes on there may make reporters' inquiries seem like harassment. But most hospital officials respect the job journalists have to do and have established procedures for releasing information. Reporters must learn them — the newsroom should have these procedures posted or filed.

Some hospitals assign the supervising nurse in the emergency room responsibility for handling all inquiries; some designate a public information officer, perhaps with the hospital's supervising nurse taking over at night. Whoever has the job should be prepared to give reporters basic information on newsworthy patients (see Chapter 18, "Ethics and Law") without unreasonable delay.

That information usually includes those familiar terms for patients' conditions — *good*, *satisfactory*, *fair*, *poor*, *serious* or *critical*. Unfortunately, this is one code that reporters can't even attempt to break. These terms simply do not have clearly defined meanings, and reporters are not qualified to speculate that *critical* means someone may soon die or that *satisfactory* means the injury will definitely not be fatal. All reporters can do is pass on the hospital's designation:

```
Six firemen died, many were hurt, two seriously . . .
                                    WNEW, New York City
```

At some small hospitals, obtaining even this basic information can be a chore. A nurse who is unaccustomed to dealing with the press may insist that the reporter wait until some hospital official arrives at nine the next morning. Aggressive reporters cannot be content with that. They must be persuasive and insistent enough to get the information.

The basic facts at the hospital can be obtained by phone, but on major stories, stations may want a reporter on the scene grabbing information as it becomes available and in a position to interview survivors and relatives.

"First, I usually check the emergency room," explains Mitch Lebe. Some of the relatives and survivors may be in the waiting room there, and the nurse in charge of "triage" — arranging for treatment according to the severity of the injuries — may have information on the victims.

Hospital officials may permit visits to the rooms of those who are not seriously injured; otherwise, reporters have no business barging into hospital rooms.

One of the firemen injured in that New York City fire was interviewed at a hospital:

```
I was lucky to be able to crawl out. I landed on my back,
but . . . I was able to get out by myself.
```

WINS, New York City

Then the wife of a fireman who was not seriously injured:

```
One of the other firemen called me up and told me about a
quarter of eleven, I guess. I hadn't heard about the
fire, but I started to assume that something had happened
because he was so late getting home; so in a couple of
minutes I was going to call the firehouse to see if there
had been an accident.
```

WINS, New York City

At a hospital the line between aggressive reporting and obstructing lifesaving efforts must be honored. There is nothing wrong with gently asking someone who is not seriously injured for a comment. But there is something terribly wrong with any action that interferes with the treatment of the seriously injured.

■ ■ ■

An additional warning to reporters covering tragedies: Double-check names! If an official says a person has died, repeat the name of that person to the official to make sure you have it right . . . and get the name of the official. The hospital, the coroner and the police should each be able to verify the name of the person. It's wise to call at least two of the three. This is no time for an error.

There are two questions the radio reporter tries to answer at tragic events: First, "What exactly happened?" That answer comes from the officials and eyewitnesses and is communicated through their actualities and in the reporter's reports. Second, "What was it like?" The witnesses, rescuers, survivors and relatives all help answer this question, as do the reporter's ROSRs.

Often, probably too often, these stories end with the standard snapper: *Police are investigating the cause of the fire.* That's a loose end, notes Irwin Gratz, former news director of WPOR in Maine. To tie it up, make sure you report the results of that investigation when it is complete:

```
Investigators say last week's fire on the 18th floor of
the Woodman building was deliberately set.
```

KEZO, Omaha

Crime

Perhaps this section should be titled "Alleged Crime" to keep the caveat—"innocent until proved guilty"—inscribed on reporters' minds. Crime must be covered with utmost care. When reporters get interested in the law, the law gets interested in their reporting. Many of the legal questions considered in Chapter 18, "Ethics and Law," are raised primarily in crime reporting.

Police

Many stations can't afford to send reporters down to police stations or to the scenes of crimes. Instead, they rely on the police radio and regular beat calls to the police. The person on the other end of these calls may be a dispatcher, desk sergeant or the entire police department. These people are not always interested in reporters finding out everything that has happened.

If reporters can visit the police station, they may find their news on the police *blotter*—a record of what the police have been up to, which is kept at the station and, in some cities, transmitted on the police teletype (see Chapter 7, "Sources"). The blotter is public information, as are arrest records (except when minors are involved), and, therefore, should be available to reporters. Most of the events recorded are too insignificant for radio time (in small towns: lost cats, cars that wouldn't start), but they're worth looking through.

Occasionally big names are listed in connection with little crimes—that's news. More significant events, which the police may not be anxious to discuss, may also have been dutifully recorded on the blotter. Nevertheless, an examination of the blotter must be supplemented by talks with the police on duty. Even at the police station, reporters are dependent on the police opening up and talking.

"Some police officers want to help; others, for one reason or another, seem to hate the press," notes Lebe. The fact is that police and reporters have had a bad marriage from the start. Reporters gripe that the police don't provide enough information. Police accuse reporters of hindering investigations or demanding information that might damage someone's rights. Reporters claim police give them the runaround. Police accuse reporters of being out to "get" cops.

But reporters must live with police for the sake of the news. Life is easier if they can establish a rapport with them. Some free time spent hanging out at the police station can be useful. A reputation for fair and accurate reporting is crucial. Even with such a reputation, it's not easy to win the confidence of the police, especially over the phone.

A beat call may elicit an answer like this: "Nope, quiet, just the way we like it." The reporter has to decide, based on experience with that officer, whether that answer can be trusted. If not, it may be necessary to run through, as inoffensively as possible, the list of potentially disquieting events, just to confirm that none of them has slipped the mind of the officer.

When a station covers a crime from the newsroom—usually because its town has more crimes than it has reporters—a reporter gathers the facts on the phone and throws in a phoner with one of the police describing the charges or the arrest.

If a reporter is sent to the scene of the crime, the first priority, again, is an interview with the officer in charge. Detectives, if they have a moment to talk, are the best source for details on the crime as well as speculation on suspects and motives.

Detectives and other police officers are not always anxious to talk. In some cities and towns the police chief has made it clear that he doesn't want to hear his people on the air. It may be necessary to interview police officers and detectives with the cassette recorder off and then convey their comments in a voicer. In most cities, however, police officers do not object to going on the air.

Here is a voicer, based on information supplied by the police:

```
It happened in downtown Flushing, the busy corner where
Kissena Boulevard runs into Main Street. The suspect,
dressed in green overalls and wearing a black wig,
reportedly walked up to a woman teller at a
Manufacturers Hanover Trust branch and demanded a bag of
money. Police say Howard Ford, an off-duty city
detective moonlighting as a teller, saw what was
happening, pulled his service revolver, identified
himself and ordered the holdup man to surrender. Police
say the response was a burst of gunfire. Ford shot back.
Customers scrambled for safety as bullets went back and
forth. The suspect collapsed outside on the street and
died. Ford, shot once in the stomach and once in the
leg, collapsed and was rushed to a nearby hospital,
where he died three hours later. -- Stan Brooks, Ten-Ten
News
```

                                          WINS, New York City

Next, interview neighbors, witnesses, the first cop to arrive on the scene, etc. — remembering that such charged matters as identification of victims and theories about suspects should be left entirely to the police. If a neighbor suggests a suspect on tape, the tape cannot be used. The suspect could sue for libel (see Chapter 18, "Ethics and Law").

A suspect's race or ethnic background should not be mentioned unless it is connected to the motivation for the crime or unless the suspect is still at large and, as part of a *detailed* description, it may aid in the arrest. This is a response to protests against the tendency to mention race only when the suspect's race is black. NBC radio received a similar protest from a Vietnam veteran who noted that the fact that a suspect had served in Vietnam, although entirely irrelevant to the crime, was frequently mentioned in news stories, whereas it was almost never noted that suspects had served in, for example, the Korean War or the Peace Corps. NBC conceded that he had a point and tried to change its ways.

The rough-and-tumble world of cops and alleged robbers is governed by some strict rules. Reporters have to understand and be able to communicate those rules, and that means they must become familiar with some legal terminology. Chapter 3,

"Meanings," noted the differences between words like *robbery*, *theft* and *burglary*. Here are some other crucial distinctions between the legal meanings of words:

C h a r g e / I n d i c t m e n t   *Charges* are accusations made before a judge when a suspect is arraigned. Then a *grand jury* often will have to decide whether there is enough evidence to produce an *indictment*.

F e l o n y / M i s d e m e a n o r   *Felonies* include violent crimes such as murder and rape as well as major crimes against property such as robbery, burglary or car theft. *Misdemeanors* are less serious. Shoplifting is generally a *misdemeanor*. People convicted of *misdemeanors* usually face only fines. People convicted of *felonies* might be sent to prison.

M u r d e r / M a n s l a u g h t e r   To murder is to kill with malice—*first degree* (in most states) if it was premeditated—*second degree* if it was not. *Involuntary manslaughter* means it was an accident; *voluntary manslaughter*, that it was intentional but committed without malice. And all these killings are *homicides*.

P a r o l e / P r o b a t i o n   Only people who have been serving jail or prison terms can be *paroled*, but people can be placed on *probation* after they are convicted of a crime *instead* of being locked up. Both are forms of conditional freedom that can be retracted if the person fails to meet the terms of the parole or probation.

S u s p e c t / C r i m i n a l   This is the most crucial distinction of all. No one is a *criminal* until he or she is proved guilty of a crime. People who have been arrested and charged with crimes are *suspects*, who are to be considered innocent until proved guilty. And, even if the suspect was caught red-handed, it's, "*Police say* the suspect was caught red-handed."

Courts

There are two separate bodies of law in this country: civil and criminal. *Criminal laws* deal with crimes against "the people"—murder, robbery, running a red light. *Civil laws* handle disputes between citizens or businesses—breach of contract, libel.

No one faces jail for committing a civil offense. People can sue in civil court because they feel they've been wronged—the wrong is called a "tort"—or because a contract has been violated. If the plaintiffs win, they are awarded "damages"—money or relief from the wrong.

It takes an unusually hot suit to draw reporters into civil court. This is unfortunate. As large corporations or even small businesses slug it out with each other in civil court, the depositions they file and the testimony they present often reveal the true nature of economic power in a community. There's news here, though it may take time and sophistication to secure it.

The criminal courts have no such trouble attracting reporters. They have most of the violence, sex and corruption. They also have an intricate structure that reporters must master.

The names and responsibilities of the different levels of trial and appellate courts vary by state. In some states, for instance, the supreme courts are near the bottom of the hierarchy—in some states they are indeed supreme. All the different courts will be mentioned in the news, so their roles must be studied.

Reporters must be concerned with all the stops a case makes on the road between arrest and prison or freedom. Courthouse regulars—lawyers, clerks, other reporters, even judges—can be pumped for information on how the criminal justice system operates in a state. The chart on pages 264–265 provides a good introduction to the basic structure.

A station has a responsibility to listeners or viewers, and to the suspect, to follow through with coverage of the legal proceedings after an arrest. In other words, if attention was paid to charges against someone, it must also be paid to the fact that those charges were dropped, that they were reduced, that the person was found innocent of them or that his or her conviction on those charges was thrown out on appeal. All that may be needed to keep up are regular calls to the district attorney, defense attorney and court clerk; or the station may decide to send a reporter to the trial.

The majority of states have now opened their courts to cameras and microphones. This can make obtaining actualities at a major trial as easy as plugging your tape recorder into the public address system and noting potential in- and out-cues during the testimony. In those state courts—and the federal courts, at this writing—where tape recorders still aren't allowed (see Chapter 18, "Ethics and Law"), reporters have to show more initiative. "You usually leave your tape recorder with the security office on the ground floor," says WCBS's Mitch Lebe. "When the day's session is over you run and pick it up and sometimes you can get interviews with the lawyers or even the principals on the way out."

If court restrictions make actualities hard to find, reporters will frequently be left to rely on voicers. These voicers are usually scrawled in a note pad while sitting through the proceedings, then filed on the nearest phone. The action is usually with the witnesses. Here is a voicer on a trial in progress:

```
Zoo director Joe Reed* is charged with abusing an 800-
pound baby hippo that died when attempts were made to
move it from the Birmingham Zoo. The Humane Society of
```

* This name has been changed.

This chart, prepared by a presidential commission, shows how cases move through the criminal justice system—from detected and reported crimes to prosecution, the courts and the corrections system. Procedures in some states may vary from those outlined here. The varying weights of the lines reflect estimates of the relative numbers of cases that reach each stage in the system. (The President's Commission on Law Enforcement and Administration of Justice, *The Challenge of Crime in a Free Society*, 7-12; 1967)

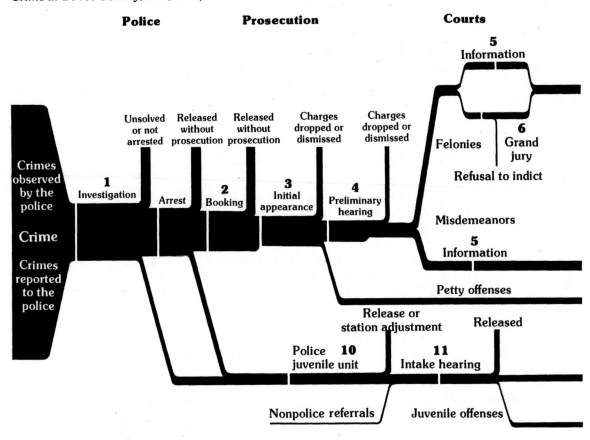

1 May continue until trial.

2 Administrative record of arrest. First step at which temporary release on bail may be available.

3 Before magistrate, commissioner or justice of peace. Formal notice of charge, advice of rights. Bail set. Summary trials for petty offenses usually conducted here without further processing.

4 Preliminary testing of evidence against defendant. Charge may be reduced. No separate preliminary hearing for misdemeanors in some systems.

5 Charge filed by prosecutor on basis of information submitted by police or citizens. Alternative to grand jury indictment; often used in felonies, almost always in misdemeanors.

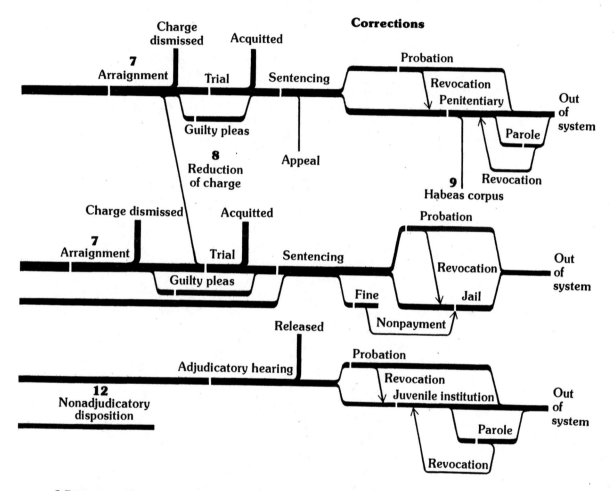

Corrections

7 Arraignment — Charge dismissed — Trial — Acquitted — Guilty pleas — **8** Reduction of charge — Sentencing — Appeal — Probation — Revocation — Penitentiary — Parole — Revocation — **9** Habeas corpus — Out of system

7 Arraignment — Charge dismissed — Trial — Acquitted — Guilty pleas — Sentencing — Fine — Nonpayment — Probation — Revocation — Jail — Out of system

Released — Adjudicatory hearing — **12** Nonadjudicatory disposition — Probation — Revocation — Juvenile institution — Parole — Revocation — Out of system

6 Reviews whether government evidence is sufficient to justify trial. Some states have no grand jury system; others seldom use it.

7 Appearance for plea; defendant elects trial by judge or jury (if available); counsel for indigent usually appointed here in felonies.

8 Charge may be reduced at any time before trial in return for plea of guilty or for other reasons.

9 Challenge on constitutional grounds to legality of detention. May be sought at any point in process.

10 Police often hold informal hearings, dismiss or adjust many cases without further processing.

11 Probation officer decides desirability of further court action.

12 Welfare agency, social services, counseling, medical care, etc., for cases where adjudicatory handling not needed.

```
the United States says Reed misused a cattle prod in the
move attempt. Prosecution witnesses testified that the
director repeatedly struck the hippo on the rear end.
But one defense witness said that use of a cattle prod
. . . even many times . . . on young animals is normal.
And defense witnesses testified that another official --
the zoo's veterinarian -- had misused a drug -- M-99 --
given to the hippo to allow the move. If convicted, Reed
could face a maximum three months at hard labor and a
500-dollar fine. Testimony will resume next week. -- Greg
Adams, WERC News
```

"I write furiously at a trial," says Lebe. "I want to get down a lot of quotes, because I'm looking for a colorful line that I can mention in a voicer. And I write down not only what was said, but my observations. Sometimes mention of the wringing of hands, the paneled walls, the brass rail can help take the listener there."

When trials wander off into procedural debates, the action shifts to the lawyers and judges; and additional pressure is put on reporters to follow the intricacies of the law involved. Appeals and some hearings also revolve around legal strategies. At these levels, lawyers are more often available for interviews—since there are no more potential jurors to bias.

WERC got the prosecutor's comments on a delay in a hearing for a death-row inmate:

```
This thing has gotten ridiculous now because two-and-a-
half years have gone by and he's still in state court.
He's gotten everything that's coming to him as far as
I'm concerned.
                                            WERC, Alabama
```

After a verdict the reporter should sum up the arguments that held sway. Participants in the trial may also be willing to talk at that point, and a story on the verdict may include their comments—taped or paraphrased:

```
After deliberating about an hour and 45 minutes, the
jury returned a verdict of innocent on all charges
against elementary school teacher Susanne Kane*. The
mother of the nine-year-old child had lodged the
criminal charges . . . accusing the 27-year-old teacher
of bruising her son. An official of the Chester-Upland
school district said that Kane's only wrong -- as far as
the rules on corporal punishment are concerned -- was
that she had inadvertently paddled the youngster without
```

---

* This name has been changed.

the presence of another witness -- because the other
teacher was suddenly distracted from the classroom.
After the verdict Kane said she'd be more careful to
have two or three witnesses in the future. She said she
expects to return to the school this fall. -- I'm Duane
Gray, 12-10 News

WCAU, Philadelphia

Politics

Governments hold meetings. Government leaders, leaders of opposition groups and candidates for office give speeches and hold news conferences. Reporters have to cover all these events: reporting on the public's business, recording positions on issues and looking for cracks in the public facade that might reveal the inner workings of political organizations.

This is covering politics—perhaps a journalist's most serious responsibility. Politicians—battling for power—and reporters—the scorekeepers and sometimes referees in the battle—have been using each other for years. Politicians feed reporters many of the stories necessary to keep the newscast stocked with news of significance; but the political news that doesn't come in the regular feedings is what elevates the good reporters above the pack.

There are two ways to cover most political stories: the routine way—and reporters do have to master this—and the enterprising way. Enterprise won't always turn up anything, but the scoops and the awards are likely to go to reporters who *are* enterprising.

Meetings

Too many stations are forced to cover meetings by phone. That means a call to an official or two afterward for a rundown of what happened. This leaves the politicians in complete control of the information the reporter gets about the meeting. And no matter how honest, politicians are not about to freely give information that hurts them. Increasing the number of phone calls, especially to opposition politicians, should help, but for important meetings the telephone is a weak substitute for being there.

If reporters are able to attend a meeting, preparation might include a visit to the city clerk or whatever official can fill them in on the agenda. This allows reporters to collect some background on the potential controversies and to do some reporting beforehand, such as contacting some of the citizens who may be affected by the discussion but who aren't likely to attend.

Some interviewing can be conducted before things get underway. If the issues to be discussed are clear, reporters can get a story on the air even while the meeting is still in progress.

WCAU in Philadelphia was covering a hearing of the Pennsylvania House Agriculture Committee on a bill to restrict the use of pain-killing drugs for race horses. Their reporter in the state capital filed an actuality with the state senator who introduced the bill. The newscaster in the studio read a lead-in noting that the hearing was about to begin; then this discussion of the effect of one of the drugs—"Bute"—was played:

> Recently there was a dramatic illustration of the
> controversial use of Bute at Pimlico, a race track in
> Maryland, when jockey Robert Pineda was killed in a
> pile-up that was caused by a horse who broke down and
> caused a multiple-horse collision, throwing their
> jockeys in the fall, killing jockey Pineda.

And the reporter also filed a voicer based on the same interview before the hearing started:

> Senator Howard says that, according to Horse Racing
> Commission statistics for the past three years, more
> than 78 percent of all horses entered at Pennsylvania
> flat racing tracks were doctored with Butazolizin --
> commonly known as ''Bute'' -- a powerful pain-killing
> drug. Howard says this interferes with the animal's
> natural protection against injury . . . which is pain.
> As a result, he says, injured animals are often fatally
> damaged when they break down on Pennsylvania tracks. --
> In Harrisburg, this is Jim Wiggins, 12-10 News
>
> WCAU, Philadelphia

Some reporters tape a meeting in case there are any heated exchanges. At hearings and meetings of larger organizations, it should be possible to plug into the public address system in the room. Otherwise, reporters have to make do with their own microphones—a poor arrangement if people are speaking from different positions.

Most of this tape is useless because most of the time meetings sound dull. Some reporters save their tape for interviews after the meeting and spend their time during the meeting taking notes and working on voicers. Afterward, it's appropriate to ask politicians questions that allow them to repeat into the tape recorder interesting comments made during the meeting.

The goal is to get statements from all sides in a dispute—politicians, the affected parties and interested spectators. At that hearing on horses and drugs, interview targets would include horse trainers, veterinarians, animal lovers and the state legislators on the committee. The reporter also puts together a voicer or a wrap, either summing up the meeting or covering a few important points. Here's a wrap on a meeting between the president and the nation's governors in Washington:

Reporter:	President Bush used the meeting to push his economic plan.
Bush:	I need your help. I'd like to ask for your help.
Reporter:	But the meeting didn't go according to script. When reporters began leaving after the president's remarks, Colorado Governor Roy Romer stopped them.
Romer:	Could I ask the press not to leave yet.
Reporter:	The Democrat then criticized Bush's plan.
Romer:	We ought not pose this meeting with the governors as how can we as governors help you go to Congress and convince them that your approach alone is the only approach.
Reporter:	Romer said Democrats want a fairer tax system and a bigger peace dividend for problems at home. The president defended his plan but promised to work with states to address concerns. -- Barry Bagnato, CBS News, Washington

Politicians can hide controversy by choreographing meetings in advance or using legal wordings as camouflage. Good reporting is distinguished from the routine by the ability to see through to the effects and political meanings of issues. That takes preparation.

Contacts help. Reporters can prepare themselves by staying in touch with the players (see Chapter 8, "Gathering News"), from the mayor and the opposition leader to the clerks. If befriended, these people can provide the analysis necessary to understand the play at the meeting. These are the people who are qualified to point out the strategies and disclose who stands to gain. It's worth the time spent waiting in their offices or tracking them down at their watering holes.

Study helps. A chart that explains the organization of the city government can usually be obtained. The city charter and a directory of city agencies also make interesting reading. And politicians' voting records and statements in legislative bodies are all matters of public record—they occasionally stand in revealing contrast to campaign statements or recent positions. Budgets, too, should be read—line by line. It's a rare shenanigan that doesn't involve money.

Similar collections of paper and people surround conferences and hearings. A reporter who is acquainted with them is better prepared to understand. It's like putting on the colored glasses at a 3-D movie—suddenly the action can be seen to have depth.

Speeches

Many reporters begin coverage of a speech with a visit to the public relations people handling the event. They are not about to whisper dirt about their bosses, but, since their job is to handle the press, they should be able to provide some early direction— at least a guide to what the politician wants the news to be.

PR people often have the text of the speech to hand reporters. This can be used to select potential actualities, but it's necessary to listen to the actual speech for digressions. Some of the biggest news gets made when the speaker leaves the prepared text.

During the speech, the tape recorder is usually plugged into the PA system, if possible. If not, it should be placed up front with the microphone near the speaker's face. Merely holding a mike up to a PA loudspeaker does not produce high-quality sound. (Sound quality is the most important consideration, of course, but if it's feasible, reporters also like to have their tape recorders near enough so that they can glance at the counter numbers when they hear a potential cut. Noting those numbers will save time later.)

If the speech promises to be long, reporters might want to try to turn their recorders off as they get to dull sections of the prepared transcript. Otherwise, reporters just listen and take notes—in-cues, out-cues and times of potential actualities. They can also begin composing voicers.

Here is an actuality recorded from the PA during a speech by the British prime minister in New York:

```
Our response to political or military adventurism must
be measured and appropriate and this is certainly true
in Africa. Because of our past history, we can't escape
involvement in Africa's struggles. Africa has shown that
she welcomes this involvement where it contributes to
redressing the evils of poverty and underdevelopment.
But there's a big gap between involvement and
intervention.
```
                                                                    ABC

The PR person should be able to answer the reporter's most pressing question at these events: "Will I be able to get the politician alone afterward?" The answer is usually "yes," in which case it may not even be necessary to record the speech. Any important points can be repeated again in the interview after the speech. There are advantages to these follow-up interviews: Extemporaneous answers may make for more pithy actualities. The reporter can attempt to get short summaries of long-winded discussions from the speech. And, as Mitch Lebe notes, it's a lot easier to find the actualities on the tape of a three-minute interview than on the tape of a 45-minute speech. These one-on-one interviews also provide an opportunity to change the subject. The real news, and therefore the best actualities, may have nothing to do with the subject of the speech.

Some years ago, an Alabama station interviewed Cornelia Wallace *after* she announced her candidacy for governor:

```
Wallace:    I just decided today that I felt it was
            something I should do. I decided to run
            'cause I wanted to insure that the people of
            Alabama have a choice, that they have an
            honest governor, a choice to vote for some-
            one honest, and there are not as many candi-
            dates in the field as I thought there would
            be.

Reporter:   So you just made this decision today?

Wallace:    Yes.

Reporter:   Anything in particular just kick it off
            today, or have you been thinking about it a
            little bit all along?

Wallace:    No, it was really today.
                                          WERC, Alabama
```

Reporters also work the audience after a speech, looking for reactions to record. These actualities can help fill subsequent newscasts with follow-ups on the speech.

Coverage of speeches is distinguished from the routine by the reporter's ability to place thoughts lifted from the speech in perspective and by the sharpness of the interviews afterward.

News Conferences

When Bill Moyers was White House press secretary, this is how he described his jousts with reporters at press briefings: "They pull it out of me until there's nothing more I want to tell them."

Like Moyers' briefings, most news conferences are a snap for newsmakers to control. There are many tricks they can employ short of Richard Nixon's eventual strategy—not holding any more news conferences. Newsmakers can filibuster—go on and on about the insignificant until there's no time left. They can also avoid direct answers to questions:

> Question: Why won't the new bus lines service black neighborhoods?

> Answer: A number of black leaders were consulted about this plan. In fact we talked with people from all areas of the city . . .

Newsmakers can dodge follow-up questions, depriving reporters of any opportunity to pin them down. They can call most frequently on those reporters least likely to ask challenging questions, and they can plant self-serving questions with friendly reporters.

The reporter's job is to break through. Every story isn't Watergate; every politician isn't Richard Nixon. There's no call for boorishness or paranoia, but reporters have to be forceful and persistent enough to challenge the newsmaker for control of a news conference. That requires standing up and asking in a strong and commanding voice whatever questions the reporter needs answered. It may require repeating questions that have been evaded, standing up again for follow-ups, changing the subject and, if the situation permits, cutting off a filibuster. One reporter who has done the homework and isn't shy may dominate a news conference.

Of course, the best way for reporters to avoid being denied in a news conference is to step outside the news conference format and engage a newsmaker one-on-one in a private interview afterward. If they can arrange such a session beforehand, many reporters will sit on their best questions during the conference—why share the fruits of their labor with the competition?

News conferences, like speeches, yield actualities. Reporters primarily file actualities and wraps.

Campaigns

Communicating to the people is how elections are won—and that is where the news media come in. Campaigns are becoming more and more media events. In a visit to a shopping center a candidate can reach hundreds of voters, but if a radio or television reporter is there, that candidate can reach many thousands.

Clearly reporters are in a position to tip the balance, so their first responsibility is to be evenhanded (see Chapter 18, "Ethics and Law").

Hot issues have a way of materializing around election time—often not to be heard about again for another two or four years. Reporters have to be ready for them. Most stations help by preparing files on each of the candidates at the beginning of the campaign; press releases, position papers and newspaper stories are collected. A reporter assigned to follow a candidate can read through the file, catch up on

WOR, New York, reporter Robyn Walensky (seated) takes notes at a campaign rally. (Mitchell Stephens)

the issues and be ready to spot inconsistencies, wavering or even the occasional fresh idea.

Candidates rarely serve meat in their speeches. They've learned that a substantive position—a detailed tax proposal, a draft of a proposed budget—can alienate as many voters as it attracts; so the political reporter is fed a steady diet of bland pledges to help all and hurt none, sprinkled with platitudes about the decency of the voters and the essential soundness of our democracy. These statements must be labeled "not news!" and kept out of actualities.

UNACCEPTABLE

```
When I go to Washington I will do my best to represent
the fine people of this great city and to uphold the
great principles on which this nation was founded.
```

Rule: If any candidate for any office could have said it, it is probably not newsworthy. News is issues, attacks, controversy and any clear portents of what these people will do if elected. If the candidate won't bring up the issues, it becomes the reporter's job to do so.

Candidates should be asked to respond to their opponent's attacks; they should be questioned about the major issues, and vague points in their positions should be pounced on. Matters of concern to the people must be covered. Reporters may have to press, probe and confront to get something of substance on tape.

As the field of press agency has advanced, reporters covering major campaigns have found themselves the recipients of prerecorded actualities featuring the candidates. They come on cassettes, ready to use. Most reporters keep them off the air; they want to use tape that results from their own questioning, not from some public relations agent's script. (See Chapter 7, "Sources.")

Campaign coverage can become a Ping-Pong match of charges and counter-charges. That's okay, until the last days before the election. When the voters are presumably making final decisions there may not be time for the opponent to prepare a response to a particularly virulent charge. At that point, reporters may avoid airing unsubstantiated attacks that cannot be answered. Coverage of a sudden charge of corruption the afternoon before the vote may have to be postponed, despite its obvious news value.

Polls

Reports on how people are likely to vote can also affect how they actually will vote. That's why one candidate or another can often be found trumpeting the results of some public opinion poll; it's also why reporters have to be so careful in their handling of these polls.

Public opinion polls have definite limitations. Reporters were reminded of that fact during the 1992 presidential election when at one point Bill Clinton was said to be leading George Bush by up to 15 percentage points in one set of polls but by as few as five percentage points in others.

Polls are limited by the wording of the questions they ask: "Do you believe that human life must be protected even before birth?" will get a different response from "Do you believe women should have the right to choose whether or not to have an abortion?" Polls are limited by the order in which the questions are asked—in 1984 polls that asked questions about issues *before* they asked who respondents favored for president came up with less support for Ronald Reagan. Polls are limited by the choice of the population that is queried—likely voters, registered voters, people who have listed telephone numbers. And polls are limited by the fickleness of that which they are supposed to be summarizing—people's opinions. That's what the pollsters mean when, after the wrong person wins, they start moaning about the "volatility" of the voters.

This is not to say that polls cannot be useful in reporting on public opinion; only that they must be handled with great care. There may not be a place in a broadcast story for all the details and numbers with which responsible pollsters qualify their findings, but there still are certain basic facts that reporters must at least keep in mind, if not in their stories.

1. Who conducted the poll? Organizations that pay for public opinion surveys have a way of getting what they paid for. And, at the very least, you can be sure that if the results were unfavorable you wouldn't have learned them. The organization that sponsored the poll must be noted in the story.

    UNACCEPTABLE
    ```
    A new poll released today shows that a majority of
    Americans believe the best way to improve our
    educational system is to pay teachers more.
    ```

    ACCEPTABLE
    ```
    A national teachers union has released a new poll. The
    pollsters say they found that a majority of Americans
    believe the best way to improve our educational system
    is to pay teachers more.
    ```

2. What was the margin of error? Polls are hardly foolproof. If a survey has been conducted scientifically, its statistical limitations will be summed up in this one number: the margin of error. If that margin is almost as large as the difference the poll found on a question, then that poll is not worth much. The margin of error should be mentioned in the story, too. "I'm fairly scrupulous about this," explains Richard Threlkeld, CBS's national correspondent. "It's something the late George Gallup worked for years to get people in the media to do."

    UNACCEPTABLE
    ```
    A new poll, published by the Desmond Times, says that
    Mayor Hanratty will beat Republican Frank Straus by five
    percentage points.
    ```

    ACCEPTABLE
    ```
    Who's ahead in the race for mayor? A new poll, published
    by the Desmond Times, says Mayor Hanratty has a five-
    percentage-point lead over Republican Frank Straus.
    However, that poll has a four-percent margin of error,
    so that lead does not mean much.
    ```

3. How many are undecided? A substantial lead after most have made up their minds is a lot more significant than a substantial lead when most of the electorate is still deciding.

    UNACCEPTABLE
    ```
    According to a new poll, conducted by this station,
    David Hauser has a big lead in the race for the
    Republican nomination for mayor. He's seven percentage
    points ahead of his nearest rival, Joan Malin.
    ```

ACCEPTABLE
A new poll has found that David Hauser is off to a good
start in the race for the Republican nomination for
mayor. He has a seven-point lead over his nearest rival,
Joan Malin. However, more than half the people surveyed
said they are still undecided.

4. When was the survey conducted? Who was sampled? This information may not
always make it into the story, but it may make a crucial difference in how
reporters choose to handle the results of a survey. Was the poll taken before or
after the debate? Were only likely voters sampled? And how many people were
interviewed? The fact that the sample included only 134 people should be
reflected in the margin of error, but this fact may also be useful in teaching a
little humility. It may help reporters remember to bill these efforts to read the
public's mind as the estimates and predictions they are, not as solid facts.

"Reporters ought to approach a poll the way they approach any other source,"
Threlkeld advises. "They should ask, 'Is this poll trustworthy? Is this information
true?' You have to check the information in polls as carefully as any other information
you get as a reporter."

Investigation

All reporting requires investigation—CBS's Bill Lynch searching through the appen-
dices at the White House (see Chapter 8, "Gathering News"), KOEL's Dick Petrik
seeking to discover what armed robbery the sheriff was after (see "Introduction")—
but the phrase *investigative reporting* is used to single out truly exhaustive reporting projects, projects that most stations cannot give their reporters time to do.
Reporters must do them anyway.

To be a reporter is to be constantly on the lookout for signs that those in positions
of trust are not trustworthy. Beginning reporters shouldn't come on like Sherlock
Holmes and fantasize a Teapot Dome scandal every time a politician gets a free cup
of coffee. But when a radio reporter is too caught up in three-car accidents to follow
a solid tip on a conflict of interest, it's time to start considering a career as a disk
jockey.

Investigative reporters keep their ears to the ground—in touch with contacts,
open to tips; they keep their eyes on the money—who stands to gain; their fingers
on the phone—pursuing tips, checking leads; and their faces buried in the records—
it's in the documents somewhere. These reporters, of course, are just doing what
all reporters do—only more so, and if they get something, the results will be that
much more satisfying.

As careers and reputations are brought into question, the need for caution naturally increases. Caution means everything is double- and triple-checked; most
investigative reporters require confirmation by at least two sources before they'll run
with a story. Caution does not mean watching out for whomever might be offended.

Investigations are not necessarily aimed at catching wrongdoing; nor do they have to be about politics. KNX-FM in Los Angeles won an award for a documentary about rape. It, too, required investigative reporting. Reporter Bob Madigan pored through police statistics, FBI statistics, statistics from the Los Angeles Committee on Assaults Against Women, statistics from the local rape crisis hotline—all to get an accurate picture of the scope of the problem. Then he talked with department of corrections officials, police, the district attorney, social workers and psychologists; then rape victims—some women who had called the rape hotline agreed to talk on tape.

This was all standard. Madigan really showed enterprise by persuading prison officials to put him in touch with convicted rapists. He was able to record their voices at a group therapy session. All of this took almost eight months. The result—a 90-minute documentary (see Chapter 13, "Public Affairs").

Incidentally, Madigan produced this documentary while continuing his regular reporting and writing duties. KNX-FM has only a three-person staff. How do they find time for such investigative reporting? News Director Christopher Ames says the secret is budgeting time well and "working their asses off."

Protests

The squeaky wheel gets greased; the media cover disputes when they disrupt. Alas, the complaints of various oppressed nationalities too often are ignored . . . until some of them go and hijack a plane.

There is something unfortunate about a system of coverage that favors yelling or violence. Ignoring protests or terrorism, however, would create a more serious problem—paranoia that there is something going on that we're not being told about. Reporters should make an additional effort to cover the gripes of groups that don't resort to loud protest, but they can't ignore serious disturbances, even if they seem to be blatant media events. They're news; they get covered.

Strikes and other protest demonstrations provide easy actualities through interviews on the street with demonstration leaders and the people doing the picketing; reporters just have to be sensitive to the difference between leaders and self-proclaimed leaders. But the real challenge is to produce voicers and actualities that cut through the rhetoric to the central areas of disagreement. This, of course, requires a talk with the other side.

In a strike, management should be easy to track down; they're not shy about expounding their views. In a protest demonstration, the officials or policy makers who are the targets of the demonstration may be less inclined to go public. Deft telephone dialing or door knocking may be necessary to give these people a chance to defend themselves—perhaps just on background (see Chapter 8, "Gathering News").

The standard routine for covering a street protest is: First, interview the protest's leaders and other demonstrators. ("Sometimes the average person who feels committed enough to come down and walk around in a circle on a cold day is more interesting than a person who is in charge," observes Mitch Lebe.) Next, piece together the meaning of their complaint for voicers and wraps. And then, search out the other side. Often there's one more task: tracking down the effect of the strike or protest on the community—services interrupted, people inconvenienced, economic ramifications. Carrying out all these assignments demands some homework on such matters as "piece goods," "attrition," the "viability" of fetuses and, perhaps, the grievances of various oppressed nationalities.

The more heated the protest, the more pressure may be placed on reporters. Angry protesters may even choose to vent their wrath on a reporter as a representative of "the media." The best policy in these situations is passivity; listen and try to understand. Reporters are there to learn, not debate.

When a protest boils over into violence, reporters find themselves in an uncomfortable position. Aside from concern over the situation, their own safety and the mine field of potentially criminal acts they have to discuss judiciously, there's the danger that their reports may further incite violence or cause panic.

This actuality about a situation in Matamoros, Mexico, was aired by ABC. How might people react when they hear something like this about their town on their radios?

> When we got to the scene of the fire, then I saw that it
> was more than a fire . . . it was a riot.

A reporter cannot use, or let a newsmaker in an actuality use, the word *riot* lightly. One poorly chosen word can touch off further trouble (see Chapter 3, "Meanings"). Being told there is a riot in your town may inspire various sorts of behaviors— not all of them safe. Reporters must remember that a bottle thrown through a store window may be called an *incident*; it is not necessarily a *disturbance*. A crowd of unruly kids may constitute a *disturbance*, but it is not automatically a *riot*. Four people were killed and about two dozen injured that day in Matamoros. City hall and dozens of stores were burned. In this case, ABC was correct in airing an actuality that labeled that situation a *riot*. South central Los Angeles in 1992 centainly a *Riot*.

Other crucial semantic distinctions: Angry demonstrators pushing against police lines do not represent an *outbreak of violence*. Violence involving blacks is not necessarily *racial violence*.

Reporters are not alchemists. *Crowds* cannot automatically be transformed into *mobs*; *mobs* into *angry mobs*; *fires* into *arson*; *shots* into *snipers*; *struggles during arrests* into *police brutality*. If such charged designations are to be used, they must come from responsible sources and be clearly attributed to them. Rumors and unverified tips are unacceptable (see Chapter 18, "Ethics and Law").

The pressure to keep reporting balanced also increases during protests or riots. Airing charges that the police shot an innocent teenager—without giving the police a chance to respond—can overheat already heated situations, as can reporting that demonstrators have begun attacking police—without giving the demonstrators' side of the story. Of course, ignoring such charges would also be a mistake.

In addition, reporters must keep the size of a protest in context. If only 100 of the 30,000 students on campus are participating, that must be noted.

These are standard rules of careful, ethical reporting—amplified in importance by a volatile situation. They may not be enough when things get rough. Supplementary rules that many news organizations have adopted for covering disorders are discussed in Chapter 18, "Ethics and Law."

Economics

Business, labor, consumer news, finance, economic policy—these are stories that reach into our pockets or pocketbooks. They are becoming increasingly important in broadcast news.

Part of the audience for economic news will have a direct personal interest in what the newscaster is saying. Business people will be waiting to hear of changes in interest rates, in commodity prices, in exchange rates. These changes may affect their decision on whether to add a late shift at the plant tomorrow. Workers will be waiting to hear whether the union accepted that six-percent wage increase, or whether it decided to strike. Investors will want information on that attempted takeover and how it will be felt on Wall Street. Consumers will want to know if that frost in Florida will push up the cost of fruit and juice.

Reporters covering economics, and few reporters escape the subject these days, will have to learn how to cater to the interests of these segments of the audience. They will have to study up on the businesses in their areas by visiting the local Chamber of Commerce and visiting the businesses themselves. They'll want to plow through the financial statements all *publicly held* businesses (companies in which the public can buy stock) must make available (an office of the Securities and Exchange Commission will release them, if the company won't), and they'll want to talk with the *securities analysts* in charge of evaluating local companies for brokerage firms.

To get smarter about labor, reporters will want to talk with union officials as well as with workers. In addition, a little reading on labor history will help provide some perspective.

The concerns of investors are hard to localize. Those locals with excess capital have probably invested as much of it on Wall Street as they have on Main Street. But if the area has a commodities market—where products such as grain or oil are traded by speculators—or a commodity that's important to the local economy, reporters will have to familiarize themselves with that.

Consumer news often comes from government regulatory agencies such as the Federal Trade Commission or the Food and Drug Administration. Allegations about unsafe products or unfair business practices can become major stories. And reporters will also want to keep in touch with local consumer groups and local retail stores to monitor changes in the availability and cost of products. A shortage of Japanese automobiles is news to one group of consumers. The introduction of a new liquid detergent is news to another.

The best economics reporting, however, goes beyond satisfying the concerns of just these parties with special interests. It looks for broader meanings and wider implications in such "money stories." The ups and downs of local businesses will affect the local economy and, therefore, will affect most listeners or viewers. A new labor settlement could help pump money into the economy . . . or raise prices. If the price of grain goes up, that boosts the economy in farm areas, but it also contributes to inflation. And a report on the introduction of that new liquid detergent might tell a tale about how things work in our society that will interest listeners who otherwise couldn't care less about laundry detergents.

Even those dry-sounding statistics on the national economy, which the federal government turns out practically every business day, can be pulled out of the business and financial section at the end of a newscast (see Chapter 12, "Newscasts") and made interesting enough for the top of the show. Here's an actuality in which an economist explains the meaning of a decline of one-tenth of one percent in retail sales in December:

```
There just was a lot of concern, so consumers
became cautious. They didn't completely leave the
marketplace . . . retail sales didn't drop much except
for cars . . . but they did temper their spending.
```
CBS

There are other possible ways for reporters to deal with a slight drop in retail sales: perhaps a call to some local stores or the Chamber of Commerce; perhaps an interview with a local college economist who will discuss consumer fears of recession; perhaps a series of quick interviews with shoppers in a large department store on whether or why they've been buying less.

Importance is the first criterion for determining newsworthiness (see Chapter 5, "Leads"). Economics stories, because their impact is often so widely felt and because they hit us in such a vulnerable spot—our wallets—are often particularly *important*, particularly newsworthy.

Features

Dick Petrik of KOEL in Iowa is talking with a judge about an upcoming trial. His final question: "Anything else interesting going on?" and Petrik has stumbled on a *feature*. The judge mentions that he plans to play golf this afternoon with three friends and that all four of the players have had open-heart surgery. Petrik gets their names and has an intriguing story about the "open-heart foursome"—a human-interest story.

Many such feature stories pop up on the trail of harder news. Reporters have to be alert for eccentric hobbies or unusual achievements, and the other exaggerations and anomalies that attract the interest of human beings.

In other words, reporters must be prepared to look beyond the story they are pursuing. The bit players—the mayor's secretary, the police dispatcher—may be newsworthy in their own right. That house with the elaborate Christmas decorations passed en route may be a story. A few minor events—local garage sales, for example—may add up to a trend and a feature.

Features are news. It didn't take public relations people long to figure out that the media have this sweet tooth and to begin feeding them features to satisfy it. Feature stories that are heralded in press releases, over the wires or by tips are then pursued like other stories. Reporters get the assignment, gather facts (the facts in features should be handled with no less care), do a couple of interviews and then file. The point of interest in the story must be captured, either on tape or in the reporter's notes; then background information must be obtained to support that point.

Features may depend heavily on emotions, as expressed in people's voices. Actualities—the participants in a program for the handicapped, the winners at an awards dinner—are essential. Features also benefit from the personal touch—the reporter's own voice. The ideal form for a feature is a wrap.

Since hard news can speak for itself, a straightforward recounting should do. Feature stories, however, require more telling. As a rule the writing should be more lively. Delayed or humorous leads work well. Puns and anecdotes, where appropriate, can be effective. And when a story's main job is to be interesting, it is even more important to use real terms—*delicious apples* and *tuna on rye*, for example, instead of *groceries*. Strong snappers also help bring out interest. Features usually leave room for creativity.

A feature wrap out of Atlantic City:

Reporter: Whether or not casino gambling can buy happiness, there are some things casino chips definitely can buy . . . things like delicious apples, barbecued chicken and tuna on rye. Ever since the Resorts casino opened, Bohack's Market, on Pacific Avenue, has been accepting casino chips as currency. Co-owners Robert Rosenfeld and Bruce Gamberg admit it's a gimmick, but it's working.

1st Owner: We did it just to get into the spirit of things. When the casino opened we put our sign up, just to get in the mood.

Reporter: What's the response been?

2nd Owner: Fantastic, we've gotten almost a thousand dollars worth of chips through here already.

Reporter: And most of those chips have been coming from out-of-towners who walk by the market

```
          on their way to and from the casino. The
          gimmick is proving to be so successful that
          a number of other stores and restaurants
          also are taking in the chips. -- In Atlan-
          tic City, Lori Yapczenski, 12-10 News
                                      WCAU, Philadelphia
```

Listeners start losing interest when the feature itself is a cliché. Treed cats or kids selling lemonade aren't much more interesting at this point than a lost dog. Keep an eye out for something different.

Live

With a telephone line or a two-way radio that can be fed directly onto the air, radio reporters can cover an important breaking story live.

Perhaps the most famous live radio-type report of recent years actually appeared, without visuals, on television . . . in the very first moments of the Persian Gulf War:

```
          Something is happening outside. The skies over Baghdad
          have been illuminated. We're seeing bright flashes going
          off all over the sky. I've never been there, but it
          feels like we're in the center of Hell.
                                      Bernard Shaw, CNN
```

Certainly "live" is radio news at its most exciting. Listeners like live coverage because it's dramatic; they are there as breaking events break. News directors like it because listeners like it; reporters, however, have some qualms. Reporting live increases the pressure and can deprive journalists of their most basic tool—their writing.

Frequently reporters have a chance to write a live report out in advance or at least to scribble some notes, but sometimes they are compelled to go on the air extemporaneously. For professionals who have been trained to care deeply about their choice of words, that is not an altogether comfortable experience. Here are some tips on reporting live:

1. *Prepare.* "As much as possible, I try to write out my live reports in advance because then I can catch my errors," says WCBS's Mitch Lebe. "If I'm lazy and don't prepare, I sometimes catch those errors after I've said them on the air." So, the first rule of reporting live is to try to get as much down on paper as possible. Jotting down the points that should be covered is invaluable. Scrawling out the sentences ahead of time helps order thoughts, even if there's no opportunity to read those sentences. And the reporter can also prepare by rehearsing the report. Of course, taped or live, the more information reporters gather before they have to report, the better the job they do.

A *live report on CNN* at the beginning of the Persian Gulf War. (© 1991 CNN, Inc. All Rights Reserved)

2. *Emphasize the timely.* Recaps may have a place, but the purpose of live reporting is to report the very *latest* developments—additional police arriving, the terrorists peeping through windows, the building still smoldering. The present tense must take command. Even if it may not prove to have been of great significance, the fact that something is happening on a major story at this moment is exciting in itself, and these breaking developments draw listeners into the live report. Reporters have to be prepared to switch to more timely topics in midsentence if necessary. Lebe offers this example: ". . . then the fire spread to the two adjoining build . . . THE FLAMES ARE SHOOTING OUT OF THE WINDOW RIGHT NOW!"

3. *Evoke.* "The whole point of live reporting," says David Heller, news director at KLOS in Los Angeles, "is to provide an evocative word picture of what is going on. Simple facts are not as important as describing the scene." This should bring to mind another type of report—ROSRs (see Chapter 9, "Tape"). Live reporting employs the same elements as ROSRs—sights, sounds, smells, the first person. Reporters here are scouts, sending back personal reports from the scene.

4. *Stay calm.* It's fine when the excitement creeps into reporters' voices, but they must keep it out of their minds. Ad-libbing into a live microphone under duress leaves reporters vulnerable to all sorts of errors. Calmness and concentration are necessary to guard against speculation, embellishment and sloppiness. Reporters should not get caught up as participants; they are observers, just reporting what they see and what they have learned.

When reporting live, reporters should be prepared to answer questions on the air asked by the newscaster or announcer in the studio. If the station favors this live exchange, the reporter might think through, and even suggest, possible questions beforehand.

One final piece of advice for reporting live from Voight Smith of WJVM in Illinois: "Try to get there *before* the fire is out."

Wrap-Up

Different types of coverage, different strategies; but it's important to remember what they all have in common. Every story—the ones mentioned here, the stories that fall in between these categories or outside these categories—requires an enterprising, thorough and responsible pursuit of facts and tape.

Practice Assignments

A. List the people you would interview on tape and the questions you would ask on the scene in the following situations:

1. A fire breaks out in a large downtown department store. Four shoppers are hurt, it is the third fire at a large store in the past two months.
2. The annual meeting of the Propertyholders' Association is held. On the agenda is a city council bill to raise annual real estate taxes five percent.
3. The mayor has announced a slash in the budget of the city's poverty programs. A coalition of minority groups comes to City Hall to confront the mayor.
4. Some of the local high school's gym equipment—valued at about 70-thousand dollars—is stolen. A night guard and a janitor were in the building when the crime occurred. Local police are on the scene.
5. College students in your town organize a one-day sit-in and boycott of classes. They're protesting the police's conduct in the arrest of a student on drug charges.

B. Cover the meeting of a local governmental body—a school board or city council, for example. Record and edit two actualities and a voicer.

C. Cover a local speech or press conference. Record and edit two actualities and a voicer.

D. Interview local police officials on departmental policy on the use of guns. Record and edit one actuality, one voicer and one wrap.

E. Visit a local courthouse and sit in on a session of a trial. Record and edit two voicers on that trial.

F. Interview management and workers at a local business on the policy of that business in granting maternity leave. Record and edit one actuality, one voicer and one wrap.

G. Obtain from a local publicly held company a copy of that company's latest quarterly earnings report. Interview company officials on the significance of that report and record and edit one actuality, one voicer and one wrap.

III

Producing

Newscasts

Larry Clark is responsible for the 12:55 p.m. newscast on KAKC in Tulsa, Oklahoma. All the stories that he and others in the newsroom have written for that show are spread out in front of him. Clark now has to **produce** the newscast. His job, once the stories have been assigned and written, is to arrange these stories so they flow and hold interest, to mix in weather and sports news, to put the commercials in place, to add the open and close and, finally, to combine all this in a package that is 5 minutes long—exactly. The newscast is the final product.

Few people are actually given the title **producer** in radio journalism, but this is one of the more important jobs anyone responsible for a newscast has to do. In the more specialized world of television news, the person with these responsibilities, the person in charge of the entire newscast, usually is called the **producer** (see Chapter 17, "Television Newscasts").

Ordering

The seven news stories that Larry Clark had to turn into his 12:55 newscast, arranged alphabetically:

1. Air Force confirms that Russian bomber flew close to the East Coast; *with actuality*.
2. Call for suspension of ban on saccharin.
3. Classes being held despite fire in school last night.
4. Local reaction to president's plan for solar energy; *with actuality*.
5. New college to be dedicated here; *with actuality*.
6. President discusses energy at news conference.
7. Weather service says that funnel-like clouds in the sky aren't tornado clouds; *with actuality*.

In what order should these stories be used? Broadcasting them in alphabetical order seems even-handed, but the jumps from national news to local news, then back again to a national story, might disconcert listeners. They also might have difficulty with the rapid switch from energy to a new college, and then back to energy again. And is that Soviet bomber the story most likely to catch the attention of Tulsa listeners?

Clearly, alphabetical organization leaves something to be desired. Stories have to be carefully placed in a newscast. The organization of a news show must meet some of the same standards as the organization of a story.

First, the newscast needs a good **lead story**—a story that gets attention and discourages dial twisting. Then the newscast must be arranged so that it flows as smoothly as possible from story to story. And finally, the newscast benefits from a good **close**, perhaps a story with a twist that leaves listeners thinking.

A sheet on which the order of stories is written down is called a **lineup.** Many veterans disdain lineups, preferring to shuffle the stories until they proceed logically or to work out the order in their heads. But, newer members of the profession should take the time to write out a lineup to help organize their thoughts on organizing the newscast.

The lineup should include the story's slug, its length and mention of any tape there is to go with it. Below is a simple lineup format. (**Spots** are commercials, and the **running time** is the total time of the newscast so far.)

STORY	TAPE	STORY TIME	RUNNING TIME
Open		:03	:03
Toxic waste	wrap	:50	:53
Spot		:30	1:23
Epner	actuality	:33	1:56
Stabbing		:18	2:14
Engoron trial	actuality	:31	2:45
Spot		1:00	3:45
Russia dollars	voicer	:35	4:20
Belfast		:16	4:36
Weather		:20	4:56
Close		:04	5:00

The somewhat more elaborate lineup reprinted on the next page was prepared by producer Hal Terkel for the CBS World News Round-Up. It includes out-cues for the tape used in the newscast as well as the name of the reporter who filed each tape. The numbers on the right are the times of the lead-in and write-out used with each tape.

The lineup gives the order of stories. There are a number of guidelines for determining that order.

```
WNR 4/10
1. HARRISBURG...ROTH                                                   :58
                              TAPE...1:12
                              OUTCUE...CBS News, Harrisburg.
                                                                      :05
------------------------------------------------------------------

2. ROYALTON, PA...LANDAY                                              :10
                              TAPE...1:33
                              OUTCUE...CBS News, Royalton, Pennsylvania.
                                                                      :24
------------------------------------------------------------------

3. WASHINGTON...SERAFIN                                               :20

                              TAPE...:52
                              OUTCUE...CBS News, Washington.
                                                                      :29
------------------------------------------------------------------

4. CAIRO...SEFTON                                                     :13
                              TAPE...:46
                              OUTCUE...CBS News, Cairo.
                                                                      :28
------------------------------------------------------------------
                                                                      :06
5. TEHRAN...PLANTE

                              TAPE...:37
                              OUTCUE:...CBS News, Tehran.
                                                                      :07
------------------------------------------------------------------

6. DAR ES SALAAM...DANIELS                                           :12

                              TAPE...:57
                              OUTCUE...CBS News, Dar Es Salaam.
                                                                      :30
------------------------------------------------------------------
```

Newsworthiness

Importance, interest, controversy, the unusual, timeliness and proximity (see Chapter 5, "Leads") are at work again here. The newscast should open with the most newsworthy story. Listeners want to hear the hour's lead story first, and the station wants to grab listeners' attention with the most powerful story.

In the example that opens this section, the most newsworthy story for KAKC was the clouds that did not harbor tornadoes. Negative news isn't ordinarily big news, but this story could not have been more timely or more local; and, since the presence of tornadoes can be devastating, their absence, if there was a chance they might have been there, while not unusual, is important. (On an earlier newscast, before the tornado story broke, the story that classes were being held in the school that had had the fire was the lead.)

In choosing the lead story, proximity often is the dominant consideration. Some stations practically insist that the lead story be a local story.

Which story is the most newsworthy can be debatable. At 6:30 a.m., ABC Entertainment (see Chapter 19, "Programming") led with a story about Russia's prosecution of two American correspondents. The second story in the newscast concerned rioting in Mexico. But just a half-hour earlier, ABC Information had led with the Mexican rioting and played the prosecution of the correspondents third. One of the more controversial differences in news judgment in broadcast journalism history came on the day Elvis Presley died. On its evening television news program ABC led with his death, NBC led with his death, even BBC Radio in Britain led with the death of the American rock star; but the CBS Evening News led with the debate on the Panama Canal treaty. CBS officials are still defending that decision.

Sometimes the lead story *is* obvious. On the day President Reagan was shot, all three networks led with the same story all afternoon and all evening.

Newsworthiness is *the* major criterion for selecting the lead story. For the rest of the newscast it is *one* criterion. All other things being equal, stories should be placed in order of their news value. Seldom are all other things equal, however.

Variety

When listeners stay tuned to a radio station for a couple of hours, they don't want to hear the same stories repeated every hour in the same order. When news stories are breaking, it's easy to freshen the lineup, but even if there are no new items, the newscast must be changed. Preserving variety, then, becomes another consideration in ordering a newscast. Sometimes a moderately newsworthy story is moved down in a newscast, or ignored completely, not because it is out of date, but because it was just aired an hour ago.

Stories of lesser import are often shifted about. For instance, on the 5:30 a.m. newscast on WMAL in Washington, D.C., a shut-down in the Alaska pipeline was the lead story. It wasn't mentioned at all on the 6:05 newscast. The Alaska pipeline returned to become the second story at 6:30, the last story at 7:00; then it was ignored completely at 7:30. The story wasn't changing, it wasn't getting much less timely, nor were the competing stories that morning changing. The writers of these newscasts were simply concerned with keeping their newscasts sounding fresh.

Stories should be reordered for each newscast. If possible, the lead story should be varied and stories should be dropped if they are not that important and have already been used several times. However, the collapse of the president of the United States at a state dinner in Japan, for example, is still the lead story no matter how many times it has been used. Proper attention must still be paid to the most newsworthy stories.

Geography

A newscast is a tour of events around the world, and anyone who presumes to be a listener's tour guide should know better than to hopscotch from Korea, to city hall, to Washington, then back to the Far East for a story about Japan. Newscasts flow most smoothly when geographical jumps are kept to a minimum. Normally this means doing national stories, international stories, regional stories and local stories in separate groups. If the newscast only includes local news, this may mean separating in-town and out-of-town news. All other things being equal, this works well.

In the example that began this section, there were four local stories and three national stories. KAKC's Larry Clark did the four local stories first, then the three national stories:

1. Weather service says that funnel-like clouds in the sky aren't tornado clouds; *with actuality.*
2. New college to be dedicated here; *with actuality.*
3. Classes being held despite fire in school last night.
4. Local reaction to president's plan for solar energy; *with actuality.*
5. President discusses energy at news conference.
6. Air Force confirms that Russian bomber flew close to the East Coast; *with actuality.*
7. Call for suspension of ban on saccharin.

Again, all other things are usually not this equal. On the same day that James Earl Ray, the man convicted of assassinating the Reverend Martin Luther King, Jr., escaped from prison, the hostages on a train in Holland were released. Most stations led with Ray's escape, but they didn't then cover all the national stories. Their second story was the release of the hostages—an international story. Newsworthiness outweighed the need for geographical coherence.

This lineup from WOR in New York City is organized primarily by geography, but it still manages to get the most newsworthy stories to the top:

1. Senator to meet with city officials on finances—*local.*
2. Letter bombs sent to corporations—*local.*
3. N.Y. Democrats split on choice for president—*local.*
4. President appoints nine regional delegate chairmen—*national.*
5. Senate hearings on legislation to break up oil companies—*national.*
6. Senator on law that would force disclosure of foreign bribes—*national.*
7. Reactions to Boston school decision—*national.*
8. Government report on cigarette advertising—*national.*
9. Report on interview with Italy's Communist Party's leader—*international.*
10. Higher customs rates in Russia—*international.*
11. 18-year-old man hit by train—*local.*
12. Parents object to graduation speaker—*local.*

13. Bank official indicted for embezzlement—*local*.
14. Newspaper changes format—*local*.

Natural Tie-Ins

A newscast is an odd program: Items on many different subjects are thrown together without a common theme to unify them. Of course this lack of coherence is unavoidable since there are so many stories to cover. But, when there is an opportunity to put two related stories together and make the show a bit less disjointed, writers should seize it.

When possible, stories with similar subjects should be placed together. KAKC went from the story on local reaction to part of the president's energy plan to his news conference where he discussed energy. Not only did this eliminate one abrupt transition between stories, it eased the even more difficult transition between local and national news. WOR employed a similar strategy by exploiting the natural tie-in between the local presidential politics story and the national story about the president's political moves.

Stories about labor disputes should be placed together, fire stories should be done one after another, economic stories make a natural grouping; except of course when other considerations are more pressing. If six firemen died in one fire, and the other fire was interesting only because it temporarily allowed a pet snake to escape, the natural tie-in should defer to news judgment. The firemen's deaths should open the show; the snake fire might close the show.

Tape

A newscast should sound smooth. It also should sound lively. A few minutes of the newscaster reading copy without breaks can get dull. A change of pace is needed.

Short of having the newscaster break into song, the only change of pace available is tape. Tape gets the newscast out into the world and brings on a fresh voice or two for a fraction of a minute. It perks up a newscast.

Tapes are valuable pieces in the organization of a newscast. (Videotape plays the same role in television newscasts.) They should be used in such a way that their value is exploited, not wasted. In KAKC's newscast four of the seven stories have an actuality. If they were all placed together in the show, that would leave one section of the newscast very busy and the other very dull. Instead, Larry Clark interspersed the tape stories with the nontape stories:

1. Weather; *with actuality*.
2. New college; *with actuality*.
3. School fire.
4. Solar energy; *with actuality*.

5. President's conference.
6. Russian bomber; *with actuality.*
7. Saccharin.

Here is an NBC newscast with Ann Taylor:

1. Kentucky fire; *with actuality.*
2. Dutch hostages.
3. Summit meeting; *with actuality.*
4. First Lady.
5. Memorial Day.
6. Italian trial; *with voicer.*
7. Belfast violence.

This is another rule that is often honored in the breach. A desire to apportion tape throughout the newscast must be balanced against the other guidelines. If the three most important stories all have tape, they might still have to be used one after another at the top of the newscast.

Blocks

When newscasts grow long, organizing them gets complicated. Often the newscast is broken down into different segments—**blocks**—that make the task of ordering stories more manageable.

Blocks are usually separated by commercials or special features. Because of this natural break between segments, they can be treated separately without having to flow smoothly into each other. Each block can be seen as having its own lead story, and maybe even its own concluding story.

Blocks may also restrict ordering options. The station may insist that the show open with a block of local news, followed by a block of regional news, no matter what the news value of the stories.

In its 7:45 a.m. newscast, WSB in Atlanta uses a commercial to separate the national and local news. The first block, before the commercial, is a brief run-down of national stories; the top local story and a more detailed presentation of the local news follow the commercial.

Blocks are invaluable on those stations with endless newscasts—all news. Lineup sheets are prepared that break each hour into separate segments. A preliminary lineup from WCBS in New York City for the hour from 3:00 to 4:00 p.m. is reproduced on the next page.

Written to the left of each block of stories is the time, in minutes and seconds after the hour, at which that block begins. The first block begins at 3:07:30—after the network news and commercials. Commercials are not listed on this sheet, but they are played between blocks. *Flanders, Nachman, Athens, Kalb, Cox* and *Cornell*

PRODUCER'S RUNDOWN

PRODUCER   CALLAGHAN

ANCHORMEN PARSON - FARNSWORTH

TIME 3:00p → 4:00p

DATE   7/21

07:30   COUNCIL - FLANDERS (T)
            - NACHMAN (T)
        BATES
        STEIN

12:00 SPORTS YANKEES
               METS

15:00 SUMMARY
          TAX
          UNIVERSE
          ATHENS - FEATURE (T)

18:30   BUSINESS - WILLIAMS

21:30 FEATURE MEDICINE

26:30   - ATHENS (T)
         HEAT DEATH

31:00   CAIRO
        BEIRUT - KALB (T)
        FLOOD (T)
        PRICES - COX (T)
        CONSUMERS / DRUGS

38:00 FEATURE SPECTRUM II

41:00   RACE #4
42:02 NEWS
       SPORTS REGATTA
        CHIEF / SPILL / SMELL

45:00 SUMMARY
          COUNCIL - NACHMAN (T)
          BATES - ATHENS (T)
          N.J. LOTTERY

48:00 BERGMAN - CORNELL (T)
        CROATIANS
        HELP

51:30 FEATURE EDITORIAL
           COPS + BLACKOUT

55:30 ROBOT / CIRCUS
        BEAD / HAND GLIDES

are reporters; their names are often written with, or instead of, the slug for a story. A *T* after a story or after the name of a reporter means that the story includes tape.

All-news stations use different formats, but all of them break hours into separate blocks to order their presentations for listeners and keep writers and editors sane.

Spots

Newscasters may have to read the commercials. Newswriters or producers have to fit them into the newscast. More properly, since commercials pay the bills, they have to fit the newscast around the commercials—the spots.

On a network, the spots may be scheduled to the second in advance. The newswriter must write a block of stories that ends at that exact second. Local stations can be more flexible. Usually a show's format specifies about when the commercials should be used, but the writer can move them around 5 or 10 seconds to allow room for a story.

KAKC puts the commercial after the first story in the newscast. Larry Clark's lead story, the funnel-like clouds, ran 45 seconds. It wouldn't have made any difference had it run 5 seconds more or less—moving the commercial a bit—as long as the whole show added up right.

Radio spots generally come in two lengths—30 seconds and 1 minute. Newswriters just have to know which they're making room for.

Kickers

> The Boy Scouts of America has sued a sportswear
> manufacturer, Popsicles Playwear Limited. The Boy Scouts
> want the company to stop making baby clothing bearing
> the scout motto ''Be Prepared'' on the seat.
>
> Bill Diehl, ABC

That's a **kicker**—an offbeat story used to end the newscast. Many stations like to leave listeners marveling, if not smiling. Most kickers are funny. They don't have to be; unlikely will do:

> A Cleveland woman has kept the ashes of her late husband
> in a hall closet since 1975 . . . waiting for a
> Cleveland shipping firm to fulfill a promise to scatter
> them on Lake Erie. The firm reneged because of publicity
> and federal anti-pollution regulations. But the company
> said it would fulfill the promise if the woman gets a
> permit from the government. Her reaction: ''If people

can throw beer cans and cigarette butts in the lakes,
why can't they scatter my husband's ashes?''

Don Budd, Mutual

A warm human-interest story also makes a good close for a newscast:

Six years ago, Larry Cox of San Diego was denied
admission to a sailing class because he's blind. But Cox
was determined to learn to sail, just as he had
conquered water skiing. He has now achieved his goal --
even to the point of sailing solo in the San Diego boat
harbor with his instructor on the dock relaying
directions by walkie-talkie. Cox jokes that the biggest
obstacle to sailing is finding his way to the boat.

KNX, Los Angeles

Most writers collect interesting or unusual stories off the wires and from the
station's own reporting for possible use as kickers:

Roger Smith of Watsonville, California, is looking for
an intruder . . . and a very good housekeeper. This
sneak slipped into Roger's house through a window he had
broken . . . took nothing, but made Smith's unmade bed
before he left.

Gil Fox, ABC

Not every newscast ends this way. Some newswriters avoid closing with a light
story because doing so has become almost a cliché in broadcast news. Offbeat stories
can be placed elsewhere in the newscast, but, since these tales ordinarily are not of
any importance, the end of the newscast is the logical place for them. At the end
of the newscast, they also can provide a bridge back to the station's entertainment
programming. It can be somewhat disconcerting to go from a minor disaster straight
into a song about dancing.

Have you ever said to yourself, ''I'm so hungry I could
eat the plate?'' Well, now you can. A company in Taiwan
says it has invented the world's first edible dinnerware
-- made out of oatmeal. The plates and bowls have a
shiny surface . . . just like china. But you put boiling
water on them, and three hours later they turn to mush.
If we ever get that hungry, we'll tell you what they
taste like.

Peter Jennings, ABC

Timing

The stories have to fit. A 5-minute newscast with a 1-minute commercial leaves 4 minutes for news. On an especially heavy news day there may not be room in those 4 minutes for a kicker, and some other stories may have to be cut or dropped.

With the time in seconds written on the bottom of each story (see Chapter 1, "Copy"), to determine how many stories will fit, the writer has to add up their times, including tape. Some more experienced journalists simply add up the number of lines of copy; they know how many lines they can read in the allotted time. Bill Diehl's ABC Entertainment newscasts have room for 3 minutes and 50 seconds of copy. Diehl reads one line in 4 seconds, so his copy plus tapes should be 58 lines long to fill the show. Diehl records the number of lines in each story, instead of the time in seconds. If he is running long, he eliminates a story or trims some lines. This story started out more than 16 seconds long:

```
Several suspects are being questioned by French police
in connection with yesterday's terrorist bombing that
caused heavy damage at the Palace of Versailles outside
Paris. The chief curator at Versailles says the damage
can be repaired in two or three months.
                                          Bill Diehl, ABC
```

Diehl's show was overstuffed, so he cut the final sentence, trimming the length to 12 seconds.

Veteran writers, who have been writing the same newscast for years, can often gauge how much copy they have room for by staring at the script. Less experienced journalists should not attempt this trick. The penalties for an inaccurately timed newscast include having to rush through the final story, leaving out the last half of the final story or having to stretch 10 seconds of copy for the 20 seconds left until the network news starts.

Sometimes each block in a show must be timed separately. ABC gives its affiliates the option of selling a 30-second commercial during the newscast. Diehl has to write one block of stories exactly 30 seconds long—called "fill"—to cover that time for the stations that don't sell the space. There's no leeway on the length of that block; hundreds of stations cut out and in for exactly 30 seconds.

Newscasters may **backtime** sections of the newscast. For example, they might backtime the sports, weather and kicker—determining that they take 50 seconds total to read. If it's a 5-minute newscast that begins on the hour, the newscaster should be at 4 minutes, 10 seconds after, when sports begins. With this knowledge the newscaster is aware of whether the show is running short or long, and can pull a story or slow down a bit to compensate. Backtiming permits double-checking in the studio.

The length of stories may also influence their position in the newscast. There may only be room for one 20-second story before the commercial; so a 30-second story, though it is more newsworthy, will have to be used later. And that 40-second piece with an actuality may be too long to fit in the newscast at all.

Timing is one rule for ordering newscasts that is often inflexible.

Completing

The newswriter's rule: Jump into a newscast, feature first. First a writer writes the light stories—the **bottom** of the newscast—then the hard news. This approach is safer because hard news stories have a way of changing. If they are written too early, they may have to be rewritten later. Also, since features require somewhat more originality, they're best written early—before the time pressure gets too intense.

Completing a newscast may mean writing some stories of a different sort from those considered so far in this book. Sports, weather, financial and farm news are often placed at the *bottom* of the newscast. Completing the newscast also may require some finishing touches—final tasks needed to turn a series of stories into a newscast ready to be read on the air.

Rewrites

In a memo distributed to the staff at NBC, Alan Walden noted the following leads to stories from consecutive newscasts:

    A Florida jury returns a guilty verdict in the murder
    trial of Theodore Bundy.

    A Miami jury returns guilty verdicts in the Theodore
    Bundy case.

Walden had three complaints: First and most important, that there is a factual contradiction between the two versions of the lead—is it guilty *verdict* or guilty *verdicts* (on more than one count)? Second, that both leads—built around a name unfamiliar to most national listeners—are, in Walden's words, "petrifyingly dull" (see Chapter 5, "Leads"). And third, that the leads are, quoting Walden again, "damned near identical." It's this third complaint that concerns us here.

Listeners want news, not reruns. A story or even a lead that has been used in the previous newscast cannot be reused in the same form, or nearly the same form, without boring everyone who was listening then. The easiest solution is to hold the story for another hour. Don't use it in this newscast; by the next newscast, those who are still listening will not remember the exact wording. Some stations let writers get away with this if the story isn't very important. If it is very newsworthy, it must be included for those listeners who were not listening an hour ago; and the story must be rewritten for those who were.

If there has been a new development on a story, the rewrite must emphasize that. But even if events do not change, the story must.

The first time through, the writer presumably chose the most powerful angle. What's left for a rewrite? Sometimes there is another equally valid approach to the story hiding in the source material.

> In Virginia, Governor Mill Godwin is tackling the
> problem of aiding drought-ravaged portions of the state.
> Farmers there have complained of barren fields and a lack
> of hay to feed their cattle. Godwin is appointing a
> water-supply task force to work on the problem . . . and
> he says state funds might be used to purchase feed and
> sell it to farmers below market value. Three localities,
> including Fairfax County, have asked for the power to
> impose local water emergency plans.
>
> WMAL, Washington, D.C., 3:30 p.m.

The version of this story used on the next newscast takes a slightly different tack and brings in some new facts:

> Worsening drought conditions in Virginia have prompted
> Governor Mill Godwin to name a water-supply task
> force. . . . The Shenandoah Valley and central Virginia
> are the hardest hit areas . . . with farmers now saying
> they're having to sell off cattle because they can't get
> the hay to feed the herds this winter. . . . Godwin says
> state funds might be used to purchase feed for re-sale
> to farmers at below market cost.
>
> WMAL, Washington, D.C., 4:30 p.m.

When there are fewer facts to choose from, and really only one possible angle, writers just use fresh sentences to say the same thing:

> The woman from Winona who helped Richard Mitchell*
> escape from a county jail last year . . . will be
> eligible for parole in October.
> The state parole board decided today to release 23-
> year-old Karen White* from the Sauk Centre Institute for
> Women in October. At that time she will have served six
> months of a three-year sentence. Mitchell is serving a
> life sentence in the Saint Cloud Reformatory for hiring
> another man to murder his wife.
>
> WCCO, Minneapolis, 11:55 a.m.

* These names have been changed.

Then, the same story half an hour later:

```
And . . . here is a prison story from Minnesota. The
state parole board says Karen White of Winona . . . .
the woman who helped Richard Mitchell escape from a
county jail last year . . . . can leave prison in
October. She will have served six months of a three-year
sentence. Mitchell's serving a life sentence for the
murder of his wife.
```
WCCO, Minneapolis, 12:30 p.m.

Stories on succeeding newscasts don't have to be entirely different, but they must be reworked enough so that listeners don't experience *déjà vu*. There is always another way to write a story. The lead is particularly important to rework in that rewrite . . . failure to do that was the source of Alan Walden's third complaint.

Tie-Ins

Even those of us with the shortest attention spans do not jump from one subject to another in conversation every 20 to 40 seconds; but newscasts have to move that quickly to cover the news. A device, borrowed from conversation, can make this skipping about seem less abrupt.

If we change subjects when talking to a friend, we usually ease the way with a phrase that leads from one topic to the next: "*Speaking of fires*, did you see the pictures of that one in Detroit last night?" That first phrase is called a **tie-in** or, to use a show business term, a *segue*.

Tie-ins have the same function as the transitions used within stories (see Chapter 6, "Stories"), but on a different level. They ease the flow from one story to another:

```
While the drought is plaguing the West, too much water
is playing havoc with the Mid-West.
```
KPNW, Oregon

There are two types of tie-ins:

Related This is the "Speaking of . . ." kind of transition. It leads into a related story. Two stories on the Mideast might be bridged with one of these tie-ins:

```
In another Mideast development . . .

The Mideast was also the scene of . . .

Mideast experts are also watching . . .
```

```
There's another story out of the Mideast today . . .

Meanwhile, in Cairo . . .

Demonstrations also broke out in Lebanon . . .
```

Most of the work in related tie-ins is often done by one of three words: *also*, *another* or *more*. Kathy Kiernan of KNX in Los Angeles did a story about firebombs disrupting service on the London "underground," then began a story on a train fire in the state of Washington with this phrase:

```
More trouble with trains closer to home . . .
```

KOA in Denver followed a story about a mountain rescue with:

```
Another search is underway in the mountains west of
Denver.
```

And KFLA in Kansas, after a story about a fire on a farm:

```
Chet Molhagen is also worried about the effects of fire
and other emergencies -- Molhagen is the head of the Red
Cross Emergency training class that will . . .
```

Transitions between stories should not be forced. It's better to have no tie-in at all than to try to relate basically unrelated stories. Loren Edward Tillett III, director of news at WROV in Virginia, notes that the lack of rain in California and the price of vegetables, for example, are related; the city council and prostitution are not. "That drought will be felt at the supermarket" is okay as a tie-in; "Another group concerned with pleasing the public" is not.

Switch   This kind of tie-in has a more difficult job. It bridges the deeper chasm between *unrelated stories*. Essentially a switch tie-in alerts listeners that the subject is changing.

Most switch tie-ins play upon geography. To go from a local story to something about the president's day, many stations use:

```
In Washington . . .
```

WSOY went in the opposite direction, from national to local news, with this transitional phrase:

```
In news of this area . . .
```

Here are some more switch tie-ins:

```
Also in the news . . .
Later this afternoon . . .
Closer to home . . .
Elsewhere . . .
Over in Europe . . .
But that was not the case for . . .
In local news . . .
Down in the state capitol . . .
```

Switch tie-ins can be reserved for the most abrupt transitions in the newscasts—from local news to international news, for example, or from a murder to the weather. "In sports" and "Here's a traffic update" are switch tie-ins.

It is possible to ease listeners into a story on a different subject without a formal tie-in. Many writers try to mention the location in the lead of the story to orient listeners. Some leads from one edition of the CBS World News Round-Up:

```
Zimbabwe this morning announced the end of its military
operation in Mozambique.
```

```
The North-South Conference moves toward its end in
Paris.
```

```
Still unresolved here in New York . . .
```

The place names in these leads warn us where we are going as we move around the world.

■ ■ ■

Most stories do not start with a tie-in. Otherwise the newscast would be a jumble of locations: "In Israel," "In England," "Back home," and forced connections: "In another story involving a person. . . ." A few tie-ins go a long way—the average 5-minute newscast might use one or two.

Following is the list of stories used in a 10-minute noon newscast on WRVA in Richmond, Virginia. When John Harding put together the newscast, he included the three tie-ins shown in italics:

1. VEPCO Attacked
2. Prisoner Walks
3. Body Murdered
   "And . . . in another homicide case . . ."
4. Matthews Arrest
5. Waste Disposal

6. Gov's Letter
7. Transplant
8. Newhart Trial
   "In Norfolk . . ."
9. Water Spout
10. Elderly
    "In Chesterfield . . ."
11. Chesterfield Schools
12. Hanover Sewers
13. Henrico Manager
14. Army Exercise
15. Wild Ponies
16. Stocks
17. Weather

Another problem with tie-ins is that many have become clichés. Here are a few that should be left in peace:

```
In a lighter vein . . .
In other news . . .
On the home front . . .
```

When used, tie-ins usually go before the lead. If the writer knows in advance where the story will be placed, the tie-in can be written with the lead; otherwise, it can be added when the newscast is organized.

Writers have found other ways to tie together a newscast. On rare occasions a common theme can be found that unites some of the stories, and the writing can bring out this theme. Notice how News Director John D. Watkins uses the words *still* and *continue* to connect the leads in this newscast:

```
The Pope still recuperating from a bout with the
flu . . .

A former attorney general still out of prison . . .

Coal miners still voting on the latest contract
proposal . . .

Peacekeeping forces continue to move into Southern
Lebanon . . .
                                    KGO, San Francisco
```

This, too, helps smooth out a newscast.

Headlines

Headlines is a newspaper term that has found a place in some broadcast newscasts:

> In the headlines . . .
>
> A U-W regents committee directs the administration to devise a plan to get rid of stock holdings in companies doing business with South Africa . . .
>
> The controversial right to privacy bill, passed by the Assembly, is aired before a Senate committee this afternoon . . .
>
> And, Assembly Democrats are coming closer to formulating that super amendment and a state budget bill . . .
>
> WIBA, Wisconsin

Some stations use headlines like this to open a newscast. Some use a headline as a "billboard"—a line before a commercial designed to encourage listeners to stay tuned.

> Bye-bye rebate . . . that story next.
>
> KAKC, Oklahoma

There are two headline styles:

Teases A *tease*, like "Bye-bye rebate," is supposed to intrigue listeners and keep them listening out of curiosity. Teases are short—designed to be catchy, not necessarily clear:

> On this Wednesday morning . . . we'll look at how NASA plans to spend our money in space, the black market in babies . . . and what IS Billy Graham going to do with those 23-million dollars? Those stereo news features upcoming.
>
> WRVQ, Virginia

Teasing fits uncomfortably in broadcast journalism, which is supposed to be in the business of delivering. The danger here, as pointed out by Rick Barber of KWBZ in Colorado, lies in a tease like this: "Three dead, twelve injured . . . we'll be back after this message." You can only go so far in manipulating and confounding an audience.

Self-Sufficient   At KFWB in Los Angeles, News Director Don Schrack insists that headlines be complete; no teasing. Schrack believes listeners should be able to tune in, hear only the headline and get a basic understanding of the story.

Of course there is a limit to what can be said in one sentence. All headlines must be written concisely, but many news directors, like Schrack, demand that a headline, no matter how slim, be able to stand on its own:

```
Sandusky woman credited with saving local boy from
drowning in swimming pool yesterday afternoon.

Sandusky Rotary Club inducts new officers in special
ceremonies today.
                                                    WLEC, Ohio
```

Headlines are usually written in an abbreviated style, often employing technically incomplete sentences (see Chapter 4, "Sentences"):

```
A federal probe into murders at the Atlanta pen.
                                                    WSB, Atlanta
```

A headline certainly is no place for wordiness:

```
WEAK
Sixth District Congressman Wyche Fowler says the Federal
Bureau of Prisons is about to begin a thorough
investigation of the Atlanta Federal Penitentiary . . .
scene of a rash of murders in recent months.
```

Weather

This conversation was overheard in a park:

```
''What's the weather like?''
''I don't know; I haven't heard a radio.''
```

Broadcast weather reports have taken over the job of keeping tabs on the troposphere from arthritic joints, knowledge of cloud formations and even our own senses. People have come to depend on radio to tell them what it's doing outside and what it's going to be doing. This is about as close as the news comes to predicting the future.

Interest in the weather varies by region: It is highest in farm areas—where there is money riding on it—and lowest in places like Southern California—where the weather often gets dull. Just about every radio station includes some weather news—mostly as part of newscasts.

On many stations the weather opens the show:

```
Clear skies and 79 degrees in Richmond at noon. . . .
This is John Harding reporting.
```
WRVA, Virginia

If the weather is making news it can force its way into the body of the show:

```
Nature continued to vent its wrath today in south-
central Texas, where 14 inches of rain pushed the
Guadalupe and Medina Rivers over their banks for the
second day in a row. . . .
```
WCAU, Philadelphia

But normally, the weather resides at the back of the newscast:

```
This afternoon . . . partly sunny and not quite so warm
with widely scattered thunderstorms . . . high 92. . . .
Tonight and tomorrow . . . partly cloudy and a little
cooler with chance of showers and thundershowers . . .
low tonight 68 . . . high tomorrow 85. . . . Currently
it's 98 degrees in Jackson . . . 98 in Kalamazoo and in
Battle Creek it's 90 degrees or 32 Celsius. -- I'm Scott
Marshall, WKNR News.
```
WKNR, Michigan

Information on the weather can be garnered from the wires, including the National Weather Service wires if the station subscribes (see Chapter 7, "Sources"). The wires transmit forecasts and current statistics for each area in a region. Some stations listen to a weather radio frequency also provided by the National Weather Service; some subscribe to private weather forecasting services such as Accu-Weather in Pennsylvania; some get weather news by telephoning airport terminals; some use their own meteorological equipment; some employ their own meteorologist.

There is one other method for compiling weather information that should never be ignored. "You'd be surprised," notes David Heller of KLOS in Los Angeles, "how up-to-date your current weather information can be simply by looking out the window and walking outside every hour or so." This supplement to other sources can prevent that unfortunate situation where the newscaster is talking about partly sunny weather while listeners are watching rain.

Many stations use the same format for the weather in each newscast, so all the writer has to do is get the latest facts and plug them in:

```
Your Fourteen forecast . . .
Sunny today . . .
Partly cloudy tonight . . .
```

```
Then, mostly cloudy tomorrow with a chance of light
showers . . .
Today's high -- 68 . . .
Overnight low -- 47 . . .
High tomorrow -- 65 . . .
Now sunny and 58 degrees.
```
WSJM, Michigan

These communicate the necessary information, but it's not a bad idea, if there's time, to go beyond lists of numbers and put the weather for an area into words:

```
Rain is in the forecast for most of us again
today. . . . A slight chance of sprinkles here in town,
but a good chance outside, especially in the mountains
and deserts. The Coachella Valley got about an inch and
a half of rain yesterday, and several expensive homes
were flooded. A lot of people were still digging out from
the tropical storm that blew through here a couple of
weeks ago. There's a flashflood warning out for the desert
areas today.
    For the rest of us, it'll be cloudy and damp, with a
high of around 75 or so. It's 70 right now in Los Angeles
. . . Orange County has 73 . . . the Valley trailing at
69 degrees. Light smog in the midst of it all.
```
KLOS, Los Angeles

A couple of pointers for writing weather copy: Fronts, barometers and the weather on the other side of the continent may be of some interest, but listeners are most concerned with whether they should wear a sweater or bring an umbrella. It's a mistake to stray too far from the chance of precipitation and the temperature.

With our present knowledge of the permutations of the atmosphere, five-day forecasts are not that far removed from five-day guesses. Listeners want to hear the odds on the weekend, but writers should not imbue long-range predictions with any more certitude than they deserve. "They're predicting rain this weekend." Not: "It will rain this weekend."

Finally, weather news should follow the rules for broadcast writing. There may be an excuse for tossing in a few extra numbers, but there is no excuse for unexplained technical terms or formal language.

```
WEAK
Variable cloudiness tonight with a high probability of
lingering precipitation.
```

```
BETTER
Cloudy off and on tonight, with a few more showers
likely.
```
WTLB, New York

And watch meanings. For instance, a tornado *watch* means conditions are such that a tornado might occur. A tornado *warning* means that conditions are so threatening that there has already been a tornado in the area.

Sports

There are listeners who care more about the fortunes of the Cincinnati Reds than China; who are more interested in the pronouncements of Don Shula than of Mario Cuomo. Don't sneer; the motivations of sports fans and news fans are not all that different. Most stations make an effort to satisfy them both.

A few stations employ a special sports reporter; most assign sports to newswriters for inclusion in the newscast—usually near the end, where it's least likely to annoy the uninterested.

The sports news can be a sentence or two:

```
On the WABC scoreboard: The Mets are leading the Padres
. . . two to nothing . . . after six in San Diego. The
Yankees took the night off.
```

Or it can include longer items:

```
At the World Track and Field Championships in Tokyo
today, Carl Lewis and Leroy Burrell both broke Burrell's
world record in the 100-meter dash, but Lewis broke it
better. Lewis was fifth at the halfway point, but then
turned it on to beat Burrell by two one-hundredths of a
second -- in 9 point eight six.
```
Ray Gandolf, ABC

Sports information is available from the wires, including special sports wires (see Chapter 7, "Sources"), or it can be tracked down on the phone with calls to the team's public relations office or to the players themselves. The audio news services (see Chapter 7) carry sports cuts, and reporters can liven up the sports news by obtaining their own actualities.

Producing a solid sports report takes enterprise; it also takes expertise. Neither a journalist's sex nor an antipathy for José Canseco is an excuse for ignorance. Sports news is important to enough people to be important enough for journalists to study.

Study sports? If that sounds like fun, it is probably not necessary. But prospective journalists who start concentrating on the traffic when their radios start emitting scores have some homework ahead of them. Newswriters have to know what Scotty Pippin does for a living, how to transform goals into "hat tricks" and how to sound excited when writing of "sudden death." It may be necessary to start reading the sports pages and possibly to secure an apprenticeship with a friendly sports nut. They enjoy nothing more than initiating the innocent into the intricacies and lore of athletic contests.

The sports likely to turn up in newscasts have expanded beyond baseball, football and basketball to include hockey, soccer, track and field, golf, tennis, auto racing and horse racing. The final entry on that list is of particular importance in radio news. Followers of the "sport of kings" have been known to have more than a rooting interest in their favorites. Occasionally they make wagers on the outcome of equestrian events, which tend to increase their concern with the results. The spread of legal off-track betting has exaggerated this tendency. Racing fans, therefore, become loyal listeners of a station that regularly supplies the latest racing results. Forgetting to give the results of the eighth race can trigger more angry phone calls to the station than omitting the results of an election.

Writing sports copy can be pleasant. Free from the portentous and often tragic content of the rest of the news, it's possible to have a little fun. Cleverness is allowed, if not required. A touch of subjectivity, such as a slight rooting interest in the home team, is occasionally appropriate. A more liberal use of slang and undefined terms is also permitted. Instead of shooting, a basketball player might, as a sports reporter on KGTV in San Diego put it, "stop and pop" or "slam" or "jam"—exhibiting "great hang time."

Bill Alford of KNOW in Texas points out that since sports news is targeted to a specific audience, there's less need to worry about background information. Those listeners who don't know what "hang time" is probably won't care. Language should be clear enough for all *sports* fans to understand.

Otherwise all the rules of broadcast news writing apply. Obviously, numbers are a problem. "The most important thing is always the score," says Lynn Woolley of KRLD, Dallas. Scores mean masses of undigested numbers. Many stations stick to scores of interest to the hometown fans, plus any unusual performances. But other stations run through the whole list of scores on the theory that listeners can pick out any scores in which they are interested and ignore the rest.

Blender manufacturers anxious to add new buttons to their machines were faced with the necessity of devising countless variations on the words "blend" and "chop": "mince," "grate," "grind," "liquefy," etc. Sports writers are faced with a similar problem, and their solution is similar. How many ways can you say that one team has defeated another? After exhausting "team A *over* team B" and "team A *tops* team B," many resort to "edged," "downed," "dumped"; then soon "slammed," "crushed," "bombed," "smashed," "clobbered," "whipped," "slaughtered," "wiped out," "annihilated." What about "grated" and "liquefied"?—even tennis can become a violent sport.

Action verbs are nice, but it's wise to stay away from the more sadistic. Even in the heat of the playoffs, they sound rather silly.

Another pitfall in sports writing is the cliché. Baseball alone may have spawned more expressions than any other human activity save war and sex. It's a "game of inches," where the "batter steps into the box," "waits as the pitcher eyes the runner, then delivers," and with "one swing of the bat, sends the game into extra innings." This language has its charm, but it's a quality best appreciated after a few beers in the grandstand, not at the end of a radio newscast. Be inventive! Play with the clichés:

```
It's wait till next year for the American League. It's
been wait till next year for six years in a row . . . and
14 of the last 15 all-star games. It happened quickly
last night in New York. The National League scored four
runs in the first inning . . . and won seven to five.
```
WMAL, Washington, D.C.

Traffic

Radio gets its largest audiences during the morning and evening ***drive times***—rush hours—which gives a good idea of where most of radio's listeners are. Until people figure out how to read a newspaper or watch television while driving, drivers will remain radio's primary audience.

It didn't take news directors long to realize that among the most useful information a person fighting rush-hour traffic can receive is information on how to sneak around that traffic. Almost all stations in areas large enough to have traffic try to say something about it, usually in their news broadcasts.

In large cities, where drivers spend an hour or two a day changing lanes and breathing exhaust, traffic reports are staples of newscasts. These reports usually include information on commuter bus and railway lines. You can't listen to the radio on a subway, but you can tune in before you leave to check on how things are running. And your wife or husband can tune in to check out your excuse if you're late.

The problem is how to find out what traffic is doing. This is the one area in which the wires are no help. Traffic changes too rapidly for even the wires to be able to keep up with any but the most serious tie-ups. No station can afford to place a reporter at all key intersections and bus depots. Some find traffic news important enough, however, to employ a helicopter to fly over the major arteries, surveying patterns and offering tips.

In New York, Philadelphia, Houston, Los Angeles and Chicago, a special network, Shadow Traffic, provides stations with traffic news. Shadow follows the starts and stops of metropolitan area traffic and mass transportation. It uses helicopters, other aircraft, "stringers" (free-lance correspondents) on the road, and information from public works crews, all fed into a computer to provide Shadow's on-the-air announcers the information for the reports they produce for over 60 TV and radio stations in the New York area alone. Shadow also monitors citizens' band radios and puts people atop tall buildings, like New York's Empire State and World Trade Center—"our Kongs" they're called. Similar traffic-monitoring networks exist in other major cities congested enough that cars frequently "crawl" and expressways "snarl." Nonetheless, the majority of stations in the country, lacking the services of a traffic network or their own helicopter, are forced to scrounge. Bits of traffic news can be gleaned from the police and police radio—often the AAA helps. News of major problems on bridges, railroads and bus lines is provided by the authorities that run them. They must be called regularly, but these people have a natural tendency to downplay their own failings. A half-hour delay may be labeled "10 minutes" or

WSB's traffic helicopter over Atlanta.

ignored completely. Tips also help. It's wise to ask a station's sales people to call in if they spot a tie-up while out on the road. And WBBM in Chicago has a simple method of getting traffic news: A traffic reporter covers the city from its studios . . . on the 102nd-floor Skydeck of the Sears Tower.

Many stations "borrow" traffic news from other stations—stations that have helicopters, for example. This is stealing and is unethical and probably illegal.

Traffic reports are difficult to verify and tough to get, but as part of the newscast, they should be treated diligently. Incorrect information still hurts a station's reputation. A scoop on a backed-up road is a substantial scoop. An extra phone call often pays off in traffic reporting.

There is little room for "great" writing; most traffic news is straightforward:

```
The Fort Worth police department is advising motorists
who normally take the North Freeway to avoid a portion
of the road between Belknap and Northside Drive. The
north-bound lanes are impassable thanks to a hole in the
```

Trinity River Bridge. They'll be closed to traffic until
nine o'clock tonight.

KFJZ, Texas

But, as in any other writing, it is still better to make the facts real rather than just
listing them.

WEAK
The West Side Highway is congested up to 96th Street.
The F-D-R Drive is clear all the way to the bridge.

BETTER
The F-D-R Drive looks like the better route out of town
tonight. It's clear all the way to the bridge, while the
West Side Highway is slow going up to 96th Street.

Financial and Farm

Some more numbers that some listeners wait for at the end of the newscast are the
Dow Jones average, closing stock prices, the price of gold, the price being offered
for soybeans at the local grain market and midwestern hog prices. Most such financial
or farm facts are available from the wires, including the special business and financial
wires and farm wires (see Chapter 7, "Sources"). The prices being paid for farm
products at local markets can be obtained with a phone call. Most stations know
where and when to call. Shown below is part of a farm report put together through
a call to a local market.

Midwestern hog prices are **steady to mostly 50 cents lower**

Southeast Virginia hog markets are **50 cents lower**

                     at **40 to 42**

Virginia broiler prices are **steady**

                     at **43 to 44 cents**

Midwestern cattle prices....

         choice steers are **39 and a half to 41 and a half**

         choice heifers **38 to 39 cents**

WRVA, Virginia

Many listeners don't own stocks; many don't care about the price of "broilers"
(chickens); but many stations find that they benefit by catering to those who do
care. Financial and farm reports can capture listeners (see Chapter 11, "Coverage").

One problem in writing these reports is, again, numbers. Lists are unavoidable, but when possible, writers should step back from the decimal points and explain, for instance, what the gross national product means. Here is a stock market report that accompanies the numbers with some words:

```
The stock market has jumped ahead on near record trading
volume today after yesterday's close at the highest
level in nine months.
```
Peter Maer, Mutual

Both financial and farm news must be localized. If there is a General Motors plant in town, a GM earnings report deserves extra attention. If the local farmers plant lots of beets, beet prices must be emphasized.

Financial and farm stories each have their own vocabularies which reporters must understand and translate. All journalists should be able to handle basics such as the gross national product or wholesale price index. A local professor or a textbook can provide instruction if necessary. And reporters in farm areas should talk to some farmers or agriculture professors if they think "futures" are just what promising students have. ("Futures" are shares in commodities purchased and traded before they are ready to be delivered.)

The Open and Close

Newscasts have been known to begin with anything from the sound of fire alarms to a prayer. The networks, however, don't waste much time on an opening:

```
NBC Radio News . . . I'm Steve Porter.
```

Mutual doesn't even identify the newscaster or the show until just before the first commercial.

Some stations sell newscasts to single sponsors, so they want to mention the sponsor's name in their opening. This is read by an announcer.

```
It's time now for the 6:30 edition of WWSR Local News
and Sports, sponsored today by _____. Now, here
with the news is _____.
```
WWSR, Vermont

And some stations make quite a production of it:

```
                                    (play WRKD news theme)
```

```
This is WRKD radio Sunday Morning News; a summary of
news from around the state of Maine and the world of
sports, plus the weather forecast for this area.
```
WRKD, Maine

Closes usually reflect the opening. NBC is equally succinct at the end:

```
Steve Porter, NBC News.
```

Mutual still doesn't say anything. WWSR mentions the sponsor again:

```
You've just heard _____ with the 6:30 edition of
WWSR Local News and Sports, sponsored by _____.
```

and WRKD:

```
                              (play WRKD news theme)
```

```
You have been listening to WRKD radio news . . . the
latest news of Maine, sports news, plus the weather
forecast . . . from the wires of United Press
International and the WRKD newsroom.
```

Such formats may or may not strike listeners' fancies. All that's needed for clarity is that at some point in the newscast the station and the newscaster be identified. The opening and the closing lines provide excellent opportunities to take care of that obligation.

Wrap-Up

Before the news is allowed on the air it should be carefully organized, with stories in a logical and comfortable arrangement, and it should be complete. In some areas, listeners may need the current humidity or the latest price of hogs to feel fully informed.

Practice Assignments

A. Order the following stories for the 11 a.m. newscast.

1. Labor Department announced this morning that unemployment increased four tenths of one percent last month.
2. Twin seals born in local zoo this morning.
3. Suspect in last week's murder of a five-year-old boy arrested last night.
4. Teachers' strike here in 4th day—still no talks; *with actuality.*
5. Opening of new Woolworth's downtown store scheduled for tomorrow.
6. General Assembly approved resolution condemning Israel last night.
7. Local sales tax to be voted on by City Council this afternoon; *with actuality.*

8. Japan agreed this morning to new trade pact with the United States.
9. Auto workers at Honda plants in United States will walk out at noon today unless contract is signed.
10. Sports.
11. Weather.

B. By 1 p.m., these new stories have come in. Selecting from the stories used at 11 a.m. and the new stories, order the 1 p.m. newscast.

1. Auto workers at Honda plants walk out.
2. City Council votes down local sales tax, five to four, for second time this year; the mayor is angry; *with actuality.*
3. President of teachers' union requests mediation; *with actuality.*

C. Order these stories for the 4 p.m. newscast.

1. Department of Health and Welfare reaffirms ban on Medicaid abortions this afternoon.
2. Flash flood warning in effect today and tonight for area.
3. Chamber of Commerce picnic today canceled due to flash flood warning.
4. Two local teenagers arrested on drug charges this afternoon.
5. State legislature passes bottle return bill this afternoon; governor vows to veto; *with actuality.*
6. President announces today he will deliver new tax reform message at end of week.
7. Bomb kills two in Rome department store this morning; terrorist group claims responsibility.
8. Study released this morning says town has lost 2-thousand, 400 jobs this year, mainly due to closing of local GE plant; *with voicer.*
9. Pope announces today a 10-day tour of France, Belgium, Portugal and Spain.
10. Dow Jones index rises eight points in anticipation of president's tax message.
11. National Institutes of Health says this morning that common food dye linked to cancer.
12. Weather.
13. Sports.

D. Order these stories for the 3:30 p.m. newscast.

1. Local residential fire this afternoon . . . causes, injuries unknown; *with voicer.*
2. Mayor announces hearings on controversial school construction contract; *with actuality.*
3. Consumer price index rises two percent last month; announcement this morning.
4. Oil companies release 3rd quarter profits today; almost all show gain of at least 30 percent.

5. Local woman indicted this morning in check-cashing conspiracy.
6. Italian Parliament elections held today; Socialists expected to gain.
7. World-wide trade talks continue in Geneva.
8. Iran announces ouster of two British newsmen today.
9. First woman judge appointed to State Supreme Court this afternoon; *with voicer.*
10. Stocks.
11. Weather.
12. Sports.

13

Public Affairs

The 25-second news story, or the 50-second story with tape, can do a remarkable job of keeping people up to date on the social, political and economic world around them. One of the major arguments of this book is that, with good writing based on sound reporting, complex understandings can be communicated in fractions of a minute.

Still, it must be acknowledged that something *is* lost in the effort to squeeze so many important stories into one newscast. There are limits to what can be done with 25 or 50 seconds. Sometimes deeper meanings rest on patterns seen only in large masses of facts; sometimes minor, seemingly forgettable details communicate nuances that may lead to fuller understandings; and sometimes the secondary or even tertiary points—those that don't fit in a newscast—prove useful in seeing a subject in the round. These patterns, nuances and lesser points require time to communicate. There's no way around that. Many stations, therefore, find a place in their schedules for programs that focus on just one or two important issues, that give that extra time to matters of particular concern to the public—"public affairs."

Most public affairs programs—*documentaries* and *interview shows*—share this goal: to go into more depth than newscasts allow. The *editorials* that also fall under the heading "public affairs" supplement the standard newscast, too, though in a different way: They allow the use of an otherwise forbidden tool in the search for understanding—opinion.

Some stations bury their public affairs offerings on Sunday mornings when few people are listening, but others have used these programs to attract listeners and to inspire whole communities to think about and even solve problems.

Documentaries

Documentaries give broadcast journalists time to stretch out. Writers move from the tight broadcast news story to the luxury of a 5- to 10-minute *mini-doc*—a short documentary—or to a series of reports on one subject, or even to a full half-hour documentary.

A new, "comprehensive" high school, three times as large as other high schools, opened in Nashville. WLAC could have covered the news in a story, perhaps including an actuality featuring the principal or the head of the school board, but news director David Tower felt this story deserved a more thorough treatment. Tower spent two days at the school and visited the new experimental classes. He interviewed students, teachers and administrators. The result?—a half-hour documentary.

There are also subjects that don't make it onto newscasts because there aren't any breaking developments—no "news peg." Lisa Bergson of WRFM, New York City, investigated such a topic, the abuse of personal records, in a series of more than 30 3-minute reports.

Too few commercial radio stations take the time to produce documentaries. Some ambitious reporters, however, will produce them on their own time.

Getting Tape

"Radio," says the British Broadcasting Corporation's David Kogan, "is a matter of noise." Kogan, a BBC producer stationed in New York, suggests that that "noise" or sound should be as evocative as possible. "It should give almost a visual impression of something you can't see," he says. That trick can be accomplished, Kogan believes, through the use of actualities—the voices of newsmakers with information about an event or, better, the voices of newsmakers who are actually *feeling* the impact of that event or, better still, those voices with **natural sound** behind them (see Chapter 9, "Tape"). "I once heard a piece on a new type of fitness club in which there were interviews with the owners and part-owners, but *not* with any of the people who used the club," Kogan says. "On a story like that you want to know what it's like to be there; you want to hear sweating and thumping and groaning. You want as much noise as possible."

The BBC, with a less hurried style of news than is common in the United States, uses many short documentaries, or **packages,** perhaps 2 to 10 minutes long. When Kogan begins working on one, the first question in his mind is what he's going to get on tape.

After he decided to do a story on an apparent epidemic of teenage suicides in the United States, Kogan used a computer file of *New York Times* stories to gather past newspaper articles on the subject. He wanted information, but more significantly he wanted potential contacts, potential "noise." One clip led to a New York State official who had taken an interest in the problem of teenage suicides. The reporter with whom Kogan worked on the documentary, Bill Turnbull, conducted a lengthy interview with that official, but nothing from that tape would be used on the air— not evocative enough. That official's voice could *not* communicate the intensity of the pain these deaths caused. It could *not* give listeners a feel for the emotional meaning of teenage suicides. Nonetheless, the official did supply plenty of useful information, including the names of two mothers whose children had committed suicide and who were working to prevent other families from undergoing similar tragedies. That was a big break. The documentary would open with one of their voices:

> My son was on track; my son lifted weights. He had a very high IQ . . . and my son killed himself.

Turnbull went on to interview a group of students at a school where there had been more than one suicide. Some of their comments were used in a **montage**—a few short, usually anonymous, actualities edited together, also known as a **vox pop** (literally, "voice of the people"). The students began by explaining why they think some of their classmates took their own lives:

> First Student: If by committing suicide my life would be easier and simpler and . . . I would live in peace. I wouldn't have all this confusion . . . I wouldn't have no more problems to face.
>
> Second Student: Couldn't it be that some of them just wanted attention that end up dead?
>
> Third Student: They should sit down and talk with one another . . . communicate . . . have a talk with your parents . . . I know that parents will understand.
>
> Fourth Student: That's the problem . . . our parents don't know who we are. A lot of people say, ''Yes, I'm close to my mother and my father,'' but yet they cannot tell you who your best friend is.

The story also included the voice of one of the mothers, speaking to other teenagers who might have been considering suicide:

> I saw my son's body lay there in the casket. He was cold; he was hard; he was dead. I watched them put the casket in the hole in the ground; I watched them pile the dirt on top of the casket. There's no coming back. There's no . . . like . . . he's hovering down over the casket looking down and saying, ''Well, now they'll love me.'' He can't see it. He's dead. Do not ever consider suicide as an option.

This documentary ran 4 minutes and 45 seconds . . . perhaps two-thirds of that time was occupied by tapes, rather than scripted narration by the reporter. This is not to say that documentary reporting is strictly the gathering of punchy cuts. To the contrary: 4 minutes and 45 seconds on a subject requires a particularly thorough understanding of that subject. Documentary reporters spend plenty of time in libraries or in the offices of dry but informative officials. That BBC package was full of information—"on average one young American takes his or her life every 84 minutes"—information that showed how much straight research went into it. Still radio documentaries depend on tape for their power, just as television documentaries depend on visuals. "I wouldn't want to turn in a package that was as much as one-half script," Kogan says.

Others who produce documentaries may not demand exactly that percentage of actualities, but they certainly agree on the importance of tape. Aside from everything else, too much uninterrupted narration quickly can get dull. David Tower relied on the teachers, students and administrators to tell most of the story of that new high school in Nashville. In each installment of her report on personal records, Lisa Bergson used at least one actuality—including interviews with people who felt their own privacy had been violated by the misuse of records on them.

Good tape can be hard to come by, especially on the sort of elusive, difficult-to-pin-down subject that tends to intrigue documentary makers. Many years ago, David Ensor, then a reporter/writer for National Public Radio, found such a subject living in the White House. Ensor had heard reports that people were beginning to perceive then First Lady Rosalynn Carter as an influential and controversial member of her husband's administration. He had become more interested when one of her speech writers suddenly resigned. Ensor decided to produce a documentary on Ms. Carter for NPR's *All Things Considered*—a program that features short documentaries on topics of national interest. The problem: where to get a tape of the First Lady?

The president's wife was not available for an interview, but she was scheduled to speak at the National Press Club. Ensor decided to record her speech there and fill out his report with tape of people who knew her. Even this wasn't easy.

Few of the First Lady's associates were willing to say anything controversial on tape. Most spoke only "on background" (see Chapter 8, "Gathering News"). Ensor talked with former employees, but not on tape. He talked with a friend of hers from Georgia who preferred that he not record the conversation. He was told, but only "on background," that the First Lady's staff was functioning less than smoothly. Ensor could use this information, but he needed sound.

Finally, Ensor got one former member of Ms. Carter's staff, whose job had been dealing with the press, to complain—on tape—that he wasn't told what to say to the press. Then a representative of the Commission on Mental Health, which she chaired, discussed Ms. Carter's performance—on tape. Ensor also got UPI's White House correspondent through five presidencies, Helen Thomas, to evaluate this First Lady—on tape. Ensor obtained a long but fascinating reminiscence from an acquaintance of Ms. Carter in New York. With Ms. Carter's own statements to the Press Club, Ensor had enough sound. Now he had to turn that sound, and the narration that would go with it, into a coherent story—obviously a more difficult trick than working just one actuality into a 50-second story.

Organization

David Kogan and Bill Turnbull began putting that BBC package on teenage suicides together by editing their interviews down to a total of about 15 minutes. They listened to that, then continued editing until they had a **rough cut** of about 7 or 8 minutes of potential actualities.

The extra time available in documentaries does not free their writers or producers from the basic rules for organizing a story (see Chapter 6, "Stories"). Those extra minutes may allow for inclusion of two or three angles, but the angles still must be carefully established and followed through. The story must still stick to one idea at a time, though that idea may be developed over a couple of pages instead of a couple of sentences. Unless a firm organizational plan is kept in mind—or, better, written down on paper—a 4-minute-and-45-second documentary can easily turn into a 4-minute-and-45-second hodgepodge.

The two members of that BBC team decided they had two jobs to do in their package: First, they wanted to indicate the extent and the seriousness of the problem of teenage suicides. Second, they wanted to discuss American reaction to the problem. They organized the documentary so that those tasks were tackled one at a time: They spelled out the problem, then gave examples of the reactions to it.

After opening with that dramatic tape of the mother whose son had killed himself, they went to a tape of another such woman, then to a mental health official who noted that there often were no obvious signs of depression in the teenagers who take their own lives. Then one of the mothers returned to talk about the pressures on people like her late son:

```
If I'm this 16-year-old boy who doesn't drive the right
car or play on the football team, well forget it. I do
not get the all-American blond cheerleader, and that's a
big setback.
```

The reporter himself supplied summaries of theories and statistics—"the teenage suicide rate in the United States has doubled over the past decade." The problem was established.

The reaction to the problem was illustrated, first, by audiotape of a recent CBS television movie on the subject of teenage suicides—evidence of how pressing a concern it had become in the United States. Then the classmates of those who had killed themselves gave their thoughts and reactions. The reporter then mentioned some programs that had been initiated in an effort to prevent teenage suicides; and the two mothers concluded with warnings both to teenagers and parents.

This documentary not only followed a fairly straight path through a couple of points, but managed to end with the same voices with which it had begun—always a neat effect. In fact, at both ends it violated a rule of writing to actualities in newscast stories: The documentary started *cold,* with the voice of the mother saying, ". . . my son killed himself"—with no lead-in at the beginning. And its last words were also spoken by a mother—there was no write-out at the very end. Of course, this won't always work, but one of the advantages of having the extra time a documentary provides, and only one subject to cover, is that you can experiment with creative techniques, techniques that might confuse in the more limited world of a newscast.

David Ensor also began organizing by doing a ***rough edit*** of each of the actualities he thought he might use in his NPR documentary on Ms. Carter. He then typed up descriptions of the better cuts and spread those descriptions out in front of him.

Ensor essentially had three issues to deal with: the "influence" question, the "competence" question and Ms. Carter's personality. How powerful was Ms. Carter? How well was she handling that power? What was she like? He would cover the three questions one at a time.

With these questions in mind, Ensor arranged the cuts he had rough edited. Most documentaries are organized around their tape. Writers order the cuts, often by shuffling index cards, each representing one cut, and then fill in the copy necessary to say what must be said between the cuts.

For the "influence" question, Ensor had a statement by Ms. Carter on the Equal Rights Amendment that helped focus discussion of her impact on issues, and he had a joking reference to her own power or lack of it from the speech he had recorded. It would make a fine introduction to the subject. As for the "competence" question, he had a complimentary tape from the representative of the Commission of Mental Health and an uncomplimentary tape from her former staff member. For insight into the First Lady's personality he had that long cut from her acquaintance in New York.

Ensor spelled all this out in an outline (most writers prepare an outline for documentaries). Then, after the outline was approved by his editor, Ensor wrote the story and prepared final versions of his cuts.

A series such as the one Lisa Bergson prepared for WRFM presents slightly different organizational challenges. But she used the same basic approach that anyone trying to make sense of a mass of material must use: She analyzed the material, picked out some basic themes, then prepared to handle them one at a time. Her material, like Kogan's, broke down into two large areas: threats to privacy created by the abuse of personal records and possible ways of preventing those abuses and threats. But Bergson had much more time to fill than Kogan—more than 30 3-minute reports—so she broke down the threats into those posed by government and those posed by business. And from the business threats she separated out the whole question of credit checks.

Bergson would have a few reports on each of these subjects, looking for natural connections to ease the jump between subjects, introducing each report with a short discussion of how it fit into her overall theme and then concluding each with a quick preview of the next segment. Each report in such a series must not only fit smoothly into the whole but also must make sense on its own—for those listeners who have not caught the other installments.

Music

Music and news? Together? Well, it would hardly be appropriate in a documentary on teenage suicide, but there are situations where music in a documentary can help highlight or even make a point. A documentary on the anniversay of the Woodstock music festival David Kogan produced for the BBC included selections from some of the performances. And a half-hour NBC documentary on marijuana farming in Northern California opened with a brief selection from a song—". . . Home-grown's alright with me . . ." The documentary was then formally introduced with music from a Bob Dylan song—". . . Everybody must get stoned . . ."—playing in the background.

Ten seconds of catchy singing or playing at a few appropriate spots can certainly liven up a documentary, but music is easily misused and overused. Documentary producers who are anxious to show off the breadth of their record collections too often end up drowning out their points with a rush of irrelevant sounds. Songs should be used in a documentary only if their lyrics are truly relevant to the subject at hand—we don't need to hear Michael Jackson's "Beat It" during a documentary on wrestling, for example. Lyrics often carry clear and specific meanings, and if the documentary is trying to say something different, the result will be dissonance.

Most documentaries won't use any music, and in those that do, a few short musical interludes usually suffice. Use music, if you use it at all, for accents, not as a substitute for tape and writing.

Writing

The tape has been selected and organized; perhaps a piece of music has been chosen. Now it's time to write, to **script** the documentary. The first things to remember are the basic rules for broadcast writing discussed in the early chapters of this book. You're trying to keep listeners interested in a story for minutes now, not seconds. This is no place for dull or confusing words or flabby sentences.

A documentary also requires a good lead, though with all that time available writers might choose to delay a bit more. Here is how that NBC documentary on marijuana farming, reported by Peter Laufer, began (after the music):

```
So many Americans smoke marijuana these days that it
rivals corn as the richest cash crop in the U-S.
```

Since documentaries are full of tape, much of the writing in them will be writing to tape (see Chapter 10, "Writing to Tape"). Lead-ins still prepare and introduce:

Lead-in: Now that so many people smoke it, it's so expensive and it's being grown commercially all over America, marijuana is again a high priority for lawmen like California Attorney General John Vandecamp . . .

Cut: We're going, mind you, not after users. We're going after those who are profiting, some people immensely profiting, from the cultivation of marijuana.

But here differences between writing documentaries and writing news stories begin to show up. For a start, in a documentary, which may include dozens of cuts, those lead-ins tend to blend into the write-outs—the write-out for one actuality becomes the lead-in for the next. In other words, documentaries are filled with **bridges** (see Chapter 10, "Writing to Tape"). Here's another section from that NBC documentary:

Cut: I've been growing for 12 years, so I've had quite a bit of experience outside, inside, downhill, uphill, flatland, growing in cornfields, growing in the delta, growing at 7-thousand feet, you know, growing in a greenhouse and taking the plants up to a high mountain meadow and sitting with them for a summer.

Bridge: Not the least of the obvious commercial benefits of home-grown is the fact that the stuff's already in this country. With no international borders to cross, a major risk was immediately eliminated, and outlaw horticulturists started refining the product, even growing the weed indoors.

Cut: I constantly work on efficiency, and I think that's really the wave of the future. It's now possible to do it low-key, without all that much danger of being caught and have a good product coming out at a regular time.

Bridge:	Jay still grows some pot outside, but he's turning his attention to indoor farming.
Cut:	These are halogen lamps and they give off a real whitish blue color and a real nice spectrum of light for pot plants.
Bridge:	Jay is a successful small businessman, not rich but paying his own way in the world. His indoor operation is an assembly line. He need not wait for harvest season; he manipulates the plants' life cycles and harvests every week. Retailing the marijuana himself for about 160 dollars an ounce.

And there is another major difference between this writing and the writing discussed in earlier chapters: There is an unhurried quality to the writing in documentaries, a quality that would cause serious troubles were it to be found in a news story. Note how long it takes to identify the person who is speaking in the above cuts. The facts on Jay (his last name is not used for obvious reasons) are brought in gradually.

Documentaries must be just as clear as news stories, but they don't have to resolve everything in a couple of dozen seconds. They might occasionally introduce the speakers in actualities *after* the cuts have played . . . as long as the cuts still make sense. They might leave some questions unanswered for a while, some controversial points unrefuted, knowing that there'll be time to return to these subjects later. In other words, documentary writers can leave a little slack.

Of course, this is another one of those freedoms that brings with it responsibilities. When they move beyond the tight format of a news story, writers assume more responsibility for pacing their work. If the copy they write for use between the tapes is too skimpy, a documentary will sound choppy and unclear:

UNACCEPTABLE

Local Store Owner:	. . . everybody is involved and benefiting economically from marijuana growing in this area.
Reporter:	Humboldt County Sheriff David Renner knows megabucks are being made in his county.
Sheriff:	500-million to a billion dollars . . . and there's a very small part of that money being spent here.
Reporter:	Businessman McKee disagrees.

| Local Store Owner: | As a matter of fact, I think more of it stays here from this kind of a business than stays here from logging. |

But write too much and the documentary starts to sag:

UNACCEPTABLE

Local Store Owner:	. . . everybody is involved and benefiting economically from marijuana growing in this area.
Reporter:	Just how much money is being brought into the economy? That's hard to tell. Since marijuana growing is a clandestine activity, it's impossible to document the value of the crop. One thing's for sure, though: Humboldt County Sheriff David Renner doesn't like the marijuana business in his county one bit. Aside from everything else he has against it, he has serious doubts that it even brings much money in. The sheriff does know, though, that someone is making megabucks in his county.
Sheriff:	500-million to a billion dollars . . . and there's a very small part of that money being spent here.
Reporter:	Not being spent here? So where's that 500-million to a billion dollars being spent? Here's the answer: Sheriff Renner is one of those who is convinced the money goes south to absentee landlords, drug kingpins who live the high life in L-A while their employees cultivate the pot and take the risks. But before you get to thinking that everyone in town shares the sheriff's view of a cash pipeline heading south, listen to what

businessman McKee has to say. He couldn't disagree more with the sheriff's view of the economics of marijuana in Humboldt County. In McKee's view it isn't the high life in Los Angeles that's benefiting; it's local merchants like him who are being helped by all that marijuana cash.

Local Store Owner: As a matter of fact, I think more of it stays here from this kind of a business than stays here from logging.

Correctly paced writing explains the tapes, provides a pause between the tapes, but does not overwhelm the tapes. When writing a documentary it's wise to keep in mind David Kogan's suggestion that a documentary be more than half tape. A good rule of thumb is to try to more or less balance the length of the tape with the length of the reporter's narration.

ACCEPTABLE
Local Store Owner: . . . everybody is involved and benefiting economically from marijuana growing in this area.

Reporter: Since marijuana growing is a clandestine activity, it's impossible to document the value of the crop, but Humboldt County Sheriff David Renner knows megabucks are being made in his county.

Sheriff: 500-million to a billion dollars . . . and there's a very small part of that money being spent here.

Reporter: Sheriff Renner is one of those who is convinced the money goes south to absentee landlords, drug kingpins who live the high life in L-A while their employees cultivate the pot and take the risks. Businessman McKee disagrees.

```
Local Store Owner:   As a matter of fact, I think more
                     of it stays here from this kind of
                     a business than stays here from
                     logging.
                                          Peter Laufer, NBC
```

Documentaries give broadcast journalists something they rarely get: a chance to build, a chance to put a series of cuts together, a chance to construct larger ideas out of a varied collection of thoughts and incidents. There is a unique writing opportunity here, too. In documentaries, broadcast writers can develop, echo and return to themes. They can develop patterns and rhythms in their wordings that play not only over sentences or groups of sentences but also over pages. For example, in a documentary produced before the collapse of the Soviet Union, Cameron Swayze, then with NBC, built his theme of misunderstandings and mistrust by repeating terms related to speaking, stating, communicating:

```
A handful of gray-faced men control the lives of 260
million Soviet citizens. . . . The world waits on their
pronouncements. . . .
```

```
They speak rarely and when they do it is often
menacing. . . .
```

```
''There would be a new order,'' Lenin proclaimed. . . .
```

```
But there is another message from Moscow: A message not
of hope but of despair. . . .
```

Interview Programs

Interview programs can fill various slots in station programming. Many stations, perhaps unwilling to put the time and effort into documentaries, leave their public affairs responsibilities to a half-hour interview with a local official every Sunday morning. Others have switched to all-talk formats and constantly fill the air with interviews (interrupted frequently by phone calls from listeners) with authors on book tours, athletes, celebrities and sex therapists, as well as those same local officials.

If the subject under discussion is insignificant enough, and the questions gentle enough, interview shows may have little or no news value. But get a guest who has just written a book on aerial reconnaissance, not one who has written on model airplanes, or ask the city council president about her vote against a plan to clean up

Kathy Novak with New York Governor Mario Cuomo. (WABC Radio)

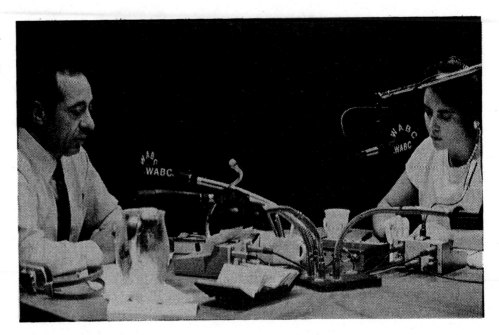

the town's water supply, not just about her frustration with broken water fountains in City Hall, and things may start getting interesting and newsworthy.

If the goal is in fact getting news—not just exercising the host's personality or filling the air with idle chatter—it helps if the guest is controversial. (As a rule, heads of local abortion clinics work better than Boy Scout leaders.) And it's necessary that the interviewer be sharp and prepared.

Before

How do you prepare for an interview? "I read everything I can get my hands on," says Ted O'Brien, who hosts a morning interview program on WRKO in Boston. When an interview is conducted live on the air, there's no way for the poorly prepared to edit out their inanities. And even if they could fool their audience, there is no way they are going to be able to dig below the superficialities if they barely understand the superficialities. O'Brien, with the help of his producer, will track down any clips he can find from newspapers and magazines on subjects he is about to consider on the air. He studies up. And if the guest has just written a book, O'Brien does the obvious: He reads the book.

The point is that it takes two informed people to have an informed conversation . . . even if the role of one of those people is just to bring out information for the benefit of presumably uninformed listeners. "I am a fiend on adequate preparation," says Kathy Novak, who for many years hosted a talk show on WABC in New York.

ABC's Ted Koppel interviews PLO Leader Yassir Arafat. (© 1989 copyright Capitol Cities/ABC Inc.)

Novak kept files full of clippings on subjects she believed she might someday want to discuss on her one-hour weekday-morning interview show. "I never will walk into a studio, look at my guest and say, 'What have you been doing since last time I talked to you?'"

Many veteran interviewers prefer not to write out their questions in advance. They say prepared questions can sound too formal on the air. (More likely they have become so used to composing their questions live that they feel no need to spend the time scribbling them down.) All good interviewers will, however, at least prepare notes for use in the studio during an interview. "The worst thing is to finish a nice 8- or 9-minute interview and then to realize that you forgot to ask a key question," O'Brien explains. Notes protect against the limitations of an over-burdened mind—trying to juggle thoughts of questions and answers and commercials and time.

Novak says she always arrived in the studio at WABC equipped with notes on the "areas" she wanted to pursue. That should be the minimum an interviewer brings into the studio. Beginners and relative beginners *should* definitely take the time to write out their questions in advance. If all is going smoothly, it may not even be necessary to refer to those prepared questions. But this is certainly no time to risk having to search a momentarily blank mind for a properly worded question. Better safe . . .

"There are brillant people like Ted Koppel who do interviews without writing questions down," notes Richard Threlkeld, who worked at ABC for many years. "Koppel has an I.Q. of about 200." The rest of us are better off having something on paper.

Interviewers should write one other thing out in advance: a scripted open and close for the show. These will introduce the interviewee and review the subjects that will be, or were, discussed. It's best not to rest an entire program on the vagaries of conversation.

The Questions

"A bad question," Kathy Novak explains, "is one with the answer already in it. The guest just says, 'Yeah, you're right.' " This should be familiar advice. (The importance of asking short-answer rather than true/false questions is discussed in Chapter 9, "Tape.") There are other similarities between interviews designed to obtain actualities for newscasts and interview programs—questions should be short and to the point, for example—but there's one big difference: While live on the air, an interviewer can't be content to guide a subject toward one or two "hot" statements. Each question must be designed both to produce an interesting response by itself and to fit some larger "line of questioning" that keeps the show, or a segment of the show, interesting and coherent.

An interview designed simply to produce a few actualities might jump from a question about the candidate's view on development downtown, to one on poverty, to one on taxes. But on an interview program the audience will require a smoother flow—perhaps two or three questions about development downtown and then a transition into the subject of poverty: "There's a lot of poor people in that downtown area. You've admitted that your plans might cost some of them their homes. Just what hope can you offer the poor of this city?" A question about taxes, then, might be saved until after a break for a commercial. The questions in such an interview don't have to follow a straight line. There can be bends and turns, but abrupt changes in subject should be kept to a minimum.

On interview programs, as in an interview taped for use in a newscast, it's a mistake to open with questions that threaten to alienate the interviewee: "If you have a question that seems to challenge their ethics or integrity, you save it for last," Novak advises. "They might walk out on you." However, like any other program, an interview program has to begin with something that is going to catch the audience's attention. So, *all* the controversial stuff can't be saved for the end. "I will generally use a question at the top that whets the listeners' appetites," Novak says. In other words, at the top of the show you might *not* confront the mayor with charges that his administration has practiced systematic discrimination in hiring—that can be saved for the end—but you might begin by getting into the mayor's attitude toward equal opportunity programs.

When those tough questions finally do come, they have heavy responsibilities. On an interview program the audience will want more than just a 12-second denial: "That's absurd; we've always tried to hire members of minority groups. Those people just don't know what they're talking about." The audience will expect that the extra time available here will allow some deeper digging. "Well, Mayor Jones, according to that N double-A-C-P survey based on city records, only two percent of the people hired during your administration are black." And: "You say you're as committed to minority hiring as anyone, yet your predecessor had a black press secretary and a Hispanic deputy mayor, but all the top people in your administration are white."

The audience will also expect to learn more about the personality of the person you're interviewing: "What were your feelings, when those blacks started booing and walking out of that town meeting?"

"I have learned that there are two ways to behave to get the most out of a person," explains Richard Threlkeld. "One is to take the prosecutorial role: You have the person in the dock and will get information out of him no matter what. Mike Wallace is the prime example of this strategy." Threlkeld says he prefers a gentler approach. "I tend to go in as somebody who is not quite conversant with the subject. You have to walk a fine line and not appear stupid, so the person dismisses you. But you do say, 'Gee, that's interesting.' Or, 'I didn't know that.' People like Charles Kuralt and Barbara Walters interview this way."

During

When a guest arrived at WABC, Kathy Novak was not exactly overly friendly. She would stick her head out of her office, explain where coffee could be found and then say, "I'll be back to get you just before the show." Novak fears that a significant conversation with a guest *before* the show can only detract from the freshness of the conversation they'll have *during* the show. She has no desire to grow more friendly with people she may have to challenge on the air. She won't review questions in advance with a guest. She won't give her opinion on what she wants the guest to talk about. Instead, she'll let her questions do the guiding on the air. Any rehearsal, she fears, and "it's going to sound canned."

Once the program begins, Novak is doing her best to *listen*. "A lot of interviewers continue to look at their list of questions and miss the opportunity to pick up on a point that's been discussed and ask a follow-up," she warns. "If you can become relaxed enough to sit back and listen, you can build a third and fourth question out of the first and second." In other words, you can build a coherent line of questioning.

Two types of guests are sure to create trouble on an interview program:

The Long-Winded When the answer to question one threatens to stretch to the first commercial break, the odds are part of the audience is going to start looking to other channels for relief. In broadcast news, *long* is usually *dull*. What to do?

"You just break in," says WRKO's Ted O'Brien. Kathy Novak, however, tries to be more subtle about interrupting long-winded guests. "You don't want to seem like you're being rude or crass," she expalins. "I try to just anticipate a pause or the end of a sentence and then jump in." No interviewers want to interrupt, but they cannot allow a guest to turn their show into a lecture. If all else fails, moving your finger rapidly across your neck may get the point across.

And Threlkeld notes that keeping questions short and to the point can encourage interviewees to maintain the same pace in their answers.

The Shy Many guests are as professional about handling interviews as the program's host. They've been interviewed on the air many times before and are conscious of their responsibility to help fill the air with interesting and engaging comments. Others, however, may be seeing the inside of a radio studio for the first time, and the thought of speaking before such a large audience of friends, neighbors and strangers may leave them petrified. What to do?

"They have to forget that they're talking to a quarter of a million people," Novak says. "I try to grab their attention with my eyes. If necessary, I'll say, just before we go on or during a break, 'Listen, you are talking to *me*.' "

A good interview program is an intelligent, informative, hard-hitting conversation. If the interviewees aren't holding up their end, reporters have to work that much harder in their questions. "You have to bring them out," Novak says. It may take repeating questions. It may take some joking to break the tension. It may take a brief detour to a more comfortable topic—the weather, if things are really desperate. But it's *your* show. In the end it's *your* responsibility to fill the air with substance.

Editorials

This is where all those opinions that have been leashed and kept away from the news can be turned loose. You think it's crazy for a man who has been convicted of embezzling to be allowed to keep his seat in the state legislature? If you are in a position to write an editorial, you can say so, in so many words:

```
It would be incomprehensible for the members of the
  House to allow this man to remain in state government.
                                              WXYZ, Detroit
```

Fairness? Well, air time just has to be given to those who disagree. The FCC's rules are now more lax than this ethical rule. It simply requires that people who have been personally attacked or candidates whose opponents have been endorsed be notified and given a chance to respond (see Chapter 18, "Ethics and Law"). The comment above might seem to be part of a "personal attack" so it would be necessary to notify the state legislator himself and offer him air time.

Editorials don't have to be argumentative. They can be used to interpret events:

It was a bitter eight-month fight, and in the end Robert
Bonin was the loser. But even with his resignation,
there was clearly no winner in the battle. The past
months have been difficult ones -- tragic ones -- for the
courts and the Commonwealth, and there is no cause for
celebration.

WEEI, Boston

Or to push civic responsibility:

So, for a stronger nation and a better state, today is
your day! Be sure you vote.

KQV, Pittsburgh

And this "Spectrum" commentary mixes entertainment with opinion:

The tomato, alas, has become a rare delicacy to be
savored quickly, once a year. Sometimes in the dead of
winter, I look at the store's offerings of pale plastic
baseballs and I understand why strong women weep. A
salad is just not a salad without a good tomato.

Marianne Means, CBS

Broadcast editorials have succeeded in ousting the corrupt, building parks, promoting health-care campaigns, raising money for various causes as well as increasing awareness on political issues. Occasionally they are demonstrably wrongheaded — that presumably is one purpose of the rebuttal time.

Editorials are usually the responsibility of the station manager, but that person often seeks writing and reporting help from the news staff. Some large stations hire full-time editorial directors to handle these duties. And an editorial committee that may include the news director and other managment staff may make policy decisions; stations are usually careful not to allow their editorials to be used for personal vendettas or idiosyncratic crusades.

Despite the conspicuous presence of subjectivity, editorials have much in common with other forms of broadcast news: They are written for the same medium and, therefore, have the same need to be conversational and clear. Facts cannot be treated any more loosely. The writing must still say what it means.

Editorials are composed of four elements:

The Issue

The city of Pittsburgh is considering a change in its
method of garbage collection in order to save money and
provide a more efficient collection service.

The Background

At present garbage is collected once a week from the backyard or rear of the residence by a crew of sanitation workers who dump the 55-gallon garbage cans into a burlap sack. One of the workers then carries the sack out to the street where he throws it into a collection truck.

This method works pretty well most of the time except when there is a heavy snowfall, hard rain or traffic obstruction on the street. Then the garbage may not be collected for two weeks, and there are lots of complaints.

The city is thinking about providing every householder who now receives collection service with an 80-gallon plastic container mounted on wheels. It would then become the responsibility of the resident of the house to wheel this container out to the curb where it could be picked up and dumped much faster by a special lift attached to the truck.

The Opinion (or Recommendation)

This might work well in some areas where it is quite flat, but, in Pittsburgh, we don't think this is the answer.

The Support

Besides the five- or six-million-dollar outlay required to furnish every home with its own 80-gallon container and to equip all the trucks with special lifts, there are too many other reasons why this system won't work.

Too many Pittsburgh residents are handicapped or are too old to push the containers out to the street. Too many streets and alleys where collections have to be made are too narrow, or too steep, or both. Even if the resident could get the container out to the curb, there is the danger of it running away down a hill and crashing into the street.

We think there must be a better way to collect garbage.

KQV, Pittsburgh

Sometimes the issue is not stated, just the opinion. Sometimes the support is combined with the background or the opinion. But these four elements, in whatever order or combinations, are the building blocks of editorials.

Susan Burdick is editorial director at WEEI in Boston, but when she is preparing an editorial she functions like a reporter. Burdick clips all relevant newspaper stories; she visits or calls the parties involved, reads through the relevant documents, attends city council meetings. Burdick also strolls over to the newsroom and chats with reporters covering the issue. Hers are, at least, informed opinions.

Like most stations, WEEI emphasizes local issues in its editorials. It tries to comment on the major problems confronting its community. Burdick discusses ideas and opinions with the station's general manager every morning and with its editorial board every few weeks. Once a position has been agreed upon, Burdick's job is to state it, explain it and make it sound convincing.

She begins with an outline. She notes what points she wants to make, then gives each point a paragraph and tries to arrange them in an order that works. She likes to lead the editorial with the issue and then the opinion—"to tell them where you stand":

```
Debating the death penalty is getting to be an annual
event on Beacon Hill. This year there are two measures
up for review. First, a bill to restore the death
penalty for certain types of murder. Second, a proposed
change in the state constitution. We'd like to say once
more for the record: We strongly oppose any move to
reinstate the death penalty in Massachusetts.
```

Giving the background can be the toughest job. Burdick's editorials can run no longer than a minute and a half. One of her major problems is keeping the background from eating up most of that time.

Burdick says she is always catching herself becoming too complex. The goal is to present just enough background on the issue so that listeners think, "Yeah, I know what she's talking about." If the issue itself is too complex, Burdick does a series of editorials to cover it. If the issue has been hanging around the news for a while, less background is needed:

```
The arguments on both sides of the issue are old hat by
now, but deserve repeating. Proponents say the death
penalty would, first and foremost, deter crime. It's
justifiable punishment, they say, for something as brutal
as murder. Many argue imprisonment isn't enough to keep
criminals off the street -- that they too often are
paroled or furloughed.
     Those who oppose the legislation say the statistics
are clear: The death penalty does not discourage would-
be killers. Most murders, they argue, are not
```

premeditated. And some opponents point out there's been
discriminatory use of the death penalty against
minorities and the poor.

Next, the heart of an editorial—the support or why you came to that conclusion.
As Burdick says, "Obviously, you have to be convincing."

We think the most compelling argument against bringing
back the death penalty is one cited by the State Supreme
Court several years ago. The death penalty, it said, is
cruel and unusual punishment. In a humane society,
there's simply no justification for such extreme revenge.
What's to be gained by taking yet another life? A man
who's convicted of murder should be punished -- but
through imprisonment, not death.

In this editorial Burdick leaves to the close the responsibility for wrapping up,
and repeating the opinion:

The death penalty has not been carried out in
Massachusetts for more than 30 years. It's a sad comment
on our society that it's even thinking of restoring the
death penalty. And it would be tragic if the legislature
and the citizens allowed it to get back on the books in
Massachusetts.

Not all of Burdick's editorials follow this same format, and editorial writers at
different stations have different styles. They all face the same problem of presenting
a clear and convincing case, but the best writers are often those who devise the most
creative solutions to this problem.

Burdick found an original and effective way to criticize the mayor in one of her
editorials. She obtained a tape in which, she says, the mayor contradicted himself
within only eight seconds. The editorial was built around that tape.

Wrap-Up

Journalists working on a documentary, an interview program or an editorial should
keep in mind what in some sense is the ultimate purpose of these programs—to dig
deeper, to reveal more. It seems a shame to give those extra minutes, or to let loose
opinions, if those tools are not going to be used to explore, investigate and understand the world thoroughly.

Visuals

By 6:30 p.m. New York time, the graphics have been selected, the videotape from around the world assembled. The executive producer, working with Dan Rather and other members of the staff, has arranged the show's 22 minutes or so of news. And Rather had edited the copy newswriters have prepared for him.

Sitting at the same desk where he worked on his script, Rather puts on his jacket and turns to face the camera. A make-up woman applies some powder to keep his nose, cheeks and forehead from shining. After a signal from the director, Rather says, "Good evening. This is the *CBS Evening News*, Dan Rather reporting."

What follows is the first run-through (some of the show will be redone when a partially videotaped, partially live version of the newscast is sent to other affiliates at 7 p.m.) of a program that is the culmination of a day's work by a team of people that makes the staff working on any radio news broadcast seem small. Including technical personnel and CBS reporters around the world, more than 90 people contribute to the production of this newscast.

Even smaller news organizations employ many more people to produce a television newscast than just about any radio newscast. KATV in Little Rock, Arkansas, has a staff of 35 working on news shows. The complexities of television news require more, and more specialized, personnel.

The focus of the preceding chapters has been radio journalism, but virtually all those discussion also apply to the work the journalists on the staffs of these television stations do. Television journalists also write copy that is to be read aloud by newscasters and must be received by the audience's ears. *All* the basic writing rules are the same on television as on radio. Television journalists also rely heavily on the wire services. They follow many of the same rules in covering stories. They look for the same things in interviews, and must write on-scene reports and lead-ins to the material they bring back from the field.

Television news, however, does follow a different schedule from radio news. Instead of a short newscast each hour, most television stations have short newscasts at breakfast time and, perhaps, at noon, then full-hour or half-hour newscasts at dinnertime and again at 10 p.m. or 11 p.m. Still, television news *is* basically radio news with one major addition—visuals. The techniques taught in the previous chapters remain relevant, but working with visuals demands an *additional* set of reporting, writing and producing skills. This chapter and the three that follow are devoted to the journalistic ramifications of visuals. They explain how news is told with images as well as with sounds. This chapter's specific job is taking a closer look at some of the images that can fill the screen during a television newscast.

Talking Heads

After a signal from the floor manager, Dan Rather looks at the camera and begins talking. We see his head, his shoulders and perhaps half of the sweater he so often wears under his jacket. Once the opening formalities have been taken care of—perhaps a shot of the members of the "news team" trotting to their desks, teases from some upcoming stories or just that brief introduction spoken by Dan Rather—the screen on most television newscasts is filled by a shot of the top third or so of a newscaster's body. This person's head, which dominates the picture, is talking, reading the opening story, and this shot, a staple of television news, is called a **talking head.**

The term "talking head" has negative connotations in television journalism because talking-head shots certainly do not make much use of the medium. (The phrase "talking head" is also used to refer to similarly unimaginative shots of the heads of people being interviewed in videotape reports or television documentaries.) The story the **anchor** is reading could have been written for radio. The only difference between a talking head on television and a newscaster on the radio is that view of the television newscaster's face—not a particularly profound addition. Still this shot has its place. Often there are no visuals available, especially on out-of-town stories, so there is no choice. And some particularly complex stories may be better understood without the added distraction of visuals. Watching Dan Rather's face may make it just a little easier to understand what he's saying.

Graphics

Visually, the next step up from a talking head is a talking head plus a **graphic.** As newscaster Debbie Knox, of WISH-TV, reads a story about the strife in South Africa, to the side of her head is a picture of a burning vehicle. That picture doesn't give viewers much information, but it helps them focus on the story. It also makes for a more interesting shot. Graphics are being used more and more in television news.

A graphic, or **still,** can be a photograph. A few stations still obtain or create color slides; a few still use photographs supplied by the wire services if they have nothing else on a story. But most stations now turn frames from videotape stories into graphics by preserving them in computerized **still stores.** And many stations now employ artists to fashion illustrations for stories. A graphic can also consist of a drawing or a chart, and fancy technical devices, "electronic paint boxes," enable moving graphics to be produced.

In addition, graphics can also include words, perhaps the word *RECALL* under a close-up of a car that is being recalled—the word here is functioning like an extremely short newspaper headline. Or the words may be a long, crucial quote—perhaps the exact words the city council president used to deny any involvement in that alleged kickback scheme. Most stations put words on the screen through use of a computerized **character generator.**

There are four ways a graphic can be used in a newscast:

Supers

Most of the hard information communicated in television news is going to be communicated, as it is in radio, to viewers' ears, because it is more natural and comfortable for people to listen to someone explaining something than it is to read that explanation off the screen. But most viewers certainly are capable of reading a few words at a time off the screen, and television journalists have discovered how useful a few written words can be in supplementing whatever is being said.

For example, in radio news where only sound is available, each time a person of some importance in a story speaks in an actuality that person's name and title must be mentioned (see Chapter 10, "Writing to Tape"). That takes valuable time. In television, however, where sound *and* sight are available, there is another alternative. The newsmaker's name and title can be flashed on the screen along with a shot of the person, relieving the copy that will be read on the air of responsibility for identifying that person. Writers may want to note the name in the copy anyway, but they don't have to. That's efficient. That's called a **super.**

Supers, produced on character generators and stored in computer memories, are used frequently in television news. On many stations, the name of each newsmaker who speaks on camera will show up below that person's head on the screen for a few seconds—long enough for viewers to read. And the station's own reporters and newscasters often are identified in this way, too. It can't hurt to build the "name recognition" of your stars.

These graphics are called "supers" at many stations because in less technically advanced days they were actually superimposed over the picture they were identifying. The are also sometimes called **lower-thirds,** after the portion of the screen they usually occupy. And in some newsrooms these graphics are referred to as **fonts,** because the character generators on which they are produced allow a choice of different "type fonts," or type styles (or perhaps because the brand name of the character generator on which they are often produced is Vidifont).

And supers are not limited to identifying people. Stations will also use graphics to give locations, exact addresses, even times; to indicate that the videotape viewers are watching is old "file footage"; to indicate a shot is "live"; or to acknowledge they are borrowing, with permission, another station's or network's exclusive pictures.

Supers, the simplest form of graphic, provide a basic demonstration of what visuals can add to television news. (Rules for using supers, it should be noted, can

The supers on screen here identify the location, the network and the fact that this event is being broadcast live. (© 1991 CNN, Inc. All Rights Reserved)

get complex. CBS has distributed a pamphlet about 15 pages long on the subject with guidelines on, for example, what type faces to use, how names should be written, where in the screen different types of supers should be placed and when the CBS "eye" should be used.)

Keys

Frequently a graphic appears to be right behind the newscaster. Usually it isn't. There may be a few stations that still employ **rear projection**—where an image actually is projected on a screen behind the newscaster—and some stations occasionally place actual television monitors behind a newscaster to show graphics or, more commonly, to show a reporter who is about to report live from the field. But most stations produce this effect through a process that takes graphics that aren't even in the studio and electronically combines them with a shot of the newscaster so that on screen they seem to be behind that person.

One method for doing this is called **chromakey.** A camera is programmed to drop out everything on screen of a particular color—usually a medium blue. The background behind the newscaster is blue, so it disappears and then is replaced by something else. That something else might be a graphic showing a car and the word

Newscaster Debbie
Knox of WISH-TV,
Indianapolis, on
camera with a
graphic, a "box."
(Steve Sweitzer)

Newscaster Debbie Knox of WISH-TV, Indianapolis, on camera with a graphic, a "box." (Steve Sweitzer)

RECALL. If the newscaster were to make the mistake of wearing a blue tie of the same shade, that also would disappear.

Using keys, any shot can be placed behind a newscaster—a weather map, some videotape, a shot from a live camera. A key enables Ted Koppel on ABC's Nightline to appear as if he is having a face-to-face conversation with someone sitting in a studio thousands of miles away. Some stations even use keys to decorate their sets— perhaps with a shot of the city's skyline made to appear as if it were right behind the news desk.

Boxes

The next step up in technical sophistication is a system that cuts a **box** out of the shot of the newscaster and then fits a graphic into that box. The effect is similar to that produced by a key, but neater, and there's no danger of the newscaster moving and covering up a few letters of the graphic.

Some newscast formats now require that a box with a graphic appear every time the newscasters in the studio appear on camera. So since there's some sort of in-studio introduction to every story, there's a graphic in every story.

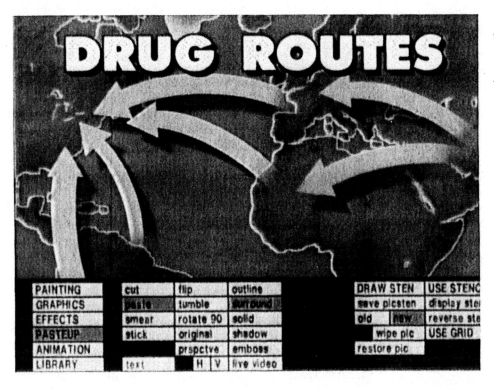

Choosing the words and/or pictures that will appear in a box is an important *journalistic* decision. If the story says the auto maker is *considering* a recall, *RECALL* won't do in the graphic; *RECALL?* might be okay. If the charge is *voluntary manslaughter, MURDER TRIAL* is unacceptable in a graphic. The words in a graphic have the same responsibility to remain faithful to the meaning of the story as the words in that story's lead. And the picture must be appropriate, too. A television station was once sued in part because it had illustrated a story on the questionable tactics of an organization with a graphic that showed a man bearing a striking resemblance to Lee Harvey Oswald, the accused assassin of President John Kennedy.

The pictures that appear in these boxes are usually just "freeze-frame" images taken from videotape stories. Words can be added to these images, and they can be easily stored in a computer—a still store—for that evening's newscast or for future use.

Computer Art

Bill Johnson's title at WRC-TV in Washington, D.C., is "art director." It is an increasingly important position in television journalism. A reporter doing a story on the flow of drugs into the United States, for example, might come to Johnson not just for a box to decorate the lead-in to her story but for a graphic, some computer art, that might shoulder some of the burden of telling this complex tale. "Can we do a map with moving arrows to show the flow of drugs from south to north?"

Johnson moves to his *electronic paint box*—an expensive computer graphics system made by Quantel. A whole selection of maps is stored in the system. He just has to pick one that covers the necessary area. Then, using an electronic pen or *stylus*, he draws some arrows, indicating the path drugs follow to various United States cities. "The paint box can animate," Johnson explains. "You can program it to make the arrows move up the map." Words—the names of the cities and countries involved—can then be added. This electronic *full-screen graphic*, can now be mixed in with videotape in the reporter's story.

In the past, stations only devoted the full screen to a graphic if they had an illustration that seemed crucial or if they wanted to use a slide or a photo of an event for which no videotape was available. These were rare occasions. Computers, however, have made possible a new kind of television art.

Electronic paint boxes are used most frequently in newscasts during the weather—when they produce those smiling suns and angry clouds that float from left to right across weather maps. (See Chapter 17, "Television Newscasts.") But they are gaining a larger and larger place in news stories. KCRA-TV in Sacramento, California, for example, used such a computer system to produce a series of images illustrating how an airplane almost crashed near San Francisco.

Diagrams, maps, charts and graphs—once almost the exclusive property of print journalists—have not only entered the world of broadcast journalism but have come alive in the process. With animated computer art, television news now really does have access to pictures that can compete—in their ability to convey information—with a thousand words.

Videotape

A short history lesson: From its earliest days, whenever television news wanted to show action that took place outside the studio, it used film. The early television film stories were direct descendants of the movie newsreel. In fact, when they began doing television news, each network contracted for footage with companies that produced newsreels. Soon television stations began producing their own 16mm film to illustrate their stories. Camera operators usually went with the reporter to the scene of a news event, shot some shots and interviews and then brought the film back to the newsroom to develop and edit. It was projected on a *film chain* directly into a television camera; then the film appeared in the newscast.

In film stories the visual potential of the medium was being used to its fullest. Neither radio nor newspapers could match shots of, for example, people fleeing a sniper or police units moving in. Yet television stations have abandoned film. CBS never uses film stories in the Evening News. It still has on-the-scene reports, but they are no longer recorded on film.

Videotape—now a familiar part of most of our "home entertainment centers"—is a first cousin of the audiotape used in radio news. Like audiotape, it records electronically coded signals that can be played back immediately or erased. The difference is that, besides sound, videotape can also record moving pictures.

Videotape has significant advantages over film: The picture quality is higher—it looks more "live." It doesn't have to be developed—it can be played back immediately after it's recorded; and it can be reused—just erase and start again.

Nevertheless, two significant technical problems delayed the adoption of videotape for *remotes*—on-the-scene reports—in television news: First, early videotape cameras and recorders were too bulky to use on the scene at news events. Second, the videotape was difficult to edit. You can see film; you just find the frames you want, cut and splice them together. But pictures are coded on videotape in invisible electronic signals. Thus it was hard to find particular shots. And the tape is too large and expensive to cut up like audiotape. To edit, it was necessary to get two precisely coordinated tape recorders rolling and then transfer scenes from one to the other.

Both these problems have been conquered by new electronic and computer technology. Compact, lightweight videotape cameras and recorders have been produced that surpass the portability of film cameras. And precise, computer-aided editing systems have been developed that make videotape much easier to edit than film.

Now on just about all stations those shots and interviews from the scene are recorded and then played in the newscast on videotape recorders. The use of videotape didn't change the selection of shots or interviews; it did make them a little easier to work with and better-looking on the air.

Since pictures are recorded electronically on videotape, reporting with videotape is often called *electronic newsgathering,* or *ENG.* Most stations use ¾-inch or ½-inch videotape cassettes to record their remotes. But there is another alternative: Videotape stories can also be sent back *live* to the newsroom. Since they are shot with small television cameras, the camera's signal can simply be transmitted back, usually by microwave transmission (occasionally with the help of satellites), and put directly on the air. The ability to go live is another tremendous advantage videotape had over film.

It is the use of this increasingly quick, flexible and portable medium that has, more than anything else, enlivened television news in recent years. With improvements in videotape technology, newscasts have become more visually exciting, and the visual opportunities open to television reporters have expanded.

"Videotape and the live capabilities of these cameras have made television better able to take the viewer *there*," says Steve Ramsey, news director of KWCH-TV in Wichita, Kansas, "Newspapers will tell their audiences about the news tomorrow. Radio lets them listen as news takes place. But television can now bring people to the news event."

Amateur Videotape

Once upon a time it was hard for television news crews to get video footage of flames shooting out the window of a building, or a tornado bearing down on a town, or to get shots of the police beating someone while making an arrest. Their crews had to be lucky enough to be at or near the scene when the event occurred. People living nearby have never had that problem. They just come out of their houses, or peer out windows and see what's going on. Increasingly, they're also aiming their home video cameras at what they see, capturing dramatic footage and offering it to local television stations.

Is it a good idea to use such amateur videotape? News Director Elbert Tucker of WBRC-TV in Birmingham, Alabama, says he asks himself three questions: "Is it newsworthy? Is it interesting? Is it air quality?" Amateur video raises other questions as well: Do you pay for it? Do you actively solicit it? These last are policy questions that different stations and networks will answer differently. But News Director Joe Rovitto of WTAE–TV in Pittsburgh says his reporters are now in the habit of asking around for amateur videos when they get to the scene of a story.

The one absolute rule about amateur video is that, if you do use it as part of a story, it must be identified as such. This is often done with a super. It can also be done in the copy, ". . . as this neighbor captured with a home video camera. . . ." Such a disclaimer explains why the picture is out of focus or shaking so much (most people don't use tripods) and why the picture is often less sharp (home VHS equipment creates a TV picture with 400 lines, compared to the 525 lines in broadcast TV).

Some media-savvy folks have also begun submitting homemade video tape along with a press release to illustrate a story. (See Chapter 7, "Sources.") News Director Roger Ball of WANE-TV, Fort Wayne, Indiana, says a group of residents, who wanted to complain that a railroad crossing gate came down too slowly, offered his station videotape of the gates in action. This videotape raised a crucial new question: Is the video credible? While it's unlikely someone would have altered the video camera's speed, might there have been a railroad repair crew just out of camera view adjusting the speed of the gates when the video was shot? This is certainly a case in which you would identify the source of your picture, but it might also be one in which you would send a station crew out to document the evidence for yourself.

Wrap-Up

Talking heads, graphics, videotape—these are the things that appear on the screen during a television newscast. When these visuals, and the words that work with them, are well chosen, television brings news to both the eyes and the ears of its audience. It is a powerful tool.

15

Television Reporting

Dennis Johnson, medical reporter for what is now KTSP-TV, Phoenix, got hold of a copy of a study on health hazards in copper smelters. The study made some strong charges about potential medical problems for workers inside these plants, and more than half of the copper smelters mentioned were in Arizona. Johnson called the director of the study in New York for further information about the problem, then made plans to cover the story at a copper smelter well out of town the next day.

He needed interviews with workers, but workers would only be free to talk at the beginning or the end of their shift. They left work at 3:30 p.m.—too late for his 6 p.m. newscast. Johnson and a camera operator had to leave the station at 4:30 the next morning to get there in time to conduct interviews before the start of the shift.

All reporters need facts. As noted in Chapter 9, "Tape," radio reporters are also after sound; radio reporters would have conducted similar interviews with the plant's workers. But television news adds an additional item to the reporter's shopping list. Johnson also had to make sure he came back with the proper visuals.

For the benefit of the visuals, after interviewing workers Johnson and his camera operator toured the smelter with company officials. The tour provided dramatic videotape footage of brilliant orange molten copper. Then they hurried back to Phoenix for an interview on camera with an official from the company that owned the smelter.

Johnson had the luxury of not having to cover any other stories that day, so he could return to the newsroom and start looking over the videotape they had shot. With the visuals in mind, he typed up a rough draft of the story.

Next, Johnson selected the sections of the interview he planned to use. He wrote a few more drafts of the story—tightening it each time—before he showed it to his producer for approval. With the producer's okay, Johnson moved to the editing room to work with a videotape editor. Again, if he had had to cover more stories that day, he might not have been able to sit in on the editing himself; the editor would have had to work from the script alone.

The copper smelter was the lead story on KTSP-TV's newscast that evening.

There is something wonderfully simple about television reporting. You go out to a copper smelter; you talk to some people; and the viewers get to see some of what you saw. They can see those people talking; they can see the incredible molten copper. Simple.

The problem is that gathering and processing those simple images is an undertaking that dwarfs in its complexity anything newspaper or radio reporters have to go through.

Shooting

Television reporters are tied to their cameras . . . loosely. They have to be free enough to get the story—to roam around in search of information at a news event and to cultivate sources and dig for facts (see Chapter 8, "Gathering News"). But on most stories they cover, television reporters are expected to return with videotape that brings viewers as close as possible to the story. To do that effectively, they must honor the whims of the camera.

The basic strategies of reporting were discussed in earlier chapters. Here are the special routines, requirements and reporting skills demanded by the television camera:

The Crew

Television reporters like Dennis Johnson need help. Unlike the radio reporter who can carry all the necessary equipment—a cassette recorder and a notebook—in one hand, television reporters need a camera and lights, in addition to sound equipment of some sort and a notebook.

Many small stations make do with one-person reporting crews. Ed Howard of KULR-TV in Billings, Montana, works for such a station and has to cover stories solo. Howard must hold the camera himself while conducting an interview. To videotape himself, Howard sets the camera up on a tripod, shoots, plays it back to see what the shot looks like; then, if it looks decent, he shoots for real. "I'm a one-man band." Howard says. His technical responsibilities curtail to some extent his flexibility as a reporter.

At most stations, such as KTSP-TV in Phoenix, reporters get help in the form of a single camera operator. This person is responsible for shooting the videotape, setting up the lighting and working the sound equipment. At the largest stations and at the networks, these responsibilities are divided among two or even three people—a *camera crew*. Union regulations at many large stations ensure that nobody does another's job; in other words, reporters don't touch cameras or any other technical equipment.

Reporters are responsible for the reporting. The camera crew or camera person is responsible for the technical quality of the videotape. However, the actual choice of shots falls into a gray area. Generally, the reporter decides what to shoot and the camera operator chooses the angle and composition of the shot. But with experience they should be able to offer each other suggestions and make decisions cooperatively.

Since antagonism between the reporter and technicians can be both unproductive and uncomfortable, the best advice on working with a crew is to work *with* the

ABC reporter Mike Von Freund with a three-person camera crew. (© copyright Capitol Cities/ABC, Inc.)

crew. Communication is essential. Reporters have to know what their photographers are shooting—it will affect their reporting and writing. And photographers have to know how reporters are seeing a story—it will affect what they shoot.

Steve Sweitzer, chief news photographer for WISH-TV, Indianapolis, recalls seeing a story that a reporter and technician must have gone out at daybreak to cover: the first moments of the first day of school. "But while the reporter was waxing poetic about the sun rising over the playground, there weren't any shots of the sun rising over the playground," Sweitzer says. "Obviously, somebody missed the boat there. You have to work as a team."

Basic Procedures

The more complex the undertaking, the more necessary it is to understand the routine and to master the procedures. It certainly helps in television reporting.

Schedules Most stations stagger their reporters' schedules somewhat so that someone is on duty early in the morning—in case anything breaks—and someone is around in the evening to get a fresh story for the 10 or 11 o'clock newscast. But the majority of a station's reporters are usually out in the field in the late morning or early afternoon, covering stories that can be comfortably edited in time for the early evening newscast.

Generally, each reporter is responsible for two or three stories a day. If there's some reason for hurry, a messenger might take the videotape back to the studio for processing while the reporter and crew move on to another story. More frequently the reporter and crew will write and edit the whole bunch themselves upon their return.

Slating   Reporters should write down in a note pad a brief description of each of the shots they get in the order they are shot. People's names, what they are doing, what the shot is showing, all may help when the videotape is replayed in the editing room. Reporters will recall the meaning of most of their shots; they may need to know the meaning of *all* of them. **Slating** shots in a notebook makes it easier to jot down a draft of the story in the car, before looking at the videotape, and also makes it easier to find the shots when editing.

Ratio   Videotape can be reused. There is no real need to worry about "wasting" it as a story is shot. However, no photographer wants to shoot *too* much videotape . . . simply because it will be necessary to wade through all those extra minutes of tape when editing the story. Photographers might try to limit themselves to shooting perhaps four times as much tape as they will actually use in a story. That's called a **shooting ratio.** Monitoring the shooting ratio was much more important in the days of film, which cannot be reused.

Each individual shot—a shot of a fireman fighting the fire, for example—should be held long enough to permit healthy portions of that image to be edited into the final version of the story. As a rule, the camera should stay on every shot for at least 15 seconds. If the shot is important enough to be used a few times in the story, the length of time the camera should hold is multiplied. Camera wiggles, loud trucks and bystanders yelling "Hi, Mom!" all require that the shot be held that much longer to compensate for the ruined moments.

Setting Up   First, you want the camera to be steady. "We've been insisting that our photographers use tripods as much as possible," says Lee Giles, news director of WISH-TV, Indianapolis. "We're striving for a quality image." People aren't as steady as **tripods**—those three-legged camera stands—and unsteady images are not quality images. If the photographer has to follow something or shoot in a hurry, it won't be possible to set up a tripod. Otherwise, one should be used.

Second, get the camera as close as possible to what you want to shoot. A veteran *60 Minutes* photographer used to say, "What we're trying to do is get into the other guy's pants."

"One of the things that separates the beginners from the pros," says Sweitzer of WISH-TV, "is that beginners stand away from their subjects and use a telephoto lens to zoom in on them. A professional gets as close as possible to the subject and then zooms all the way back. In TV that physical closeness is essential." Why? Part of the answer is that being near something makes you more aware of it and, presumably, better able to capture its essence. But also, the further back you are, the wider the focal length will be, and the more vulnerable you will be to inadvertent camera movements.

Types of Shots

Camera shots are usually divided into three groups: close-ups, medium shots and long shots.

A *close-up* (CU) is a shot of a person's head and perhaps shoulders. (Occasionally the camera will come in even closer so that the screen is filled with eyes, nose, cheeks, mouth and little else—an "extreme close-up.") Tight shots of a sign or a person's hand nervously fiddling with something, or a charred doll at a fire, would also be labeled close-ups.

In general, *medium shots* (MS) show objects and a little of their surroundings—the charred doll surrounded by a few yards of rubble, the business sign and some of the store window. A medium shot of a person usually includes everything from the waist up.

Long shots (LS) place things in perspective—a whole row of stores, a view of the entire burnt-out building. Long shots of people include their whole bodies and, necessarily, much of what is around them.

The role these shots can play in telling a story is discussed in later sections. One technical point, though: Our eyes are drawn to motion, whether it's rioters jumping up and down on a police cruiser or a building jumping up and down because the camera operator can't hold the camera steady. For shots of the exteriors of buildings, tripods become essential. The riot, since there's motion in the scene and a little extra motion won't be noticed, can probably be shot "from the shoulder." As photographer John DeTarsio of KNSD, San Diego, says, "If it doesn't look like an earthquake in real life, then it shouldn't look like that on videotape." Also, the more tightly a camera focuses on a subject, the more apparent any inadvertent camera movements are. So beginning camera operators, who may have some trouble keeping a camera steady, might want to emphasize longer shots.

Pans and Zooms

There are two basic ways in which cameras or their lenses can move: They can pan and they can zoom. Both tend to be overused by beginners.

In a *pan* the camera slowly turns to sweep a large area. Pans are used to follow movement—perhaps a police car arriving; to show the scope of something—a crash site; or to pinpoint physical relationships—how close the X-rated movie theater is to the high school.

Still, some news directors warn new reporters against using any pans at all. For one thing, they are difficult to do well. The camera must be moved slowly and steadily or the result will be a jerky blur. Too many pans in a story and viewers get dizzy. And there is never any excuse to "spray the garden"—pan back and forth across a scene. One pan should be sufficient.

There is a simpler way to shoot two things that are near each other. Instead of panning from one to the other, shoot one, then the other. This avoids all those wasted seconds while the camera moves between them. Steady shots are also much less vulnerable to a slip by unsteady hands.

If a pan is going to be attempted, it is always wise to pause for 10 seconds or so at the beginning and end of the pan. Shoot the X-rated movie theater for a few moments, then pan, then shoot the high school for a few moments. That way it is possible to edit out the pan and still use the shots.

In a *zoom* the camera doesn't move, the lenses do—gliding from a close-up to a long shot or vice versa. This can add meaning to a story. The camera can start with a long shot of the crowd, then zoom in on the speaker; or zoom from a close-up of a business sign to a shot of the whole store and maybe the neighboring stores.

But, if a camera does not have an electronic zoom, zooms too can be difficult to do smoothly, and they are easily overused. Instead, it is often best to shoot the close-up and long shot separately and edit them together in the story (when reporting live, this isn't possible, so zooms might be more valuable live). And if you are going to zoom, the rule is the same as with pans: Hold the shots at both ends of the zoom, so they can be used if the zoom is edited out.

Motion makes for good footage, but as a rule it's best if what is being shot does the moving, not the camera or its lenses. Moving pictures are often best shot by nonmoving cameras. "The photographers here use zooms and pans sparingly," says Carissa Howland, news director of KCWY-TV, Casper, Wyoming. "One zoom or pan is enough in a story. There's very little that beats a straight shot. We're a news team, not artsy-craftsy movie makers."

Shooting Order

Two rules determine the order in which videotape or film should be shot: The first is to get the *temporary scenes* first. Anything worth shooting that may not be there later gets top priority. Certainly the flames themselves at a fire story fit into this category; so do interviews with eyewitnesses or survivors—they may leave. On a police story, often the police arrange to parade suspects they have arrested in front of reporters before arraignment—that scene is temporary and gets first priority. "On a breaking story, get the pictures first, facts later," says Howland of KCWY-TV.

After those temporary scenes have been shot, the reporter and crew can deal with the more permanent subjects—an interview with the fire chief, shots of the fire trucks or shots of the gutted building. And then they can worry about getting those facts.

The second consideration when determining shooting order is the order in which the shots will probably be used in the final version of the story. All other things being equal, it's helpful if stories are shot in approximately the order they will be used. This is called *editing in the camera,* and it should make it easier to edit the story in the editing room.

Composition

What makes a good shot? In television news the major concern is the event, not the aesthetics. Good shots show clearly what happened. The more exciting the happenings, the more exciting the shots.

However, anyone who aims a camera should be conscious of some aesthetic notions. It certainly can't hurt, as Sweitzer of WISH-TV advises, to think about how the master artists have filled their paintings or how the best film makers, like Orson Welles or Martin Scorcese, have filled their screens. And there's no doubt that once the camera has located the event, an understanding of some basic technical and aesthetic rules can help make shots of that event easier to follow and more attractive to look at.

Framing Televison monitors are not all adjusted the same. Often, something that is visible on the edge of one screen is off screen on another. So camera operators must allow for what is called a *ten-percent cutoff.* They have to figure that anything that appears in a band around the edge of the screen—the outer ten percent of the picture—may not be visible on some monitors. Therefore, they keep important subjects, such as the top of someone's head or the top line of a protest placard, out of that unreliable area.

Headroom A good portion of the shots used on television news are of people. People look silly with their foreheads cut off. Except in extreme close-ups, it is necessary to leave them some headroom—enough so that even after the ten-percent cutoff is taken into account, there will be a bit of space between the top of their head and the top of the screen.

Many beginners go too far in this direction; they leave as much as a third or a half of the screen on top of a person's head. Since there usually isn't too much going on above our heads, that's usually wasted picture. The solution is either to tilt the camera down so we can see more of the person, or even better, to zoom in to a closer shot. All that is necessary is enough headroom to separate the hair from the top of the screen on any monitor.

Balance Shots should be composed so that they direct attention on the screen to whatever is most important. The simplest way to do that is to put the proper center of attention in the middle of the screen. Certainly it would look strange if the person doing the talking was way off to the side.

Nevertheless, too much symmetry is rather dull. Interesting shots are often less than completely symmetric. In fact, some broadcasters believe that the viewer's attention on the screen does not focus on the center of the picutre, but on two points, one third of the way from the top and one third of the way from either side. This is called the "rule of thirds." Many standard television news shots are built around these points instead of the center of the screen. (Note the position of the newscaster's eyes and the box on p. 344.)

Leading the Action   If the camera is panning to follow a jogger, it's important to leave more room in the picture in front of the jogger than behind the jogger. That way it appears as if the jogger has some room to run into. Leaving more room behind the jogger would make the person seem to be constantly on the verge of running out of the picture. Always "lead"—keep the camera a little ahead of—the action.

The same rule applies when shooting somebody talking. Interviewees usually are not looking directly into the camera. They have their heads turned a bit toward the right or left. When videotaping people talking, leave extra space in front of them—on the side of the picture they are facing. Give people space to talk into.

Depth   Television is a two-dimensional medium. In order to keep shots from appearing too flat, photographers try to compose their shots to give an impression of depth. "If you're shooting a story on an accident on the interstate and you want a shot of incoming traffic," Sweitzer explains, "you might get a flare on the road in the bottom left-hand corner of the shot—in the *foreground*. At a fire, you might get a fire truck in a corner in the *foreground* with the fire in the background, to give some proportion and depth to the shot."

This use of *foreground objects* might create focus problems indoors or on dark days. But in most outdoor shooting, it will succeed in adding a sense of that third dimension—depth.

The Line   Some events move in set directions—parades, football games, even conversations. When shooting a parade or a football game it is important to shoot it all from the same side of the action. Otherwise, when the shots are edited together, the parade will keep flip-flopping—moving from left to right on the screen, then from right to left—or it will not be clear which way the football teams are trying to move the ball.

It is necessary to imagine a line in the direction of the action and to stay on one side of that line only. The line for a parade runs down the middle of the street on which people are marching. The line for a football game runs from goal post to goal post through the middle of the field. When shooting a conversation, the line runs from one person's head through the other person's head. No matter where the camera is placed, if it doesn't cross that line, one person in the conversation will always seem to be speaking toward the left and the other toward the right. If shots of them talking are edited together, it will be clear that they are facing each other. However, if the camera shoots one of the participants from one side of the line between them and the other from the other side of that line, they will both seem to be facing the same direction, rather than facing each other.

If people are milling about during a demonstration, there is no set direction of motion and the line becomes unimportant—it doesn't matter where the camera shoots from. But as soon as those people start marching, the camera must stay on one side of the line of march to keep the images it captures coherent.

In sports, a baseball game has no set direction of motion. Shots taken from the third-base line, first-base line, behind home plate and centerfield can all be mixed together without disorienting viewers. But in football, basketball, hockey, soccer and tennis, the cameras have to pick one side and stay on that side. Otherwise, it would be unclear who is trying to accomplish what. Stations broadcasting a game live are usually careful to warn viewers that they are seeing a "reverse action" shot on those few occasions when they do employ a camera on the other side of the field or court.

Telling the Story

Some videotape is so evocative and clear that it can stand alone—without a reporter's narration. Cameraman John DeTarsio of KNSD-TV in San Diego produced such a piece—a "video essay" he calls it—on a post-Christmas party for tens of thousands of children at a race track in Tijuana, Mexico.

After lugging his equipment out of the car, DeTarsio began by shooting long shots of the race track itself, with which he might open his piece. At the track's entrance, he saw a woman giving out free lunches to the children on their way in. For some natural sound, he placed a wireless microphone on the woman, then photographed her in action, making sure to get some close-ups of the children's faces.

Next, it was off to find the track owner. An *audio track* of him explaining the history and purpose of this charity event would play under some of DeTarsio's pictures—the closest thing this story would have to a narration.

DeTarsio would also place his wireless mike on a man handing out presents and on a face-painting clown. "You look lovely," the microphone caught the clown telling a little girl. The cameraman always made sure to get shots of the interactions with children and of the joyful, sometimes painted, faces of those children. He videotaped a talent show: young kids dancing, young kids belting out songs. Finally, he photographed some of the children leaving, framed by a sign that read: *Gracias*.

An hour after he arrived, DeTarsio was on his way back to the station. After a couple of hours of editing, he had a story that would run just over a minute—without a reporter.

Most television stories, of course, do make good use of reporters. Nevertheless, all videotape reports should have a little "video essay" in them. The idea is always, as DeTarsio tried to do, to get as much of the meaning of the story into the camera as possible. Shooting a story, in other words, is a journalistic activity—another way of telling the story.

If the angle from which a story is being approached changes, the shots required will also change. Sweitzer, of WISH-TV, was once sent out on a story that seemed to be about a routine traffic accident—a truck had hit a disabled car and overturned. "Not much of a story, and we didn't plan to shoot much," he recalls. There would be a few shots of the truck, of the car and of the effects of the accident on traffic. But when police reported that they suspected three people might have been in that car when it was hit, Sweitzer's job suddenly changed: Now he needed to shoot much more (it would be a longer story), and he needed shots of rescue efforts and ambulances. And then another possible angle presented itself: There were suggestions that police had taken too long to respond to the disabled car that may have caused the accident. Sweitzer now had to get shots of police cars to use if the reporter decided to discuss this angle.

"You have to decide what you're trying to say about an event." Sweitzer says. In other words, reporters and photographers have to decide what story they're telling and then make sure their pictures do the best possible job of telling it.

There are five things to look for:

Impact   "You have to ask, 'What would viewers want to see if they were here?'" Sweitzer suggests. "What television news wants to do is to show events in even more detail than viewers would get if they were on the scene themselves."

When shooting a story, television reporters and photographers follow the guidelines for newsworthiness outlined in Chapter 5. "Leads": importance, interest, controversy, the unusual, proximity and timeliness. They look for shots that demonstrate important points, are interesting or show controversy. But there's an added consideration when measuring *visual newsworthiness*, when determining what viewers would want to see if they were there: the amount of excitement or impact.

News cameras must be on the lookout for the spontaneous debate on the street as the governor walks by the protesters, a scuffle on the picket line, the embarrassed mayor dashing away from reporters, the suspects trying to hide their eyes from the cameras, firemen battling the flames—action.

Television news is often attacked for distorting events by emphasizing the moments of violence or conflict and underplaying the hours of calm. Reporters, especially when covering a demonstration, must be sure to place events in context and provide complete and accurate accounts (see Chapter 18, "Ethics and Law"). But, if a demonstration lasts 4 hours and must be recounted in a 2-minute videotape report, some telescoping of events is inevitable, and television reporters would be foolish if they didn't emphasize the most dramatic, the most newsworthy, developments.

Of course, a shot does not have to be violent to have impact. Sometimes there is as much excitement in a survivor's face as in the battle between the firefighters and the fire. And if a suspect has been arrested for arson, a shot of that person's face—"Who would do such a thing?"—has as much impact as the flames.

People "There are two things you can take pictures of: people and things," notes Carissa Howland, news director of KCWY-TV, and she doesn't hide her preference. "You've got to relate a story to people. You've got to see some human beings. It's human beings who are watching the news. I've seen stories with 30 seconds of just buildings and sidewalks. Things don't make good TV news, people do."

This is another important reason why we need the survivor's face, the suspect's face. People relate to people. If the story is a new building going up, get some shots of the construction workers. If the story is a new topless bar in a residential neighborhood, get shots of the *people* who object and, if possible, of the owner, of the patrons and of the faces, at least, of the performers.

"You are always focusing on people," Sweitzer says. "When I was looking over a batch of videotape stories from stations in other areas, I probably saw four or five shots where the camera person was walking behind the subject. You have to get *in front* of the people you are photographing. I want to see their faces. A good video photographer has got to learn to walk backwards."

Cover Shots The few moments of excitement and the participants' faces, alone, do not tell the story. Around the action and the people, reporters and photographers must insert scenes that illustrate the basic issues, introduce the protagonists and set the scene. When shooting a story, reporters must be conscious of how they will write that story (see Chapter 16, "Writing to Visuals") and choose shots that **cover**—match, illustrate—the points they want to make. For example, at the scene of a protest, aside from whatever dramatic footage may be available, reporters need cover shots of the police to use if they are likely to discuss the police's presence; they need pictures of the building in front of which the demonstration is being held to cover discussion of the target of the protest; plus the signs protesters are carrying to cover discussion of the issues; shots of traffic congestion if blocked traffic is an issue; and street signs for possible use when the location of the demonstration is mentioned.

In addition, it is always smart to shoot some general scenes of crowds, buildings and signs. These shots can be used during discussions for which there are no more specific illustrations.

A story can be ruined by failure to come back with the appropriate cover shots. "What usually happens," explains Lee Giles, the news director at WISH-TV, "is that the photographer and the reporter just don't talk on the scene, and the reporter just assumes the photographer got the shot." So, reporters have to think carefully about what they are going to want to say, and then they have to communicate their thoughts to whoever is taking the pictures.

Reaction To communicate the meaning of an event it is not always sufficient to show the event itself. The meaning of something often becomes clear only when we see its *effect*, the reaction it causes.

Rather than simply shooting the candidate's plane arriving, reporters make sure they get a shot of the people waiting for it at the airport. Editing in that *reaction shot* adds meaning to the arrival. Rather than simply showing a smashed-up car, reporters get shots of the skid marks, the pole it knocked down and the backed-up traffic. Rather than just that person sitting on the flagpole, reporters include shots of the crowd gathered below. People, especially their faces, are the best visual conveyers of meaning; so getting reaction shots often means getting shots of people reacting to an event or action. That's why John DeTarsio's camera was so often drawn back to the faces of the kids at that racetrack party.

Howland provides a similar example: "Somebody brought an injured eagle to a grade-school class around here. The cameraman stood behind the guy who was holding the eagle and got a shot of a row of kids with their mouths open—their reaction to that eagle. The expression on those kids' faces was priceless."

Sequence We arrive in a park. The first scene we see is the trees and benches of the picnic area off in the distance. As we walk closer we notice that the normal crowds of people are missing. When we arrive in the picnic area, it is clear that all the picnic benches are empty. Then we look closely at one of them. The bench is covered with large, red ants. Only then do we look up to see a park worker who explains that the area has been closed because of the ants.

That is the way people generally see things: first from afar, then closer and closer—with more of the meaning of the scene becoming available as they begin to see the details. Television reporters often imitate this sequence—far away, closer, close. They start with a *long shot* of the area—an **establishing shot.** This orients viewers; it tells them where we are—in an auditorium for a speech, on a middle-class block with police and onlookers gathered around, or at the scene of a fire.

Next, a *medium shot.* We are approaching the meaning—we see who is speaking in that auditorium; the specific home where police attention is focused; the smoldering building itself. Finally, *close-ups.* Now we get the picture—the speaker's face talking, the body on the floor of the house, an exhausted firefighter.

Not every scene is revealed in this way. Sometimes the videotape is edited so that it begins with a close-up and opens out to an establishing shot. But reporters should make sure they get this logical sequence of shots—establishing, medium, close-ups—so they have the pieces with which to put together a logical presentation. Reporters don't just jump up to objects and events. They get a sequence of shots that may be used to lead the viewer step by step to the meaning.

■ ■ ■

Notice how this videotape of a fire can pretty much tell the story, using these techniques, without any words:

LS Burning building and fire trucks
MS Firefighters fighting fire
CU Chief giving orders

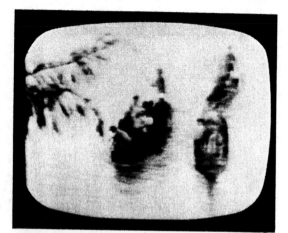

Telling the story of the Vietnamese boat people: long shot, medium shot, close-up. (CBS News Photo)

The networks and larger stations sometimes send "field producers" out with camera crew to cover stories. Pat Leahy, field producer at WCBS-TV, New York, is listening for potential sound-bites at a campaign rally. (Mitchell Stephens)

LS	Huddled survivors
CU	Face of a survivor
MS	Covered bodies
CU	Crying relative
MS	Bodies being carried away
LS	Building smoking (no flames)
CU	Exhausted firefighter

Sound-Bites

Up to this point the emphasis has been on *silent* videotape or film. Most television news reporters also include selections from interviews with, or statements by, newsmakers. These short sections in which people talk on camera are called **clips** or **sound-bites**—a word that has entered our political vocabulary since the first edition of this book was written.

The shrinking sound-bite has, of course, spurred considerable criticism of television news. One study determined that the average length of an uninterrupted statement by a presidential candidate in a television news report had declined from 43 seconds in 1968 to 9 seconds in 1988. Such criticism—often launched by print journalists—is not entirely fair. The average quotation in a newspaper story is hardly much longer than the average television sound-bite.

Nevertheless, during the 1992 presidential campaign many television journalists were making a conscious effort to give candidates a bit longer to state their case. Getting clear, meaningful statements on the air is a more important goal than keeping a newscast moving at a snappy pace. Before shortening a sound-bite, reporters must always ask themselves: Would it still make sense? Would it still say something important?

Shots Television interviewing follows the same basic rules as radio interviewing (see Chapter 9, "Tape"). However, television reporters not only have to worry about guiding and listening and microphones, they also have to worry about the shot the camera is getting.

The wrong way to shoot an interview is to place the camera off to the side so that it forms a triangle with the interviewer and the interviewee.

UNACCEPTABLE

reporter
            camera
subject

There are two things wrong with that shot: First it enables us to see only the side of the face, the profile, of the subject of the interview. Sweitzer of WISH-TV calls that "a talking ear shot." Second, if the camera pulls back to a **two shot** of the interviewer and interviewee, the space between them—unless they consent to embrace—will dominate the screen, and that's empty space, dead space.

In an interview, the camera should be placed behind and over the reporter's shoulder.

ACCEPTABLE

            camera
reporter
subject

That way, when the subject of the interview is looking at the reporter, he or she is also looking in the direction of the camera. The subject will pretty much be facing the camera; both eyes should be visible. And should the camera pull back to a two shot, the interviewee will dominate the screen, framed on one side by the side of the interviewer—no dead space.

The person being interviewed should be told to try to ignore the camera. "I say, 'Try as much as possible to pretend I'm not here,'" says photographer Sweitzer. Not many people are comfortable looking right into the camera and addressing it (former New York Mayor Edward Koch is an exception), so interviewees should be told to look only at the interviewer. If their eyes start wandering between camera and reporter, they'll look shifty-eyed. Many reporters go out of their way to maintain eye contact with interviewees in an effort to help them keep their eyes steady.

Interviews for use in television newscasts are shot primarily with *close-ups* of the person being interviewed. But some other shots (discussed below) will be needed to avoid a problem that often arises when trying to edit sound-bites into a videotape report: the problem of jump cuts.

Natural Sound Background sounds are as valuable in television news as they are in radio (see Chapter 9, "Tape"). It's always useful to have the sound of the chanting, the marching or the scuffling recorded on videotape. In fact, in television it would look a little funny to have shots of an angry demonstration without hearing any of those sounds. When the camera is shooting something that makes an interesting noise, a microphone should be aimed at it.

Cutaways The president of a dog food company is discussing on camera the settlement he has just reached with a union. The reporter wants to include the section of the interview where the president blasts the union leader and a later section where he responds to the reporter's question by predicting a hugh price hike. The reporter wants to edit out the section in between where the company's president discusses the quality of his dog food.

Throughout the interview the company's president is being videotaped in a close-up. If the ode to his dog food is removed and the attack and prediction put next to each other, two **matching shots** would be placed together—both close-ups of the company's president. The problem here is that while these shots are *almost* identical, they can never be *exactly* identical. In each shot the man's head is in a slightly different position. If the shots were edited together, his head would seem to jump at the edit point, the place where the videotape has, loosely speaking, been "cut." This would be a **jump cut.** Most news directors believe jump cuts look a little funny and a little unprofessional. What to do?

One possible solution is to do nothing. A study by Dan Drew and Roy Cadwell at the University of Wisconsin found no evidence that the presence of such "editing discontinuities" makes much difference to viewers in stories with an audio track. And in fact, CBS and some other news organizations have taken to allowing the occasional jump cut into a story with sound-bites with few if any complaints. Nevertheless, even at these news organizations reporters are going to have to know how to eliminate some jump cuts, and at the large majority of stations they will be asked to eliminate them all.

Here's the trick: Jump cuts can be made to disappear if another shot is inserted between the two close-ups of the interviewee. This extra shot is called a **cutaway**—the picture cuts away from the person being interviewed for a few seconds. There are two kinds of cutaways:

Reverses A shot of the reporter asking a question can serve as a cutaway. With that inserted, we see the company's president blasting the union leader, followed by the reporter asking the question about prices and then the president predicting. There's no jump cut because the two close-ups of the president are no longer next to each other.

But how does the camera get shots of the reporter asking questions to use as cutaways? There is only one camera covering the story and that camera cannot instantly pan back and forth between the reporter and newsmaker. Instead, what reporters do is wait until the interview has ended and then, with the camera aimed at them, re-ask the questions. These repeated questions are called **reverses** because the camera position is reversed.

There is something a little dishonest about reverses. Those tough questions Mike Wallace on *60 Minutes* is hurling at some defensive individual were actually reshot after the interview, perhaps with the interviewee no longer in the room. There's little choice. This is the only way to fully cover such an exchange with one camera, but it puts an ethical burden on reporters. They have to be careful as they repeat their questions not to change their phrasing or tone in any way that would distort the meaning of the answers that have already been recorded.

Video Only It is possible to edit two sections of an interview together without putting a reverse, a question, in between. A **video-only cutaway** also does the trick. Here the two sections of the interview *are* edited together, but another shot is used to replace a few seconds of the close-up of the interviewee talking. The interviewee talks straight through; the audio track is unchanged. But the picture goes from the close-up to the cutaway and back to the close-up again. As long as the cutaway is placed at the very end of the first section of the edit or at the very beginning of the second section or so that it covers both the end of the first and the start of the second, the jump cut will be gone.

For use as video-only cutaways, camera crews take shots of reporters nodding their heads before or after the interview, or shots of the crowd at a speech or news conference, or shots of the back of the newsmaker's head, or the newsmaker's profile, or the newsmaker's fingers fiddling nervously. A few seconds of any of these can be inserted unobtrusively in the middle of the interview. Reporters shooting an interview must always be sure that the crew has gotten one or two of these shots to use in case it's necessary to use a video-only cutaway.

And video-only cutaways do not have to be as meaningless as shots of reporters nodding their heads. Sometimes it is possible to cut away to a shot that covers— illustrates—what the newsmaker is talking about. For example, if the interviewee is discussing dog food prices, the reporter might decide to cut away to a shot of dog food on the shelves at a supermarket.

Video-only cutaways require separating sound and picture on videotape. This is no problem on modern videotape editing equipment.

Stand-Ups

If sound-bites resemble actualities, stand-ups resemble voicers. At some point in most videotape stories, the reporter appears on camera at the scene to relate information garnered there. These on-camera reports are called **stand-ups** for the simple reason that reporters usually deliver them standing up.

Roma Torr-Lopez from News 12, Long Island, New York, records a stand-up.

Justification Some news directors love stand-ups: "The reporters in the field are the station's representatives," says Jeff Wald, news director of KTLA, Los Angeles. "We believe they should be seen in the story." Giles, of WISH-TV, agrees: "We want viewers to see our reporters. We want them to establish an identity." Others have more mixed feelings toward stand-ups. There may be more interesting things to show on camera than a reporter, and there may turn out to be more interesting things to say than what that reporter could come up with on the scene. "I always tell my reporters, 'Make the stand-up count.'" says Howland of KCWY-TV.

Most stories on most stations will include at least one stand-up, but even if they feel obligated to include a stand-up, reporters should try to make sure it "counts." To justify their existence, stand-ups should contain important information, they should not be allowed to squeeze out other more visually interesting shots and they should themselves be as visually interesting as possible.

Points Stands-ups, like voicers, are written on the scene, without the benefit of computers or the other conveniences of the newsroom. Reporters prefer to read the stand-up while looking straight into the camera; so it has to be memorized. And, while the stand-up is recorded on the scene, the rest of the story won't be written until the reporter has returned to the newsroom. So, the stand-up must be written with an as-yet-unwritten story in mind.

All these limitations point to the need for simplicity in a stand-up. A stand-up with too many points in it is more difficult to compose on the scene, more difficult to memorize and more difficult to fit into the rest of the story. Few stand-ups attempt to make more than one, or at the most two, points.

A stand-up at the end of a story on Democrats running for president in New Hampshire:

```
And economic despair in New Hampshire translates to
political hope for the state's Democrats. They are
beginning to believe that any of these candidates, even
if untested, just might have a chance against a
president who once seemed unbeatable. -- Cokie Roberts,
ABC News, Manchester
```

As is a voicer, the stand-up is enhanced by information that points up the value of having a reporter on the scene (see Chapter 9, "Tape"). The first person and a personal angle can help. Incidentally, stand-ups can be recorded over a few times to get them right. Reporters can also try a few different stand-ups, each emphasizing different points. The final version can be selected when editing the story.

"Cute" stand-ups are in fashion. They fit in comfortably with the "happy talk"—light banter—now emphasized at many stations. Still, whatever a station's favored mix of show biz and news, reporters must try to get something meaningful into their stand-ups, even when encouraged to record them while standing in a lion's cage (it has been done). If nothing else, include an interesting fact about lions. Stand-ups can't say much, but if they don't say something, no matter how photogenic the reporter, they are a waste of time.

"Make sure the information you're imparting is significant," Howland advises. "Nothing is more appalling than the stand-up that says nothing, such as: 'The traffic accident is under investigation.' I've seen lots of wasted stand-ups."

Length Most stand-ups are short—10 to 20 seconds. Occasionally they run longer, especially in complex stories that require a lot of explaining but don't offer much in the way of visuals.

Background A stand-up employs a variation of the talking-head shot. To increase visual interest, reporters try standing in front of something interesting. At a protest, the stand-up can be recorded in front of the marchers; at a fire, in front of the smoking building (not too close); at a speech, with the audience in the background.

Zooms are used frequently in stand-ups—starting with a shot of the reporter and zooming out to show the angry demonstrators nearby, or starting with a long shot that includes a view of the store that was robbed and zooming in on the reporter.

The search for interesting backgrounds has brought reporters to some strange places. A reporter with the Canadian Broadcasting Corporation ended a story on wind surfing while standing on one of those contraptions. After saying his ID, he fell into the water.

It's generally not necessary to go this far, but news directors look with disfavor upon reporters who return from a colorful festival with a stand-up recorded in front of a blank wall, and they're even less pleased with reporters who wait until they return to the newsroom to record a stand-up. "That's my pet peeve," says Wald of KTLA. "Stand-ups in a newsroom drive me crazy."

Openers   Occasionally stories start with a stand-up—an **opener**. Since reporters generally want to begin a story with a shot that catches the viewer's eye and since a stand-up is usually among the duller shots in a story, openers are rare. They are used most frequently in stories about economics, or in political analyses that don't lend themselves to good visuals, or perhaps for a crime story for which no shots of the scene or the characters are available. Once in a while, too, a reporter has produced an unusually clever stand-up and decides to use it to kick off a feature story. Openers are also used on live stories to emphasize at the start that the reporter is there:

```
It has been a very confusing night for reporters, for
the airlines and the passengers. When we arrived here at
Newark Airport amid all the confusion, we found one D-C
Ten preparing for take-off.
                              WCBS-TV, New York City
```

Then the videotape and the rest of the story.

Bridges   A stand-up can also be used in the middle of a story to **bridge** two other sections of the report. These aren't easy to do well, and they aren't easy to justify. It's difficult to write something that will fit neatly in the middle of a story that hasn't yet been written. And again, there are usually more visually interesting shots to use in the middle of a story.

"There ought to be a reason for using one," argues Sweitzer. "Generally what you're trying to do is use the reporter to tell something about a story that you don't have pictures of. On a story about police catching some robbers, you're not going to have pictures of the capture, so you can use the reporter to point to a bush and say the suspect was caught here." Sweitzer recalled this additional example of a bridge stand-up that justified its existence: "In a story about an aircraft carrier, the reporter walked from one plane to another on the carrier's deck while she was talking about the proximity of planes on the deck."

Bridges work especially well when the reporter demonstrates something. Here a reporter does a bridge stand-up while opening a door to the roof from which the brick that killed a woman was thrown:

> Tenants say one of the problems here is that anyone who wants to get to the roof can. The door here is always unlocked.
>
> WNYW-TV, New York City

If enough good shots of an event are available and if nothing needs demonstrating, it's hard to see what, besides a little promotion for the news team, a bridge stand-up adds. However, since it doesn't require much videotape to record a stand-up, it is not a bad idea on some stories to try a bridge. If it fits and adds something, it can be used. If not, no harm done.

Closes   This is where stand-ups usually appear—at the end of the story. They lead naturally into the reporter's ID—"Garrick Utley, NBC News, London." Reporters should generally record one or two **closes**. Most of the time they end up using one.

To write a close that fits comfortably at the end of a story, reporters choose from the same set of options available for a snapper (see Chapter 6, "Stories") or a write-out (see Chapter 10, "Writing to Tape"): another fact, a future ramification, the other side, a punch line, a restatement of the main point. Of these, the first two are the most common and often the easiest to tag onto a story. Another fact (at the end of a story about a man who hiked to safety after a small plane crashed):

> Searchers today at last found the wreckage of the tiny plane and the bodies. And Norman Ollestad left the hospital. He said he would never fly again. -- Terry Drinkwater, CBS News, Los Angeles

A future ramification stand-up:

> The search for more radium will take several days. And medical tests are to begin on the brickyard workers who were closest to the radium dump. The problem, said one state official, will be here for a long time. -- Harold Dow, CBS News, Denver

Live

Live reports from the scene of news events cast the same spell on television audiences that they do on radio audiences. Here is an excerpt from another live report from Baghdad on the early moments of the Persian Gulf War:

. . . What we saw was about five bombs dropped in the center of the government part of the city. There is a bomb every few minutes. The bombing is intensifying now, and the explosions are coming closer to this part of town.

Peter Arnett, CNN

Live reports are immediate and exciting . . . but for television reporters—even those who are not in a city being attacked by American missles and planes—they can also be nerve-racking.

Sometimes a whole report is done live—essentially as one long, extemporaneous stand-up. Sometimes a videotape on the news event is played in the studio and the reporter adds the stand-ups (usually an open and a close) live from the scene. Some of the potential problems here are obvious: Trucks, airplanes and defective microphones all can mess up sound quality; the hands and heads of overeager spectators can interfere with the picture. In addition, reporters are going on the air without the chance to reshoot if they make an error and without the benefit of someone in the newsroom to look over their work.

Preparation, as always, is crucial. But unlike radio reporters, television reporters generally cannot expect to read these live stand-ups word for word from a script they have scribbled down in advance. "If they rely on a handwritten script they may not communicate effectively," cautions Marvin Rockford, news director at KCNC-TV in Denver. "They will probably lose eye contact with the camera and their delivery may become more wooden, less natural." Rockford also warns against efforts to memorize the entire report. "Most experienced reporters have a story about the time they memorized a live report . . . and forgot their lines in mid-sentence," he says.

The solution, "If the story is particularly sensitive, a written script may be necessary," Rockford says. "But otherwise, we encourage our reporters to work from notes." Report the story backward and forward. Think out exactly what you want to say. Sketch it out in a note pad. Rehearse it a few times mentally and, if possible, out loud. Then relax and wait for the signal.

As with live radio reports, live television reports should try to emphasize the timely and communicate the sights, sounds and smells of an event (see Chapter 11, "Coverage"). Of course, television reporters have an advantage: They can actually show those sights. Reporters should be prepared to point out, or even walk over to, newsworthy sights, and the camera should be prepared to leave the reporter at some point, through a pan or a zoom, to take in more of the event.

Satellite News Gathering

The use of satellites in reporting stories—so that reports can be produced dozens of miles from the newsroom—has become so common that it is now known by its initials: *SNG*—for satellite news gathering.

SNG begins with a well-outfitted truck. The truck will have an electrical gen-

*Frank Turner
of WTVF-TV,
Nashville,
reporting live.*

erator to power everything, a camera and videotape recorder, some videotape editing equipment, a satellite dish on top and, in most cases, a technician/camera operator and a reporter riding inside. It will park somewhere near the news event (cables have limited lengths), somewhere reasonably level and somewhere with a decent view of the sky.

After the crew arrives, one of their first tasks will be to "acquire"—lock the dish in on—the satellite. The truck can now communicate with the newsroom via the satellite. "The toughest part of the SNG business is communication," says Raymond Conover of Conus, the video news service. (See Chapter 7, "Sources.")

Once the basic story has been shot and a script written, it can be edited in the truck and transmitted back to the newsroom by satellite. But the truck will usually stick around: The reporter will be asked to introduce and conclude that videotape live from the scene.

When the time to go on the air live arrives, the communicating gets rather complex. Live audio and video of the reporter and the news event are being sent by satellite back to the studio, but an audio track from the studio is also being fed, by satellite, into an earpiece worn by the reporter. The reporter is hearing an "interruptible feedback"—IFB—circuit, which includes whatever is being said on the air at the moment, minus the reporter's own live comments (which would be distracting because they would be delayed a half second or so), plus the comments—interruptions—of people in the studio.

The reporter hears the anchor introduce the live report, then begins to talk. "Hurry up!" the producer yells into the earpiece. The videotape plays, with the reporter listening for an out-cue, then it's back on the air live to conclude the story.

Editing

Tom Nugent sits in a small room at WTNH in New Haven, Connecticut. In front of him to his left and right are ¾-inch videotape recorders with color monitors; between them sits a videotape editor covered with buttons and capable of controlling each of the recorders. Nugent is a photographer/*tape editor.* With reporter Rad Berky he spent the morning and early afternoon covering two stories. Now, with Berky, he has to edit the most important of those stories—a follow-up on the suspension of a police officer after a suspect he was arresting died—into a videotape report that can be played on the station's evening newscast.

Nugent and Berky have discussed this story in detail. Berky, who had to write the script, had looked at the videotape Nugent shot. Berky had begun working on his *narration* (see Chapter 16, "Writing to Visuals") for the story in the car on the way back to the station. He was even able to make some preliminary decisions on sound-bites by listening to a rough audiotape he had made of the interviews they videotaped (many reporters carry an *audio* cassette tape recorder for this purpose). After looking through the videotape, Berky sat down behind a typewriter and began writing his *script* for the story. When it was complete he checked it with his producer, walked into a small *audio booth,* recorded his narration and then handed the script to Nugent.

That script is crucial. On it are not only all the words in Berky's narration but also notes on exactly what sound-bites he wants to use—with in-cues, out-cues and counter numbers from the videotape recorder—along with the reporter's suggestions on what silent shots to edit in where and what supers (see Chapter 14, "Visuals") will be needed in the story.

Nugent now *lays* that audiotape of the reporter's narration onto an audio track of the videotape on the recorder to his right. The videotape he shot on this story is all on a videotape cassette in the recorder to his left. Now he will select cuts from the tape to his left and record them, with that narration, on the tape to his right. This is called *electronic editing.*

"The other type of editing would be film editing, which is physically taking the film, cutting it and splicing it back together," Nugent explains. "With videotape you electronically take pictures and audio off one tape and electronically place them on another tape."

Nugent begins by *laying in* all the shots with sound. Using Berky's counter numbers, he locates the beginning of a sound-bite of the police chief: "The rules that he violated had to do with. . . ." Then, following the script, Nugent locates the spot where that sound-bite should go in the videotape with Berky's narration

Reporter Rad Berky, WTNH, New Haven, reports a story and reviews the videotapes for editing. (WTNH 8)

recorded on it: "But Chief D'Errico says Redding* was suspended, based on witness reports that Redding kicked Shaw in the face while he was lying handcuffed on the ground." By pressing a button, Nugent can **preview** what it would look like to insert the sound-bite there. The edit looks smooth; the audio levels are fine. Nugent presses another button and makes the edit for real, pressing a button after the out-cue of that sound-bite to prevent any more of the interview from being recorded.

After the sound-bites and stand-up are in place, Nugent begins editing in shots to go with Berky's narration. Berky wanted a shot of a club, called the "Casino," on screen when he says, "Redding had been working extra duty at the Casino club." Nugent finds a long shot showing the club and a sign with its name, and he edits it in, video only, over that sentence. To *cover* his line introducing that sound-bite of the chief, Berky wanted a medium shot of him interviewing the chief, then a cut-away—Berky nodding his head at that interview. As Nugent edits in these shots he is careful to place an electronic signal, an automatic out-cue, at the start of the chief's sound-bite. That ensures that the shot he is editing in before the sound-bite will end exactly when the sound-bite begins.

"These machines are real precise," Nugent explains. "The videotape recorders play 29 frames a second. I can cut within a frame or two."

The story Berky and Nugent produced will be the lead story on the 6 o'clock newscast. It runs 1:45. Videotape stories usually average 1¼ to 2 minutes in length. "But everything's negotiable," says News Director Kris Ostrowski of WRC-TV in Washington, D.C. Reporters can occasionally win more time for their stories—if they can make the case that their stories deserve the extra time.

The editing routine followed in putting videotape reports together at other stations and on other stories may vary somewhat from that outlined here: At smaller stations reporters may have to work these machines themselves. At the largest stations photographers might surrender responsibility for editing their stories to tape-editing specialists. And on some stories it may be necessary to edit a story before a script is written. But the basic principles involved in editing a videotape story do not vary: The pictures must proceed in a logical, coherent order and they must coordinate with the words (see Chapter 16, "Writing to Visuals").

Here are some important notes on editing:

Cuts　Each shot or portion of a shot used in a story is called a **cut**. A cut is an edited version of the shot. That long shot of the Casino club is one cut, the medium shot of the interview another, the cutaway of Berky nodding his head still another.

Silent cuts should be on screen just long enough for the viewer to comprehend whatever information is in them. For example, a shot of two people should be held, as a rule, longer than a shot of one—there is more information in it.

This is clearest when words are in the picture. A shot of words should be edited so that it is long enough for viewers to read comfortably. A cut featuring a stop sign

---

* This name has been changed.

doesn't deserve more than 3 seconds by this standard; a shot of a sign reading, "Passengers Only Beyond This Point"—5 seconds. Too short and viewers might be confused and even frustrated; too long and viewers might get bored.

Long shots generally contain more information than close-ups. Hence, long shots are usually given more time on the air when editing. Cuts with action in them hold interest longer than static shots. When tape is edited, action shots usually are held longer. Of course, there are other considerations. Some shots may have to be held a little longer than they deserve because the reporter has a lot to say that needs to be covered by that shot.

The average silent cut runs from 3 to 10 seconds. Shots may run shorter if they are very simple—the stop sign, for example; or if a group of shots is combined in a **montage**—a series of short shots edited together (perhaps different shots showing gas prices or faces in a crowd); or if they are just providing views from different angles of the same scene—perhaps a series of medium shots of a crowd.

As a gimmick, NBC once ran a videotape story that was all one cut, with the camera starting in a truck and then being lifted up by a helicopter. But shots must be very interesting to run more than 10 seconds; viewers tire of scenes rapidly—more and more rapidly it seems, as anyone who has studied a recent beer commercial or music video knows. "We have to renew our commitment to the viewer every 15 seconds," is how reporter Michael Settoni, of KNSD-TV in San Diego, puts it.

Order A television videotape story has the same job as any broadcast story: clearly communicating information. It is not surprising, therefore, that many of the rules for arranging shots reflect the rules for arranging thoughts in broadcast news stories. For example, as writing that presents too much information, too quickly, sinks a broadcast story (see Chapter 6, "Stories"), too many cuts that are too busy make a videotape piece confusing. As too many long sentences make a story drag, too many long cuts make videotape boring. And varying the cut length helps pace a videotape piece, as varying sentence length paces a story. Editors of both words and visuals have to maintain a snappy but comprehensible pace.

Similarly, the rule that stories should deal with one subject at a time (see Chapter 6, "Stories") also applies when editing videotape. It makes no sense to sprinkle cover shots of police throughout a story on a protest. Viewers understand best when presented with one issue at a time—keep the cop shots in one section of the story. Even if the videotape survives violation of these basic storytelling rules, the copy that has to go with these haphazard cuts will suffer.

A videotape story also has a lead shot, as any broadcast story has a lead sentence. Reporters differ on the importance of the lead shot. Phil Barnouw of KCBS-TV, Los Angeles, is among those who believe a story should lead with its best shot. A fire story might lead with the flames or the bodies, a protest story with the most dramatic confrontation; a story on unhealthy conditions in mental hospitals with the grisliest scenes inside. The strategy here is obvious—catch their eyes.

Other reporters are more interested in establishing what a story is about than in dazzling the audience with that opening shot. "You must allow viewers to get their bearings," says Jeff Wald of KTLA. The mental hospital story might begin with an establishing shot of the outside of the building. The idea is to build up to the more dramatic footage.

Subscribers to both these schools of thought agree that attention should be given to both preparing and engaging viewers with the lead shot. They just disagree on which should be emphasized—preparing or engaging. Sometimes it's possible to do both. Steve Sweitzer of WISH-TV recalls seeing a videotape on a judge who was also a race car driver. "The story opened with a long shot of the judge walking down the hall to his chambers," Sweitzer says. "To me that's backing into the story." The most visually exciting element of this story was the judge in a race car, not the judge in a corridor, and the race car angle of the story also needed establishing. Sweitzer's suggestion? "I would have preferred intercutting the shot of the judge walking with a shot of him getting into a race car. Then just as he gets to his desk, you could have the race car take off."

This attention to order and form should persist throughout the story. "Stories need a strong beginning, a good middle *and* a strong end," Sweitzer says. "I saw a story yesterday from another station that had to do with motorcross racing. It ended with a freeze frame of the race. To my way of thinking, since the story began with a shot of the beginning of the race, it should have ended with a shot of the end of the race."

Most videotape stories aren't going to exhibit perfect form. It's certainly not always possible to echo the beginning in the end of a story, especially a hard news story. But form must be kept in mind while editing videotape.

Other rules for ordering cuts follow from the rules for shooting visuals that tell the story, discussed earlier in this chapter. Editors must take into account the logical sequence for approaching scenes: long shot, medium shot, close-ups (although good editors frequently play with this pattern). Editors also want to mix in reaction shots as they order the cuts to bring out meanings.

Visual Continuity   In one shot a firefighter is wearing a hat; in another shot his hat is off. That's no problem if the two shots are used at different points in the story, but it would be disconcerting if the shots were placed next to each other. Proximity in a story implies proximity in time. Viewers would wonder how that hat had suddenly disappeared. Editors must be aware of the need to preserve **visual continuity.**

If a fire truck is moving in one picture, it can't be parked in the next. There are two ways around this problem. First, when shooting the moving fire truck, allow it to drive out of the frame. That hints at off-camera activities and makes it possible for viewers to accept seeing the truck standing still in the next cut. The second solution works for most of these situations where visual continuity is a problem: Edit in a shot in between. Go from the moving fire truck to a shot of the fire, then back to the parked fire truck. This technique also solves the problem of the firefighter's hat; just cut away to a shot of the fire truck; then it's possible to return to the now hatless firefighter without breaking the visual continuity. It's similar to using a cut-away to avoid a jump cut.

Sound First, the sound-bites must be edited down. As in radio, the editing often will be brutal, but meanings *cannot* be changed (see Chapter 9, "Tape"). "I suggest thinking of a sound-bite or an interview as a piece of meat," Howland of KCWY-TV says. "You want to cut out the fat. People complain that you interviewed them for an hour and only used 10 seconds, but those 10 seconds were the best, most memorable part of the interview."

Next, the sound-bites must be placed in the story. As in radio documentaries (see Chapter 13, "Public Affairs"), the sound is usually selected and edited into a story before the other shots. That's how Nugent handled the story on that officer who was suspended.

The average videotape story uses a couple of sound-bites and a stand-up. Most of the time a story won't open or close with a sound-bite—that can be confusing. In fact, the sound-bites usually are delayed for a while to allow the cover shots to set up the story. There is nothing wrong with editing a couple of different sound-bites together, but, more often than not, the sound-bites are spread out in the story. And the stand-up, more often than not, is a close.

If more than one sound-bite is used, reporters usually go first with the most objective, then they use the more opinionated comment. In other words, first the doctor, then the patient; first the police officer, then the victim. This seems the logical way for a story to unfold, though it is certainly not a rule.

Once the sound-bites and stand-up have been selected and roughly placed, the story should begin to fall into place around them. Here is a fairly standard version of a fire story:

```
LS Smoldering building and firefighters: 10 secs.
MS Firefighters fighting: 5 secs.
CU Chief giving directions: 5 secs.
Sound-bite: Chief explains: 20 secs.
LS Huddled survivors: 10 secs.
CU Survivor's face: 5 secs.
Sound-bite: Survivor describing: 10 secs.
LS Gutted building: 10 secs.
MS Exhausted firefighters: 10 secs.
Stand-up: 15 secs.

TOTAL: 1:40
```

Natural sound deserves mention here. Background sounds can easily be edited into a story on a separate audio track so that they play under a reporter's narration—

like a *bed* in a radio voicer (see Chapter 9, "Tape"). This is done frequently, and much of the videotape that has been referred to, for simplicity's sake, throughout this chapter as "silent" will in fact have some quiet natural sound on it.

Sometimes the natural sound is allowed to get louder. In television, where the picture is around to clarify the meaning of a sound, there is no reason not to let particularly newsworthy noises stand on their own—with a break in the narration. For example, in a videotape report on the funeral of a World War II veteran who ended up dying, homeless, on the streets of Washington, Independent News let a bugler play taps for about 14 seconds, under a montage of shots of the funeral, before the reporter resumed talking over the music.

And the sound and picture don't always have to match exactly. There's room for a little creativity here. Sometimes editors let the audio track from a sound-bite keep running for a few seconds *after* they have switched to the next cut, or they keep a shot on after the sound-bite begins. A **split end** that's called. It can make a story seem smoother, seamless. If the fire chief ends by talking about the survivors, why not bring the shot of the survivors on a little early? And sometimes there is meaning in the contrast between sound and picture. John DeTarsio of KNSD-TV used old natural sound from the last day of racing at a local track under pictures he had just taken of the empty race track awaiting demolition.

Wrap-Up

A word of caution, from Steve Ramsey of KWCH-TV, Wichita: "We often become so aware of our shots, our words . . . and the way our hair is combed that we forget the story. But that's what really matters. The very best television news reports allow the viewer to forget the reporter and the camera and become involved in the story."

Practice Assignments

Describe how you would shoot the following stories at the scene. Indicate whether each shot is a LS, MS, or CU.

1. Policemen's Union pickets City Hall at noon, protesting layoffs. The mayor comes out to meet the protesters. Lunchtime crowd gathers.
2. Your town's largest bank is robbed of 600-thousand dollars on a weekday morning. One teller is shot and seriously injured. A bank customer is abducted as a hostage.
3. It's discovered that the water in the seals' pool at the zoo has been poisoned. One seal has died and several are ill. Police say the culprit climbed over a metal

picket fence in the middle of the night and contaminated the water while the night guards were patrolling other parts of the zoo.

4. A 24-year-old woman is found strangled in her home in a prosperous section of town. Police are at the scene. Neighbors gather. Her body is carried out.

5. A city commission publishes a study charging that at least half of the apartment buildings in the poorer sections of town violate city building codes. The mayor, accompanied by aides and various community leaders, goes on a walking tour to check out the situation for herself.

16

Writing to Visuals

The copy on the bottom of the next page, written for the *CBS Evening News*, follows the rules for broadcast writing outlined in earlier chapters. The edits were made by an important figure in the history of this field: Walter Cronkite, then newscaster *and* managing editor of the program. Note how Cronkite saved time and words.

If anything, television newswriting must be even more conversational and clear than radio newswriting. When we can actually see the newscaster talking, stiff, formal language seems even more uncomfortable. And, with visuals to distract us, dense, convoluted copy is even more difficult for us to follow. So the basic writing style is the same for television, but again the presence of visuals complicates matters. Television writing must work in partnership with visuals, which places tough demands on the writer. There's a new set of rules to master.

Copy

First, a basic difference in the copy: Each page of television news copy is divided in half. The copy that the newscaster reads, at most stations, is written on the right-hand side of the page only.

```
11/21 6pm pug
OC CHRISTY
```

This is <u>the</u> day for
thousands of Kentucky
farmers. . . . This is pay
day. The state's biggest
cash crop -- tobacco -- went
on sale this morning . . .
amid fears that farmers
would be getting a poor
price. We have two reports
on the long-awaited
auctions. The first is from
Ferrell Wellman in Lexington

```
                          . . . where this year's
                          market officially
                          opened . . .
ENG SOT: #6
OUT: . . . WAVE-TV News
RUNS: 1:48              (SOT)
```

The heading on this page of copy about tobacco sales should be familiar from radio ("pug" is the nickname of the man who wrote the story—Ferrell Wellman). But after the heading there are some obvious differences. The right-hand side of the page is the *audio column*—anything the newscaster reads goes there. The left-hand side of the page is reserved for video information. In this lead-in to a videotape report on WAVE-TV in Louisville, Kentucky, "OC CHRISTY" tells the newscast's director that newscaster Christy Callahan is to be *on camera* at that point. Callahan's face will fill the screen until the end of the lead-in, when the director will switch to a videotape. That videotape will be played on an "ENG"—for *electronic news gathering*—machine; in other words, a videotape recorder. There is sound on the videotape—*sound on tape*, "SOT." ("SOT" is repeated in the audio column to remind

```
14. CRONKITE        For the record,
                    the National Weather
                    Service says, the
                    experts have figured
                    out that last month
                    was the coldest
                    January in the
                    eastern United
                    States in at least
                    177 years.
                        The forecast for
                    the next 30 days:
                    More of the below-
                    normal cold, WHICH,
                    The weather service
                    SAYS COULD MAKE
                    said if the bitter
                    cold continues
                    through March, "this
                    winter could be the
                    coldest since the
```

```
                    founding of the
                    Republic."
                                  (THANKS TO
                    (Incidentally, the
                    recent warming &
                    (BARGE TRAFFIC HAS)
                    trend was a break for
                    RESUMED
                    Mississippi River
                    barge operators.
                    Commercial traffic
                    has been restored
                    (along a 160-mile
                    (OF THE MISSISSIPPI)
                    stretch from St.
                    Louis down to
                    Cairo, Illinois, A
                    I  STRETCH
                    that had been  clogged
                    BY ICE
                    by ice for almost a
                    month.)
```

Walter Cronkite timed his copy as he edited, while working on the CBS Evening News. (CBS News Photo)

the newscaster to stop reading at that point and let the videotape do the talking.) And each of the videotapes to be used during the newscast has been given a number to help make sure the right one plays at the right time. This is videotape *number six*. The final information included here—the "out"-cue and the length of time the story "runs"—should be familiar from the lead-ins to radio voicers (see Chapter 10, "Writing to Tape").

All the style rules for copy discussed in Chapter 1, "Copy," still apply in the right-hand column of television news pages. Of course, the time it takes to read a line changes because the lines are half as long.

Obviously, basic broadcast copy rules do not apply on the left—the video column. "ENG SOT: #6" manages to break a few of the rules for typing broadcast copy all by itself, but that is no problem. The standard broadcast copy rules all but disappear on the left-hand side of the page because the information written there is not read on the air. During the show those notations are just read by the director and the technical staff.

The technical cues in the video column must be precise and legible, but they may include abbreviations, numerals below eleven, code, and they may be handwritten. The information that needs to be included in that video column varies for different types of stories.

Tell Stories

A television story that uses no videotape or film is called a ***tell story***—the newscaster just *tells* the story. The visual here is a talking head or a talking head plus a graphic, and the copy in the right-hand column is really no different from a radio story.

If no graphics are being used, all that's necessary in the video column is the name of the **anchor**, or newscaster. The name should be lined up with the first line of the story, so it is clear that the anchor is on the air from that point on in the copy.

Here's a tell story written when Walter Cronkite hosted the *CBS Evening News*, Cyrus Vance was secretary of state and Jimmy Carter was president:

```
Cronkite                          Good evening. Secretary of
                                  State Vance put the Carter
                                  Administration's foreign
                                  policy into full gear today.
                                  Arriving in Israel on the
                                  first stop of a six-nation
                                  Middle East tour, Vance
                                  talked of peace and the U-S
                                  commitment to Israel's
                                  security and survival.
                                              CBS Evening News
```

Such straight tell stories are becoming rarer and rarer in television news—one reason why it was necessary to go back in time for this example. In fact, the term "tell story" is increasingly used for the now much more common situation where the newscaster reads a story *with* some sort of graphic.

Graphics

The director usually needs to know exactly where in the copy the graphics come up and exactly where they should disappear. To keep things precise, the notation in the video column should be lined up exactly with the line in the audio column at the start of which the graphic is supposed to appear.

In this page from a story, a full-screen graph of unemployment rates is used. The place where the graph should come up is made extra clear by the arrow. "OC" means that it's time to lose the graphic and return to a shot of the anchor *on camera.*

```
                                  That pushed the nation's
                                  unemployment rate back up --
        Start GRAPH →             this time, to seven percent.
                                  Since the beginning of the
                                  year, unemployment has
                                  declined only slightly and
                                  in the past seven months, it
```

                    has hovered stubbornly
                    between six-point-nine
                    percent and seven-point-one
                    percent.
        α⟶   Last month's increase
                    reflected layoffs in the
                    steel industry and strikes.
                                    CBS Evening News

The codes stations use for graphics vary widely. Anything that is clear to everyone in the newsroom and studio is acceptable. For example, a simple set: for a key of a plane crash: *Key—Crash*; for a super reading "Houston vs. Green Bay": *Super—Houston vs. Green Bay*; for a box including a picture of a car and the word "RECALL?": *Box—RECALL?* Finally, to lose a graphic, just write the anchor's name, indicating that the anchor is back on screen, alone.

Videotape

Sometimes a newscaster in the studio reads the narration for a videotape story live in the studio. In that case, the copy is written up just like copy to graphics. In the left-hand column, lined up with the proper line of copy in the right-hand column, a cue is written that tells the director to play the videotape at that moment. There should be a cue at the point where the videotape ends, too.

Notice the spot where the director is asked to play, or "take," the videotape in this story. (It is to be played on one of the station's Sony videotape recorders.) "VO" means that the newscaster, Jay Young, will be reading a **voice-over** narration to this *silent* videotape—videotape that will begin playing as Young says the words "Ethyl said today . . ."

        Jay   The Ethyl Corporation has
                                    announced that a large part
                                    of its Baton Rouge plant
                                    will shut down . . .
                                    resulting in almost 200
                                    layoffs.
        TAKE SONY/VO   Ethyl said today it has
                                    agreed to sell its polyvinyl
                                    chloride-resin and compound
                                    business to the Georgia-
                                    Pacific Corporation.
        SUPER: ETHYL BR PLANT   According to Ethyl officials,
                                    the sale will result in the

```
                    shutdown of its plant in
                    North Baton Rouge. . . .
                        WBRZ-TV, Baton Rouge, Louisiana
```

More often, the soundtrack has been prerecorded on videotape. The entire story is ready to play as a *package*. All that is included in the newscast script in this case is a lead-in with certain basic information about the videotape in its video column. This is similar to the way wraps and reports are handled in radio newscast scripts (see Chapter 10, "Writing to Tape").

The video column on such a lead-in should include some identification of the videotape—either a slug, a number or the number of the machine that will be playing it—plus the length of the videotape and the out-cue. Sometimes the terms "track" or "SOT" are included to emphasize the fact that the story includes a soundtrack.

Here is the lead-in to a videotape story. The videotape is ready to be played on the station's third ENG (videotape) machine.

```
                    Last night we reported on
                    two tax shelter schemes
                    currently operating in North
                    Dakota.
                    Tonight Karen Lockett
                    takes a look at fraudulent
                    investments and ways to spot
                    them.

TAKE ENG 3
TIME 2:10
OUT: STANDARD

                        KXMB-TV, North Dakota
```

The lead-in is sufficient for the newscast script. But at some point in the production of the story the reporter will have to sit down and write a script for that story which includes detailed information on the videotape. That copy must match up the cuts and the narration.

If the narration is written before the videotape is edited, the script for the story may be used as a guideline for the editor and should contain the reporter's plan for editing the story. Some reporters who have gone through the shots carefully in advance include on the script the numbers from the unit counters on the editing machine that indicate exactly where they want the shots cut.

If the videotape has already been edited, reporters may first work from a *spot sheet*—a simple list of the cuts and their lengths in order. But, as the story is written, the information on the spot sheet is transferred onto the script. These scripts often are shown to the newscast's producer for approval before they are recorded or before the story is edited.

In the script for a videotape story each cut (very short cuts that essentially show the same thing may be combined) is listed in the video column, next to the first line that should be read when the cut is on screen. Times and out-cues have to be noted for sound-bites and stand-ups:

```
Loggers marching/natural
    sound
4 secs.
Loggers marching
    4 secs.

Cheering audience
    3 secs.
Panel on stage
    4 secs

Hecocta/SOT
Runs: 8 secs.
Out: ''. . . who live
    there.''
Super: Calvin Hecocta
American Indian Movement

Hanel/SOT
Runs: 9
Out: ''. . . of their
    needs.''
Super: Bob Hanel
Lumber Company Owner

Panel on stage
    3 secs.
Logger cutting tree
    4 secs.

Owl in tree
    4 secs.

Rodman/SOT
Runs: 9
Out: ''. . . to
    extinction.''
Super: Andrew Rodman
Environmentalist
```

Several thousand loggers marched in Portland today to save their jobs, while environmentalists tried to convince a government ''god squad,'' as it's been called, to save the northern spotted owl.

The top level federal committee has to decide if jobs and the economy of timber towns in Oregon are more important than protecting the habitat of the owl in old growth forests.

Stand-up/SOT
Runs: 18
Out: ''. . . the act
    itself.''
Super: Roger O'Neil
Portland, Oregon

Inside lumber plant
    4 secs.
Construction site
    4 secs.
Zoom on still of bird
    3 secs.

Power plant
    4 secs.

Salmon
    3 secs.

The loggers say 5-thousand
jobs are at stake in Oregon.
Builders in California claim
20-thousand jobs will be lost
if a little bird known as
the gnat catcher is
protected.
And in Washington state,
power company officials
predict rates will go up
200-million dollars annually
to save three species of
salmon.

Szabo/SOT
Runs: 10
Out: ''. . . to all
    species.''
Super: Robert Szabo
Business Reform
    Coalition

Alligators
    2 secs.
Bald eagle flies to nest
    11 secs.

The act has saved the
alligator.
And the bald eagle is on its
way to recovery. But this is
an election year. There's a
recession and worries about
jobs. The Endangered Species
Act may be endangered.
-- Roger O'Neil, NBC News,
Portland

NBC Nightly News

There is no need to write out the sound-bites or the stand-up in the story's script—
the reporter doesn't have to read them.

As usual, stations don't pass up the opportunity to use slightly idiosyncratic formats and their own jargon. But most videotape scripts contain the same basic information as in the example above.

Narration

Writing narration to go with visuals is one of the most difficult skills in broadcast journalism. The language must be sharp, the timing exact and the words have to click with what appears on the screen.

Background Graphics

These aren't too difficult to write to. Graphics using boxes or keys are unobtrusive additions to television news stories. The lead-in for the story on logging used as an example in the last section was read by Tom Brokaw with a graphic appearing behind him that featured a sketch of some trees. It's not necessary that Brokaw's copy say anything about that graphic.

```
UNACCEPTABLE
The dispute between loggers and environmentalists . . .
which we've illustrated in this graphic . . .
```

As long as the background graphic refers to the major point of the story, as it should, viewers themselves should be able to connect the picture or words and the story. An example ("VTR" means *videotape recorder*):

```
Brokaw                          Protecting endangered
Box: logging                    species in these hard times
                                has led to a major economic
                                and environmental showdown.
                                A hearing in Oregon today
                                had all the players and all
                                the issues. NBC's Roger
                                O'Neil . . .

VTR -- Logging
Runs: 1:47
Out: Direct
                                               NBC Nightly News
```

Writing to background graphics, therefore, is really the same as writing a tell story, or a radio news story, for that matter. The only trick is to avoid redundancy. If the graphic says "Peace?" it is foolish to start the story, "Peace? That question is being asked. . . ." Incidentally, the beauty of one type of background graphic—the super—is that it removes the need to mention a name in the copy. Merely repeating what is said in a super is usually a waste of words, if not redundant.

There is an exception to this redundancy warning, however. Character generators are sometimes used to print important statements—perhaps the exact words the candidate had used in his controversial letter—on the screen. The goal here is *extra* clarity, so in this case repeating those words in the copy makes sense.

When graphics are given the whole screen they are no longer in the background; more complex writing requirements come into play.

Writing Away

A newscaster is discussing the weather. On screen is some videotape of young people throwing a Frisbee in a city park. That's an extreme example of **writing away** from videotape. The writing has little to do with the visuals except insofar as they demonstrate that it was a nice day.

Sometimes it is necessary to write copy that relates only marginally to the visuals. It's an alternative to a talking head when presenting information for which no relevant illustrations are available. No videotape of the weather tomorrow is available; so after the weather maps and under the graphics, it's either shots of Frisbee players or the weather person's head.

Discussion of a proposed city income tax might present similar problems. Graphics with the numbers help, but under them a reporter might decide to use videotape of people going to work, people walking into a bank or shots of the city council debating the tax.

```
Crowds on sidewalk          How much would people have
Graphic -- tax rates        to pay in city income taxes?
        8 secs.             Its sponsors say the average
                            worker would pay less than
                            200 dollars a year.
```

Situations like these, where it is necessary to write away from the visuals, are not that common. Clever reporters should return to the newsroom with shots that cover most aspects of the story (see Chapter 15, "Television Reporting"). Information on inflation can be illustrated with supermarkets and stores; details of a proposed highway can be matched with shots of the present roads, the projected right-of-way and the meeting at which the new road was debated. And then writers should make sure they save their discussion of these topics for the point in the videotape where the appropriate cover shot appears. There may be a subject or two in a story that is difficult to cover, necessitating writing away for a cut or two. But writers try to write close to the visuals whenever possible.

The real danger when writing away from visuals is words and images that not only don't help each other but also actively conflict.

```
UNACCEPTABLE
Crowds on sidewalk          Few people would be affected
Graphic -- tax rates        by the new city income tax.
      9 secs.               Its sponsors say only ten
                            percent of the people who
                            work here would even have to
                            fill out the forms.
```

The narration is talking about few people; the picture shows crowds? This could be saved by writing at least a little closer to the visual.

```
ACCEPTABLE
Crowds on sidewalk          Most people would not be
Graphic -- tax rates        affected by the new city
      11 secs.              income tax. Its sponsors say
                            90 percent of the people who
                            work here would not even
                            have to fill out the forms.
```

Spotting

This is the other extreme:

```
Stalled caravan of          Two drivers parked their
    trucks                  rigs at the front of this
    5 secs                  caravan on I-94.
                                         Jim Cummins, NBC
```

The writer here is writing extremely close to the videotape—*spotting* the videotape. With the word "this," he is almost pointing to the shot for the viewer. Once in a while this helps. It may not be clear in the picture that this is a truck caravan. Spotting the visuals can help clarify unclear shots, but usually it isn't necessary. Just show a shot of a gas station blocked by protesting truckers and write what happened at that gas station; viewers will understand that the station on screen is the very same one being discussed in the narration. It is not necessary to write "This is the gas station where. . . ." If the visuals and writing are good, viewers can spot things themselves.

```
WEAK
Trucks parked on highway    These were some of the 300
      7 secs.               big trucks that lined both
                            sides of the Indiana
                            turnpike . . . two and three
                            abreast.
```

BETTER

Trucks parked on highway
        6 secs.
	The big trucks -- 300 of
	them -- lined both sides of
	the Indiana turnpike . . .
	two and three abreast.
	                    Matt Quinn, ABC

Writing too far away from the visuals is usually a mistake. Writing too close can sound phony and simplistic. The solution is usually the middle way.

Coordinating

A writer has to write a story about an air crash. No videotape is available yet, so the station is using a black-and-white photograph of the wreckage-strewn site obtained from a photo wire. It has been transferred to a slide for use on the air, full screen. The writer begins the story as it would begin on radio:

Anchor	A D-C Ten jet crashed this afternoon seconds after taking off from Chicago's O'Hare airport. Officials say there were more than 270 people on board American Airlines flight 191 headed for Los Angeles.

Now it's time to use the slide. The words here do not have to tell viewers they are seeing the crash site.

WEAK

Slide: Crash site 6 secs.	This was the scene on the ground where the plane crashed. Notice the twisted and charred pieces of metal.

However, neither is this the time to discuss unrelated matters, to write away from the slide.

WEAK

Slide: Crash site 10 secs.	Eyewitnesses say that one of the plane's engines fell off shortly before the plane crashed. There's no word yet from officials as to whether

                                            this may have caused the
                                            crash.

What is needed is writing that relates to the slide without overexplaining it. The
writer chooses those facts in the story that fit the slide most closely and brings them
in here, facts that concern the visual but tell viewers things that aren't obvious when
looking at the visual.

         BETTER
         Slide: Crash site   The plane crashed and
             10 secs.   exploded in a vacant lot a
                                        quarter of a mile from the
                                        airport. Ambulances rushed
                                        to the scene, but it was
                                        soon apparent that there
                                        were no survivors.

This information **coordinates** with the slide. The writing makes the visual clearer
and the visual makes the writing clearer.
   The writer then decides to lose the slide as the story concludes:

         Anchor   Eyewitnesses say they saw an
                                        engine fall off one of the
                                        plane's wings shortly before
                                        the plane hit the ground.
                                        There's no word yet from
                                        officials on whether this may
                                        have caused the crash -- the
                                        worst ever in this country.

Coordinating visuals and copy requires matching shots and information.

         UNACCEPTABLE
         Body carried out   Police have charged 24-year-
             4 secs   old Robert Silversmith with
                                        the murder.

         Suspect being arraigned   The victim -- Fred Hardy --
             6 secs.   was a 30-year-old father of
                                        two. He was a neighbor of
                                        the suspect.

To put it bluntly, the victim goes with his body; the suspect goes with shots of his
arraignment.

ACCEPTABLE

Body carried out 4 secs.	The victim -- Fred Hardy -- was a 30-year-old father of two.

Suspect being
    arraigned
    6 secs.
	Police have charged a
	neighbor -- 24-year-old
	Robert Silversmith -- with
	the murder.

Notice how the videotape and the narration fit together in this section of a report on Pope John Paul II's visit to his hometown.

Pope arrives in open car 5 secs.	The Pope came home to his birthplace . . . and to the church he worshiped in as a boy.

Pope in front of church
    and crowd
    4 secs.
	Here -- as elsewhere in
	Poland -- a huge throng was
	waiting for him.

Pope shakes hands in
    crowd
    4 secs.
	But this one was different
	. . . there was less awe,
	more familiarity.

Pope talks with elderly
    woman.
    8 secs.
	Old people talked with him
	about his student days when
	he sat in the back of the
	classroom hoping his teacher
	would not see him.

John Cochran, NBC

In this section from a videotape report, Cochran always changes shots at the *end* of a sentence. As a rule this is a good idea. "It improves the coordination between the writing and the videotape," suggests Lee Giles, news director of WISH-TV. Nevertheless, it is possible to **write through** a cut. In other words, not every new shot has to be accompanied in the script by a new sentence. Often copy is matched with a sequence of shots rather than an individual cut. When this is done, it is not always possible to put the word at which the cut begins flush left in the audio column. It's sufficient if the cut is lined up with the line *during* which it begins.

Pope shakes hands in
    crowd
    5 secs.
	But this one was
	different. . . . In his
	hometown the Pope found
	people,

Pope talks with elderly
    woman
    5 secs.
	especially old people, who
	knew him . . . and treated
	him with less awe, more
	familiarity.

One additional note: The most important words to coordinate with a visual are the first group of words said when that visual comes on. Notice how the narration Cochran wrote to that shot of the Pope talking with an elderly woman opens with mention of the fact that he talked to "old people." With those words our minds make the connection between audio and visual . . . then we can accept the narration wandering off a bit into a discussion of the Pope's school days, a discussion that does not directly connect with what we are seeing. Had the narration opened with talk of school days, before getting to the words that make the connection, it would not have worked as well.

```
WEAK
Pope talks with elderly          As a student he had sat in
    woman                        the back of the classroom,
    8 secs.                      hoping his teacher would not
                                 see him, and he talked about
                                 that with old people.
```

Keeping Eyes Open

The demands of the visuals necessarily modify the standards by which information is selected for a story (see Chapter 6, "Stories"). For example, anything the Pope did out of reach of the television cameras would be less likely to find its way into the story—no cover shots available. Major facts should not be ignored just because there are no visuals to use with them. They can be included in the lead-in, or, if necessary, the reporter can write away from the videotape for a couple of cuts to get them in. However, when reasonable, the visuals affect the choice of facts, just as the facts affect the choice of visuals.

Jeff Wald, news director of KTLA, recalls seeing a story on a major-market station about a fire in which one person was killed. The videotape of that fire included shots of a firefighter rescuing a child, yet the writer ignored that rescue and went on talking about the death. Wald calls that "writing blindly." A radio story might not have mentioned that rescue attempt—the death may be more newsworthy. But on television, pictures will change standards of newsworthiness. If you have dramatic shots of a rescue, you write about the rescue as well as the death. "You have to pay attention to what the video is saying," Wald notes.

If the story is about the city's problems staffing its parks and the photographer got some great shots of kids in a park playground, it may be necessary to include a brief discussion of the effects of the staffing problems on playgrounds. If the story is about the local college's important victory in a basketball game and the photographer got some excellent shots of a "human wave" performed by the fans in the arena, the story might include some mention of fan reaction to enable a cut or two of that wave to be used. Narration for videotape has to be written with eyes open.

Reporter Rad Berky of WTNH knew he had a limited number of shots to work with on his story about a police officer who was suspended (see Chapter 15, "Television Reporting"). He knew his tape editor would want to include some previously used shots of the funeral of the man who died while being arrested by that officer . . . to add some more visual interest to the story. So Berky went out of his way to bunch together a few lines about the death for use under those shots. The visuals must be considered.

Exact Timing

The visuals may also affect the wording itself. If only 4 seconds of videotape are available of the Pope standing in front of the crowd at his old church, there is not time for:

```
Pope in front of church        Huge crowds have showed up
    and crowd                  everywhere the pope has gone
    8 secs.                    in Poland . . . and the
                               square here in front of the
                               church where he was baptized
                               was jammed.
```

That won't fit. Facts must be abandoned and the language changed to fit the videotape:

```
Pope in front of church        Here -- as elsewhere in
    and crowd                  Poland -- a huge throng was
    4 secs.                    waiting for him.
```

And, if there had been 5 seconds of that shot that were too good to ignore, the wording could have been changed to accommodate the videotape:

```
Pope in front of church        Here -- as elsewhere in
    and crowd.                 Poland -- a huge and
    5 secs.                    enthusiastic throng was
                               waiting for him.
```

If that shot had really deserved 6 seconds:

```
Pope in front of church        Here -- as elsewhere in
    and crowd                  Poland -- a huge and
    6 secs.                    enthusiastic throng came to
                               listen to him and pray with
                               him.
```

If the videotape has been edited before the narration has been written, getting the timing of the copy right becomes crucial. Add an extra second here or there to the script and the entire narration will be thrown off: Shots won't coordinate and sound-bites may begin while someone is still reading the copy for the previous shot. Seconds count when writing to videotape.

There are many accurate and pleasing ways to word thoughts. To coordinate copy and visuals, writers must be prepared to explore these alternative phrasings. The needs of the visuals may force them away from their first-choice sentences. Visuals do limit writing options, so radio newswriters have more freedom than television newswriters. But these sacrifices are repaid when the visuals and the sentences begin to harmonize.

Sound

Writing to sound-on-tape sections of television news stories requires some of the same skills used to set up actualities and voicers in radio lead-ins (see Chapter 10, "Writing to Tape").

In television news, people who are plucked off the street for interviews and sound-bites do not have to be identified; seeing their faces tells us about as much as we need to know about them. But anyone with significant impact on the story who appears in a sound-bite must be identified. If there's no super, the writing must do the job, as it has to in radio (see Chapter 10, "Writing to Tape"). A television throw line:

```
Precht                        . . . Catholic Church
     10 secs.                 leaders such as Christian
                              Precht note the improvement
                              in human rights statistics,
                              but press for guarantees
                              that the improvements are
                              not temporary . . .
                                          David Dow, CBS
```

Then Precht appears on the videotape to speak his piece.

Even when there is a lower-third to handle the details of the identification, the sentence before the sound-bite must still set up the statement, at least indirectly. In his throw line to a sound-bite with a child psychologist in a report on teenage suicide, Morton Dean, then with CBS, leaves the name to the super but takes responsibility for introducing the statement in his narration:

```
Dr. Brodlie                   The advice from adolescent
     9 secs.                  psychologists is for
                              troubled young people to
                              talk . . . to someone. And
                              for parents to listen to
                              their children . . . to hear
                              their message.
```

Then Dr. Brodlie speaks, with a super giving his full name. In the same report, Dean uses a short but even more explicit throw line:

Young woman 3 secs.	She's 23 . . . and has tried to kill herself.

A Q and A with the young woman follows.

So, if a super during the sound-bite takes care of the exact identification, it's not necessary to mention the person who talks in that bite, but it still is necessary to make sure viewers are prepared to understand what they will be seeing and hearing next. This is the throw line to a sound-bite with a painter on Capitol Hill who discusses some of the frescoes in the Capitol building:

Frescoes 7 secs.	Most folks scurry by here without really noticing, perhaps thinking this is all wallpaper, but not everyone is so naive. <div align="right">Susan Spencer, CBS</div>

The painter, who speaks next, is obviously one of those who is not so naive.

Writing throw lines for television doesn't seem any more difficult than writing them for radio, but there's a catch: The sound-bite has to be introduced *while* the videotape is playing; so the throw line has to both introduce a speaker and coordinate with a visual. To make this work when editing the videotape, it is necessary to include cover shots for the throw lines. Frequently a shot of the person who is about to speak is used, as in most of the previous examples; perhaps a long shot and then a cut to a close-up as the person begins speaking—to avoid a jump cut and the need for a cutaway. Sometimes the sound-bite is just started early, with the audio turned down—producing an effect known as "lip flap." However, it is not always necessary to show the speakers before they speak, as Susan Spencer's example demonstrates. She introduces the sound-bite with a shot of the frescoes the painter is about to describe.

Let It Breathe

This book has already warned of the dangers for broadcast news of newspaper-style writing—where the facts come fast (see Chapter 4, "Sentences"). Those dangers are even more pronounced when writing to visuals, because the visuals themselves are throwing additional facts at the viewer's already overburdened mind. Television writers frequently go wrong by trying to say too much. Some television news directors call it "machine-gun-style" writing.

UNACCEPTABLE LS Fire trucks and burning house 5 secs.	The fire started at eleven thirty this evening and burned out of control for three hours.

House burning 6 secs.	Officials say the colonial-style house, owned by Victor Racid, of Elmhurst, was vacant when the fire started.
Firefighters 8 secs.	The 18 firefighters, from the First Engine Company, struggled to keep the flames from spreading from the first to the second floor . . .
ACCEPTABLE LS Fire trucks and burning house 5 secs.	It took three hours for firefighters, working into the night, to bring the fire under control.
House burning 6 secs.	The house is owned by an Elmhurst man, but fire officials say no one was home when the flames broke out.
Firefighters 8 secs.	They say their main concern was to keep the fire, which began on the first floor, from spreading up to the second floor . . .

The homeowner's name can be mentioned elsewhere in the story.

Sometimes the narration should simply stop for a while. For example, in a story about President Fidel Castro on WBBM-TV in Chicago, the writer let us listen to Castro talk for a few seconds in Spanish before even starting the narration. Television newswriters should be prepared to pause so that viewers can listen to the natural sounds on a videotape: the sound of the helicopters arriving, the sound of the demonstrators, the sound of the bugler playing taps. The story on the Pope's visit might have opened with some natural sound, perhaps 4 seconds of crowds cheering:

```
Crowds cheering/SOT
Runs: 4
```

On the script there would be nothing in the audio column and no out-cue unless the crowd was audibly chanting.

At WISH-TV they call this "letting the videotape breathe," and they actually type "LET IT BREATHE" on their scripts. News director Lee Giles thinks videotape is generally given too little time to breathe. "We tell our people not to try to say too much," Giles says. "We would rather they underwrite than overwrite."

■ ■ ■

Here is a complete story with lead-in, sound-bites and stand-up. The words of the sound sections are included to make the story easier to follow, though they would not be included on the script.

Tennant	One of Canada's most esoteric and expensive sports is hot air ballooning. There are only about 50 balloons and qualified balloonists in all of Canada. This weekend, several of them are at an international balloon meet in New York State. Russ Patrick went along for the ride and has this report . . .
CU Rosenthal at coffee machine 6 secs.	Karen Rosenthal is Canada's newest certified balloonist -- she got her pilot's license just two days ago.
LS Briefing room 7 secs.	She was up at five o'clock this morning with two dozen other balloonists from Ontario and the northeastern
Rosenthal and pilot friend 5 secs.	U-S . . . for the first meet in which she'll pilot her own balloon . . . without an instructor on board.
Leaders at table 9 secs.	At this morning's briefing for the pilots, the ''go-'' or ''no-go'' decision . . . based largely on how stable the air is . . . was announced by the meet's leader.
Meet leader/ Runs: 7 Out: ''. . . this morning.''	''If we're going to go, people, we ought to go this morning. Anyone that feels strongly that they don't want to go this morning?''
Balloons on field 4 secs.	Balloons are an expensive hobby. Karen Rosenthal's British-made

Rosenthal's balloon
4 secs.

Balloons on field
3 secs.

Fan
2 secs.
Burner
2 secs.
Rosenthal's balloon
5 secs.

Balloons taking off
3 secs.

Patrick and Rosenthal in
balloon/SOT
Runs: 20
Out: ''. . . any of
them.''
Cutaway to people
waving up
6 secs.

Cutaway -- horses in
field below
10 secs.

CU Champagne bottle
opens
10 secs.

craft cost 10-thousand
dollars. She'd been saving
for three years to buy it.
All these hot-air balloons
have three things in
common --
giant fans are used to fill
them
with air . . . propane
burners are used to heat
that air . . . and the
balloons themselves . . . in
the air or on the ground
. . . are a riot of bright
color.
Balloonists refer to an
event like today's as a mass
ascension.
''What happens to people as
you float over them? What's
their attitude toward
balloons?''

''Oh, they . . . they all
wave and think it's great
and wish they could be up
here.''
''How about the animals?''
''Well, some of them don't
like us too much. But you
try and fly . . . you put the
burner on before you get to
them and fly over them, high,
and so you don't disturb any
of them.''
One of the great traditions
of ballooning is champagne.
It would be sacrilegious for
a balloon to head up into
the skies without a bottle
of bubbly to share later
with the chase crew and the
farmer in whose field it's
landed.

Stand-up SOT Runs: 11 Out: Direct	Karen Rosenthal says she makes all her ascensions now with one great ambition in mind. She wants to be the first woman to solo across the Atlantic Ocean. -- Russ Patrick, CBC News, near Batavia, New York Canadian Broadcasting Corporation

Wrap-Up

Television newswriting changes to meet the needs of the visuals. But, with the exception of the shot or two that is allowed to explain itself, television stories still are written so that the writing can stand on its own. The words, meanings, sentences, leads and stories of television news do the same jobs as in radio news, plus a few more.

Practice Assignments

A. Two full-screen slides are available to illustrate this story. Write a 25- to 30-second story based on the wire copy, and indicate in the video column where you want to use the slides.

   Slide 1: A condor. *Slide 2*: Brush fire burning.

FILLMORE, CALIF. -- A TWO-DAY BRUSH FIRE THAT INCHED
ACROSS THE LAST REMAINING BREEDING GROUND OF THE GIANT
CALIFORNIA CONDOR WAS DECLARED FULLY UNDER CONTROL
TODAY.

THE BLAZE, BELIEVED STARTED BY ILLEGAL FIREWORKS,
BLACKENED 120 ACRES OF STEEP, ROCKY TERRAIN IN THE LOS
PADRES NATIONAL FOREST.

A U.S. FOREST SERVICE SPOKESWOMAN SAID NONE OF THE
CONDOR NESTS WERE HARMED. THERE ARE BELIEVED TO BE ONLY
ABOUT 40 OF THE ENDANGERED BIRDS ALIVE.

THE FOREST SERVICE SPOKESWOMAN SAID THE FORCE OF 240
FIREFIGHTERS WAS REDUCED TO 45 MEN WHO REMAINED ON THE
LINES THROUGH THE NIGHT. THE BLAZE WAS DECLARED UNDER
CONTROL AT 8 A.M., BUT FIREFIGHTERS REMAINED TO MAKE
SURE THE LAST EMBERS WERE OUT.

STEEP TERRAIN HAMPERED CONTROL EFFORTS AND
FIREFIGHTERS HAD TO BE FLOWN INTO THE AREA BY

HELICOPTER, USING MOUNTAIN-CLIMBING TECHNIQUES TO CLIMB
UP THE ROCKY HILLSIDES AND HACK OUT FIRE LINES.

THE BLAZE STARTED SUNDAY AND QUICKLY SPREAD INTO THE
HUGE 53,000-ACRE CONDOR REFUGE IN THE LOS PADRES
NATIONAL FOREST. HOWEVER, THE FIRE DID NOT ENDANGER ANY
OF THE NESTS OF THE GIANT BIRDS.

''THERE ARE NO KNOWN ACTIVE NEST SITES THAT WE'RE
AWARE OF IN THE AREA WHERE THE FIRE WAS BURNING,'' A
SPOKESMAN SAID.

NO STRUCTURES WERE THREATENED AND ONLY ONE
FIREFIGHTER WAS INJURED WHEN A FALLING ROCK HIT HIS
HEAD. HE WAS NOT SERIOUSLY HURT.

B. The following silent videotape has been shot for this story:

```
LS   smashed trains   20 secs.
CU   crushed front of train   25 secs.
MS   injured people being removed   20 secs.
CU   face of uninjured but shocked survivor   5 secs.
```

Write a lead-in plus a 30- to 35-second story with videotape. You can edit the videotape any way you want. For example, 8 seconds of the long shot may be used at one point in the story and another 10 seconds at another point. But no more than 20 seconds of the long shot can be used. Indicate the cuts in the video column. Here are notes on the story:

```
2 commuter trains collide . . . crash at 8:58. . . .
both trains packed -- rush hour. . . . head-on
crash. . . . police say trains not going that fast --
estimate 15 mph each at time of crash . . . police say
about 400 people on board both trains plus 12 crew
members . . . police say at least 80 injured . . . at
least 20 injured seriously. . . . injured taken to St.
Vincent's Hospital. . . . no report of any fatalities at
this time . . . one passenger: ''All of a sudden there
was this horrible sound like an explosion, and we were
all thrown about. It was terrible, people were bleeding
and screaming.'' Railroad officials say they have no idea
what went wrong . . . unconfirmed report here that a
signal problem may have been at fault. Authorities
promise a full investigation . . . trains were the 8:20
from Pennsylvania Station downtown and the 8:15 from
Merrick. . . . crash site one mile from Jamaica Station
in Jamaica.
```

C. The following silent videotape has been shot for this story:

```
LS   abortion clinic with protesters in front  25 secs.
MS   clinic and protesters  20 secs.
CU   sign: ''Women's Clinic''  20 secs.
MS   protesters with signs: ''Abortion is murder'';
     ''Right-to-life''  15 secs.
CU   protester's face while chanting  10 secs.
MS   Reynolds marching in protest line  10 secs.
CU   Reynolds  10 secs.
CU   reporter nodding head  10 secs.
```

In addition, the following sound-bites are available:

```
Reynolds:    ''Abortion is immoral, it is murder. It's as
             simple as that. We can't allow this in our
             community.''  7 secs.

Reynolds:    ''We're protesting today and we'll continue
             to protest any attempts to open abortion
             clinics here. They are going to be taking
             human life in there.''  11 secs.
```

Write a lead-in plus a 45- to 50-second story with videotape using at least one sound-bite. You can edit the videotape any way you want. The sound-bites cannot be edited. Indicate the cuts in the video column. Here are notes on the story:

```
Opening of abortion clinic today -- first in town . . .
some doctors at local hospitals had refused to do
abortions. . . . clinic will have sliding fee scale --
to enable people in all income brackets to afford
abortions. . . . named ''Women's Clinic.'' . . . founded
by coalition of local women's groups. . . . will also
provide family counseling, diet information,
prematernity care and contraceptive counseling. . . .
staff: 6 doctors, 13 nurses, 5 counselors, 2
psychologists. Clinic expects to do about 100 abortions
a week. Group of about 30 pickets from local Right-to-
Life group here this morning to protest. Marched for
over two hours in front of clinic. Leader of group Wilma
Reynolds, a housewife in the city. Reynolds vows further
protests at the clinic. Reynolds says will call mayor,
council members and governor in attempt to shut clinic
down.
```

17

Television Newscasts

It is the week before Christmas at WTNH in New Haven, Connecticut, and the station's assistant news director, assignment editor, news planner and six o'clock producer are sitting around a table in the news director's office . . . laughing.

WTNH, Channel 8—the number-two-rated station in a two-station market—has a young staff intent on "trying harder." It may not be a typical television station (if there is such a thing) but its news operation—coordinated each day at this meeting—offers a pretty good example of who does what in the production of a television newscast. And that's what this chapter is about.

News Meetings

A group similar to the one gathered around that table at WTNH meets at least once a day at most television stations (at most large news organizations of any kind, for that matter) to discuss plans for that day's news coverage. At WTNH the meeting is supposed to begin as close to 10 in the morning "as humanly possible." (It began today at 10:25.) Its purpose is to go over the stories the station will cover that day and then to make preliminary decisions on which stories will be used in which newscasts. The laughter now convulsing the participants isn't required, but on a day like this, when a couple of producers are out with flu, it helps.

The meeting had been moving along seriously enough, with the **assistant news director** leading discussion in the news director's absence. The assignment editor, Al Blinke, and the news planner had prepared a list of the stories reporters will be covering. Today the list, dubbed the "situationer," includes the recall of some unsafe toys, a local police officer who has been suspended after a suspect he was arresting died, the deportation of a local man accused of being a Nazi and local police stepping up their efforts to catch drunken drivers with the use of blood- and breath-analysis equipment. (Such lists and the *future files* they are based on—see Chapter 7, "Sources"—are now kept on computer at many stations.) As Blinke outlined each story, the other participants asked questions and made suggestions:

"What's the point of that drunk-driving story?" assistant news director Wendie Feinberg asked. "Is it the danger of driving drunk or the hassle of being stopped?"

"Both," Blinke responded.

"Well, then let's see someone actually go through the testing," Feinberg said.

"She [the reporter] is already out on the story," Blinke answered. "I don't know if I can get to her, but I'll try."

As they run through the stories, the participants in the meeting also make decisions on how the stories will be used in the newscasts. Will they ask the reporter to produce a **package**—a videotape story complete with sound-bites, stand-up and reporter's narration—or will they ask for only a videotape that one of the newscasters in the studio can read to live during the show—a "VO," in the station's jargon, for *voice over*, or a "VOSOT" if it will include a sound-bite, a *sound on tape* segment? Sometimes they want both. That *UNSAFE DOLLS* story is scheduled to be the package that opens the station's 5:30 p.m. newscast. It will also be used as a VOSOT on the 6 p.m. newscast.

The participants in this meeting also have to decide which stories to cover live . . . and that's when the laughter begins. The assignment editor had scheduled a live report on the arrival of Santa Claus—in the form of the station's popular consumer affairs reporter—at what is being billed as the state's largest office party. For better or worse, that's standard fare at this time of year in local television news, but it caused the staff to remember their experience with this type of story a year ago: Last Christmas season someone had decided to provide Santa Claus a lift on WTNH's news helicopter. A camera was broadcasting Santa's descent live, when suddenly the winds produced by the helicopter knocked over the television lights. The screen went black. Santa and his helicopter disappeared.

"Don't worry! He's not coming in a helicopter . . . this time," the assignment editor says above the guffaws and wisecracks inspired by the memory.

Assignment Editors

WTNH divides this job in half. Pam Burke is the **news planner**—which means she's in charge of new assignments that can be planned in advance. Burke keeps the future files (see Chapter 7, "Sources"); she gets the press releases; she receives the calls from area residents who think the station should report on their spectacular array of Christmas lights. In other words, Burke's job is to handle the *predictable* news. At the news meeting each morning she presents a list of assignments for the *next* day.

Today's *UNSAFE DOLLS* story was based on a call a state consumer safety official made yesterday to the newsroom announcing a news conference. Burke found the drunk-driving story in a local newspaper and arranged to send a reporter to a small-town police station to report on it. The office party today was announced in a press release she filed. Yesterday Burke also spotted an item in *USA Today* noting that college radio stations have become among the few stations in the country playing "new music," and she suggested sending a reporter to a college in the state for a local angle on that national story.

Assignment editor Al Blinke began his search for *breaking news* at 6:30 that morning. He read through the wire copy; he made a series of calls to local police and fire departments; he looked through the newspapers. The bulk of the unplanned stories the station's reporters are covering today, however, are stories the station had been following on its own for a while. In fact, the news that that policeman had been suspended had been a WTNH exclusive the previous evening. "Most of the stories are day-to-day stories you already are familiar with," Blinke explains. "You just have to keep on top of them."

Sometimes, however, something breaks. Shortly after the meeting ends, Blinke is listening to a police radio scanner behind his desk when he hears a call for the fire department to come to an exit on the interstate. Then he hears that the interstate is being closed in the area of the incident. Blinke quickly directs a reporter with a photographer there, makes some calls himself and learns that a truck is leaking gas. The reporter will get some videotape.

Blinke also makes the preliminary decisions on who is to go where. While most television reporters are prepared to cover all kinds of stories, the station does encourage some specialization. Blinke bases some of his decisions on these formal or informal *beats*—a reporter who does a lot of police stories will keep up with that suspended officer; the station's investigative reporter will look into the files police apparently kept on a Judge Speziale. When making assignments, Blinke may also consider a reporter's interests—one of the station's reporters loves "new music," so he gets *COLLEGE RADIO*.

In trying to cover an area as large as the state of Connecticut, logistics becomes another crucial consideration. For example, the reporter and photographer driving up to the state capitol in Hartford to cover *UNSAFE DOLLS* will also be asked to stop by a Hartford department store which, according to a just-arrived press release, has a four-foot by four-foot "talking box" greeting customers in front of the store. "We try to get the most out of our crews," Blinke explains.

The assignment editor spends the rest of the morning and much of the afternoon staying in touch with his reporters, making sure they're getting the stories they should be getting, keeping the producers informed and, of course, keeping an eye and an ear open for any breaking stories. Most of Blinke's reporters wander back into the newsroom by the middle of the afternoon. A **desk assistant,** or assistant assignment editor, is there to make follow-up calls on still-developing news events, and the station's nighttime assignment editor arrives early in the afternoon to keep the desk running and to prepare for the station's 11 o'clock newscast. Nevertheless, Blinke usually sticks around until about 6:30 in the evening . . . "to make sure all the live reports go well."

Producers

"Based on our morning news meeting, I'm starting to formulate what's going to be in what order in the show," Steve Sabato, **producer** of the 6 o'clock newscast, is saying at 11 in the morning. "We have two shows—a 5:30 and a 6 o'clock—and we have to keep the two shows different, so we don't find ourselves repeating the same stories. We've decided at this point to lead the 5:30 show with the *UNSAFE DOLLS* story, and a likely 6 o'clock lead at this early point looks like the story on the suspended cop."

Sabato began his day at about 9 in the morning by **reading in**—catching up with the day's news. By the time he arrived at the news meeting he had read through national and local copy on the UPI and AP wires; he had looked through the *Hartford Courant*, the New Haven *Journal-Courier*, the *New York Times* and *USA Today*. The producer has to be familiar with all the day's news in order to make intelligent decisions about what to include in the show. He is thinking not just about stories the station's reporters will cover but also about *tell stories*, stories that may be used without videotape ("readers" they're called at WTNH)—he'll have to assign these stories to newswriters. He is also looking for any national stories that should be included in his newscast.

And it *is* the producer's newscast. Unlike theater or movie producers, who usually are basically business executives, one step removed from the content of a production, broadcast journalism producers are specifically responsible for the content. They are the top *journalists* working on a program. A newscast's producer is like a newspaper's managing editor.

Some producers, at larger stations than WTNH, get more assistance than Sabato gets. There may be an **executive producer** supervising all the station's newscasts, along with some associate producers coordinating stories and helping out. And even at WTNH, where Sabato produces alone, he still depends on the work of newswriters and reporters, and on the station's technical staff. He still will consult with the news director and assistant news director throughout the course of the afternoon, and he will also discuss his work with the assignment editor, the anchors and with other staffers. Producers do have help in running the ship. Nevertheless, they are at the helm. Steve Sabato is responsible for steering all the stories into place. He has control. Here's how Sabato does it:

Until noon Sabato burrows through wire copy and newspapers. He calls up the three video news services from which he can take national and international videotape—Cable News Network, ABC's Daily Electronic Feed (a television version of its News Call) and Newsfeed, which is owned by Westinghouse. (Sabato believes the major national story today is news of some miners trapped in a Utah mine. Someone on the desk at ABC says they'll probably have some videotape on that.) Then Sabato runs down any *file footage* or *file tape* he might need; in other words, any videotape saved from past stories that can help illustrate a current story. (File tape will be used this evening in a follow-up to a story about thousands of deaths in Bhopal, India, caused by a leak in a plant owned by a Connecticut company.)

From noon to 1 o'clock Sabato roughs out his **rundown**—a listing, in order, of the stories he'll use (sometimes called a "routine" or, as in radio, a "lineup"). The producer's primary responsibility is organizing the newscast, and the rundown puts that organization onto paper or, increasingly, into a computer. Sabato checks decisions with the news director or assistant news director, compares notes with the assignment editor and then, from 1 to 2, types up a working draft of that rundown.

When organizing his show, Sabato is not, fortunately, just staring at a blank, wide-open hour. The show *has* a set format: There are eight *blocks* of news to be filled between commercials; the 6:30 block will be dominated by the weather; the

6:45 block by sports; the final block by a weather update and the kicker. To keep viewer interest throughout the show, Sabato knows that each of the other blocks will need a strong opening story.

COP SUSPENDED (see Chapter 15, "Television Reporting") still looks like his top story; that'll kick off the opening block. Sabato decides the *UNSAFE DOLLS* is his second most newsworthy story, so he'll open his second block with that (in a version different from that used at 5:30). Other important stories—such as *SPEZIALE* and *DRUNK DRIVING*—are placed in the body of the first block, but *GAS LEAK* is saved to open the third, and the top national story—*UTAH MINERS*—to open the fifth.

The rundown Sabato types up (see pages 410–411) also has a set format. It's divided into columns:

1. In the first column, Sabato notes the initial of the anchor who will read the story, or the lead-in to the story—either Janet *P*eckinpaugh or John *L*indsey.
2. In the second, he types the number of the page the story will appear on in the script. (Notice that Sabato saves some page numbers for late-breaking stories.)
3. The story's slug goes in column three.
4. The initials of the reporter or newswriter who'll write the story go in column four. (Steve Sabato, "SES," will write the headlines and teases—"teez"— himself.)
5. Column five is for information on graphics—Sabato, for example, wants the word "SUSPENDED" to appear along with a picture in a box above the shoulder of the anchor when the lead-in to that story is read.
6. Column six explains what kinds of video will be included in the story. ("VCR" stands for ¾-inch videotape cassette recorder—either in a package or to be used with a voice-over narration; "TCR" and "VPR" are two other sizes of videotape recorders used in the show's opening and in teases.)
7. Column seven details the source of any pictures—other than graphics, studio shots or videotape produced by the station's reporters—to be used in a story. (The live reports will come from a station wagon equipped with microwave transmission facilities, dubbed "van-8"; *UTAH MINERS* should come from ABC's Daily Electronic Feed; and a few stories—like *BHOPAL*—will use file tape.)
8. One of Sabato's major responsibilities is making sure all this adds up to an hour (actually 58 minutes, 27 seconds). So, he writes the time he wants—or has scheduled—each story to run in the second-to-last column.
9. And he keeps a "running time" for the whole show in the final column. (Newsroom computers now handle this math automatically.) If by the end of sports, for example, it's earlier or later than 6:46:15, Sabato will have to make adjustments. *THUMBS* is "pad," a videotaped promo for the news staff that Sabato can play for up to a minute and a half at the end of the show if he turns out to be short. He'd rather not have to play it.

After the rundown is finished, Sabato makes sure his newswriters and reporters are aware of what he wants them to write and how long their stories should run.

Then, at 2, it's time for the preproduction meeting with the artist who will prepare the graphics and the videotape editors who will edit the tape for his teases and headlines. The major problem today is finding enough different pictures to use in graphics for the show's many Christmas-oriented stories. There's a shot of a wreath, of some candles, of Santa. . . .

From 3 to 4 Sabato is working on his headlines and teases: "Coming up next on Action News, we'll have information on those Christmas toys consumers are being warned about. . . ." As he works, he has an eye on a television set where Cable Network News is playing and an eye on the wires: Is anything breaking? (Producers have also taken to monitoring the C-Span cable network, with its live coverage of political speeches, meetings and legislative sessions.) By 4 o'clock his copy is starting to come in.

Sabato, wearing his editing hat now, tries to read over everything—the work of his newswriters and his reporters. He suggests a line here, deletes a line there and checks some facts. There's only one major problem today: The script for a videotape package on plans for repairing the state's "infrastructure" of roads and bridges is filled with too many numbers. Sabato wants a rewrite. Everything else he has seen looks usable. Could this be a hassle-free show?

No. The first piece of bad news arrives at 5 p.m. when ABC moves its Daily Electronic Feed: The *UTAH MINERS* story Sabato has been waiting for is not among the batch of videotape reports ABC has transmitted to its affiliates for use in their newscasts. Sabato asks a newswriter to write a *reader*, or tell story, on the trapped miners—it's too important to leave out of the show. Then he asks for a lead-in for another videotape report from ABC, which he has reluctantly decided to use.

Problems two, three and four arrive in quick succession: *INFRASTRUCTURE* isn't in yet—that reporter's still rewriting; *COLLEGE RADIO* isn't in yet—it's being put together by the same reporter who is stuck on *INFRASTRUCTURE*. And the reporter who is supposed to do *SPEZIALE*—the second story in Sabato's newscast—hasn't even returned to the newsroom.

The tension is reflected in Sabato's hurried movements: He shuffles the stack of papers in front of him on his desk, looks up to talk with a newswriter, calls across the room to the assignment editor to check on that laggard reporter, then returns his attention to those papers. With his rundown as a guide, Sabato is trying to organize and number the pages of the newscast's script. He's inserting blank pages for those stories that are still missing. It's 5:30 and there are too many blank pages.

Newswriters

Not every television station has people designated only to write news. At WTEV in New Bedford, Massachusetts, for instance, the newscasters and reporters between them write all the copy that will be used on the air. But at WTNH Steve Sabato has had three newswriters at his disposal at various times during the course of the day.

		DATE 12/20	SHOW	PRODUCER SES		DIRECTOR TOB		
ANCH	PG	SLUG	WTR	GRAPHIC	VIDEO	SOURCE	SKD	RT
P/L	1	HEADS (NH COP/DOLLS/ XMAS DONATE/LIVE-PAR	SES		TCR	VAN-8	:30	:30
	2	OPEN-PECK	SES		TCR		:20	:50
P	3	N-H COP SUSPENDED	RB	SUSPENDED	VCR/PKG		1:45	2:35
L	4	SPEZILAE FILES	AH	SPEZIALE	VCR/PKG		1:45	4:20
P	5	E HARTFORD OBSCENITY	TN	CRACKDOWN	VCR/VOSOT		1:00	5:20
L	6	FORAN HS BUST	DR	DRUG BUST	VCR/VOSOT		1:00	6:20
P	7	DRUNK DRIVING HAMD	DR	DRUNK DRIVING	VCR/PKG		1:45	8:05
L	8	SULLIVAN OBIT	SR	SULLIVAN			:20	8:25
P/L	9	TEEZ # 1 FEDDER	SES		VPR/TCR		:30	8:55
	10	BREAK # 1					2:00	10:55
L	20	UNSAFE DOLLS	DH	XMAS	VCR/VOSOT		1:00	11:55
P	21	FEDDERENKO-REAX	PD	FEDDERENKO	VCR/PKG		1:45	13:40
L	22	BHOPAL/DANBURY	LT	BHOPAL	VCR/VO	FILE	:30	14:10
E	23	FAIRFIELD STUDENTS	LT		VCR/VOSOT		1:00	15:10
P	24	XMAS DONATIONS	DS	XMAS	VCR/PKG		1:45	16:45
L/P	25	TEEZ # 2 LIVE-PARTY	SES		VPR/TCR	VAN-8	:30	17:15
	26	BREAK # 3					2:00	19:15
P	30	95: GAS LEAK	RB	GAS LEAK	VCR/VOSOT		1:00	20:15
L	31	INFRA STRUCTURE	TN	HIGHWAYS	VCR/VOSOT		1:00	21:15
P	32	*LIVE-OFFICE PARTY	LS	XMAS/LV		VAN-8	2:00	23:15
L/G	33	TEEZ # 3 WXR	SES		VPR/TCR		:30	23:45
	34	BREAK #3					2:00	25:45

DATE 12/20   SHOW 6:00   PRODUCER SES   DIRECTOR   TOB

ANCH	PG	SLUG	WTR	GRAPHIC	VIDEO	SOURCE	SKD	RT
L	40	WEATHER	SES				3:30	29:15
P	41	G-FOX BOX	DH	XMAS	VCR/PKG		1:45	31:00
L/P	42	SUPERTEEZ	SES		VPR/TCR		:30	31:30
	43	BREAK FOUR					2:00	33:30
C	50	UTAH MINERS	LT	MINERS	VCR/PKG	DEF	1:30	35:00
P	51	NYC NATIVITY	LT	XMAS	VCR/VO		:30	35:30
E	52	CABBAGE PATCH	JP	CABBAGE PATCH	VCR/VC		:30	36:00
P	53	T-DAY CHILD	JP	T-DAY	VCR/PKG		2:15	38:15
L/B	54	TEZ-SPORTS	BP	3-SHOT	VPR/TCR		:30	38:45
	55	BREAK FIVE					2:00	40:45
P	60	SPORTS	BP		VCR		5:30	46:15
L	PRE 61	TBA	LT	CU/L	VCR/PKG		1:45	
L/P	61	TEEZRADIO	SES		VPR/TCR		:30	46:45
	62	BREAK SIX					2:00	48:45
D	P70	REMINGTON SUIT	SR	REMINGTON	VCR/VO		:30	
L	70	SIKORSKY S-76	SR	SIKORSKY	VCR/VONAT	FILE	:30	48:15
P	71	EB VOTE	SR	E-B	VCR/VONAT	FILE	:30	48:45
L	72	CPI	JL	CPI			:20	49:05
L	73	STOX	JL	ˮ	TCR		:15	49:20
P	74	RADIO COLLEGE	TN	RADIO	VCR/PKG		1:45	51:05
L/P	75	TEEZ KICKER LIVE-8	SES		VPR	VAN-8	:30	49:50
	76	BREAK SEVEN					2:00	51:50
P	80	LATE EDITION TEZ	RT	LATE EDITION			:20	52:10
L	81	WEATHER UPDATE	SES				:30	52:40
P	82	KICKER LIVE PARTY	LS	XMAS/LV		VAN-8	2:00	54:40
	83	BYES/CLOSE/THUMBS	SES		VCR-THUMBS		1:00	55:40
		OFF AT 58:27						
		TEEZ						
		BREAK						

Sara Robins began work at 9 o'clock and has spent her day writing the station's noon, 5:30 and 6 o'clock newscasts. She writes a good chunk of the words the newscasters on those shows will read. Some of her stories are tell stories; some employ videotape. However, since reporters write the lead-ins and narrations to their own stories at WTNH, the videotape Robins works with is usually file tape or silent tape taken from one of the three national and international news services.

Yesterday between noon and 6 Robins had written 12 stories, averaging 30 seconds each, for the 6 o'clock newscast. Today turned out to be a relatively easy day—Sabato asked that she write only five.

One of those stories concerned a suit being filed against a Connecticut company—Remington shaver. Some basic shots of shavers moving down the assembly lines were available from a profile of the company's president one of the reporters has been working on. They would not coordinate particularly well with a story on a lawsuit, but the videotape would be more interesting than a talking head. Robins looks at the videotape; she reads through whatever wire copy she can find on the suit; she calls up the company to clarify its reaction; then she begins to write.

The first part of the story will be read with a shot of the newscaster and a graphic on camera:

Anchor

The company whose president said he liked its shavers so much he bought the company is being sued over an advertising claim. Consumer Reports magazine says

Shortly after the start of the second sentence in the story, when she introduces the name of the company, Robins indicates in the video column that the shot of the shavers should play:

Shavers
7 secs.

Remington Products illegally used its name in an ad for microshavers. The ads mention the magazine's favorable rating for the shaver. . . .

After Robins finishes writing her story, she gives a copy to a tape editor, who edits the videotape based on the cues and times she typed in the video column. (This one won't take much editing.) Then Robins begins working on the next story.

Weather and Sports

There is hardly a newscast on television that does not spend some minutes on these two subjects . . . usually more minutes than are expended on all but the most important news stories and usually at a set time in the show so that viewers can easily find them.

Weatherman, *weathercaster* (neither title sounds quite right) Geoff Fox had many years of broadcasting experience when he interviewed for a job at WTNH, but he says what got him the job was a floppy disk he brought with him. "I showed the news director what the computers he had could do," Fox explains.

Weather forecasting has become one of the most computerized components of television journalism. Fox uses a computer to call up his readings, forecasts and maps from a *data bank* operated by a company called Weather Services Incorporated. (Most of the information in the data bank comes from the National Weather Service.) "I use it as if it were a huge filing cabinet," Fox explains. "They've put everything where I know how to get at it, and then, depending on situations, I will reach into the right file and get out the right facts."

Fox spends most of the afternoon translating forecasts and weather maps into graphics . . . again using a computer—an "electronic paint box" (see Chapter 14, Visuals). He moves an electric pen on a large white tablet, and by pressing a few keys on his computer keyboard he can make colorful fronts, snowflakes, raindrops, lows or highs appear on his monitor and later on viewer's television screens.

"Television has always had difficulty presenting things that are not by themselves visual," Fox notes. "The weather happening is visual. A forecast is not. There was a time when TV weather people tried to illustrate forecasts with magnetic boards. You could put a smiling cloud up or a sun, but you were limited to a couple of maps—as many as you could get on the set and roll away and use. Now in the course of the newscast at 6 o'clock I will use anywhere between 9 and 14 graphics. With this computer we can for the first time make what's *going* to happen really visual." (There is, however, another side to this argument. Some of the people who report the weather on television believe that all those fancy maps and graphics can confuse as easily as they can clarify. One magnetic board with a map of the country and a few clouds, Ls and Hs may be enough for them.)

Fox spends most of his day drawing maps on the computer—three forecast maps, a high- and low-temperature map, a radar map and a satellite map. In addition, he prepares a series of listings of past, current and future weather conditions that will be produced on a character generator. None of these graphics will actually be in the studio with him. They will remain in a computer memory to be called up during the 3½ minutes he is on the air by the director or by Fox himself (using a little switch in his hand). The chromakey effect makes them appear to be behind him as Fox gives his report. The trick is learning to point out threatening low-pressure areas on maps that you can see only on the television monitor in the studio.

Sportscasters don't have to rely much on computers to illustrate their stories. Sports is filled with dramatic visuals of end-zone catches, close plays at second, reverse dunks, slap shots and human waves in the stands. WTNH's Bob Picozzi gets most of his facts on scores, transactions and schedules from the wires and some calls to local teams, but the key to his report will be his videotape.

Today Picozzi has videotape that the station shot at a Hartford Whalers hockey match last night, videotape that is being shot this afternoon on a local college basketball team, plus various national highlights and interviews that he's taking from

*Sportscaster
Bob Picozzi in
the newsroom
at WTNH,
New Haven,
Connecticut.*

ABC's Daily Electronic Feed and Westinghouse's Newsfeed.

Picozzi's lead story will be a big trade involving the Yankees. To illustrate that story he searches his own memory. Picozzi remembers one of the players in that trade getting a game-winning hit in a day game and the other player winning a game late in August. He checks a copy of last summer's baseball schedule, then walks over to the rows of sports videotape the station has saved. File tape of those two game-winning hits will open Picozzi's 5½ minutes of sports this evening.

Directors

If the producer leads the journalistic troops that prepare a television newscast, the **director** leads the technical troops. Directors are trained not in leads and lead-ins and interview techniques, but in camera angles and electronic effects. Directors are broadcasters, not broadcast journalists. They belong in this book only because they work so closely with broadcast journalists. They, literally, call the shots.

At 5:30 producer Steve Sabato hands a copy of his script, blank pages and all, to the director of the 6 o'clock newscast, Jeff Winn. Winn sits at a desk in the newsroom and begins marking the script—**blocking out** the show—while Sabato tries to fill those blank pages.

In the video column on each page either Winn writes the number of the camera he'll use at that point to show one of the two newscasters, or he writes the number

CNN's control room in Atlanta. (© CNN, Inc. All Rights Reserved)

of the machine that he'll use to play the videotape in that story. He circles the supers that have been typed into the script and gives each graphic or *still*—and there's one in almost every story—a number. Winn also writes up separate lists of stills and of videotapes. Those lists will go to the people who ready the stills and the tape.

While Winn works, Sabato is able to hand him the lead-ins to *INFRASTRUC-TURE* and *COLLEGE RADIO*. Both stories came in at about 5:45. But at 5:57, when Sabato and Winn walk toward the control room to the station's television studio, the scripts they hold still have a blank page where the lead-in to *SPEZIALE* should be. The reporter has returned, but his videotape package is still being written and edited.

In the control room at 5:59, Winn sits on a stool in front of a desk covered with labeled buttons, called the **switcher.** The wall he faces is teeming with TV monitors, two of which will receive most of his attention: a **preview monitor,** which he will use to check out everything he is *about* to put on the air, *before* it goes on the air, and an "air" or **line monitor** that shows what *is* going on the air at that moment (at this moment, it's a commercial). By pushing the buttons in front of him, Winn can fill either of these monitors with the picture produced by any of the three studio cameras and one live remote camera he is using, or with video from his three videotape machines . . . and he can combine those images with various types of graphics and effects.

At larger stations a **technical director** would actually manipulate the switcher and an **assistant director** might be available to help line up camera shots and ready videotape. But as the clock nears 6 in the control room of WTNH, Winn, alone, is shouting out instructions to his camera operators, readying the videotape, and finally, pushing the buttons that play the introduction to the show and the opening headlines.

It is nervous work. One wrong button and a shot of a reporter preparing to report live on the huge office party will appear instead of the *COP SUSPENDED* videotape; a 7-second mistake in timing and the super with the name of the policeman's lawyer will appear under a shot of the police chief.

And *SPEZIALE* still isn't in. . . .

Technical Staff

The 6 o'clock newscast on WTNH had already benefited from the work of photographers, tape editors and a graphics artist. Now as the newscast goes on the air, a group of broadcast technicians joins in: Three ***camera people*** move the large studio cameras around and, under Winn's direction, choose close-ups and medium shots of the newscasters and the chromakey background behind them. (At most larger stations they would be joined in the studio by a ***floor manager*** who would be responsible for signaling the newscasters.)

In a room to the right of the control room, two ***tape operators*** insert the videotape in playback machines as the time approaches for the various videotape reports to air; then they cue the tapes up so that there is a 2-second countdown before the stories on them play. (That 2-second ***preroll*** ensures that the machines are up to speed, and it means that Winn has to start rolling the tapes 2 seconds before he puts them on the air.)

In the station's ***master control room***, one person operates the still store—the computer in which the graphics are stored—and another plays the commercials and readies supers to appear at the director's command.

And finally, in a room behind the control room that would look familiar to a radio journalist an ***audio person*** opens, closes and adjusts the level of microphones and the audio input from tape machines. While the first videotape story is playing, it's the audio person's job to make sure that the newscasters' discussions with the producer about the still-missing *SPEZIALE* story don't accidentally end up on the air.

Anchors

The newscasters who host, or hold down, the studio end of a television newscast are often called ***anchors.*** The amount of writing and editing they will do on the scripts they read varies from station to station. Still they are the most visible, and usually the highest paid, members of the news team. Janet Peckinpaugh and John Lindsey, who anchor the 6 o'clock newscast on WTNH, have both done extensive writing at other stations. They do little writing here, but both have reporting and community relations responsibilities to fill the hours before they go on the air.

As the show approached they were reading through their copies of the script, taking 10 minutes or so to put on their make-up and working whatever psychological magic is necessary to keep the tension all around them out of their faces and voices. "This is a very hectic, deadline-oriented type of business," says Lindsay. "It never changes; it's always going to be that way. You have to take the time to take a deep breath and find your communicative self."

WTNH's small news set sits in one corner of the station's cavernous studio. By 5:59 Lindsey and Peckinpaugh are making themselves comfortable behind the anchor desk on that set. They each have scripts in front of them, but they will read the news on the air while looking directly at a camera. To make this eye contact with the viewers possible, a news assistant in the control room is feeding another copy of the script, pages taped together, under a small camera which then transmits the image to television monitors jutting out from the front of the studio cameras (a job that is now often handled by computer). One-way mirrors in front of the lenses make those monitors appear as if they were on top of the lenses and, consequently, make Lindsey and Peckinpaugh appear as if they were talking directly to viewers when they are, in fact, reading. The two anchors wear tiny, barely visible earphones so that producer Steve Sabato can talk to them even while they are on the air.

"The things that you worry about most when you go on the air are last-minute changes, dropping stories," Peckinpaugh says. And that is exactly what is happening this evening. With *SPEZIALE*, the second story in the newscast, still not in by 6:01, Sabato instructs the anchors to "float," or hold, the story. But wait! The tardy story miraculously arrives sometime within the next 60 seconds, and the producer wants *SPEZIALE* returned to its original place in the script . . . 20 seconds before Lindsey is to read it on the air (see "Introduction"). He reads it in his usual calm, relaxed style.

On the Air

After the *SPEZIALE* uncertainty, which was completely invisible to viewers, things settle down in the control room. There *is*, as the assistant news director wanted, a short scene during the *DRUNK DRIVING* story of the reporter taking a breath test. And the "POS"—people on the street—"reax"—reaction—from some local Jews to the deportation of an accused Nazi, Feodor Fedorenko, is particularly powerful: "Maybe in some small way this will show that there is some justice being done . . . after this great outrage that happened in the past," one person says on videotape.

Producer Sabato even seems to be relaxing a bit . . . but then one of the telephones in front of him rings, just after the first live report from that huge office party. It's assistant news director Wendie Feinberg, who has been watching the show in her office. Feinberg observed that the reporter failed to mention where she was for that live report—a serious oversight. While the next commercial is on, Sabato asks the anchors to throw in that information just before they introduce Geoff Fox and the weather. ". . . It's at the Shubert Theater, so if you'd like to go down . . . ," Lindsey is saying on the air a few moments later.

Weather, Sports. They're running long. Sabato, who has been carefully timing the show, decides to *pull*—skip—the national package from ABC. And now the producer, for a different reason, is starting to have second thoughts about that live appearance by the station's reporter dressed as Santa Claus.

"Can we really tell everybody who Santa is?" he asks the others in the control room at 6:50. "What about the kids out there?" There's a moment of silence, and then director Jeff Winn suggests that their reporter be billed as "just helping Santa, who is busy at the North Pole." Sabato so instructs the reporter, remembering to remind her again to say where she is.

The reporter follows instructions. Santa, make that Santa's helper, appears, and the 6 o'clock newscast on WTNH ends smoothly, with no need for *THUMBS*.

Wrap-Up

Putting the news on television requires a coordinated effort by many people and many technically sophisticated machines, under stiff deadline pressure. Nerves are inevitably going to be strained. And in the search for ratings on a medium that is more used to entertaining than informing, cuteness, frivolity and an attractive smile will too often triumph over toughness and thoroughness. But on those occasions when the people and the machines are working together intelligently, television news is perhaps the most effective method for communicating news humans have devised.

18

Ethics and Law

Consider the power of a broadcast news story to blacken reputations, to invade privacy or, on the other hand, to expose corruption and inform the public. This power burdens the reporter, newswriter or producer with ethical responsibilities that approach those of the lawyer or the doctor. And many of these dictates of conscience have been imbued with the force of law.

Lawmakers and the courts have constructed a complex structure of laws around broadcasting and journalism—at least intended to protect the rights of journalists to report the news without constraint, along with the rights of the people they report on and the rights of their audience.

Final responsibility for decisions on the legality of broadcasting certain material may rest with station management, but reporters and writers must be aware of the web of laws and regulations that surrounds their activities. Similarly, if they are to do their jobs conscientiously, they must be aware of the ethical questions they may confront.

This section raises the major ethical issues broadcast journalists face, and it considers the laws and regulations that govern their work from the perspective from which they were written—ethics. Fortunately, in this country ethical reporting is in most cases legal reporting.

Some of these legal questions are quite complex, and new developments in the courts and legislatures promise to throw some of the answers given here out of date. It is suggested that broadcast journalists supplement this discussion with further reading in books on mass communication law (see Suggested Readings) and newspaper and magazine articles on breaking developments in mass communication law.

Standards

This is a craft, a profession. Its practitioners must abide by certain standards. One of the most important of these—objectivity—has already been discussed (see Chapter 3, "Meanings"). There are others—some formulated in laws or regulations, some merely a matter of conscience.

Accuracy

Accuracy is the journalist's religion; an error of fact is a professional sin. Some might argue whether there is such a thing as truth, but there certainly are such things as facts—the fact that the victim lives on Orchard Street, not Grove Street; the fact that the commissioner said the contractor wasn't her *brother*, but she did not say the contractor was not her *friend*. Reporters must play "slow and tight" with the facts; they must struggle with them until they know them.

There are four basic attitudes that lead to inaccuracy:

Fudging It's easier to guess than to check. It's easier to write down what people probably would say than to interview them. It's easy to exaggerate a bit to give the story more weight. These energy-saving strategies are tempting but fraught with peril. It might not seem very important whether "more than 100," "fewer than 100" or "about 100 people" were trapped in that building, but when a reporter says "more than 100" while colleagues and listeners read "96" in the newspaper the next day, a chunk of that reporter's credibility is lost. Can that reporter be trusted with a storm warning, a charge of corruption, or even a basketball score? Reporters can't keep their jobs if they're not believed.

Assuming William Snee, news director at WHEN in New York, tells this tale: "At a fire scene our reporter noted that there had been an explosion. Actually, firefighters had used an item called a jet axe which makes a loud boom and throws debris. Now he checks."

And a reporter for a local wire service in a major city stumbled on a report that a truck full of turkeys had crashed on a busy freeway. The reporter, naturally enough, assumed that the turkeys were running all over the freeway. That's how he wrote it; that's how it was aired on many local radio stations. Unfortunately, the turkeys turned out to have been frozen. Many a journalist has tumbled into the gap that sometimes yawns between cause and effect. Don't assume!

Sloppiness Reporters' handwriting doesn't have to be neat, as long as they can read a name off their notes. They don't have to ask the officer to repeat that name, as long as they're confident they heard it right the first time. They don't have to double-check the pronunciation, as long as they're positive they have it right. Almost right doesn't count.

Trusting Reporters should not rest their reputation on someone else's credibility. If the police supply a name, reporters should try to double-check it in the phone book or with other officials. If a politician accuses an official of conflict of interest, reporters should double-check to see if that official really has responsibility for sewer contracts. Some newsmakers speak with forked tongues; some make errors. Double-check.

The following story, from ABC's *World News Tonight*, is an example of some misplaced trust and of the proper response to such an error: a correction.

> Just before our final report this evening, a word about last night. We were had -- by the editor of the <u>Forbes</u> business publication <u>FYI</u>. On the strength of <u>Forbes</u>'s reputation, we quoted a report from its current issue that says the Soviet Interior Ministry, in part to raise foreign currency, was going to auction off Lenin's body -- which still lies in state in Moscow. We said last night it was an extraordinary story. More to the point: it isn't true. Just a little joke by <u>Forbes</u> editor Christopher Buckley. . . . We were gullible.
>
> Peter Jennings, ABC

The number of pranksters trying to pull such hoaxes seems to have increased in recent years. Indeed, duping the media is considered something of an art form in some circles. In New York City, for example, someone hired an actor to pretend to be a homeless man willing to sell a body organ for money. Many news organizations were taken in. Double-checking is the best way to avoid being had.

Misunderstanding Small differences in meaning can have large consequences. If the United States signs an arms control agreement with Russia *limiting* the production of a certain missile, calling this a *cutback* is an error. If a policeman had *applied* for a transfer before he was shot, saying that he was about to be transferred is an error—the transfer may not have been approved. If a person has been *indicted* for a crime, it is an error to say the person has been *convicted*. These are all serious misunderstandings. Journalism is nonfiction. Accuracy is the first goal.

Libel

If reporters need the threat of prosecution to keep them accurate, they have it. Inaccurate reporting can lead the station into paying heavy damages for **libel**.

Individuals and clearly defined groups can claim to have been libeled if something reporters have published or broadcast about them **defames** them; in other words, according to the standard definition, "if it exposes them to public hatred, contempt or ridicule; or causes them to be shunned or avoided; or tends to injure them in their occupation."

The term *libel* used to be reserved exclusively for written defamation. Spoken defamation was **slander** and potentially less serious. However, since the advent of the broadcast media, spoken charges can carry as much sting as written charges, and many state laws label defamation on radio or television *libel*—especially if the defamatory statement was read from a prepared script, as most news reports are. But it should be understood that what is called *libel* in this discussion may be known in some states as *slander*.

Only in exceptional circumstances is libel a criminal offense, but a person who claims to have been defamed can sue in civil court.

There are a number of **red flag** words that tend to be defamatory and, therefore, should be used with care. Some—including criminal terms such as "murderer," "rapist" or "thief"—are considered *libelous per se*—in themselves. Here are some more terms that can automatically defame:

adulterer	drunkard
bigamist	ex-convict
briber	fascist
cheat	fool
Communist	gangster
confidence man	grafter
corrupt	mentally ill
crook	Nazi
defaulter	perjurer
drug addict	plagiarist

It also can be libelous per se to use terms that suggest that a person has engaged in clearly improper professional conduct—calling a doctor a quack, for example.

Some words aren't libelous per se, but they can be libelous in context. Saying that a person dislikes blacks may not be automatically libelous, but if that person owns a store in a black neighborhood, it may be judged to be defamatory.

These words or charges are labeled "red flag" because they should be used with care, not because they should never be used. For example, there's nothing necessarily wrong with airing charges that show someone to be corrupt—as long as those charges are true. Similarly, there's nothing necessarily wrong with being sued for libel—as long as the reporter has a solid defense, although it should be noted that mounting a defense against a libel suit can be quite expensive for a station—even if the station wins.

The media have four major defenses to use in court against libel suits. Understanding them is the best way to understand what is and what is not permissible.

Truth This defense is of paramount importance from an ethical standpoint. If the station can prove that that person is corrupt, the station will win in court. If it cannot be proved, why was the charge made in the first place?

Most defamatory charges should be confirmed by trusted sources or, when possible, by documentary evidence before they're aired. If a suit develops, the courts may lean harder on the documentary evidence than the reporter did, but if it's true that the person is corrupt, the lawyers should be able to prove it.

Truth is an absolute defense against a libel action. When libel is at issue, assume that reporting the truth is safe, while an error of fact leaves the reporter vulnerable. If it turns out to have been the person's brother who was taking those bribes, there's no truth defense.

Errors in reporting on criminal proceedings are particularly hazardous. Mistaking an indictment for a conviction can be libelous. Reporting that John Q. Smith was arrested for robbery, when it was John Z. Smith, is cause for legal action by John Q.

One station carried this sentence about allegations of mass murder in California:

```
Two avowed homosexuals are telling police in Riverside,
California, they've been in the murder business for ten
years . . . and may have killed as many as 40 people.
```

It turned out that *both* men had not confessed to these murders; one was released. (And why was it necessary to mention their sexual preference?) Had that man sued for libel, there would have been no truth defense. Once aware that an error like this has been made, the first thing to do, for legal and ethical reasons, is to correct the error, clearly and in such a way that those who heard the false charge are most likely to hear the retraction. In other words, the correction usually should be broadcast on the same hour's newscast—as soon as possible.

Privilege What if a newsmaker makes a false, libelous charge and the reporter merely airs a tape of the newsmaker's statement? Can a reporter and a station be held responsible for airing someone else's defamation? Generally, yes. The station, reporter and newsmaker could all be sued.

Reporters are responsible for the truthfulness of just about everything they air, including quotes or taped statements. Otherwise a reporter could get away with quoting any outlandish charge a person's enemies were willing to make. There are probably people out there who could be inspired to defame quite a few of us. With the exceptions noted below, potentially defamatory charges should be checked and double-checked before being allowed on the air. When in doubt, leave them out.

Still, there are certain charges that the public has a right to hear—whether they're true or not. The second libel defense protects reporters who air charges made in special situations.

Court proceedings couldn't proceed if the participants needed to be concerned with defamation suits. And reporters couldn't cover such proceedings if they had to worry about getting sued for libel for reporting that a witness called someone a murderer. So, the courts have ruled that people have the "privilege" of making such statements in court proceedings and that reporters have the "privilege" of reporting these statements—if their reports are "fair and accurate" and the source of the statement is clearly indicated—without fear of having to pay damages for libel. It doesn't matter whether the charge is true or not. If reporting of that charge was fair, accurate and properly attributed (see Chapter 3, "Meanings"), the fact that it was made in a **privileged** situation is an absolute defense.

Along with judicial proceedings, the administrative or legislative proceedings of governments are privileged. Fair, accurate and properly attributed reports of defamatory charges made by officials in official proceedings are protected. If at a city council meeting the mayor calls the president of the city council a Nazi, reporters can report that charge with impunity. Good reporters will immediately try to determine whether there is any evidence that he is a "Nazi," but the public deserves to hear their mayor's charge anyway.

Some courts have ruled recently that statements made by officials at any public meeting, not just official meetings, are privileged; so even if the mayor made the charge at a press conference, it could still be reported.

Fair Comment What if a film critic reviews a particularly unfortunate movie and accuses the director of being a "sadist"? Or a sports reporter says the local college's basketball coach is "incompetent"? Or a political commentator calls the mayor a "fool"? It would be hard to prove these seemingly defamatory statements to be true. Certainly they are of a different order than the straight news reporting this book has focused on. But such subjective and hyperbolic charges have a role in criticism. Must critics worry about libel when they are expressing their opinions?

The courts have ruled that *fair comment* on matters of public interest is protected; fair comment is a defense in libel suits. Still, there are a few qualifications. Lawyer Robert Lystad, general counsel to the Society of Professional Journalists, points out one: "The statement published must be purely comment or criticism and not an allegation of fact." If facts are involved, they must be correct—it's not "fair" to accuse the coach of never having a winning record when his team won 15 and lost only 12 games two years ago.

Next, the criticism must confine itself to matters relevant to the performance in question—it's not "fair" in a film review to falsely accuse the director of engaging in adultery. Finally, the criticism cannot be purely malicious—it's not "fair" if the reviewer hasn't even seen the play whose director he's defaming, but instead is criticizing the director to satisfy a personal grudge.

The Times *Rule* In recent decades the Supreme Court extended the freedom to criticize public officials and public figures even further. In a case involving the *New York Times*, the court ruled that even defamatory statements about public officials relating to their official conduct or fitness for office in which the facts were wrong *are* protected. All the Court required was that statements be made without *actual malice*—which was defined as "knowledge that a defamatory statement was false or reckless disregard of whether or not it was false." In later cases the Court ruled that public figures, as well as public officials, could be subject to such defamatory statements, as long as the reporting was done without "actual malice." Plaintiffs from a real estate developer to a retired baseball player to retired General William Westmoreland have been treated by the courts as public figures or public officials.

So a reporter can air an attack on the governor in which that official is accused of having been committed to a mental institution, then find out that the governor was really there on an inspection trip, and use *the Times rule* as a defense if the governor sues for libel. To win damages the governor would have to prove that the station knew the charge wasn't true or showed reckless disregard of whether it was true. If it was an honest or even just a negligent mistake, the station is safe.

Haven't the law and ethics diverged here? Why should the courts be protecting false charges that decent reporters would not allow themselves to make? The point is not to protect the false charges, but to protect the news media from being inhibited from reporting any potentially defamatory charges against important people by a fear that these charges might be difficult to prove true in court. By removing the liability for false charges in these situations, the court hoped to free the media to make true charges—their constitutionally protected role.

Nevertheless, the *Times* rule should not be used as a license for sloppy reporting on subjects where people's jobs and reputations are at stake.

■ ■ ■

The bottom line for reporters who are not doing commentary or criticism is this: No charges against people should be aired unless the evidence demonstrates that they are true. The only exceptions are charges made in privileged situations.

The FCC and Fairness

The First Amendment to the Constitution says that Congress shall pass no law abridging freedom of the press. Despite the use of the word *press*—apparently few of the Founding Fathers listened to broadcast news—this sentence does prevent the government from keeping stories off radio and television, too. However, as the courts have interpreted it, the First Amendment does not prevent the government from enforcing some controls on broadcast news.

Radio and television news, unlike any other form of journalism, is specifically regulated by the federal government. This special treatment is generally justified by three arguments—hotly disputed by many broadcasters.

First, it is argued, since the air waves belong to the people—in a way that printing presses do not—the people have some right to control how they are used. Second, since the number of broadcast frequencies is physically limited—in a way that the number of printing presses is not—someone has to determine who gets to use the frequencies and how they're used. Third, since broadcast stations have unusual power to penetrate into people's homes and lives, there is the need for some sort of minimal control over their content.

Broadcasters respond that there are now many more broadcast stations than daily newspapers in most cities; that broadcasters have shown little inclination to misuse their welcome into our homes and that open-market competition is sufficient incentive to keep them from doing so; and, most significantly, that any government regulation of news media opens up frightening possibilities of government censorship and control. In recent years, broadcasters have begun to win this argument.

The Federal Communications Commission is the agency Congress has charged with regulating the air waves. It is composed of five commissioners appointed by the president. With the help of a large staff, they have responsibility for licensing all broadcast stations in the United States. The FCC has the power to refuse to renew the license of a station that it has decided is not acting in the public interest. That's a severe punishment. Essentially, the FCC has the power to put the owners of a broadcast station out of business. To maintain their licenses broadcasters must abide by FCC regulations.

But, in the spirit of deregulation and in deference to the First Amendment, the FCC has been reducing the number of those regulations. The *fairness doctrine*—the FCC regulation that seemed to come closest to limiting news coverage—has been almost completely withdrawn.

The thrust of the fairness doctrine, according to an old FCC informational memorandum, had been this: "If a station presents one side of a controversial issue of public importance, it must afford reasonable opportunity for the presentation of contrasting views." In other words, if a station broadcast an editorial calling for large cuts in military spending, it would have had to give those who believe in less drastic cuts a chance to respond.

That's no longer necessary. As of this writing, only a few small vestiges of the old fairness doctrine remain in effect. They include the requirement that individuals be notified and given a chance to respond if they are the subject of a "personal attack" in a station editorial and the requirement that candidates be given a chance to respond to editorials endorsing opponents during election campaigns. And these vestiges of the old doctrine also were under review.

With most of the fairness doctrine gone, broadcast journalists no longer have a *legal* reason to be fair. *Ethically*, however, nothing has changed. A station should still give opposing voices a chance to respond to its editorials—as most newspapers do in their opinion pages and in letters to the editor. And fairness is obviously an important *ethical* consideration in news coverage: In reporting on federal budget squabbles, for example, it wouldn't do to cover only one side of the debate on military spending.

Being fair is not always easy. Total fairness, like true objectivity (see Chapter 3, "Meanings"), is an unrealizable ideal. In the fraction of a minute a reporter has to devote to an issue, even in a series of reports, it is not feasible to acknowledge all possible points of view, each possible shade of opinion. On military spending, for example, aside from the moderates who argue about the size of cuts in post-cold war military spending, there are some "hawks" who believe that the military budget should be increased, not cut; there are some "doves" who believe we can now do without any army altogether; and there are a myriad of subpositions and subtle variations on each of these points of view. There's no way reporters can be fair to them all.

Somehow, journalists must decide which positions on an issue are the most significant. They must create a working definition of the ethical requirement of fairness. There are many factors that can be considered: how widely positions are held; which positions are most often being discussed in public debates or by governmental bodies; which are most likely to be adopted. Applying these standards to the military spending debate would tend to reduce it to a debate between those who argue that appropriations should be cut by a lot and those who think the cuts should be smaller, so there would be some justification for a reporter emphasizing these positions in a story. The danger here is that unpopular points of view will never get a chance to become popular since the media will never cover them. Therefore, somewhere in a working definition of fairness an attempt should be made to balance this bias toward conventional wisdom.

With most stories, being fair isn't this difficult. It simply requires that in a story about construction of a new downtown expressway, for example, reporters give expression to the argument that it is needed to relieve downtown traffic and the argument that it will merely serve to increase the number of cars downtown.

On a story about welfare, reporters might seek out those who think welfare doesn't provide needy people enough to live on, as well as those who call it a rip-off. If they then give some time to the intermediate position—that the present system is about as good as we can make it—that'll pass for fair.

Reporting fairly means keeping in mind the claims of all groups to coverage and then making decisions without allowing personal beliefs, even if shared by most listeners, to interfere. It is not always possible to be perfectly fair. It is necessary to try. Reporters who have evaluated issues intelligently and who are making such a conscientious effort would not have run afoul of the old fairness doctrine anyway. The withdrawal of the doctrine did not have any real effect on their behavior.

Campaigns and Equal Time

Political campaigns required the most sensitive applications of the fairness doctrine. As of this writing the doctrine still includes special provisions for dealing with candidates for election. For example, if a station endorses one candidate for election, that candidate's opponents must all be notified within 24 hours and offered a chance to respond. If the endorsement was made within 72 hours of the election, the other candidates must be notified *before* the endorsement is aired.

The fairness doctrine was not a law passed by Congress. It was a regulation imposed by a commission empowered by Congress to regulate broadcasting. However, Congress was so sensitive to the power of broadcasts to influence political campaigns that it included in the law establishing the FCC a rule specifically requiring that candidates for political office be given equal time on the air. So, what is called the **equal-time rule** is a law—Section 315 of the Communications Act of 1934. As of this writing, this law was still in effect.

Here's what Section 315 says: "If any licensee shall permit any person who is a legally qualified candidate for any public office to use a broadcasting station, he shall afford equal opportunities to all other such candidates." Station owners, of course, are the "licensees."

Section 315 also requires that candidates not be charged excessive rates for air time. And if one candidate gets time free, all the other candidates must be given

Camera crews
covering an
appearance by a
presidential
candidate.
(Mitchell Stephens)

equal free time. After Johnny Carson invited the mayor of Burbank onto his show, he found he also had to invite the mayor's opponents in an upcoming election. That's the equal-time rule.

There are, however, some very important exceptions to this rule. The equal-time rule does *not* apply to any "bona fide newscast, bona fide news interview, bona fide news documentary . . . or on-the-spot coverage of bona fide news events (including but not limited to political conventions and activities incidental thereto)." In recent decades, the FCC has been steadily lengthening the list of programs that are exempt from the equal-time rule. Broadcasts of news conferences no longer must comply with the rule, nor must debates between candidates for office—so a station can sponsor and broadcast a debate between the Democratic and Republican candidates for mayor, without necessarily including the Burn-the-Textbooks candidate. And shows like *Donahue* and *Geraldo* now count as news programs, which means they, too, are not required to provide equal time.

This is a long list of exemptions. It includes all the types of programs covered by this book. Broadcast journalists do not have to worry about about the equal-time rule. However, they do have an *ethical* responsibility to give all the candidates for an office a reasonable shot at having their views heard. Reporters should be conscious of the need to contact and cover each candidate. Walter Dibble of WTIC in Connecticut points out that sometimes, especially in smaller towns, one candidate will be significantly more articulate than another and much more adept at making news.

In order to maintain balance Dibble won't go so far as to keep the articulate candidate off the air, but he will notify the quiet one of the imbalance and make a special effort to get that candidate's point of view.

Balanced reporting gets difficult when there are minor party candidates in the race. They will get very few of the votes; do they deserve an equal share of the coverage? Most stations will offer some coverage, but not equal coverage. These candidates certainly should not be ignored; that way, predictions about their poor showings in the election become self-fulfilling.

Behavior

If reporters fail to behave responsibly at news events, they can subject already distraught people to additional torment. They must be tactful enough to know when to be pushy and when to be gentle. If reporters fail to behave responsibly in reporting events, they can invade people's privacy, spread violence and throw their own reputations into doubt. This section will also point out that at times, even if they do behave responsibly, reporters can find themselves in jail.

Conflict of Interest

It's simple.

First, reporters shouldn't accept any gifts from the people they may have to write about—no bottles of Scotch, vacations, fountain pens or dinners. Reporters don't even want to be in the position of having to distinguish between a gift and a bribe. Return them all with a polite thank you.

The only gift reporters should accept is information. Good information sources may get their names on the news once or twice in return for a hot tip, but they won't get the news biased in their favor (see Chapter 8, "Gathering News").

Second, reporters should not cover stories in which they have a vested interest. This may require getting rid of stock in potentially controversial companies or resigning from some political or community groups. Or it may require withdrawing from coverage of related issues when they come up—asking someone else to do the story. This is not to say that reporters have to be eunuchs—they can vote, talk politics, do business. But when these concerns become pressing enough so that they spill over into reporting, or even *appear* to, something has to be sacrificed.

Third, there should be no deference in news coverage to the demands of advertisers or other business considerations of the station—no feature story on radishes as a favor to the radish company that sponsors some newscasts; no withholding of a few nasty details about a strike at the local newspaper because that paper happens to be owned by the same gentleman who pays reporters' salaries. Honest hunger for news may require that reporters bite the hand that feeds. And the hand that feeds should know better than to try to manipulate the news.

Privacy

Reporters are in the business of poking their noses into other people's business, and their power is such that they can do a lot of harm to these people. Reporters have to sniff around; that's their function. But there are large areas of people's lives that are off limits.

Nevertheless, the first thing to remember is that there basically is no legal right to privacy *in news*. The name of the victim, the name of the suspect—after arrest—and the name of the person who helped to catch the suspect are all matters of public record and can be broadcast. Any facts about people who appear in the news that are relevant to the story—what they were doing in the area at the time, their ages, marital status, personal characteristics—are fair game.

The only regular exceptions are the names of children—usually under 18—arrested for crimes. Most states have voluntary codes that police and journalists follow which call for these names to be withheld. And most stations also will not broadcast the names of alleged rape victims—in order to make it less painful for victims of this crime to come forward. During the well-publicized William Kennedy Smith date-rape trial in Palm Beach, Florida, in 1991, NBC decided that withholding the name simply reinforced the stigma attached to rape victims. Most other news organizations, however, refused to air the alleged victim's name (until she herself went public after Smith was found innocent). Several states have enacted laws making it a crime to publicize the name of a rape victim. However, the constitutionality of such laws is questionable. This remains more an ethical than a legal question.

Other situations arise that may not be covered by the codes but may call for similar tact. For example, some stations might choose not to carry the names of the people injured in a fire at a homosexual bar.

What's clearly neither acceptable nor legal is dredging up potentially embarrassing facts about people who are *not* directly connected with breaking news. It would be wrong, for instance, to walk into a homosexual bar and broadcast a story revealing the names of the people there. Their **right to privacy** would be protected by privacy laws in most states. They are not involved in news. Reporters have no right making people's private lives public to create a story.

However, the courts have ruled that public figures have surrendered much of their legal right to privacy. If a senator is seen at a gay bar, he would not have the same *legal* right to keep that fact private as would an ordinary citizen. But is it *ethical* to broadcast information about the private lives of public figures? This is a question that has become considerably more pressing in recent years . . . as widely publicized allegations of infidelity surfaced during the presidental campaigns of Gary Hart and Bill Clinton.

The traditional answer was to draw a line for politicians between aspects of their private lives that affect their performance in office and personal quirks that have no bearing on the job they're doing. If the mayor—the argument went—has a mistress, that's his business. If he puts that mistress on the city's payroll, that's our business. But this answer has seemed unsatisfactory lately, for two reasons: First, private behaviors sometimes appear to speak to the public issue of character. If a candidate is a compulsive adulterer, don't voters have a right to know this? Second, these private behaviors sometimes become so widely discussed that a news organization cannot avoid them—if only to report on how they are being discussed.

Most journalists dislike watching presidential campaigns deteriorate into debates on a candidate's sexual behavior. Most would prefer to return to the traditional answer: If it doesn't affect their performance in office, it's none of our business. But few have figured out a way to ignore these stories honestly when they do break. This is a privacy issue that has yet to be settled.

Disorder

When violence erupts, the standard rules of reporting take on added urgency. Those waiting to take to the streets and those prepared to flee to the hills will be listening to broadcast news. An inaccurate report or a sloppily chosen word can spread panic. (The basic guidelines for covering these disturbances are discussed in Chapter 11, "Coverage.") But under the intense pressure of a riot or a terrorist action, these standard rules for reporting disorders may not be enough. The last few decades have taught that responsible reporting of such volatile situations demands a code of behavior for reporters that is stricter than that employed in other types of reporting.

During a riot the line between reporting news and making news may be blurred, with dangerous consequences. Rioters have been known to perform for reporters, and by publicizing a riot reporters may be encouraging others to join in. The solution is certainly not to ignore riots. Overly restricted coverage would leave listeners confused and susceptible to rumors. Nor should reporters become cheerleaders for the police and law and order to the point where the news becomes distorted by this rooting interest.

Much thought has been devoted to preparing special ethical guidelines that reduce the chance of inciting further violence while protecting the public's right to know what's going on. The following list was compiled from the instructions given to reporters at a few major news organizations:

1. *Stay in the background.* This is no time to trumpet the fact that a station has a reporter on the scene. Awareness that reporters are there may amplify the disturbance. Using cars *without* the station's call letters displayed may help. Reporters should also keep their conversations to a minimum and forsake the loud pursuit of interviews.

2. *Wait.* This is one situation where broadcast reporters slow down! Most stations don't carry live reports on a disturbance. CBS requires the permission of the network news division's president or vice president before it will report live on a riot. And stations delay their taped reports until some perspective is available on the situation. Reporters should secure appraisals of the seriousness of the situation from responsible officials *before* they file reports. Tape of angry rioters or scared witnesses should not be used unless their statements can be placed in clear perspective—shouted charges balanced, rumors of destruction verified and made specific.

3. *Hold addresses.* The exact location of the violence tells thrill seekers and looters exactly where to go. Most stations will hold the exact address until police have control of the situation. Occasionally, however, police will ask that the address be broadcast to keep people out of the area—obviously this is a time to be in close contact with police and city officials.

Riots, hijackings and terrorist actions resemble small wars, and, as in war coverage, reporters may become responsible for withholding additional information to help police. With terrorists inside, for example, it would not be too smart to reveal on the air exactly where the police are waiting for them outside. Terrorists, too, can tune in.

Again, communicating with officials is all-important. They cannot be allowed unnecessary censorship—reporters aren't going to withhold the fact that there are terrorists in that building; but police officials must be given an opportunity to go about their business without having their tactical secrets given away over the air.

Disorders are situations where a healthy extra dose of discretion must be added to the reporter's standard considerations.

Panic

Reporters also run the risk of needlessly causing panic in situations of less magnitude than riots.

"There's been a wreck involving a green, late-model Chevy." Tom Black, news director at WOHS in North Carolina, heard that on the radio one day and wondered how many people must have been "worried to death" in a town where so many might have a family member or friend in that kind of car. The tactful decision here would have been just to report the accident without the description of the car or to wait until the families were notified and then use names. The power of radio or television to induce panic must be considered.

For another example, ABC and most other news organizations never mention an air crash until they have the flight number. Too many listeners would start shaking if they heard "An airplane crashed while landing at Chicago's O'Hare Airport this evening." (Incidentally, most stations reschedule all airline commercials after news of a crash—the sensitivities being protected here are those of the sponsors.)

Staging

Events don't always behave. Demonstrators may stop chanting before reporters turn their tape recorders on. The police officer may put down his walkie-talkie before the television crews have begun filming. The black students may enter the previously all-white school before reporters are in position to describe the scene.

It's tempting, therefore, to stage events—to ask demonstrators to start chanting again, to ask the police officer to fake that call-in for the camera, to ask the mothers to take their children and repeat their walk into the school. This is especially seductive when radio reporters are working with tape or when television reporters are working with videotape. Getting good sound or good visuals can be an important part of getting the story. News directors may frown on reporters who come back without tape of the chanting demonstrators.

Be that as it may, *staging* is clearly unethical. Reporters observe events; they do not direct events. Once they cross that line and help shape events, those events lose their integrity and reporters lose their integrity. Staged events are phony. The news should include only what "really" happens.

Better to come back without tape of the chanting. Asking demonstrators to repeat it is wrong. Asking rioters to throw another rock through a window so a reporter can get the sound—the ultimate example of staging—is outrageous.

Reenactments

As the competition in "nonfiction television" increased during the late 1980s and early 1990s, some journalists began chafing under the restriction that they show only events their cameras had actually witnessed. Why not *reenact* some dramatic events? If we missed the scene where the alleged spy turned over the briefcase, why not have actors re-create that scene? Soon even network news departments were including reenactments on one or two of their shows—with the segments carefully labeled, of course.

It didn't take long, however, before journalism critics and other journalists began coming up with the "why nots?" Reenactments blur a crucial line: between fiction and nonfiction. That alleged spy, to pursue the example, denies ever having turned over that briefcase. Even if he had, how do we know what expression might have been on his face, what he might have said, what he might have worn? All that is guesswork, yet the actors portray it as if it were fact. To what extent might this scene have been distorted? How are we to judge whether the "journalists" behind it can be trusted? Once journalists enter the world of fiction, their credibility seems to slip away.

The reenactment fad rapidly faded. Few news organizations will now engage in it. There are enough dramatic events happening within reach of television cameras. Journalists are wise to confine themselves to those events.

Hidden Mikes

In the course of investigations, reporters have occasionally resorted to the use of hidden microphones to reveal unsavory practices or catch newsmakers dissembling. This sort of trickery is illegal under federal law unless at least one party to the conversation is aware that it's being taped—that party can be the reporter. What this means is that a conversation between two unaware people cannot be "bugged," but reporters can record conversations in which they themselves or their agents participate.

The FCC also outlaws surreptitious recording that uses hidden transmitters. The tape recorder has to be on the scene. The conversation cannot be transmitted elsewhere.

Some state laws go even further. They require the consent of both parties before a conversation can be recorded. Hidden mikes are not allowed in these states, and they're treated circumspectly by most newsrooms even where they are legal. Some avoid the technique entirely; others use it only in connection with police or prosecutors who are working on a case.

Clearly, hidden microphones, if used at all, should be reserved for crucial stories—official corruption, organized crime—not to catch a football coach verbally attacking one of his players. There's something shady about trapping someone with a hidden mike. The alleged crime has to be pretty serious to warrant it.

Protecting Sources

Some newsmakers only talk to the press if their names, or some of their information, will be kept secret. That's fair enough. Often these people fear for their jobs; occasionally they're discussing potentially criminal behavior. Reporters are willing to trade confidentiality for important information. And this bargain may be more than just ethically binding. The Supreme Court has held that the First Amendment does not protect the news media from being sued for breaking a promise of confidentiality. Depending on what state law applies, a source may successfully sue a TV or radio station if it publishes his or her name after a reporter promised to keep that name confidential.

But what happens if the confidential information or the name of that informant becomes relevant to criminal proceedings and a judge orders the reporter to turn it over to help determine someone's guilt or innocence? Do reporters have any more right to withhold information from a court, even the name of a confidential source or something they have sworn to keep secret, than other citizens? Most reporters say that, like doctors, lawyers or priests, they do have such a right. Otherwise, they argue, they can't do their jobs. But the Supreme Court says reporters have no absolute right to conceal information from courts.

The Supreme Court reached that conclusion while considering the cases of several reporters, including Paul Pappas, a television reporter with WTEV in Massachusetts. Pappas had been allowed to enter Black Panther Party headquarters to cover a police raid that was expected that evening. In return, he promised not to disclose anything else he observed at the party's headquarters. There was no raid. Pappas did no story, but a grand jury investigating the Panthers subpoenaed him to testify about what had happened while he was at Panther headquarters. Pappas refused—unwilling to violate his pledge. The Supreme Court ruled that the grand jury's right to subpoena witnesses superseded Pappas's pledge.

This is an issue on which reporters' own ethical codes and in some cases their legal responsibility to their sources collide with the legal right to a fair trial. Reporters' moral sense and their view of what is required to do their jobs effectively may tell them that they have to keep their word and keep sources confidential. But the Supreme Court says that defying a court by refusing to reveal sources is illegal. Reporters have spent as many as 46 days in jail in defense of their position.

Many states have made the situation less difficult for reporters by enacting *shield laws*—laws that give reporters the legal right to withhold confidential information and the names of their sources in court. Reporters should check whether there is such a law in their state. But the case of *New York Times* reporter M. A. Farber has thrown the power of shield laws into question. Farber was jailed for refusing to turn over to the judge some information a defense attorney wanted in a state that has a shield law (New Jersey). Also, the absence of a federal shield law leaves reporters unprotected in the federal system.

Where confidential material is involved, reporters may have to consider—*before* agreeing to protect the identity of a news source—whether they are prepared to go to jail.

Access

So far this chapter has outlined reporters' responsibilities. Now it's time to consider some of their rights.

Reporting is gathering information. Access—the ability to get to that information—is essential. There are some special procedures that help reporters get close to the news. Reporters are given their own seating areas by governmental bodies; they are often permitted to visit areas that are off limits to the rest of the public; a press card can often get them past police or fire lines. Hospitals and police departments have also set up special procedures for releasing information to the press.

Nonetheless, the courts so far have generally been unwilling to concede that the news media have the right to special access to information. No one has any more legal obligation to talk to a journalist than to any other private citizen. Recent court rulings would also seem to imply that reporters have no more legal right than others to "trespass" on private property. Reporters certainly can be kept out of homes. Privacy laws specifically protect people who are not involved in news from "intrusion upon their seclusion or solitude." And courts have ruled that reporters can be evicted from public places such as restaurants if they are causing a nuisance.

So, with the exception of the special procedures some organizations have set up, reporters are in the same position as the rest of the public when it comes to gaining access to information. Fortunately, the public's right to know at least what its government leaders are up to has been broadened considerably in recent years.

Courts

As a rule, trials are open to the public and therefore open to reporters. Most hearings and appellate proceedings are also open to reporters. In exceptional circumstances, however, judges have closed the proceedings in which they are presiding to the public and the press. In most states that requires an awfully compelling excuse — such as the need to protect secret testimony — and the judge has to open proceedings when the excuse is no longer valid. Reporters cannot be excluded just to punish them.

One area where reporters are always denied access is grand jury hearings. These hearings, which determine whether there is enough evidence to indict a suspect, are secret — to protect suspects from publicity in connection with crimes of which they may never even be formally accused.

Judges' deliberations are also private, and sometimes out of their deliberations have come alarming strategies for keeping what goes on in open courtrooms private. Desire to control publicity and reporters has inspired some judges to impose **gag orders** specifically prohibiting reporters from broadcasting or printing certain information. These gag orders would seem to be direct violations of reporters' First Amendment right to report without prior restraint, and they have consistently been overturned on appeal. Unfortunately, by that time the damage may already have been done. The Supreme Court has ruled that courts should protect defendants' rights to trials untainted by excessive publicity through their own efforts — sequestering juries, changing the location of trials, ordering participants in a trial not to talk to the news media — rather than by abridging reporters' rights.

Reporters' rights to get into courtrooms are generally protected, and their right to report on what they see is certainly protected; but once in a courtroom, reporters have no right to interfere physically with proceedings. They are as vulnerable as anyone else to contempt citations for disruptive or unruly behavior. Judges cannot tell reporters how to report, but they can tell them not to hound the trial's participants in court, not to smoke in court, or, occasionally, even what to wear in court (in Maine: ties and jackets for men, dresses or skirts for women).

And judges' control of their courtrooms can go beyond decorum. In some state courts and most federal courts, broadcast journalists lose their major tools, cameras and tape recorders, when they enter a courtroom or even a courthouse. This fear of cameras and recording devices dates back to the wild courtroom scenes at the Lindbergh kidnapping trial in 1934. Even in states where cameras and mikes are allowed at trials, the judge may retain control of such key matters as the placement of microphones and cameras and may limit the numbers of cameras and mikes (often requiring broadcast crews to "pool" their efforts). There may be additional restrictions against showing pictures of child witnesses or victims of sexual crimes. But most states now allow cameras and microphones at most trials, and the federal courts may be moving to open up as well.

Police

Laws, codes or official guidelines in many states spell out what information on crimes the police *should* make available to reporters. Here's the standard list:

1. Basic factual information on the defendant including name (unless underage), age, address, job and marital status.

2. The exact charge.
3. The name of the agency that made the arrest and information on the investigation, if there was one.
4. Basic facts on the arrest, including where it happened, whether the suspect resisted, whether there was a chase, any weapons that were used and a description of anything that was seized.

Reporters should insist that they be provided with all this information within a reasonable period of time. However, there are some facts that laws, codes or guidelines require that the police not disclose. The idea is to protect the defendant's right to a fair trial by keeping potentially prejudicial statements from potential jurors. The standard list of information police are instructed *not* to release:

1. Reports of confessions.
2. Statements about polygraph tests, fingerprints, ballistic tests or laboratory tests.
3. Statements about the credibility of potential witnesses and anticipated testimony.
4. Opinions on evidence or arguments that may be used at the trial.
5. The criminal records of suspects.

News organizations often join with police and prosecutors in pledging to withhold such material. Nevertheless, the police on occasion do let information slip, and this restricted material—especially in major cases—has been known to find its way onto the air.

Incidentally, such official documents as the police *"blotter"*—a record of what the police have been up to—and arrest records are public records and therefore open to inspection by the public. Reporters should be able to look them over (see Chapter 11, "Coverage").

Hospitals

Medical personnel are obviously more concerned with treating their patients than satisfying journalists, but most hospitals recognize their responsibility to keep the public informed. Hospitals should be expected to designate someone (see Chapter 11, "Coverage") to provide reporters with this basic information on newsworthy patients within a reasonable period of time:

1. The name, address, age, occupation and marital status of patients.
2. The general nature of the injuries—what parts of the body have been injured, what bones broken, the degree of seriousness of burns.
3. If the person is dead, the time of death and the person's name—after next of kin have been notified. (Even if reporters can get the name elsewhere, they should give officials reasonable time to tell relatives.) Hospitals should also release the cause of death—but only after it has been confirmed, and that may mean waiting for an autopsy.

4. The condition of patients—usually labeled with one of these terms (in increasing order of severity): *good, satisfactory, fair, poor, serious* or *critical.*

These guidelines represent standard practice, but they're not legal requirements. At some smaller hospitals, reporters may have to employ all their persuasiveness, aggressiveness and moral authority to get hospital officials to satisfy their ethical obligation to keep the public informed.

Hospital officials generally do not, and should not be expected to, speculate on matters with legal implications, such as whether a patient was drunk, shot or a suicide victim. They leave that information to the police to release.

Hospital officials should be expected to cooperate with journalists. And journalists have an even more serious responsibility to hospital officials—staying out of the way. Lifesaving efforts come first (see Chapter 11, "Coverage").

Government Records

Officials push lots of paper. Written on those papers can be material of interest to the public and therefore of interest to reporters. Often the material is embarrassing to the officials who control it. In the past there were many ways to hide embarrassing papers. Federal officials stamped them "secret"; local officials locked them in cabinets. But in recent decades legal moves have helped get these documents out in the open. These laws are often called **sunshine laws,** and they bring to mind the expression, "Sunshine is the best disinfectant."

The federal *Freedom of Information Act* strictly limits the information the federal government can classify as "sensitive," and it streamlines the process of getting information released. Hundreds of employees of the FBI and CIA alone are now involved in finding information the public has requested under the law. Although the process requires time and lawyers (the Reagan Administration made it more difficult), reporters have been able to use this law to shed light on some of the less savory activities of the government.

For instance, NBC reporter Carl Stern once used the law to expose a questionable FBI counterintelligence program. Stern had noticed the code name "COINTELPRO New Left" on the bottom of some documents that had been stolen from an FBI office. He became curious. Stern asked the FBI director to explain and was rebuffed. His contacts on Capitol Hill didn't know what COINTELPRO was and Stern's best official sources wouldn't say anything—even off the record. All this secrecy made the story sound even more intriguing.

With his traditional means of getting information exhausted, Stern filed an official request with the FBI for the documents on the program under the terms of the FOI Act. He asked for anything they had on the "establishment, disestablishment or modification" (these are not words Stern would use on the air) of COINTELPRO New Left. The FBI said "sorry" and argued that this was sensitive material. So Stern and his lawyers filed an official complaint in U.S. District Court, asking the judge to examine the documents "in camera"—in private—to determine if the FBI's excuse for withholding them was valid under the FOI Act. The judge ruled that release of the documents would not threaten national security and ordered the FBI to turn them over.

There was plenty in those papers that was newsworthy. With the help of the FOI Act, Stern had uncovered evidence that the FBI had set up a program of spying on and disrupting radical groups, using methods that were of questionable legality. Stern had quite a story. Congressional and judicial investigations soon followed.

All 50 states now have sunshine laws that provide some form of public access to *state* and *local* government documents. These laws are not specifically designed for reporters. They are designed for all citizens, but reporters, as the eyes of the public, are often in a position to do the most with them.

Reporters should get a copy of their state's sunshine law, as well as the FOI Act, and familiarize themselves with them. Often they won't have to take "no" for an answer when they ask to see a document. The law will be behind them.

Government Meetings

Much reporting on government is reporting on meetings; yet again there are government agencies that feel more comfortable if no one is watching them go about their (or our) business. Reporters often have to fight to keep meetings open. Fortunately, most states now have laws to help reporters win those fights.

Such laws generally require that all meetings of state and local government agencies at which business is being discussed be open to the public. The only exceptions usually are portions of meetings where personnel matters, business transactions, litigation or investigations of wrongdoing are being discussed.

Despite these laws, the public's elected representatives often go to great lengths to keep the public out. They may look for such loopholes as the word "meeting" itself, and call their meeting a "work session" because work session may not be specifically mentioned in the **open meeting law**. All else having failed, an Iowa school board once met in the men's room to keep a female reporter out.

It's the reporter's responsibility to challenge these dodges and keep meetings that should be open open, even if it requires threatening, or going through with, legal action. Again, knowledge of the state open meeting law is invaluable. Reporters have to be prepared to mind not only their own ethical and legal responsibilities but others' responsibilities as well.

Wrap-Up

These laws and ethical requisites are complex. Is it necessary that broadcast reporters master them? Yes. Simply behaving decently gets reporters through most situations, but good reporters inevitably reach situations where what they are doing hurts someone, or what someone else is doing is hurting reporters' ability to do their job. At these times, reporters need to have a clear picture of their rights and responsibilities.

Here is one summary of the responsibilities of broadcast journalists:

RADIO–TELEVISION NEWS DIRECTORS ASSOCIATION
CODE OF BROADCAST NEWS ETHICS

The responsibility of radio and television journalists is to gather and report information of importance and interest to the public accurately, honestly and impartially.

The members of the Radio–Television News Directors Association accept these standards and will:

1. Strive to present the source or nature of broadcast news material in a way that is balanced, accurate and fair.

   A. They will evaluate information solely on its merits as news, rejecting sensationalism or misleading emphasis in any form.
   B. They will guard against using audio or video material in a way that deceives the audience.
   C. They will not mislead the public by presenting as spontaneous news any material which is staged or rehearsed.
   D. They will identify people by race, creed, nationality or prior status only when it is relevant.
   E. They will clearly label opinion and commentary.
   F. They will promptly acknowledge and correct errors.

2. Strive to conduct themselves in a manner that protects them from conflicts of interest, real or perceived. They will decline gifts or favors which would influence or appear to influence their judgments.
3. Respect the dignity, privacy and well-being of people with whom they deal.
4. Recognize the need to protect confidential sources. They will promise confidentiality only with the intention of keeping that promise.
5. Respect everyone's right to a fair trial.
6. Broadcast the private transmissions of other broadcasters only with permission.
7. Actively encourage observance of this code by all journalists, whether members of the Radio–Television News Directors Association or not.

19

Programming

One of the first experiments in transmitting the human voice through the air was a newscast, Lee De Forest's broadcast in New York City of the 1916 presidential election results. Unfortunately, if this was the birth of broadcast journalism, the profession got off to a bad start. De Forest mistakenly announced that Charles Evans Hughes had been elected.

The first broadcast by a commercial radio station, KDKA in Pittsburgh, was a news broadcast—also presidential election results, the election of 1920. This time they got the results right.

Radio and radio news moved into living rooms together. After a long but eventually successful battle with newspapers for the right to use the wire services, radio news established itself as the most sprightly news source, as radio was establishing itself as the country's dominant communication medium.

About 20 million people heard the name of the winner of the 1924 presidential election on their radios before they read it in a newspaper. Only about 500 had been listening to KDKA four years earlier. Charles Lindbergh's flight across the Atlantic in 1927 and the kidnapping of his baby in 1932 provided radio with further opportunities to show off its speed and its ability to dominate the coverage of breaking events.

But the most striking exhibition of the power of radio came on December 7, 1941, with these words from CBS newsman John Daly: "The Japanese have attacked Pearl Harbor, Hawaii, by air. . . ." That news broke on a Sunday afternoon. Since there are no Sunday afternoon newspapers, many Americans spent the remainder of the afternoon and evening by their radios, and radio stayed on top of the story.

If the Spanish-American War and World War I were newspaper wars, World War II certainly belonged to radio. Newspapers, and even newsreels, could not match the drama of Edward R. Murrow's voice describing the German bombing of London:

> The fires up the river had turned the moon blood-red. The smoke had drifted down till it formed a canopy over the Thames. The guns were working all around us, the bursts looking like fireflies on a southern summer night.*

After the war, the era of families gathering around the radio ended as it had begun—with the introduction of a new medium. Television stole radio's variety

*Robert Metz, *CBS: Reflections in a Bloodshot Eye* (New York: Signet, 1975), p. 99.

442

shows, soap operas, comedies, dramas, game shows and much of its audience. It also started moving in on the news.

When primitive experiments in remote televison reporting were conducted in 1937, it took two buses to house all the necessary equipment. The introduction of commerical television was delayed by World War II, but in 1945 NBC set up a television news service, staffed initially by veterans of movie newsreels. By 1947, NBC was telecasting the Camel News Caravan with John Cameron Swayze and CBS its Television News with Douglas Edwards. The progression of network television anchors that was to lead through Huntley, Brinkley, Cronkite, Reasoner, Walters, Chancellor, Reynolds, Mudd, Brokaw, Jennings and Rather was underway. Over the next two decades, television news cameras captured and transformed everything from presidential election campaigns to abuses at mental hospitals. And in Vietnam, we had our first televised war.

Despite the competition, however, radio journalism also continued to develop and to expand.

According to the Federal Communications Commission, there are about 5,000 AM and 6,100 FM radio stations in the United States. In addition, there are about 680 VHF (very high frequency—channels 2 to 13) and more than 800 UHF (ultra-high frequency—channels 14 and beyond) television stations. Almost all these broadcast stations carry some news and public affairs programming; most feature regular newscasts. And most of the thousands of cable television systems snaking from house to house across the country also transmit some news. Why?

There are two factors that have kept the news on radio and television: First, it's something the broadcast media do well. Newspapers can't keep up with the speed of broadcast news, nor can they compete with the sounds or sights broadcast news features. On radio, frequent newscasts are a relatively inexpensive service to provide listeners. On television, newscasts cost considerably more, but they attract large audiences and are frequently a local station's most profitable shows. And the Cable News Network has demonstrated that cable can do at least one type of news well— all-news television.

The second factor that kept the news on broadcast television was the FCC (see Chapter 18, "Ethics and Law"), which has the power to license radio and television stations. A radio license must be renewed every seven years, a television license every five years. The FCC used to make it clear that the amount of news and public affairs programming was one of the criteria it used when deciding if a station met the "public interest needs and desires of the community in which it is located." But in recent years the FCC has retreated from this position, and a number of radio stations have, consequently, reduced their news programming.

Formats

Important as the news is, it still plays second fiddle on most broadcast stations. This doesn't mean much for television newscasts. These shows have their own identities, and whether they come on after a silly situation comedy or a tear-jerking, made-for-TV movie won't have much effect on the content of the newscast. That's not the case on radio.

Competition from television forced radio programmers to figure out what they could do better than television. In most cases the answer turned out to be: play recorded music. Although with the introduction of music videos television is moving in on this area too, most radio stations have chosen to attract audiences by playing records, tapes and CDs, as this list of the percentage of people (12 and older) who listen to each radio format makes clear:

1.	Adult Contemporary	18.35
2.	News/Talk	14.6
3.	Top 40	11.9
4.	Country	11.0
5.	Album-Oriented Rock	9.1
6.	Urban Contemporary	8.8
7.	Oldies	6.3
8.	Spanish	4.0
9.	Adult Standards	3.5
10.	Classic Rock	3.3
11.	Easy Listening	2.5
12.	Adult Alternative	2.1
13.	Religious	2.0
14.	Classical	1.7
15.	Modern Rock	0.9
16.	All Other	0.1

With the exception of number 2, and perhaps number 13, on this list, these are all music formats. So the news is something of an interruption in the programming of most of the radio stations in the United States. Listeners get a few minutes of the latest murders, meetings and markets, with something from Washington, Moscow and the state capitol; then it's back to Michael Jackson. That's why many radio newsrooms are conscious of the need to complement their stations' formats—to make the jump from music to news as smooth as possible. Of course, this does not mean that contemporary stations stick to news about REM or that classical stations include items about the 19th century. News is still news, and no adjustment to a format is going to turn it into music.

But newsrooms *have* found less direct ways of reflecting their stations' formats. Top-40 stations, for example, make an attempt to copy the tempo of their music—snappy and fast—in their newscasts. The news director of KWEB, Minnesota, Brad Larson, explains: "Ours is an up-tempo, contemporary music station, and we design our newscasts to be upbeat and current. Newscasts are short and to the point." This might mean stories that are only 15 to 20 seconds long and newscasters who read at a slightly faster pace. John Erickson, a news director in Portland, Oregon, puts it succinctly: "KGW is a rocker, and we keep the tempo up."

The writing on a rock station also tends to be more dramatic and colorful:

> A fiery accident involving a sports car and an Amtrak
> turbo-liner has claimed the lives of two I-S-U students.
>
> WBNQ, Illinois

A classical music station, on the other hand, might go in the opposite direction and make its stories somewhat longer and less hectic. These stations try to strike a straightforward, sober note:

> A group of former mental patients has released a
> previously unpublished state report . . . detailing
> charges of beatings, contraband and deaths at the
> Fairview state hospital. The group opposes involuntary
> psychiatric treatment . . . and wants the state to close
> this hospital for the criminally insane.
>
> WFLN, Philadelphia

Most news directors are conscious of who listens to their station and are conscientious about providing information of value to them. Peter Tonks, news director of WWLE, a middle-of-the-road station in New York State, says, "Our target audience is 40-plus in age; therefore we attempt to gear our news reports to subjects and information of interest to an older, often retired audience." Tonks looks for health-care stories and may use a story about Social Security that other stations in the area would pass up.

KWSO in California is a religious station, and the news staff there too lets the station's format affect the news they write. News director Gary Hurley says he focuses on information his listeners would like to hear and leaves the "gore and smut" to others. If the station felt called upon to report a story about a rape, Hurley says his station would substitute the word "assault."

Here we're beginning to run afoul of basic journalistic principles. KWSO seems to hide facts so as not to offend its listeners. Fitting the news to the format should not require suspending the rules of honest journalism. In any case, some news directors will have none of it. They refuse to make any concessions to whatever is filling the time between newscasts. The news is the news, they maintain, and should be done properly.

Markets

The product that commercial radio and television stations market is their audience. Essentially they are selling their listeners' or viewers' ears or eyes to advertisers. The more people who tune in—measured by rating services such as Arbitron or Nielsen—the more they can charge for commercials. The more they charge, the more they can pay for salaries and equipment.

That's one effect of station size on the news. There's another effect: A station with a view of Manhattan's East Side looks for different things in the news than a station that looks out on Iowa cornfields. To understand broadcast news, it is important to understand how a station's size, usually measured by its potential audience, shifts its view of what's news. This variation in news judgment is apparent in television as well as in radio, but it's demonstrated here using three radio stations as examples.

Small

KOEL's offices sit between a park the station's editorials helped build and acres of corn and soybeans. Oelwein's small downtown area is just down the road.

A majority of the radio stations in this country operate in small towns like Oelwein, Iowa (population 7,800); towns small enough so that a good portion of the station's listeners have at one time or another exchanged pleasantries with every person mentioned in a news story; small enough so that a fender-bender on South Frederick Street can be the station's lead story because many of the station's listeners will either have seen the sheriff's car zip by or will be driving on South Frederick themselves sometime that day. There aren't many murderers, world leaders or movie stars passing through, but there is still plenty of important news. People in these towns rely on their radios to tell them whether the school board has decided to build a new high school, what the markets are paying for soybeans this morning and whether rain is going to force them to get the crops in fast. News in a small town is measured more by effect than by interest.

These are called **small-market** stations because the audience they offer to advertisers is small. Generally any area smaller than the metropolitan areas with the 100 largest populations is considered a small market. The neighboring towns of Waco and Temple, Texas, are together labeled a small market, as is Bakersfield, California, or Americus, Georgia. Because these stations sell advertisers the smallest audiences, they charge the lowest rates—often under 25 dollars to play a 30-second spot 12 times. In big cities that same spot could cost hundreds of dollars.

Small-market stations take in less money, so they have less money to spend on news staff. Often disk jockeys themselves move over to the computer and the wire-service printer to put together a newscast. Stations that can afford a news director may expect that person to double as a record spinner. According to an Associated Press study, the average small-market radio station has between two and three people on its news staff.

Even when a small station can hire full-time newspeople, there's no room for specialists who can write the news but not report it on the air or who have a great voice but no ability to write a lead-in or work the audio board. If a small station has a news staff, the people on it must be versatile.

The news on KOEL in Oelwein? A robbery at gunpoint in a store in a nearby town is news, as is a plan introduced at a council meeting to turn an old school building into a health clinic, or two people hospitalized after a car accident or someone's plan to challenge a speeding ticket in court. Almost anything exceptional that happens to the area's citizens is news on KOEL.

KOEL's news director, Dick Petrik, believes in getting as many names on the air as possible. The station broadcasts death notices from local funeral homes, and someone phones the local hospitals to put together special reports on patients. In a small market, listeners know many of those names.

Petrik looks through a pile of stories from last night's newscasts for anything that is still timely or could be updated. He finds an item about a local man injured in an automobile accident. A quick call to the hospital; Petrik gets the man's condition and in a few moments has written up a second-day story. Soon he's back on the phone dialing one of the many people he'll check with during the morning. "Got anything good, bad or indifferent for me?" Petrik asks.

Medium

In the middle of the newsroom at WRVA in Richmond, Virginia, are a large desk, a typewriter and a board covered with so many tape recorders, switches, blinking lights and dials that the news director himself says he isn't sure how to work all of them. Five different police and fire radio frequencies are constantly monitored here. Tapes are recorded on two reel-to-reel recorders, then edited and transferred to carts. Reports are received from a two-way radio system, direct lines to the State Capitol and City Hall and five regular telephone lines. One of these lines was used to patch in reporter Dave Miller's conversations with a sniper who eventually shot himself. (This is the incident illustrated in the photograph on page 3.)

Sitting at a desk in front of this electronic display is the editor on duty, John Harding. Right now all this gadgetry isn't doing Harding any good. He has a 10-minute newscast to do in less than an hour and not enough fresh news to fill it.

Harding has the misfortune of working the morning shift in what is generally considered to be an "afternoon news town." All morning WRVA has been leading with a story on a heart transplant at a local hospital—but it's the third transplant this week, and the novelty had worn off the story even before it was broadcast over and over this morning.

Reports on the police radio of car thefts and minor accidents continue to interrupt Harding's thoughts. But these stories are not significant enough to be news in an area this size where few listeners are likely to know any of the people involved.

Richmond is considered a *medium market*. With its suburbs, it has the 45th largest population of any metropolitan area in the country. The 30th to the 100th largest metropolitan areas are generally labeled medium markets. Salt Lake City is one, as are Green Bay and Peoria.

WRVA has three women and five men hired to fill their newscasts with stories more newsworthy than minor accidents. (That AP study says the average medium-market radio station employs four people to do the news.) The entire news staff at WRVA can write, report and read the news on the air. At this moment, one reporter is covering a hearing on teacher certification at the State Capitol; another is at a hearing on waste disposal at City Hall; a third reporter is with Harding in the newsroom, using the phone and preparing copy for later newscasts.

Harding doesn't have much news worthy of a medium-market station until he hears a report on the police radio about a suspect mistakenly released from jail—that's news. Then, he finds out police have a new theory about a body that was fished from the James River a couple of days ago. They are now calling it a homicide—that's news. Harding's newscast is beginning to fall into place. He needs murders and escapes, not robberies and accidents, to interest his listeners.

Other stories he uses this hour: A former home for the elderly is being turned into an apartment complex; a new elementary school gets the okay in a Richmond suburb; another suburb postpones discussion of a county sewer plan.

Minutes before Harding goes on the air, reporter Dave Miller at the State Capitol phones in a story about an attack by a candidate for governor on the state's power company (see "Introduction"). "There's nobody alive who isn't interested in electric rates!" Harding exclaims. That's news. That's also the hour's lead story on WRVA.

Large

Almost one out of every ten people who listen to radio in the Unted States turns to a New York City station. This is the largest of the large markets. Here names don't attract listeners; people barely know their neighbors, let alone some guy who smashed his car in Queens. Robberies of grocery stores do not make news here; murders have to be creative to get coverage. New suburban elementary schools and sewer plans are usually ignored—unless someone has organized a demonstration.

The **large markets** are the 30 largest metropolises in the country. These are the cities with major league sports teams. Los Angeles is second largest, Chicago third, Philadelphia fourth. Hundreds of thousands of people may hear a spot broadcast on a station in one of these cities. Advertisers have to pay for all those potential customers.

If New York City listeners tune to WCBS-AM, they hear news—that is all the station broadcasts. WCBS is one of two stations in the city, and about 100 in the country, that broadcasts all-news. Even in a town that's filled with spicy events like New York, all-news is a hungry business. Instead of having to put together a newscast that lasts 5 or 10 or even 20 minutes, WCBS's staff has to fill the whole hour with news, and as soon as that's done, there's the next hour to fill.

The person responsible for filling two of the most important of these hours is staring at the wire copy on her desk. Associate producer Liz Shanov writes and orders the news that is broadcast from 5 to 7 p.m.—most of the evening drive time. (It can take quite some time for New Yorkers to drive home.)

Actually Liz Shanov will end up writing only 30 minutes of copy herself. The rest of her two hours of news will be filled with reports produced by one of the largest radio news organizations in the world, supported by the money advertisers are willing to pay for all those listeners. Of course not every New York City station makes a big production out of the news. Some make do with a news staff of two or three. All-news is the most expensive radio format, however, and WCBS does not stint on staff or resources. (According to the AP's study, the average major-market radio station employs between six and seven news people. All-news stations, obviously, need much larger news staffs.)

Three reporters are now out in the field collecting the evening's news for WCBS. Another reporter in a **tape-operations room** is recording phoners. The editorial director is recording opinions next door. A helicopter pilot/reporter is getting ready to follow the evening's traffic jams. A traffic reporter in the newsroom is on the phone with the police. A business expert at *Business Week* magazine is preparing a report on the gross national product. A sports reporter is next to a radio, listening to an afternoon game on another station. A meteorologist is studying the dials in a weather center the station built in his home. Other CBS-owned stations are phoning in stories they think New York may be able to use. And of course, the CBS network is preparing to feed national and international news on the hour, plus sports and a separate tennis report.

Besides Shanov, two other people in the newsroom are now writing copy for earlier or later hours. Two desk assistants are collecting news on the phone or ripping it off the wires. And all this activity is being coordinated by an executive producer sitting at a large desk at one end of the WCBS newsroom. At the other end is the studio where two of WCBS's least formal newscasters are going on the air: "When the temperature's higher than my golf score," one says, "I know it's getting hot."

Shanov begins choosing news with a stop at the executive producer's desk. All the material that has come into the newsroom that day is either sitting on his desk or in his wastepaper basket. For instance, it's the executive producer who decides that a murder at a bar is not of much interest to the listeners—there are a few murders most days in New York City. But the executive producer decides to save a story off the wires about the strange death of 60 ducks on Long Island.

There are whole wires in the major markets devoted just to local news (see Chapter 7, "Sources"). More copy ends up in the executive producer's wastepaper basket than on his desk.

The news in New York that day? Finger-pointing following a recent power blackout; the cousin of the late mob leader Carlo Gambino sentenced to jail; sewage washing up on five Long Island beaches. Shanov says: "These beaches are immediately to the west of Jones Beach, where everybody goes to escape the heat. That's what makes this a much bigger story." Not that every story she uses is crucial. There's room for a kicker on a PR stunt that went bad:

```
That giant salad they were supposed to make in a 24-
foot-wide swimming pool in Albany . . . ended up as a
big wilt . . .
```

Liz Shanov, WCBS

A WCBS reporter is with the Israeli prime minister, who is visiting the city, but the reporter's first report notes that there is only one small group of demonstrators there. Shanov decides not to use the story again in her second hour. There's too much else going on in New York this evening.

Ted Koppel on the premier of the ABC News program Nightline, *on March 24, 1980. (© copyright Capitol Cities/ABC, Inc.)*

Networks

At 5 p.m. David Johnson and Peggy Finnegan do the news on WPXI, a television station in Pittsburgh. At 6:30 p.m. Tom Brokaw does the news on WPXI. That is what networks mean to viewers and listeners around the United States. They bring nationally known journalists, like Brokaw, and international reporting staffs to places that ordinarily could not afford such high-priced talent or wide-ranging coverage.

Television

WPXI is an NBC *affiliate*. NBC doesn't own the station. The FCC restricts the number of television stations one company is allowed to own. NBC presently has 209 affiliates (the exact number will vary somewhat over the years), which together can reach more than 99 percent of the nation's television audience, but most of these stations, like WPXI, are not owned by NBC.

WPXI doesn't have to pay a cent for the programs—from the *Tonight Show* to the *NBC Nightly News* with Tom Brokaw—it takes from NBC. To the contrary: NBC pays WPXI for the audience it brings to NBC's programs. The larger the station's audience, the more the network will pay. WPXI does broadcast some of its own programs each day, including an hour and a half of news at 5:30, but for much of the day and most of the evening WPXI carries pretty much what the 208 other NBC affiliates in the United States are carrying.

It should be noted that the network-affiliate relationship doesn't work only one way. Networks sometimes rely on their affiliates to cover breaking stories in their areas, and career-minded reporters take advantage of these opportunities to get their reports on a network.

ABC   Through its 212 affiliates, ABC News broadcasts three programs every weekday: *World News This Morning, World News Tonight* and *Nightline.* In addition, the news department is responsible for the news segments of *Good Morning America,* scattered news briefs during the evening, the weekly news magazine shows *20/20* and *Prime Time Live,* Sunday morning's *This Week with David Brinkley,* some additional weekend newscasts and occasional documentaries and special news programming.

NBC   NBC's affiliates receive a similar set of news programs. At NBC, though, the news department is responsible for the entire morning *Today* show. The network's news staff includes about 1,000 people, working out of 7 domestic and 17 foreign bureaus.

CBS   The *CBS Evening News* with Dan Rather, a direct descendant of 1947's Television News with Douglas Edwards, is one of the most watched newscasts on television. CBS News also produces *60 Minutes,* one of the most popular programs of any kind on television. The network has more than 200 affiliates, as its competitors do, and it sends these affiliates a selection of shows similar to those produced by the other network news departments.

Cable News Network   Ted Turner began this, the first national all-news television network, in 1980. Millions of dollars of losses later, CNN is beginning to show signs of becoming a profitable operation. CNN and its sister network, Headline News, are now carried by about 9,700 cable systems. It can reach a *potential* audience of 53.8 million homes in the United States. In addition, broadcast stations often use these networks to fill late-night hours. And CNN is also available in 93 other countries. Turner makes his money by selling advertisements and charging cable operators for the right to transmit the channel. CNN and Headline News are produced by a staff of 1,700 in Atlanta and around the world.

PBS   Public broadcasting's major news effort is the daily *MacNeil/Lehrer News-Hour,* an amalgam of interviews and videotape reports. The *NewsHour,* produced by WNET in New York City and WETA in Washington, is seen on 275 noncommercial television stations. It often succeeds in covering major stories in more depth than the shorter, faster formats of the commerical networks allow. PBS also carries some news-oriented talk shows and documentaries produced by various public television stations around the country.

Other Networks Fox Television's 138 affiliates do not yet receive any regular news programs. However, Fox does offer them live coverage of major news events and a video news service (see Chapter 7, "Sources"), featuring videotape reports produced by the various local stations themselves. Independent News had attempted to distribute a prime-time national and international newscast to television stations not affiliated with ABC, NBC, or CBS. That effort finally failed in 1990, though Independent News lives on in a couple of examples in this book.

Radio

Before television, the radio networks broadcast news and entertainment programs that are similar to what the television networks show today. When television moved in, the radio networks were left primarily with news.

Local radio stations needed the networks to bring them stars such as Jack Benny and Bing Crosby, but they didn't need networks to provide disk jockeys and records. So, most radio programming started being produced locally, with that one exception—news.

A local radio station still could not afford to hire a London or Washington correspondent. The wire services provided the information but not the expert correspondents or the sound: "From where I stand on the battlefield, you can hear the guns." The networks were still needed for national and international news. For a time they broadcast one type of program exclusively—hourly newscasts.

Four networks have survived the big-time radio era: NBC, CBS, ABC and the Mutual Broadcasting System. They have been joined by a few others. Like the television networks, each has many affiliates in cities and towns across the country. Like the television networks, they can themselves own only a limited number of those affiliates—no more than 30 AM and 30 FM stations. Like the television networks, most pay affiliates to carry their shows. Unlike the television networks, however, most radio companies in the network business now send out more than one network, or group of programs, to more than one group of affiliates.

One more thing needs to be said right off the bat about network radio: It's booming. With the ability of satellites to carry a few separate channels of programming to each affiliate at low cost (see Chapter 7, "Sources"), broadcast companies have been spinning off new networks, especially targeted to reach specific audiences, at a frantic pace. This is good for national and international news; there are a lot more services supplying it around the country. However, it may be bad news for local news. The growth in the number of national networks (along with the FCC's new, more relaxed, policies) has already crowded some local newscasts off the air.

ABC ABC was the first of the new multi-network networks. The process of mitosis, dividing and growing, began at ABC in 1968 with a split into four different networks. Now there are seven (plus 10 Satellite Music Networks, which have their own news staff in Dallas). One sends out talk shows and doesn't concern us here. The other six ABC networks concentrate on news.

There are three reasons six news networks are better than one. First, they allow ABC to have more than one affiliate in each market and, therefore, a larger audience. In Chicago, WBMZ-FM, WLS-FM, WLS-AM and WGN are all ABC radio affiliates. Second, the networks can be tailored to fit the specific music formats stations are using. A top-40 station, for example, can get fast-paced, youth-oriented news on the ABC Contemporary Network. Third, since each of the networks is aimed at a clearly defined audience, they're exceptionally efficient buys for advertisers. For example, a company selling an acne remedy can be sure of reaching its intended teenage audience by advertising on the Contemporary Network.

WBBQ-FM in Augusta, Georgia, and WAPI-FM in Birmingham, Alabama, are two of the approximately 200 stations that carry the *ABC Contemporary Network.* They get news written to fit the style of the top-40 or CHR (contemporary hit radio) station . . . broadcast at 52 and at 56 minutes after the hour (stations have a choice). ABC Radio's then-general manager for news programing, Kathy Lavinder, calls this "up-tempo news." Here is ABC Contemporary's lead-in to a voicer on an upcoming Supreme Court decision:

```
One of the hottest potatoes to be handled by the Supreme
Court in recent years is the Alan Bakke Case . . . Bakke
filed a reverse discrimination suit last year after being
turned down for entrance to a California medical school
because of a minority quota. In Washington, we asked
ABC's Tim O'Brien what's been holding up the
ruling . . .
```

The *ABC FM Network* is also aimed at a young—18 to 44—audience, but its newscasts, aired at 45 and 48½ minutes after the hour, are more "laid back," knowing and informal:

```
You may or may not have been on pins and needles waiting
for a decision by the Supreme Court in the reverse
discrimination case of Alan Bakke . . . but ABC's Tim
O'Brien tells us it's on its way . . . this week . . .
```

ABC FM has about 148 affiliates, including WRNO-FM in New Orleans and KSJO in San Jose.

ABC's third youth network is *ABC Rock.* This is designed for album-oriented rock stations like KLOS in Los Angeles and KOME in San Francisco. The news, aired at 45 minutes after the hour, is supposed to be short and clever. Here's the entire Rock Network lead-in for an actuality on a space shuttle mission in which the voice of "Mission Control Houston" introduces itself:

> Lead-in: It was another one for the Guinness. Two astronauts grabbed a disabled satellite in space and put it into a cargo bay of the shuttle . . .
>
> Actuality: Mission Control Houston . . . Joe Allen now qualifies as the first human in history to hold a 12-hundred-pound satellite over his head for one trip around the world.

For the benefit of the Rock Network's approximately 110 affiliates, ABC has sent a reporter to interview young American soldiers on duty overseas and a reporter to follow Bruce Springsteen around on one of his concert tours.

News on the **ABC Entertainment Network** is transmitted at the top of the hour to about 640 affiliates, mostly "modern country" or adult contemporary stations. WIVK in Knoxville and WSIK-FM in Nashville use news from ABC Entertainment. The network is designed for listeners in the 25–54 age group. "The news is more humanistic, more people-oriented," says Lavinder. This was how the Entertainment Network led into that same actuality on the space shuttle:

> He only weighs 130 pounds . . . the smallest astronaut in the U-S space program. But Joe Allen managed to wrestle a wayward satellite back to the space shuttle Discovery today. . . . Then, Allen held it steady for an hour and a half, while fellow astronaut Dale Gardner locked the satellite down in the cargo bay, for transport back to earth . . . winning applause from the crew back on the home planet . . .

When a young boy was lost while playing in the snow, then found dead as the snow started melting 15 days later only five feet from the front door of his parents' house, ABC Entertainment, in the words of Peter Flannery, then president of ABC Radio News, "played the hell out of the story." Flannery says the network is looking for the kind of story that gets people saying, "You'll never guess what I heard on the radio."

ABC aims at a similar audience with its **Direction Network.** The network is on at 50 and 54½ minutes after the hour and is carried by, for example, WALK on Long Island and WMUS in Muskegon, Michigan.

The **ABC Information Network** is the most traditional of the six. It has about 625 affiliates, including WABC in New York City and WJR in Detroit. "It's geared toward stations with a heavy news commitment," says Lavinder. The news is broadcast at the traditional time—on the hour (with an update at 27 after the hour)—and presented in a somewhat less folksy, more analytical style. Here's ABC Information's lead-in to that voicer on the upcoming Supreme Court decision:

The U-S Supreme Court is wrapping up its spring term this week. Among the crucial decisions yet to be announced is the Alan Bakke reverse discrimination case. Apparently part of the delay is due to a backlog of paper work. Tim O'Brien has details from Washington. . . .

CBS   The CBS Radio Network dates back to 1927. It offers six minutes of news on the hour to its approximately 440 affiliates, not all of which use the full six minutes. In addition, the network transmits a variety of features and news analysis programs, as well as radio coverage of most major sporting events, including Major League Baseball and NFL football. CBS estimates that the network reaches an audience of 23 million people. CBS also has two other networks—CBS Spectrum and CBS Hispanic Radio Network—but they do not offer newscasts.

NBC and Mutual   After General Electric bought NBC, it sold the radio network to Westwood One, the country's largest producer and distributor of national radio programming (mostly rock music features and concerts). Almost all the original staff of NBC Radio News—including a number of journalists whose comments and writings appear in this book—eventually left. NBC Radio retained the right to use reports produced by NBC television correspondents around the world; otherwise there is no connection between the two organizations. NBC Radio is connected, instead, with Mutual, which is also owned by Westwood One. The two share a building in Arlington, Virginia. NBC Radio's hourly newscasts are broadcast on about 700 affiliates, either at ten minutes before the hour or on the hour. The Source, a separate NBC Radio network, is heard on about 150 rock music stations at ten minutes after the hour. A third NBC Radio network—Talknet—does not produce newscasts. Mutual offers its approximately 700 affiliates the choice of a newscast on the hour, at ten after or on the half hour.

NPR   National Public Radio is a first cousin to television's PBS. The network has been struggling financially for much of the time since it was founded in 1971, but it still manages to produce two widely respected news and information shows each day: the two-hour Morning Edition and the 90-minute All Things Considered, broadcast in the evening. The reports on these shows run much longer than on the commercial networks (see Chapter 18, "Public Affairs"). According to NPR's news director, they aim for completeness rather than timeliness. These two programs are carried on more than 300 noncommercial stations.

■ ■ ■

The audio news services distributed by UPI and AP (see Chapter 7, "Sources") both include hourly newscasts, so they must be considered networks too. In addition, there are a number of smaller radio networks that serve specific constituencies such as blacks, Hispanics or business people, or regional networks, such as the Texas State Network, that serve specific areas.

When a local station is affiliated with any one of these networks, it gets network programs either by satellite or by lines leased from the telephone company or a combination of the two. Affiliates don't have to carry the newscast each hour, but usually they are obligated to broadcast at least the commercials in those newscasts.

It's important that journalists at a local station pay attention to what the network is doing. It would be foolish to repeat a national story the network has just done, for example.

In most cases network newscasts are introduced by a tone that can cue the station's machinery automatically to switch the network on to the air. So KREW listeners in Sunnyside, Washington, can hear Bill Lynch broadcasting live from the CBS newsroom in New York.

Wrap-Up

When they pass the disk jockey or talk-show host on their way to the coffee machine, when they hear the network newscast, when they look through the window and see the cows outside, broadcast journalists should be reminded that their news is not being written in a vacuum and that their newscasts have to take into account the situation of the station that carries them. Writers and reporters have to know what stories their network is covering. They also must consider the size of the market when selecting news, and they may have to consider the station's format. But these are mere adjustments. The basic principles of broadcast journalism outlined in this book stay the same no matter how big the station, whether or not it is a network affiliate and no matter what the station's format.

Careers

The road to careers in broadcast journalism used to start in newspaper journalism. Many of the first broadcast journalists began that way, and they directed newcomers to the same path. This has changed. Broadcast journalism has established itself as more than just a wayward cousin of the press. It has emerged as a distinguishable, and occasionally distinguished, profession with its own academic foundations and its own self-contained career ladder.

A background in print journalism still has value because the newspaper reporter employs the same standards of accuracy, fairness and thoroughness; and the newspaper reporter gets more of a workout in collecting and presenting details. The rigors of wire service reporting provide especially good training in finding facts. But not only is a stint in print no longer necessary, it leaves the prospective broadcast journalist lacking skills in writing broadcast style and reporting with tape, without which it's hard to get a job in a broadcast newsroom. And the fact that most radio journalists also must handle announcing and audio production, and most television journalists must go on the air and work with camera crews, makes crossing over from a newspaper even more difficult.

On the Air

At a big-city radio station in the 1940s the announcers and writers might never have seen each other. Scripts might be sent over a teletype from the corner of a newspaper's newsroom, where they were written, to the radio studio where the announcers ripped them off and aired them. Announcers didn't write; writers didn't announce. Each was a specialist, and neither was initiated into the secrets of audio production.

No longer. Money, as usual, was the catalyst. Station owners soon realized that it is cheaper to hire a writer who can enunciate or an announcer who can punctuate than to spend twice as much for two specialists.

The newsrooms of most of the radio stations in the country today are populated by people who can write, report, order and air the news. Most of these journalists can also edit tape, work an audioboard and read commercials. There are a few more specialists left in television news, but it's still harder to get started without on-the-air skills and some knowledge of production.

News Director Neil
Offen of WCHL,
North Carolina, on
the air. (Mitchell
Stephens)

The emphasis in this book is on journalism skills. As Michael Gross of WRKD in Maine says, "A journalist can learn to become a broadcaster, but it's tough for a broadcaster to learn to be a journalist." The following discussions, however, touch on broadcasting skills that are invaluable to a broadcast journalist: newscasting and audio production.

Newscasting

You don't have to know how to read the news on the air to work in broadcast journalism. There are jobs at some of the large stations and networks, especially in television, for writers, editors or producers. But writers who can read are qualified for positions at many more stations.

Broadcast news is supposed to be written conversationally. It would be easy to say that it should be read on the air conversationally *if* in conversation a person pronounced every word perfectly clearly and exaggerated the emphasis on certain key words to bring out their meaning and *if* that person talked slightly faster than most of us.

"Talk into the mike, don't read into it," advises Robert Samek of WSUB, Connecticut. But plain talking is not enough to hold the attention of people who are looking at traffic or their ironing, not the newscaster's eyes, as the newscaster attempts to explain complex developments. Even television newscasters have to compete for attention with household events.

Newscasting should incorporate some of the friendly style of conversation, but it is not mere talking. Lee Giles, news director of WISH-TV in Indianapolis, puts it this way: "What you're looking for is a natural conversational style. You should communicate to people as if you were talking to them in person, yet still you have to be a bit larger than life. You emphasize a bit more."

Enunciation Accomplished singers are said to have "good ears," not "good mouths." The secret to perfecting what comes out of the mouth is learning to use the ears. Newscasters must hear how they sound. A tape recorder is invaluable; borrowing others' ears, especially other newscasters', is wise; but newscasters must also learn to listen to themselves as they speak.

Are they pronouncing every word carefully? If friends frequently respond with "huh?" or "what?" there is trouble. "Rom d'Gate Lake te d'Lantic Seabor keep d'umbrellas 'andy" won't do on the air. Every word must be pronounced clearly; syllables enunciated precisely: "From the Great Lakes to the At-lan-tic sea-board . . . keep the umbrel-las han-dy." These syllables must pass through a microphone, amplifier, transmitter, receiver, speaker and ear. They should leave the mouth firm and precise. Swallowed words choke meanings. You can usually tell when you are talking to experienced newscasters; they don't mumble.

One trick: concentrate on pronouncing the last letter in every word.

Air Robert Seiden of WNAE, Pennsylvania, points out that the voice is a wind instrument. Without air passing over the vocal cords, they don't make a sound. With too little air, the voice is small and stays in the back of the throat; too much air, and the voice tends to be forced and distorted. Seiden says, "A buoyant, well-supported sound floating on top of a column of air is the desired effect."

The resonant sound that most good newscasters achieve is powered by a solid breath behind each syllable, with the lungs and throat open wide. Junior high school music teachers lecture about the need to breathe from the diaphragm. Newscasters should heed that advice.

Emphasis Read this sentence *without* emphasizing one word more than another:

```
A decision has finally been reached in the bribery trial
of the state's biggest contractor. A jury has found him
innocent.
```

That dull, monotone voice is the enemy! It buries meaning and bores listeners. Emphasis is one defense against the monotone.

Newscasters must sculpt sentences as they read them. To keep sentences attractive and allow meaning to come through, they should pronounce some words with added force and pause for an instant to dramatize others. Try reading this sentence, accentuating the underlined words and pausing at the slashes:

```
A decision has finally been reached / in the bribery
trial of the state's biggest / contractor. A jury has
found him / innocent.
```

Writers call for some accenting and pausing in their copy (see Chapter 1, "Copy"), but not enough for newscasters. Whereas a writer may underline a couple of the most important words in a story, newscasters want to emphasize perhaps a couple of words per sentence. Some newscasters go over their copy before reading it on the air and scrawl lines under the key words and slashes to pinpoint the pauses. The late Douglas Edwards of CBS added lines and slashes to this copy before he read it on the air.

```
Members of the city council of Chicago have voted

themselves a 60-percent raise in salaries / over a four-

year period. That would push their pay from 17 thousand

500 a year to 28-thousand dollars. And the White House

is upset about it, inflation fighter Alfred Khan saying

so. But the Chicago city fathers / apparently / are

unimpressed. Bob Crawford of WBBM has the story . . .
```

It's not necessary to mark up the copy like this as long as newscasters understand that they cannot treat words evenhandedly. Words have meanings; sentences must be interpreted. This doesn't mean overdramatization or that newscasters should scold criminals and celebrate heroes with their voices. It means that newscasters must understand what they are reading and use proper emphasis to share that understanding with listeners. And emphasis isn't conferred on words randomly; the key words and the most pertinent facts should be highlighted.

Newscasting employs more emphasis than conversation. "If you feel as though you are overemphasizing, you're probably using the correct emphasis," advises Todd St. Claire of WXLS in Connecticut.

Inflection   A second defense against the monotone is inflection—altering the pitch through the course of a sentence.

Newscaster Dave Pauli of KGW, Portland, Oregon.

Inflection usually conveys one of two basic meanings. When the voice gets higher at the end of a phrase, it means the thought is incomplete:

```
Calling it one of the

                              heard . . .
                    ever
worst proposals he has
```

Questions that are about to be answered also require a rising inflection:

```
                         meeting?
          accomplished      the
What was                 at
```

Complete thoughts, on the other hand, should be signified by the voice getting lower—a falling inflection:

```
He voted against the
                        new
                          plan.
```

Stories should end with the voice dropping in pitch; so snappers should be read with a falling inflection:

```
He says he'll
            never
                  go back.
```

Inflection helps punctuate stories. Too much inflection sounds sing-song and irritating; too little, and the news sounds flat.

Pace Most newscasters read the news a little faster than they normally speak to keep things lively and avoid boring the listener.

In an ambitious effort to come to some scientific conclusions about announcing, tests were made in the 1940s to determine the ideal pace for a newscaster. It was determined, somehow, that 140 words per minute was too slow to maintain interest and 200 words per minute too fast for the average listener to follow. Their ideal pace—175 words per minute.

It's hard to believe that any aspect of our lives has slowed in the past five decades, but today most news directors would say they want newscasters to average about 150 words per minute. That's just a guideline; the best pace remains the most natural pace.

Speeds vary widely from station to station and newscaster to newscaster. Beginners, nevertheless, should compare themselves with other newscasters and use the 150-word-per-minute standard to get a fix on how their pace compares with the average. Most beginners have a tendency to hurry their reading, especially when nervous.

Reading Newscasters should read in advance all copy they are going to read on the air. For one thing, they have the last shot at catching an error before it is aired, and they will read more comfortably if familiar with the copy. To avoid getting surprised by an unclear correction or an unfamiliar name, for example, it's worth the time to read everything over at least once. Unfortunately this time is not always available. Stories can break as the newscaster is walking to the studio; they sometimes have to be read cold, right off the wire or the computer screen.

These situations are saved by the prodigious capabilities of the human eye. The eye can scan a few words ahead on a line while it is reading other words. Newscasters must strengthen that faculty and learn to anticipate and prepare for the words that lie ahead. That way they can see trouble coming—an error left in the copy, an unfamiliar word—and prepare for it by occasionally editing and rewriting as they read. This is a difficult trick, to be sure, and a risky one; an ad lib lowers all defenses against errors. Best that newscasters are never put in this position; but if a mistake sneaks into copy that has to be read cold, they must be adept-enough readers to catch it.

Microphones Keep a distance from them—six inches in the radio studio. On television, tiny mikes are now clipped to newscasters' lapels. It's not necessary to yell or whisper. A natural volume is fine—loud enough so that someone across the room could hear. Microphones are sensitive. They pick up the sound of papers being rustled—slide the sheets aside, don't turn the pages of the script. Mikes are also overly sensitive to *p*'s, *t*'s and *b*'s popping, and *s*'s sizzling (see Chapter 1, "Copy"). It's often necessary to underplay these letters when talking to a mike. And it sounds most friendly when a newscaster talks as if that mike were a person.

Voices Many people used to believe that news could be read only by a baritone. This kept a lot of tenors, altos and sopranos unemployed until women's liberation helped rid us of this particular bugaboo. Most news directors are probably still fans of deep, resonant voices, but they are learning to accept some variety in their station's news sound.

Almost all news directors would agree that it is a mistake for beginners to attempt to force their voices to sound lower. Forced voices sound forced and foolish. "Through use the voice will find its own comfortable timbre," says Ray Kendall of KNDE in California.

Of course, not everyone has the pipes to broadcast the news. Some need work—accents must sometimes be eliminated, enunciation perfected. Some voices will never make the grade—too squeaky or nasal, perhaps. Voices can be improved, but there are people who are better off aiming at a behind-the-scenes position.

On Camera The television newscaster has to read the news while being watched by the audience. Thus appearance becomes important; dress, neatness and, alas, looks enter into the calculations. Eye contact becomes important—most stations use **teleprompters** or monitors that place the script so that it appears right on top of the camera lens. That's how television newscasters manage to read and look at the camera at the same time (see Chapter 17, "Television Newscasts"). The newscaster's **business**—where the hands are kept, how the papers are shuffled—becomes important too.

There is, perhaps, a subtle difference between television- and radio-reading styles. On TV things are toned down a bit. Overemphasis can look phony, and the extra sense available for communication with the audience removes some of the need to bring out the meanings. Television newscasting involves significantly more emphasis and intonation than conversation, but somewhat less than radio newscasting.

Audio Production

Packaging all the elements of broadcast news into a form that fits neatly on the air requires an ability to work a collection of electronic machines. Most radio stations prefer that their journalists have this ability.

Radio journalists should know how to gather and file tape using a cassette tape recorder, and how to edit taped reports and transform them into tape cartridges ready to use in a newscast. (These skills are discussed in Chapter 9, "Tape.") Carts then have to be combined with commercials, live reports, perhaps some theme music and live microphones to produce a newscast on the air.

Some large stations have engineers to handle this job; many stations don't. So radio journalists should be familiar with the basic techniques of **audio production.** It may also be valuable if they get to know the electronics that explain how it all works.

Television journalists should know how to report with and edit videotape. (These skills are discussed in Chapter 15, "Television Reporting.") They also should have some familiarity with the role of directors and other broadcast technicians (see Chapter 17, "Television Newscasts"). A detailed consideration of what those television technicians are doing would be too complex to include here, so the following discussion confines itself to radio production.

The Audioboard The newsroom and the news studio at WBLG in Lexington, Kentucky, share the same room. Russ Clarkson is finishing his copy for the 6:30 p.m. newscast when he hears a disk jockey in the studio across the hall announce on an intercom that Clarkson has one minute till air time. There are no engineers on duty at WBLG. Clarkson and the disk jockey alone are responsible for getting his newscast on the air.

Clarkson puts on a set of earphones, so he can hear the final minute of the disk jockey's show; then he swivels to the right in his chair. Now he is facing the **audioboard.** Directly in front of him and behind his microphone is a series of switches, gauges and **pots**—dials for controlling volume. These devices, which make up the audioboard, enable him to monitor and control all the sounds that leave the news studio.

Clarkson glances at the pot that controls his microphone. During his first few days at the station he had tested it to see where it should be set for his voice to come through at the optimum level—so that the needle on the nearby gauge moved freely, near but not into, the red area. Now he just has to check to make sure that it's set at his predetermined level.

To Clarkson's left are three separate tape cartridge playback machines. Clarkson takes the three carts he is using in the newscast and pushes them into the machines—they cue up automatically.

Through the earphones Clarkson hears the disk jockey play the news jingle. He switches on his mike; the disk jockey flips a switch putting the news studio on the air; and Clarkson begins reading the first story.

There is an actuality in his lead story. After he has finished the lead-in, Clarkson pushes a remote-control switch on the audioboard that plays the first cart machine. His hand automatically moves to the pot that controls his mike to turn it down—in case he sneezes or coughs. The cart ends. His mike is turned back up, and the pot that controls that first cart machine is turned down—carts dubbed from cassette recorders may have a "whhittt" sound at the end, which shouldn't be permitted on the air.

Clarkson reads the time; that is the cue to the disk jockey that it's time for a commercial. At WBLG, spots are played on cart machines in the main studio. Clarkson listens for the end of the commercial in his earphones, then returns with the rest of the news.

A reporter is ready for a live report over the telephone. By flipping a switch, Clarkson **patches** that phone line into one of the pots on the audioboard. After reading a lead-in, he turns on that pot and the reporter is on the air. Through the report Clarkson is **riding the gain**—checking the reporter's volume on a gauge and making minor adjustments when it gets too loud or soft by gently nudging the pot. On a bad connection, turning up the volume for the reporter also raises the volume or the background hiss. These considerations must be weighed to get the clearest possible sound.

After the reporter closes, Clarkson instantly turns up the studio mike, turns down the pot that carried the reporter and reads the rest of his stories, playing his other two carts. Then the time again, and the disk jockey plays a second commercial. Clarkson returns with the weather and sports, then reads his close and it's back to the disk jockey for the remainder of the hour.

Clarkson swivels back to the left and starts writing the next hour's newscast.

Electronics   A newscaster leans over a microphone in a radio studio and begins to read the news. The newscaster's voice produces sound waves that wiggle an element in the microphone. That wiggling produces small pulses of electricity that reflect the pattern in the sound waves. Those pulses are magnified by an amplifier and then converted again, this time into a pattern of radio waves that still reflects the original sound waves produced by the newscaster's voice. In AM, *amplitude modification,* broadcasting, the signal is coded into the radio waves through variations in the amplitude—strength—of the waves. In FM, *frequency modulation,* changes in the frequency of the waves—how fast they come—reflect the pattern of sound waves.

Radio waves travel through the air and are picked up by a radio antenna. The receiver converts the waves back into electrical pulses. They are amplified again and, finally, are used to pull a magnet that wiggles a cone in the radio speaker in such a way that it produces sound waves that exactly imitate the newscaster's voice.

This process relies on a complex series of electronic devices ranging from tiny capacitors to mammoth transmitters. Does a radio journalist have to understand how all this works? Not necessarily, but it helps. It's easier to handle the machines involved in audio production with an understanding of what they are up to, and some small radio stations demand that their journalists possess such an understanding.

A loosening of FCC regulations has lessened the value of an FCC license—signifying a certain understanding of broadcast electronics—for potential broadcast journalists. There was a time when a third-class FCC license would be required for a job at some stations. According to Jim Farley, of ABC News, that day has pretty much passed. Nevertheless, it's certainly easier to handle the machines involved in audio production if you're clued in to how they perform their tricks. Ohms and watts may seem a long way from leads and stories, but when your business is getting the news on the air, an understanding of how messages are sent through the air can't hurt.

Getting There

How to build a career in broadcast news? There are as many different routes to the top jobs as there are people in those jobs. Journalists are too informal to stick to one or two recruiting strategies. But there are certain qualities that most people who do the hiring look for, and there are ways of investing yourself with those qualities.

The Bottom

The bottom is, of course, where you start. There are two "bottoms" in broadcast news:

Gopher "*Go for* coffee; *go for* pencils; *go for* wire copy." The largest newsrooms entrust beginners with these responsibilities. Their job titles are **desk assistant** or perhaps production assistant, editorial assistant, copy person; these are the only positions in the top news organizations that recent college graduates, without professional experience, have a shot at.

A desk assistant's journalistic duties are usually ripping and distributing wire copy, listening to the police radio, getting traffic reports, recording actualities or transporting videotape. Generally, they are given no real chances to write or report. At unionized stations, gophers are specifically prohibited from doing writers', reporters' or engineers' jobs—"touch that computer and it's a union grievance."

The advantage of such a position for a beginner is the eight-hour-a-day opportunity it affords to study how a top news organization works. The disadvantage is that such jobs don't really give young journalists a chance to do journalism. After a year as a gopher, they may be a lot more knowledgeable, but not necessarily any better.

Some desk assistants do succeed in moving up to writing, reporting or newscasting positions at their stations, but too many find themselves stuck as desk assistants. Jim Farley, someone who climbed from gopher at WINS to the top post at NBC Radio News and then on to an executive position at ABC, still cautions that once you've worked as a desk assistant there is a tendency for others always to look at you as a desk assistant. You can get overlooked. So Farley recommends a second method of entering the profession.

Small Stations "This route," Farley explains, "means you go out to a small market in the 'boondocks' where you will do everything. You'll water the transmitter—if the ground is wet the signal radiates a little further. (Against FCC regulations, incidentally.) You'll sweep the floors, run your own board, announce, write, report, maybe sell some commercials. The five-day work week doesn't exist in a small market. You work six days, and you're on call on your day off." At a small television station reporters may get a chance to anchor, edit, work the remote cameras and maybe set up the teleprompter.

Small stations tend to be in small towns, where they pay small salaries, which may be less than comfortable for potentially big stars. But it is here in the small markets that the trade is best taught and learned. Few news directors would disagree that a year spent in Oelwein, Iowa, doing everything is more productive than a year ripping and distributing wire copy in Los Angeles.

Of course not every broadcast station adheres to the highest standards of journalism. Beginners may have to demand a little more of themselves than the station requires.

■ ■ ■

Gopher or small-station positions are both labeled **entry-level** jobs, but broadcast journalism has become so competitive that even to watch the wires or to apprentice in the smallest markets it is usually necessary to get some background in the field. Despite the title "entry level," full-time jobs rarely go to pure beginners. This sounds like the old conundrum, "You need experience to get a job, but you need a job to get experience." Nevertheless, there are methods of preparing for entry-level positions, ways of sneaking up on that experience. They all require hustle and dedication. For better or for worse, radio journalism is no longer a field dilettantes can "just try."

Education

Courses in broadcast journalism help; there is no longer any doubt about that. It was, and still is to some extent, fashionable for news directors to debunk an education in broadcast journalism—their line being that they want young people who studied politics, economics and literature in college. The techniques of newswriting and reporting, they say, can be taught in six months on the job.

That's all true. You can't underestimate the value of a strong liberal arts education. Anyone who allows college to slip by without meeting the great ideas and thinkers, and learning to use advanced tools of thought, may be handicapped. A few weeks in a newsroom trying to explain complex statistics about the local economy, or writing about the meaning of a revolution in Africa, will reveal the handicap.

It's also true that news directors, if they're good, can teach broadcast journalism skills in a half-year of on-the-job training. The catch is that there are few news directors left who bother to take the time to do the instructing. Why should they waste half a year on a economics major when they can hire people who were trained in broadcast news in school?

It is now practically impossible to walk in off the street and tell a news director, "Hire me! I've got a good liberal arts education." Even the most strident critic of journalism schools wants to see whether the applicant can write a couple of 20-second stories or put together a wrap. They don't teach those skills in political science courses. Liberal arts help; courses in broadcast journalism may be decisive.

Experience

News directors are practical-minded. They like to hire people who have shown they can do the job somewhere else. "The first thing I look at is what a person's done," says Jeff Wald, news director of KTLA in Los Angeles. Experience is the key listing on a resume.

Beginners can start assembling their list of credits at a college radio station. Some college stations do good work; others can be made more professional. College radio may not be the real world, but any time people are listening, some of the real pressures of the profession are there. College television stations are rarer but obviously just as valuable.

Beginners can also get experience by creating their own "subentry-level" positions. These are jobs that are not offered; they are asked for, often invented. They don't pay much, if anything, and they don't provide much of a chance to play Dan Rather. Still, they get feet in doors.

Some stations hire **stringers** to cover government meetings, high school sports or campus activities. Covering a high school basketball game may not be the most pleasant way to spend a Friday evening, but it's professional experience. It may be necessary to call some local stations and remind them that they could use some coverage of campus activities.

Similarly, someone who can show up at a breaking event other reporters may be missing and record a few professional-quality actualities may be able to get some cuts on a local radio station. The AP audio news service, for instance, buys such free-lance actualities.

Getting experience in broadcast journalism may take aggessiveness and creativity, but these are qualities that keeping a job in this field also requires.

Job Searches

Broadcast news is not a profession that can be conquered simply by doing well in school and being a good person. Most broadcast stations do not recruit on college campuses. There is no systematic method for them to uncover the best job candidates. Instead they often end up hiring the most diligent and pushy, the people who write, call, and visit and sell themselves.

An organized search for a person to fill a position in broadcast journalism generally means that the news director places a classified ad in a trade publication. *Broadcasting Magazine* is the main forum of such advertisements. The jobs are waiting under "Help Wanted—News." The *RTNDA Communicator*, the publication of the Radio–Television News Directors Association, and *Earshot*, a radio news publication (88 First Street, San Francisco, CA 94105), also contain some classifieds.

Beyond these "help wanteds," the responsibility for making contact rests with the applicants. They can place their own "situations wanted" ads in these same publications or use the mails, the telephone or personal visits to bring their credentials before news directors.

Are news directors the people to contact? Usually, yes; they run the news operation. However, at small stations with one-person news teams, news director itself is the entry-level position. The hiring at these stations is done by the general manager or the station's owner.

A mass mailing is another good first step. Since there are more applicants than jobs, it's wise to try as many different stations as possible to try to equalize the odds. *Broadcasting Magazine* publishes a "year-book" that lists all the radio and television stations in the country, along with facts about their formats, their phone numbers and addresses, and the names of their news directors and other key personnel. One strategy is to choose 100 or so stations in selected areas of the country and to send their news directors or general managers a letter and resume. (Try to address each letter personally. "I get tired of Xeroxed 'Dear News Director' letters from people who obviously haven't done their homework," complains Wald at KTLA.) Most news directors will not take the time to respond. Most of the rest will say, "Sorry." One or two may express interest—that's a start.

The next step is to follow up the letters with a phone call.

Some people get in a car, pick a bunch of stations in one area, set up some interviews by phone and then spend a couple of days visiting and talking with news directors, resume in hand.

As in reporting, there's a line between aggressiveness and obnoxiousness. It may make sense to call back every couple of months to see if anything has opened up, but calling every week may seem like pestering. The idea is to make sure as many news directors as possible are aware of your qualifications . . . and feeling positive about you.

Mechanics

When looking for a job, the tools used in the search must be sharp, the person prepared. All of this is for naught, of course, if the person isn't capable, but too many capable people fail to find jobs because they couldn't master the mechanics of looking for a job.

Resumes A **resume** is a sheet of paper that sums up a person's background and qualifications. It should be neat, concise—rarely more than a page—and it should be organized so that the most flattering details stand out. Resumes want to get attention, but the prospective journalist who wrote in bright red letters across the middle of his resume, "STOP! YOUR SEARCH IS ENDED!" was going a little too far.

Resumes are not works of journalism; they are advertising. They don't have to be balanced; they should stress the positive. This is no place for humility. If someone won an award for a piece of journalism, that has to be on the resume. If a person was captain of the basketball team, that should be there too. But there is no need to mention failing to make the team.

Since experience is what news directors want to see, that is what they should be shown first. If the person has any experience, that's the first listing on the resume—after the name, address and phone number. Experience should be noted in reverse chronological order—the latest job first. Then education. Forget elementary school and high school, unless there's a chance the news director went to the same one. Colleges and graduate schools, if any, are important. Relevant courses should be mentioned; relevant extracurricular activities noted. Throw in grades or the grade-point average if they are good.

If there is something to fill it, honors and awards make a nice listing: dean's list, Kappa Tau Alpha journalism society, etc. References may be listed; otherwise it should be made clear that they are available on request.

Some potentially good journalists write poor resumes: bloated, self-deprecating or sloppy. A resume should be lean and proud.

When resumes are sent through the mail, they should be accompanied by a well-written, personally addressed cover letter that notes the position in which the person is interested and briefly sums up the person's qualifications for that position. The cover letter might request an interview. Some cover letters are abrupt—"I can write. Let's talk." Some are long arguments for their authors. Whatever works. . . .

Of course, grammatical, word-usage or spelling errors in a resume or cover letter are sure routes to failure. The following sentence, if you can call it that, is from a "job-wanted" letter Carissa Howland received while news director of KRCR-TV in Redding, California: "Having been a four letter athelete thru high school and college, plus a coach for five years and sports writer you'll receive a great talent without having to spend alot of money." Needless to say, Howland was not anxious to "receive" this "talent."

Audition Tapes If a decision to hire is going to be based in part on how a person sounds on the air, news directors want to hear the voice that is being considered for the job. And television news directors want to see what an applicant looks like on the air. News directors may request an **audition tape.**

An audition tape should sound or look professional. It should demonstrate a wide range of skills: good writing; preferably some reporting; the ability to handle different types of stories—breaking news and features, perhaps sports and a kicker; the ability to read a commercial. A person already working at a station might just record a newscast and send it out—that's called an *air check*. Otherwise, an audition should be recorded on the best equipment possible. Gaining access to a radio or television studio is best; a good reel-to-reel tape recorder will do for radio. Of course, the tape should be error-free.

Radio audition tapes can be on reel-to-reel or cassette tapes. For television, most news directors prefer ¾-inch videotape cassettes, though ½-inch is becoming more common. A few clean copies of the audition tape should be made, and then the resume, cover letter or classified ad should specify that it's available on request. Stations have a responsibility to return tapes they have requested.

Some stations make their own tapes of job applicants by having them read some copy in a studio when they come in for an interview.

Interviews Letters, phone calls, resumes, classified ads and audition tapes are all methods of getting into the news director's or general manager's office. It is there that the final decision on whom to hire is made, and the impression a person makes in an interview in that office will be a determining factor.

First, do your homework. "It's a good idea to call the local chamber of commerce once you've set the interview date," advises Terrence Finnegan, professor of journalism at the University of Illinois. "You can have a pack of information about the town where the station is located mailed to your home. Ask them to include a couple of local newspapers if possible. Then, arrive a day early, if you can, and watch or listen to the station's newscasts. Have some questions or comments prepared for the interview based on what you've learned about the town and those newscasts."

And once the interview begins? Here's Jim Farley of ABC: "Without being pushy, obnoxious, overaggressive or overanxious, you want to communicate the idea that you want this job very badly, that you're willing to work harder than any of the other applicants sitting outside the door.

"The idea you want to get across is, 'Hey, I'll work any hours you give me.' A problem in the radio business is that somebody's got to work overnights. Throughout radio, the important shifts start at three or four o'clock in the morning. You've got to communicate that you'll work overnights with no complaints, weekends with no complaints.

"And," Farley adds, "you've got to mean it."

Applicants shouldn't give the impression that they are ready to turn the newsroom upside-down, but they shouldn't be shy and intimidated, either. The best way to inspire confidence is to be confident. Applicants shouldn't interrogate the news director, but should ask questions, show an interest in the workings of the newsroom and demonstrate that they understand how broadcast news works. News directors are looking for reasons to justify their eventual decision. Hand them justifications for hiring and withhold justifications for saying, "Sorry."

Writing Tests Many stations combine the interview with a writing test to get a quick fix on the applicant's journalistic skills. There is no simpler way to determine whether a person can handle the news.

Generally, in a writing test applicants are handed a batch of print-style copy, perhaps some stories from a newspaper or a roll of wire copy, and asked to transform this copy into broadcast style, perhaps a complete 5-minute newscast. Speed counts.

Writing is like athletics—the more you do, the better you get. People looking for jobs in broadcast news should go into training for a month or so. Every day they should sit down at the computer with a newspaper and spend a couple of hours banging out broadcast stories and newscasts. Practice makes writers fast and confident, if not perfect. And since a number of broadcast stations have taken to giving current events tests—"Who is William Rehnquist?"—as well as writing tests, this is no time to slack off on the newspapers and newscasts.

Rigors

Broadcast journalism is a career you have to want badly because a lot of other people want it too. It's an employer's market. Journalism schools are turning out many more applicants than stations have jobs for. Indeed, the journalism business as a whole has been suffering in recent years.

After the first rejection letters, the whole enterprise may seem hopeless. For a person who hasn't really learned how to write and report broadcast news, it may *be* hopeless. But someone who is prepared, and good, has to remember to be resolute.

In a profession where doggedness counts, persistence in looking for a job is recognized as a virtue. The person who keeps calling back, without being obnoxious about it, to see if a job has opened up, the person who sends out follow-up letters and volunteers to do some part-time work while waiting for something full-time to develop, may be the one who comes to mind when a position is available.

The person who sends out 100 letters has a better chance than the person who sends out 25. The person who answers the ads in *Broadcasting* for a few months has a better chance than the person who answers them for a week or two.

And what kind of work is it when you get it? This is how Michael Owens of KSIS, Missouri, describes broadcast journalism: "Low pay, long hours, griping with city officials and the most exhilarating work in the world."

Wrap-Up

Stan Zimmerman of WSPB in Florida insisted that this book make one final point: "Be sure to tell them they won't get rich [in small markets, at least], but they'll have one hell of a lot of fun."

Suggested Readings

The following books were helpful to me as I prepared this book. I recommend them.

Writing
Strunk, William, Jr., and E. B. White. *The Elements of Style.* New York: Macmillan, 3rd ed. 1979.
Zinsser, William. *On Writing Well.* New York: Harper & Row, 1976.

Journalism
Burrows, William E. *On Reporting the News.* New York: New York University Press, 1977.
Stephens, Mitchell, and Gerald Lanson. *Writing and Reporting the News.* New York: Holt, Rinehart and Winston, 1986.

Television
Yoakam, Richard D., and Charles F. Cremer. *ENG: Television News and the New Technology,* Carbondale, ILL.: Southern Illinois University Press, 2nd ed. 1989.

News Media Issues and History
Barnouw, Erik. *Tube of Plenty: The Evolution of American Television.* New York: Oxford University Press, 2nd ed. 1990.
Fornatale, Peter, and Joshua E. Mills. *Radio in the Television Age.* Woodstock, NY: Overlook Press, 1983.
Stephens, Mitchell. *A History of News.* New York: Penguin, 1989.

Mass Communication Law
Overbeck, Wayne. *Major Principles of Media Law.* Fort Worth, TX.: Harcourt Brace Jovanovich, 1991.

Index

Italic page numbers refer to photographs.